FIGURING

MARIA POPOVA

CANONGATE

First published in Great Britain in 2019 by Canongate Books Ltd,
14 High Street, Edinburgh EH1 1TE

canongate.co.uk

1

First published in the United States by Pantheon Books,
a division of Penguin Random House LLC, New York, USA

British Library Cataloguing-in-Publication Data
A catalogue record for this book is available on
request from the British Library

ISBN 978 1 78689 724 4

Typeset in by North Market Street Graphics, Lancaster, Pennsylvania, USA
Designed by M. Kristen Bearse

Printed and bound in Great Britain by Clays Ltd, Elcograf S.p.A.

For Bella

Whoever requires the suffrage of others, has at once placed his life in the power of calculation and of chance; to such a degree, that the labours of calculation cannot secure him from the accidents of chance, and the accidents of chance cannot exempt him from the pains of calculation.

—Germaine de Staël, *A Treatise on the Influence of the Passions Upon the Happiness of Individuals and of Nations* (1796)

How should we like it were stars to burn
With a passion for us we could not return?
If equal affection cannot be,
Let the more loving one be me.

—W. H. Auden

CONTENTS

FIGURING

0

All of it—the rings of Saturn and my father's wedding band, the underbelly of the clouds pinked by the rising sun, Einstein's brain bathing in a jar of formaldehyde, every grain of sand that made the glass that made the jar and each idea Einstein ever had, the shepherdess singing in the Rila mountains of my native Bulgaria and each one of her sheep, every hair on Chance's velveteen dog ears and Marianne Moore's red braid and the whiskers of Montaigne's cat, every translucent fingernail on my friend Amanda's newborn son, every stone with which Virginia Woolf filled her coat pockets before wading into the River Ouse to drown, every copper atom composing the disc that carried arias aboard the first human-made object to enter interstellar space and every oak splinter of the floorboards onto which Beethoven collapsed in the fit of fury that cost him his hearing, the wetness of every tear that has ever been wept over a grave and the yellow of the beak of every raven that has ever watched the weepers, every cell in Galileo's fleshy finger and every molecule of gas and dust that made the moons of Jupiter to which it pointed, the Dipper of freckles constellating the olive firmament of a certain forearm I love and every axonal flutter of the tenderness with which I love her, all the facts and figments by which we are perpetually figuring and reconfiguring reality—it all banged into being 13.8 billion years ago from a single source, no louder than the opening note of Beethoven's Fifth Symphony, no larger than the dot levitating over the small *i*, the *I* lowered from the pedestal of ego.

How can we know this and still succumb to the illusion of separateness, of otherness? This veneer must have been what the confluence of accidents and atoms known as Dr. Martin Luther King, Jr., saw through when he spoke of our "inescapable network of mutuality," what Walt Whitman punctured when he wrote that "every atom belonging to me as good belongs to you."

One autumn morning, as I read a dead poet's letters in my friend Wendy's backyard in San Francisco, I glimpse a fragment of that atomic mutuality. Midsentence, my peripheral vision—that glory of instinct honed by millennia of evolution—pulls me toward a miraculous sight: a small, shimmering red leaf twirling in midair. It seems for a moment to be dancing its final descent. But no—it remains suspended there, six feet above ground, orbiting an invisible center by an invisible force. For an instant I can see how such imperceptible causalities could drive the human mind to superstition, could impel medieval villagers to seek explanation in magic and witchcraft. But then I step closer and notice a fine spider's web glistening in the air above the leaf, conspiring with gravity in this spinning miracle.

Neither the spider has planned for the leaf nor the leaf for the spider—and yet there they are, an accidental pendulum propelled by the same forces that cradle the moons of Jupiter in orbit, animated into this ephemeral early-morning splendor by eternal cosmic laws impervious to beauty and indifferent to meaning, yet replete with both to the bewildered human consciousness beholding it.

We spend our lives trying to discern where we end and the rest of the world begins. We snatch our freeze-frame of life from the simultaneity of existence by holding on to illusions of permanence, congruence, and linearity; of static selves and lives that unfold in sensical narratives. All the while, we mistake chance for choice, our labels and models of things for the things themselves, our records for our history. History is not what happened, but what survives the shipwrecks of judgment and chance.

Some truths, like beauty, are best illuminated by the sidewise gleam of figuring, of meaning-making. In the course of our figuring, orbits intersect, often unbeknownst to the bodies they carry—intersections mappable only from the distance of decades or centuries. Facts crosshatch with other facts to shade in the nuances of a larger truth—not relativism, no, but the mightiest realism we have. We slice through the simultaneity by being everything at once: our first names and our last names, our loneliness and our society, our bold ambition and our blind hope, our unrequited and part-requited loves. Lives are lived in parallel and perpendicular, fathomed nonlinearly, figured not in the straight graphs of "biography" but in many-sided, many-splendored diagrams. Lives interweave with other lives, and out of the tapestry arise hints at answers to questions that raze to the bone of life: What are the building blocks of character, of contentment, of lasting achievement? How does a person come into self-possession and sovereignty of mind against the tide of convention and unreasoning collectivism? Does genius suffice for happiness, does distinction, does love? Two Nobel Prizes don't seem to recompense the melancholy radiating from every photograph of the woman in the black laboratory dress. Is success a guarantee of fulfillment, or merely a promise as precarious as a marital vow? How, in this blink of existence bookended by nothingness, do we attain completeness of being?

There are infinitely many kinds of beautiful lives.

So much of the beauty, so much of what propels our pursuit of truth, stems from the invisible connections—between ideas, between disciplines, between the denizens of a particular time and a particular place, between the interior world of each pioneer and the mark they leave on the cave walls of culture, between faint figures who pass each other in the nocturne before the torchlight of a revolution lights the new day, with little more than a half-nod of kinship and a match to change hands.

1

ONLY THE DREAMER WAKES

This is how I picture it:

A spindly middle-aged mathematician with a soaring mind, a sunken heart, and bad skin is being thrown about the back of a carriage in the bone-hollowing cold of a German January. Since his youth, he has been inscribing into family books and friendship albums his personal motto, borrowed from a verse by the ancient poet Perseus: "O the cares of man, how much of everything is futile." He has weathered personal tragedies that would level most. He is now racing through the icy alabaster expanse of the countryside in the precarious hope of averting another: Four days after Christmas and two days after his forty-fourth birthday, a letter from his sister has informed him that their widowed mother is on trial for witchcraft—a fact for which he holds himself responsible.

He has written the world's first work of science fiction—a clever allegory advancing the controversial Copernican model of the universe, describing the effects of gravity decades before Newton formalized it into a law, envisioning speech synthesis centuries before computers, and presaging space travel three hundred years before the Moon landing. The story, intended to counter superstition with science through symbol and metaphor inviting critical thinking, has instead effected the deadly indictment of his elderly, illiterate mother.

The year is 1617. His name is Johannes Kepler—perhaps the

unluckiest man in the world, perhaps the greatest scientist who ever lived. He inhabits a world in which God is mightier than nature, the Devil realer and more omnipresent than gravity. All around him, people believe that the sun revolves around the Earth every twenty-four hours, set into perfect circular motion by an omnipotent creator; the few who dare support the tendentious idea that the Earth rotates around its axis while revolving around the sun believe that it moves along a perfectly circular orbit. Kepler would disprove both beliefs, coin the word *orbit,* and quarry the marble out of which classical physics would be sculpted. He would be the first astronomer to develop a scientific method of predicting eclipses and the first to link mathematical astronomy to material reality— the first astrophysicist—by demonstrating that physical forces move the heavenly bodies in calculable ellipses. All of this he would accomplish while drawing horoscopes, espousing the spontaneous creation of new animal species rising from bogs and oozing from tree bark, and believing the Earth itself to be an ensouled body that has digestion, that suffers illness, that inhales and exhales like a living organism. Three centuries later, the marine biologist and writer Rachel Carson would reimagine a version of this view woven of science and stripped of mysticism as she makes *ecology* a household word.

Kepler's life is a testament to how science does for reality what Plutarch's thought experiment known as "the Ship of Theseus" does for the self. In the ancient Greek allegory, Theseus—the founder-king of Athens—sailed triumphantly back to the great city after slaying the mythic Minotaur on Crete. For a thousand years, his ship was maintained in the harbor of Athens as a living trophy and was sailed to Crete annually to reenact the victorious voyage. As time began to corrode the vessel, its components were replaced one by one—new planks, new oars, new sails—until no original part remained. Was it then, Plutarch asks, the same ship? There is no static, solid self. Throughout life, our habits, beliefs, and ideas evolve beyond recognition. Our physical and social environments change. Almost all of our cells are replaced. Yet we remain, to ourselves, "who" "we" "are."

So with science: Bit by bit, discoveries reconfigure our under-standing of reality. This reality is revealed to us only in fragments. The more fragments we perceive and parse, the more lifelike the mosaic we make of them. But it is still a mosaic, a representation—imperfect and incomplete, however beautiful it may be, and subject to unending transfiguration. Three centuries after Kepler, Lord Kelvin would take the podium at the British Association of Science in the year 1900 and declare: "There is nothing new to be discovered in physics now. All that remains is more and more precise measurement." At the same moment in Zurich, the young Albert Einstein is incubating the ideas that would converge into his revolutionary conception of spacetime, irreversibly transfiguring our elemental understanding of reality.

Even the farthest seers can't bend their gaze beyond their era's horizon of possibility, but the horizon shifts with each incremental revolution as the human mind peers outward to take in nature, then turns inward to question its own givens. We sieve the world through the mesh of these certitudes, tautened by nature and culture, but every once in a while—whether by accident or conscious effort—the wire loosens and the kernel of a revolution slips through.

Kepler first came under the thrall of the heliocentric model as a student at the Lutheran University of Tübingen half a century after Copernicus published his theory. The twenty-two-year-old Kepler, studying to enter the clergy, wrote a dissertation about the Moon, aimed at demonstrating the Copernican claim that the Earth is moving simultaneously around its axis and around the sun. A classmate by the name of Christoph Besold—a law student at the university—was so taken with Kepler's lunar paper that he proposed a public debate. The university promptly vetoed it. A couple of years later, Galileo would write to Kepler that he'd been a believer in the Copernican system himself "for many years"—and yet he hadn't yet dared to stand up for it in public and wouldn't for more than thirty years.

Kepler's radical ideas rendered him too untrustworthy for the pulpit. After graduation, he was banished across the country to teach mathematics at a Lutheran seminary in Graz. But he was glad—he saw himself, mind and body, as cut out for scholarship. "I take from my mother my bodily constitution," he would later write, "which is more suited to study than to other kinds of life." Three centuries later, Walt Whitman would observe how beholden the mind is to the body, "how behind the tally of genius and morals stands the stomach, and gives a sort of casting vote."

While Kepler saw his body as an instrument of scholarship, other bodies around him were being exploited as instruments of superstition. In Graz, he witnessed dramatic exorcisms performed on young women believed to be possessed by demons—grim public spectacles staged by the king and his clergy. He saw brightly colored fumes emanate from one woman's belly and glistening black beetles crawl out of another's mouth. He saw the deftness with which the puppeteers of the populace dramatized dogma to wrest control— the church was then the mass media, and the mass media were as unafraid of resorting to propaganda as they are today.

As religious persecution escalated—soon it would erupt into the Thirty Years' War, the deadliest religious war in the Continent's history—life in Graz became unlivable. Protestants were forced to marry by Catholic ritual and have their children baptized as Catholics. Homes were raided, heretical books confiscated and destroyed. When Kepler's infant daughter died, he was fined for evading the Catholic clergy and not allowed to bury his child until he paid the charge. It was time to migrate—a costly and trying endeavor for the family, but Kepler knew there would be a higher price to pay for staying:

> I may not regard loss of property more seriously than loss of opportunity to fulfill that for which nature and career have destined me.

Returning to Tübingen for a career in the clergy was out of the question:

I could never torture myself with greater unrest and anxiety than if I now, in my present state of conscience, should be enclosed in that sphere of activity.

Instead, Kepler reconsidered something he had initially viewed merely as a flattering compliment to his growing scientific reputation: an invitation to visit the prominent Danish astronomer Tycho Brahe in Bohemia, where he had just been appointed royal mathematician to the Holy Roman Emperor.

Kepler made the arduous five-hundred-kilometer journey to Prague. On February 4, 1600, the famous Dane welcomed him warmly into the castle where he computed the heavens, his enormous orange mustache almost aglow with geniality. During the two months Kepler spent there as guest and apprentice, Tycho was so impressed with the young astronomer's theoretical ingenuity that he permitted him to analyze the celestial observations he had been guarding closely from all other scholars, then offered him a permanent position. Kepler accepted gratefully and journeyed back to Graz to collect his family, arriving in a retrograde world even more riven by religious persecution. When the Keplers refused to convert to Catholicism, they were banished from the city—the migration to Prague, with all the privations it would require, was no longer optional. Shortly after Kepler and his family alighted in their new life in Bohemia, the valve between chance and choice opened again, and another sudden change of circumstance flooded in: Tycho died unexpectedly at the age of fifty-four. Two days later, Kepler was appointed his successor as imperial mathematician, inheriting Tycho's data. Over the coming years, he would draw on it extensively in devising his three laws of planetary motion, which would revolutionize the human understanding of the universe.

How many revolutions does the cog of culture make before a new truth about reality catches into gear?

Three centuries before Kepler, Dante had marveled in his *Divine Comedy* at the new clocks ticking in England and Italy: "One wheel moves and drives the other." This marriage of technology and poetry eventually gave rise to the metaphor of the clockwork uni-

verse. Before Newton's physics placed this metaphor at the ideological epicenter of the Enlightenment, Kepler bridged the poetic and
the scientific. In his first book, *The Cosmographic Mystery,* Kepler
picked up the metaphor and stripped it of its divine dimensions,
removing God as the clockmaster and instead pointing to a single
force operating the heavens: "The celestial machine," he wrote, "is
not something like a divine organism, but rather something like a
clockwork in which a single weight drives all the gears." Within it,
"the totality of the complex motions is guided by a single magnetic
force." It was not, as Dante wrote, "love that moves the sun and
other stars"—it was gravity, as Newton would later formalize this
"single magnetic force." But it was Kepler who thus formulated
for the first time the very notion of a force—something that didn't
exist for Copernicus, who, despite his groundbreaking insight that
the sun moves the planets, still conceived of that motion in poetic
rather than scientific terms. For him, the planets were horses whose
reins the sun held; for Kepler, they were gears the sun wound by a
physical force.

   In the anxious winter of 1617, unfigurative wheels are turning
beneath Johannes Kepler as he hastens to his mother's witchcraft
trial. For this long journey by horse and carriage, Kepler has packed
a battered copy of *Dialogue on Ancient and Modern Music* by Vin-
cenzo Galilei, his sometime friend Galileo's father—one of the era's
most influential treatises on music, a subject that always enchanted
Kepler as much as mathematics, perhaps because he never saw the
two as separate. Three years later, he would draw on it in composing his own groundbreaking book *The Harmony of the World,*
in which he would formulate his third and final law of planetary
motion, known as the harmonic law—his exquisite discovery,
twenty-two years in the making, of the proportional link between
a planet's orbital period and the length of the axis of its orbit. It
would help compute, for the first time, the distance of the planets
from the sun—the measure of the heavens in an era when the Solar
System was thought to be all there was.

   As Kepler is galloping through the German countryside to prevent his mother's execution, the Inquisition in Rome is about to

declare the claim of Earth's motion heretical—a heresy punishable by death.

Behind him lies a crumbled life: Emperor Rudolph II is dead—Kepler is no longer royal mathematician and chief scientific adviser to the Holy Roman Emperor, a job endowed with Europe's highest scientific prestige, though primarily tasked with casting horoscopes for royalty; his beloved six-year-old son is dead—"a hyacinth of the morning in the first day of spring" wilted by smallpox, a disease that had barely spared Kepler himself as a child, leaving his skin cratered by scars and his eyesight permanently damaged; his first wife is dead, having come unhinged by grief before succumbing to the pox herself.

Before him lies the collision of two worlds in two world systems, the spark of which would ignite the interstellar imagination.

In 1609, Johannes Kepler finished the first work of genuine science fiction—that is, imaginative storytelling in which sensical science is a major plot device. *Somnium,* or *The Dream,* is the fictional account of a young astronomer who voyages to the Moon. Rich in both scientific ingenuity and symbolic play, it is at once a masterwork of the literary imagination and an invaluable scientific document, all the more impressive for the fact that it was written before Galileo pointed the first spyglass at the sky and before Kepler himself had ever looked through a telescope.

Kepler knew what we habitually forget—that the locus of possibility expands when the unimaginable is imagined and then made real through systematic effort. Centuries later, in a 1971 conversation with Carl Sagan and Arthur C. Clarke about the future of space exploration, science fiction patron saint Ray Bradbury would capture this transmutation process perfectly: "It's part of the nature of man to start with romance and build to a reality." Like any currency of value, the human imagination is a coin with two inseparable sides. It is our faculty of fancy that fills the disquieting gaps of the unknown with the tranquilizing certitudes of myth and superstition, that points to magic and witchcraft when common sense and reason fail to unveil causality. But that selfsame faculty is also what leads us to rise above accepted facts, above the limits of the possible established by custom and convention, and reach for new summits of previously unimagined truth. Which way the coin flips depends on the degree of courage, determined by some incalculable combination of nature, culture, and character.

In a letter to Galileo containing the first written mention of *The Dream*'s existence and penned in the spring of 1610—a little more than a century after Columbus voyaged to the Americas—Kepler ushers his correspondent's imagination toward fathoming the impending reality of interstellar travel by reminding him just how unimaginable transatlantic travel had seemed not so long ago:

> Who would have believed that a huge ocean could be crossed more peacefully and safely than the narrow expanse of the Adriatic, the Baltic Sea or the English Channel?

Kepler envisions that once "sails or ships fit to survive the heavenly breezes" are invented, voyagers would no longer fear the dark emptiness of interstellar space. With an eye to these future explorers, he issues a solidary challenge:

> So, for those who will come shortly to attempt this journey, let us establish the astronomy: Galileo, you of Jupiter, I of the moon.

Newton would later refine Kepler's three laws of motion with his formidable calculus and richer understanding of the underlying force as the foundation of Newtonian gravity. In a quarter millennium, the mathematician Katherine Johnson would draw on these laws in computing the trajectory that lands *Apollo 11* on the Moon. They would guide the *Voyager* spacecraft, the first human-made object to sail into interstellar space.

In *The Dream*, which Kepler described in his letter to Galileo as a "lunar geography," the young traveler lands on the Moon to find that lunar beings believe Earth revolves around them—from their cosmic vantage point, our pale blue dot rises and sets against their firmament, something reflected even in the name they have given Earth: Volva. Kepler chose the name deliberately, to emphasize the fact of Earth's revolution—the very motion that made Copernicanism so dangerous to the dogma of cosmic stability. Assuming that the reader is aware that the Moon revolves around the Earth—an anciently observed fact, thoroughly uncontroversial by his day— Kepler intimates the unnerving central question: Could it be, his story suggests in a stroke of allegorical genius predating Edwin Abbott Abbott's *Flatland* by nearly three centuries, that our own certitude about Earth's fixed position in space is just as misguided as the lunar denizens' belief in Volva's revolution around them? Could we, too, be revolving around the sun, even though the ground feels firm and motionless beneath our feet?

The Dream was intended to gently awaken people to the truth of Copernicus's disconcerting heliocentric model of the universe, defying the long-held belief that Earth is the static center of an immutable cosmos. But earthlings' millennia-long slumber was too deep for *The Dream*—a deadly somnolence, for it resulted in Kepler's elderly mother's being accused of witchcraft. Tens of thousands of people would be tried for witchcraft by the end of the persecution in Europe, dwarfing the two dozen who would render Salem synonymous with witchcraft trials seven decades later. Most of the accused were women, whose inculpation or defense fell on their sons, brothers, and husbands. Most of the trials ended in execution. In Germany, some twenty-five thousand were killed. In Kepler's sparsely populated hometown alone, six women had been burned as witches just a few weeks before his mother was indicted.

An uncanny symmetry haunts Kepler's predicament—it was Katharina Kepler who had first enchanted her son with astronomy when she took him to the top of a nearby hill and let the six-year-old boy gape in wonderment as the Great Comet of 1577 blazed across the sky.

By the time he wrote *The Dream,* Kepler was one of the most prominent scientists in the world. His rigorous fidelity to observational data harmonized with a symphonic imagination. Drawing on Tycho's data, Kepler devoted a decade and more than seventy failed trials to calculating the orbit of Mars, which became the yardstick for measuring the heavens. Having just formulated the first of his laws, demolishing the ancient belief that the heavenly bodies obey uniform circular motion, Kepler demonstrated that the planets orbit the sun at varying speeds along ellipses. Unlike previous models, which were simply mathematical hypotheses, Kepler discovered the actual orbit by which Mars moved through space, then used the Mars data to determine Earth's orbit. Taking multiple observations of Mars's position relative to Earth, he examined how the angle between the two planets changed over the course of the orbital period he had already calculated for Mars: 687 days. To do this, Kepler had to project himself onto Mars with an empathic leap of the imagination. The word *empathy* would come into popular use three centuries later, through the gateway of art, when it entered the modern lexicon in the early twentieth century to describe the imaginative act of projecting oneself into a painting in an effort to understand why art moves us. Through science, Kepler had projected himself into the greatest work of art there is in an effort to understand how nature draws its laws to move the planets, including the body that moves us through space. Using trigonometry, he calculated the distance between Earth and Mars, located the center of Earth's orbit, and went on to demonstrate that all the other planets also moved along elliptical orbits, thus demolishing the foundation of Greek astronomy—uniform circular motion—and effecting a major strike against the Ptolemaic model.

Kepler published these revelatory results, which summed up his first two laws, in his book *Astronomia nova—The New Astronomy*. That is exactly what it was—the nature of the cosmos had forever changed, and so had our place in it. "Through my effort God is being celebrated in astronomy," Kepler wrote to his former professor, reflecting on having traded a career in theology for the conquest of a greater truth.

By the time of *Astronomia nova*, Kepler had ample mathematical evidence affirming Copernicus's theory. But he realized something crucial and abiding about human psychology: The scientific proof was too complex, too cumbersome, too abstract to persuade even his peers, much less the scientifically illiterate public; it wasn't data that would dismantle their celestial parochialism, but storytelling. Three centuries before the poet Muriel Rukeyser wrote that "the universe is made of stories, not of atoms," Kepler knew that whatever the composition of the universe may be, its understanding was indeed the work of stories, not of science—that what he needed was a new rhetoric by which to illustrate, in a simple yet compelling way, that the Earth is indeed in motion. And so *The Dream* was born.

Even in medieval times, the Frankfurt Book Fair was one of the world's most fecund literary marketplaces. Kepler attended it frequently in order to promote his own books and to stay informed about other important scientific publications. He brought the manuscript of *The Dream* with him to this safest possible launchpad, where the other attendees, in addition to being well aware of the author's reputation as a royal mathematician and astronomer, were either scientists themselves or erudite enough to appreciate the story's clever allegorical play on science. But something went awry: Sometime in 1611, the sole manuscript fell into the hands of a wealthy young nobleman and made its way across Europe. By Kepler's account, it even reached John Donne and inspired his ferocious satire of the Catholic Church, *Ignatius His Conclave*. Circulated via barbershop gossip, versions of the story had reached minds far less literary, or even literate, by 1615. These garbled retellings eventually made their way to Kepler's home duchy.

"Once a poem is made available to the public, the right of interpretation belongs to the reader," young Sylvia Plath would write to her mother three centuries later. But interpretation invariably reveals more about the interpreter than about the interpreted. The gap between intention and interpretation is always rife with wrongs, especially when writer and reader occupy vastly different strata of emotional maturity and intellectual sophistication. The science, symbolism, and allegorical virtuosity of *The Dream* were entirely lost on the illiterate, superstitious, and vengeful villagers of Kepler's hometown. Instead, they interpreted the story with the only tool at their disposal—the blunt weapon of the literal shorn of context. They were especially captivated by one element of the story: The narrator is a young astronomer who describes himself as "by nature eager for knowledge" and who had apprenticed with Tycho Brahe. By then, people far and wide knew of Tycho's most famous pupil and imperial successor. Perhaps it was a point of pride for locals to have produced the famous Johannes Kepler, perhaps a point of envy. Whatever the case, they immediately took the story to be not fiction but autobiography. This was the seedbed of trouble: Another main character was the narrator's mother—an herb doctor who conjures up spirits to assist her son in his lunar voyage. Kepler's own mother was an herb doctor.

Whether what happened next was the product of intentional malevolent manipulation or the unfortunate workings of ignorance is hard to tell. My own sense is that one aided the other, as those who stand to gain from the manipulation of truth often prey on those bereft of critical thinking. According to Kepler's subsequent account, a local barber overheard the story and seized upon the chance to cast Katharina Kepler as a witch—an opportune accusation, for the barber's sister Ursula had a bone to pick with the elderly woman, a disavowed friend. Ursula Reinhold had borrowed money from Katharina Kepler and never repaid it. She had also confided in the old widow about having become pregnant by a man other than her husband. In an act of unthinking indiscretion, Katharina had shared this compromising information with Johannes's younger brother, who had then just as unthinkingly circulated it around the small town. To abate scandal, Ursula had obtained an abortion. To cover up the brutal corporeal aftermath of this medically primitive procedure, she blamed her infirmity on a spell—cast against her, she proclaimed, by Katharina Kepler. Soon Ursula persuaded twenty-four suggestible locals to give accounts of the elderly woman's sorcery—one neighbor claimed that her daughter's arm had grown numb after Katharina brushed against it in the street; the butcher's wife swore that pain pierced her husband's thigh when Katharina walked by; the limping schoolmaster dated the onset of his disability to a night ten years earlier when he had taken a sip from a tin cup at Katharina's house while reading her one of Kepler's letters. She was accused of appearing magically through closed doors, of having caused the deaths of infants and animals. *The Dream*, Kepler believed, had furnished the superstition-hungry townspeople with evidence of his mother's alleged witchcraft—after all, her own son had depicted her as a sorcerer in his story, the allegorical nature of which eluded them completely.

For her part, Katharina Kepler didn't help her own case. Prickly in character and known to brawl, she first tried suing Ursula for slander—a strikingly modern American approach but, in medieval Germany, effective only in stoking the fire, for Ursula's well-connected family had ties to local authorities. Then she tried bribing the magistrate into dismissing her case by offering him a silver chalice, which was promptly interpreted as an admission of guilt, and the civil case was escalated to a criminal trial for witchcraft.

In the midst of this tumult, Kepler's infant daughter, named for his mother, died of epilepsy, followed by another son, four years old, of smallpox.

Having taken his mother's defense upon himself as soon as he first learned of the accusation, the bereaved Kepler devoted six years to the trial, all the while trying to continue his scientific work and to see through the publication of the major astronomical catalog he had been composing since he inherited Tycho's data. Working remotely from Linz, Kepler first wrote various petitions on Katharina's behalf, then mounted a meticulous legal defense in writing. He requested trial documentation of witness testimonies and transcripts of his mother's interrogations. He then journeyed across the country once more, sitting with Katharina in prison and talking with her for hours on end to assemble information about the people and events of the small town he had left long ago. Despite the allegation that she was demented, the seventy-something Katharina's memory was astonishing—she recalled in granular detail incidents that had taken place years earlier.

Kepler set out to disprove each of the forty-nine "points of disgrace" hurled against his mother, using the scientific method to uncover the natural causes behind the supernatural evils she had allegedly wrought on the townspeople. He confirmed that Ursula had had an abortion, that the teenaged girl had numbed her arm by carrying too many bricks, that the schoolmaster had lamed his leg by tripping into a ditch, that the butcher suffered from lumbago.

None of Kepler's epistolary efforts at reason worked. Five years into the ordeal, an order for Katharina's arrest was served. In the small hours of an August night, armed guards barged into her daughter's house and found Katharina, who had heard the disturbance, hiding in a wooden linen chest—naked, as she often slept during the hot spells of summer. By one account, she was permitted to clothe herself before being taken away; by another, she was carried out disrobed inside the trunk to avoid a public disturbance and hauled to prison for another interrogation. So gratuitous was the fabrication of evidence that even Katharina's composure through the indignities was held against her—the fact that she didn't cry during the proceedings was cited as proof of unrepentant liaison with the Devil. Kepler had to explain to the court that he had never seen his stoic mother shed a single tear—not when his father left in Johannes's childhood, not during the long years Katharina spent raising her children alone, not in the many losses of old age.

Katharina was threatened with being stretched on a wheel— a diabolical device commonly used to extract confessions—unless she admitted to sorcery. This elderly woman, who had outlived her era's life expectancy by decades, would spend the next fourteen months imprisoned in a dark room, sitting and sleeping on the stone floor to which she was shackled with a heavy iron chain. She faced the threats with self-possession and confessed nothing.

In a last recourse, Kepler uprooted his entire family, left his teaching position, and traveled again to his hometown as the Thirty Years' War raged on. I wonder if he wondered during that dispiriting journey why he had written *The Dream* in the first place, wondered whether the price of any truth is to be capped at so great a personal cost.

Long ago, as a student at Tübingen, Kepler had read Plutarch's *The Face on the Moon*—the mythical story of a traveler who sails to a group of islands north of Britain inhabited by people who know secret passages to the Moon. There is no science in Plutarch's story—it is pure fantasy. And yet it employs the same simple, clever device that Kepler himself would use in *The Dream* fifteen centuries later to unsettle the reader's anthropocentric bias: In considering the Moon as a potential habitat for life, Plutarch pointed out that the idea of life in saltwater seems unfathomable to air-breathing creatures such as ourselves, and yet life in the oceans exists. It would be another eighteen centuries before we would fully awaken not only to the fact of marine life but to the complexity and splendor of this barely fathomable reality when Rachel Carson pioneered a new aesthetic of poetic science writing, inviting the human reader to consider Earth from the nonhuman perspective of sea creatures.

Kepler first read Plutarch's story in 1595, but it wasn't until the solar eclipse of 1605, the observations of which first gave him the insight that the orbits of the planets were ellipses rather than circles, that he began seriously considering the allegory as a means of illustrating Copernican ideas. Where Plutarch had explored space travel as metaphysics, Kepler made it a sandbox for real physics, exploring gravity and planetary motion. In writing about the take-off of his imaginary spaceship, for instance, he makes clear that he has a theoretical model of gravity factoring in the demands that breaking away from Earth's gravitational grip would place on cosmic voyagers. He goes on to add that while leaving Earth's gravitational pull would be toilsome, once the spaceship is in the gravity-free "aether," hardly any force would be needed to keep it in motion—an early understanding of inertia in the modern sense, predating by decades Newton's first law of motion, which states that a body will move at a steady velocity unless acted upon by an outside force.

In a passage at once insightful and amusing, Kepler describes the physical requirements for his lunar travelers—a prescient description of astronaut training:

No inactive persons are accepted . . . no fat ones; no pleasure-loving ones; we choose only those who have spent their lives on horseback, or have shipped often to the Indies and are accustomed to subsisting on hardtack, garlic, dried fish and unpalatable fare.

Three centuries later, the early polar explorer Ernest Shackleton would post a similar recruitment ad for his pioneering Antarctic expedition:

Men wanted for hazardous journey, small wages, bitter cold, long months of complete darkness, constant danger, safe return doubtful, honor and recognition in case of success.

When a woman named Peggy Peregrine expressed interest on behalf of an eager female trio, Shackleton dryly replied: "There are no vacancies for the opposite sex on the expedition." Half a century later, the Russian cosmonaut Valentina Tereshkova would become the first woman to exit Earth's atmosphere on a spacecraft guided by Kepler's laws.

After years of exerting reason against superstition, Kepler ultimately succeeded in getting his mother acquitted. But the seventy-five-year-old woman never recovered from the trauma of the trial and the bitter German winter spent in the unheated prison. On April 13, 1622, shortly after she was released, Katharina Kepler died, adding to her son's litany of losses. A quarter millennium later, Emily Dickinson would write in a poem the central metaphor of which draws on Kepler's legacy:

Each that we lose takes part of us;
A crescent still abides,
Which like the moon, some turbid night,
Is summoned by the tides.

A few months after his mother's death, Kepler received a letter from Christoph Besold—the classmate who had stuck up for his lunar dissertation thirty years earlier, now a successful attorney and professor of law. Having witnessed Katharina's harrowing fate, Besold had worked to expose the ignorance and abuses of power that sealed it, procuring a decree from the duke of Kepler's home duchy prohibiting any other witchcraft trials unsanctioned by the Supreme Court in the urban and presumably far less superstitious Stuttgart. "While neither your name nor that of your mother is mentioned in the edict," Besold wrote to his old friend, "everyone knows that it is at the bottom of it. You have rendered an inestimable service to the whole world, and someday your name will be blessed for it."

Kepler was unconsoled by the decree—perhaps he knew that policy change and cultural change are hardly the same thing, existing on different time scales. He spent the remaining years of his life obsessively annotating *The Dream* with two hundred twenty-three footnotes—a volume of hypertext equal to the story itself—intended to dispel superstitious interpretations by delineating his exact scientific reasons for using the symbols and metaphors he did.

In his ninety-sixth footnote, Kepler plainly stated "the hypothesis of the whole dream": "an argument for the motion of the Earth, or rather a refutation of arguments constructed, on the basis of perception, against the motion of the Earth." Fifty footnotes later, he reiterated the point by asserting that he envisioned the allegory as "a pleasant retort" to Ptolemaic parochialism. In a trailblazing systematic effort to unmoor scientific truth from the illusions of commonsense perception, he wrote:

Everyone says it is plain that the stars go around the earth while the Earth remains still. I say that it is plain to the eyes of the lunar people that our Earth, which is their Volva, goes around while their moon is still. If it be said that the lunatic perceptions of my moon-dwellers are deceived, I retort with equal justice that the terrestrial senses of the Earth-dwellers are devoid of reason.

In another footnote, Kepler defined gravity as "a power similar to magnetic power—a mutual attraction," and described its chief law:

The attractive power is greater in the case of two bodies that are near to each other than it is in the case of bodies that are far apart.

Therefore, bodies more strongly resist separation one from the other when they are still close together.

A further footnote pointed out that gravity is a universal force affecting bodies beyond the Earth, and that lunar gravity is responsible for earthly tides: "The clearest evidence of the relationship between earth and the moon is the ebb and flow of the seas." This fact, which became central to Newton's laws and which is now so commonplace that schoolchildren point to it as plain evidence of gravity, was far from accepted in Kepler's scientific community. Galileo, who was right about so much, was also wrong about so much—something worth remembering as we train ourselves in the cultural acrobatics of nuanced appreciation without idolatry. Galileo believed, for instance, that comets were vapors of the earth—a notion Tycho Brahe disproved by demonstrating that comets are celestial objects moving through space along computable trajectories after observing the very comet that had made six-year-old Kepler fall in love with astronomy. Galileo didn't merely deny that tides were caused by the Moon—he went as far as to mock Kepler's assertion that they do. "That concept is completely repugnant to my mind," he wrote—not even in a private letter but in his landmark *Dialogue on the Two Chief World Systems*—scoffing that "though [Kepler] has at his fingertips the motions attributed to the Earth, he has nevertheless lent his ear and his assent to the Moon's dominion over the waters, to occult properties, and to such puerilities."

Kepler took particular care with the portion of the allegory he saw as most directly responsible for his mother's witchcraft trial—the appearance of nine spirits, summoned by the protagonist's mother. In a footnote, he explained that these symbolize the nine Greek muses. In one of the story's more cryptic sentences, Kepler wrote of these spirits: "One, particularly friendly to me, most gentle and purest of all, is called forth by twenty-one characters." In his subsequent defense in footnotes, he explained that the phrase "twenty-one characters" refers to the number of letters used to spell *Astronomia Copernicana*. The friendliest spirit represents Urania—

the ancient Greek muse of astronomy, which Kepler considered the most reliable of the sciences:

> Although all the sciences are gentle and harmless in themselves (and on that account they are not those wicked and good-for-nothing spirits with whom witches and fortune-tellers have dealings . . .), this is especially true of astronomy because of the very nature of its subject matter.

When the astronomer William Herschel discovered the seventh planet from the sun a century and a half later, he named it Uranus, after the same muse. Elsewhere in Germany, a young Beethoven heard of the discovery and wondered in the marginalia of one of his compositions: "What will they think of my music on the star of Urania?" Another two centuries later, when Ann Druyan and Carl Sagan compose the Golden Record as a portrait of humanity in sound and image, Beethoven's Fifth Symphony sails into the cosmos aboard the *Voyager* spacecraft alongside a piece by the composer Laurie Spiegel based on Kepler's *Harmony of the World*.

Kepler was unambiguous about the broader political intent of his allegory. The year after his mother's death, he wrote to an astronomer friend:

> Would it be a great crime to paint the cyclopian morals of this period in livid colors, but for the sake of caution, to depart from the earth with such writing and secede to the moon?

Isn't it better, he wonders in another stroke of psychological genius, to illustrate the monstrosity of people's ignorance by way of the ignorance of imaginary others? He hoped that by seeing the absurdity of the lunar people's belief that the Moon is the center of the universe, the inhabitants of Earth would have the insight and integrity to question their own conviction of centrality. Three hundred fifty years later, when fifteen prominent poets are asked to contribute a "statement on poetics" for an influential anthology, Denise Levertov—the only woman of the fifteen—would state that poetry's highest task is "to awaken sleepers by other means than shock." This must have been what Kepler aimed to do with *The Dream*—his serenade to the poetics of science, aimed at awakening.

In December 1629, Kepler funded the printing of his *Dream* manuscript out of his already shallow pocket and set the type by hand himself. The first six pages took him four months, and then his money ran out. He left his family at their temporary home in Sagan and, already in precarious health, traveled to Leipzig, where he borrowed fifty florins—a substantial amount, about as much as a skilled craftsperson made in a year. He then put on his warmest brown stockings, belted a pistol and a powder flask into his tattered black woolen cloak, and made his way to Nuremberg, where he bought a famished mare as bony as himself. The two fragile creatures rode a hundred kilometers through the autumn rain to the Bavarian courts in Regensburg, where Kepler would seek permission to sell some Austrian bonds to repay his debt and finish printing *The Dream*. Days after he arrived and settled into an acquaintance's house, now named after him, Kepler came down with an acute illness. Used to frequent attacks of fever and bodily ailments, he paid little mind. Bloodletting was performed to attempt alleviating the symptoms, but he began slipping in and out of consciousness. Pastors were called in.

At noon on November 15, 1630, Johannes Kepler died, six weeks shy of his fifty-ninth birthday. Three days later, as his body was lowered into a grave in the Lutheran churchyard of St. Peter's Gate, a pastor proclaimed: "Blessed are they who hear and preserve the word of God." The Thirty Years' War, waged unblessed and unblessing on the alleged word of God, would soon swallow the cemetery and erase any trace of Kepler's bones.

The night after the funeral, a full moon passed through Earth's shadow in a lunar eclipse governed by eternal forces deaf to human words—fundamental truths of nature, which Kepler had spoken in the native tongue of the universe: mathematics. Three hundred thirty-nine years later, his *Dream* would come true as the first human foot stepped onto the Moon, leaping humankind via a trajectory calculated by his laws.

. . .

The Copernican model was the first major idea to challenge our self-importance. The challenge has taken many guises in the centuries since, as new world orders have been introduced—from evolutionary theory to civil rights to marriage equality, which society has initially met with antagonism comparable to that shown by the denizens of Kepler's hometown. What is at the center—be it of the universe or of our power structures—must stay at the center, even at the cost of truth. "The same, precisely the same conflicts have always stood as now, with slight shifting of scene & costume," Ralph Waldo Emerson would write in his journal in the middle of the nineteenth century.

Exactly two hundred fifty years after the solar eclipse that first gave Kepler the idea for *The Dream,* a report on the Woman's Rights Convention of 1852 appeared in the *New York Herald.* Its author—a man who vehemently opposed the idea that women were equal to men—wrote that the convention consisted of "old maids, whose personal charms were never very attractive" and women who have "so much virago in their disposition, that nature appears to have made a mistake in their gender—mannish women like hens that crow." His op-ed contained this pinnacle of illogic buoyed by emotional hysteria:

> If it be true that the female sex are equal to the male in point of physical strength and mental power, how is it that from the beginning of the world to the present time, in all ages, in all countries and climes, in every variety of the human species, the male has been predominant, and the female subject politically, socially, and in the family circle? . . . How did woman first become subject to man as she now is all over the world? By her nature—her sex—just as the negro is and always will be, to the end of time, inferior to the white race, and, therefore, doomed to subjection; but happier than she would be in any other condition, just because it is the law of her nature.

In the wake of his mother's witchcraft trial, Kepler made another observation centuries ahead of its time, even ahead of the seventeenth-century French philosopher François Poullain de la Barre's landmark assertion that "the mind has no sex." In Kepler's time, long before the discovery of genetics, it was believed that children bore a resemblance to their mothers, in physiognomy and character, because they were born under the same constellation. But Kepler was keenly aware of how different he and Katharina were as people, how divergent their worldviews and their fates—he, a meek leading scientist about to turn the world over; she, a mercurial, illiterate woman on trial for witchcraft. If the horoscopes he had once drawn for a living did not determine a person's life-path, Kepler couldn't help but wonder what did—here was a scientist in search of causality. A quarter millennium before social psychology existed as a formal field of study, he reasoned that what had gotten his mother into all this trouble in the first place—her ignorant beliefs and behaviors taken for the work of evil spirits, her social marginalization as a widow—was the fact that she had never benefited from the education her son, as a man, had received. In the fourth section of *The Harmony of the World*—his most daring and speculative foray into natural philosophy—Kepler writes in a chapter devoted to "metaphysical, psychological, and astrological" matters:

> I know a woman who was born under almost the same aspects, with a temperament which was certainly very restless, but by which she not only has no advantage in book learning (that is not surprising in a woman) but also disturbs the whole of her town, and is the author of her own lamentable misfortune.

In the very next sentence, Kepler identifies the woman in question as his own mother and proceeds to note that she never received the privileges he did. "I was born a man, not a woman," he writes, "a difference in sex which the astrologers seek in vain in the heavens." The difference between the fate of the sexes, Kepler suggests, is not in the heavens but in the earthly construction of gender as a function of culture. It was not his mother's nature that made her ignorant, but the consequences of her social standing in a world that rendered its opportunities for intellectual illumination and self-actualization as fixed as the stars.

2

TO FIND DISMOONED AMONG THE STARDUST

Maria Mitchell is standing in the front parlor of her humble family home at 1 Vestal Street on the island of Nantucket—a place "undecked, unlovely," as she would later write in a poem, but beloved. Beside her, a shiny brass telescope points out through the removed windowpanes. She is too ablaze with excitement to feel the gusts of February freeze rushing in. A glass bowl filled with water hangs overhead, dappling the room with rainbows. Through a piece of smoked glass, she lifts her big brown eyes to the darkening noonday firmament, ready to count the seconds of the eclipse.

Upstairs, a notecard in her neat hand hangs on the door of a former closet, transfigured by her father into a study for the ten Quaker children to share, but in use by Maria alone: "miss mitchell is busy. do not knock."

Twenty-one minutes past noon, on this particularly biting winter Saturday in 1831, a metallic light begins to turn the houses, the hills, the harbor into a living daguerreotype. I imagine someone across the narrow cobblestoned street stopping Beethoven midbar. I imagine a young whaler down in the bay leaning on his harpoon to look up.

A hundred miles north, under the uncanny skies of partially eclipsed Concord, Ralph Waldo Emerson has just buried his beloved young bride, dead of tuberculosis at twenty.

Against the deepening cobalt of the sky, the Moon glides before the sun and carves a slowly slimming crescent. When it settles for a moment into a glowing ring, Maria counts 117 seconds and feels like she is peering down the gun barrel of time, gold-rimmed and eerie.

She is twelve. She is besotted with the splendor of the cosmos and the sturdy certitude of mathematics—a coruscating intellect undimmed by the limitations of her time and place. No woman can vote. No woman can receive a formal education in higher mathematics or astronomy anywhere in the world. No woman has yet been hired by the United States government for any technical job. Maria Mitchell wouldn't live to reap the vote, but she would become many firsts: America's first professional woman astronomer, the first woman admitted into the American Academy of Arts and Sciences, the first woman employed by the government for a "specialized non-domestic skill" as a "computer of Venus"—a one-person GPS performing complex celestial calculations to help sailors navigate the globe.

The year of her ecliptic revelation, the king of Denmark—Europe's supreme patron of the sciences—announced a major astronomical prize: The first person to discover a new telescopic comet would be awarded a gold medal valued at 20 ducats, a fortune. Such a discovery would be no small feat or mere fluke—the patient observer would have to discern a small, blurry, tailless coma of light amid the cosmic wilderness of existing objects, with which he or she must be intimately familiar in order to detect the interloping apparition.

Night after night, year after year, Maria Mitchell would point her steadfast instrument at the nocturne and sweep the skies with quiet systematic passion, searching for a new celestial object against the backdrop of familiar bodies. One autumn evening in her twenty-ninth year, she would slip out of her parents' dinner party to climb onto the roof and station herself at the telescope, wrapped in what she called her "regimentals"—her uniform of plain Quaker clothing. I imagine this contained young woman surprising herself with a spontaneous gasp when she sees what she saw at half past ten on that first day of October in 1847, before beckoning her father to the roof to show him the momentous speck she had isolated from the vast cosmic background: a new telescopic comet.

What invigorated Maria Mitchell that evening, and what would drive her for the remaining decades of her life, was not the king's medal, nor the luster of worldwide recognition, but the sheer thrill of discovery—the ecstasy of having personally chipped a small fragment of knowledge from the immense monolith of the unknown, that elemental motive force of every sincere scientist.

Despite Maria's reluctance to make the discovery public, her father insisted that they alert the Harvard Observatory. He finally persuaded her by framing it as a patriotic act—she would be claiming a victory not for her ego but for American astronomy, still in its infancy and wholly uncompetitive with the gravitas of European institutions and the millennia of Middle Eastern and Chinese credibility. But nature itself intervened—on this small island so beholden to the elements for its basic operations, stormy weather delayed the postal pickup for two days. By October 3, as Mitchell's announcement was traveling to Harvard, an astronomer in Europe also observed the comet, reported it to the local astronomical authorities, and swiftly claimed the medal.

When the letter from Nantucket arrived on October 7, the president of Harvard instantly recognized in Maria Mitchell's discovery an opportunity to celebrate a first major triumph for American astronomy—and for the still-nascent Harvard, which had established its Lawrence Scientific School, home to the university's first graduate program, earlier that year. "It would be a pity that she should lose the medal on a mere technical punctilio," he appealed to the American ambassador in Copenhagen. Word soon traveled around Europe. In a heartening case of solidarity and integrity, the Old World's scientific community acknowledged Maria Mitchell's priority of discovery, turning the medal over to her—a three-inch disc of solid gold with a bas relief of the king of Denmark on the front and of Urania, the ancient Greek muse of astronomy, on the back. Four months after the discovery, the Royal Astronomical Society bulletin published an article about "Miss Mitchell's Comet," as it would be known for more than a century before being renamed the unromantic C/1847 T1. Mitchell had provided the journal with her original calculations of the comet's orbit—an impressive feat, for this particular comet travels along a mathematically complex hyperbolic trajectory. Nearly half a century later, Margaretta Palmer would become the first woman to earn a Ph.D. in astronomy in America, at Yale, for her study of the irregular orbit of Mitchell's comet—a crooked cosmic boomerang flung earthward from the far reaches of the cosmos long ago, never to return to our Solar System again.

Months before Mitchell's discovery, Ralph Waldo Emerson had written in his debut book of poetry:

I tire of shams, I rush to be.
I pass with yonder comet free,
Pass with the comet into space.

Within months, the discovery would make Mitchell the first woman elected, unanimously, to the American Academy of Arts and Sciences. On her certificate of admission, the salutation "Sir" is crossed out, as is the word "Fellow," over which "an Honorary Member" is handwritten in pencil. It will be almost a century before the Academy admits the second woman—the anthropologist Margaret Mead. But Mitchell would always remain unmoved by such recognition. "Medals are small things in the light of the stars," she would later write. "There's only one thing in the world of any real importance, and that is goodness."

Over the years, Ralph Waldo Emerson, Herman Melville, Henry David Thoreau, Elizabeth Peabody, and Frederick Douglass would all visit Nantucket to peer through the same telescope the twelve-year-old girl had once pointed at the annular eclipse, at the stars, at her celestial dome of possibility—a telescope not much worse than the one Harvard then had, not much better than the one by which Galileo had unsettled the universe two centuries earlier.

Visiting Mitchell's childhood home turned museum nearly two centuries later, I glide a surreptitious hand over the four parallel dents on the side of her telescope's cool brass body and wonder how it acquired them. I imagine the young Maria Mitchell tripping on her heavy Quaker gown one night as she climbs the eight narrow wooden steps to the widow's walk on the roof while carrying the large brass instrument, a small observing notebook, and a whale oil lamp, as she did nearly every night of her youth.

Over and over, Maria's umbral brilliance would rise above the shadows cast by her society. "Mingle the starlight with your lives," she would later tell her students at Vassar—America's first class of women astronomers—"and you won't be fretted by trifles."

Still. We hunger for straightforward stories of improbable achievement against towering cultural odds, stories that excise the trifles, the messiness, the inconsistencies of personhood that mark every human life. But Mitchell's life is infinitely more interesting when considered for the questions it raises rather than for the answers it bestows. Some questions: Where does it live, that place of permission that lets a person chart a new terrain of possibility, that makes her dare to believe she can be something other than what her culture tells her she is, and then become what she believes she can? How does something emerge from nothing? It is a question baffling enough to ask about the universe, but simply obtuse to consider about the self—there is no such thing as a self-made person. Maria Mitchell had an uncommon gift for mathematics, yes, and was animated by a quiet obstinacy that allowed her to shoulder the obstacles her culture placed before her. But she was also the product of myriad factors outside her own nature—she grew up in an uncommonly loving family, with an uncommonly erudite mother and an uncommonly present father who treated her like an intellectual peer, in a maritime town where mathematics was not a lofty indulgence in abstraction but a vital practical aid in navigation, in the Quaker faith, which insisted on the equal education of boys and girls, on an isolated island, where long and dreary winter nights turned astronomy into popular entertainment. In the final years of her life, Mitchell would point to her natural proclivity for mathematics and her father's steadfast encouragement as the wellspring of her scientific achievement, but she would add: "The spirit of the place also had much to do with the early bent of my mind in this direction."

Mitchell, who had learned Latin in childhood and was among antebellum America's few astronomers to use Latin texts, must have known the Latin term *genius loci*—"the spirit of a place." Although the modern use of the word "genius" has allocated it to the individual, this original use encodes the indelible role of place in personhood. Comets of chance and tides of circumstance sculpt the shorelines of the self to make us who we are—we can no more claim all credit for our achievement than deflect all blame for our impediments, and it is often difficult to separate the elements of life that make for fortune from those that make for misfortune. Were Mitchell's accidents of birth lucky or unlucky—to have been born a woman, and brilliant, in the nineteenth century, in a small and secluded whaling community? Would she have reached further, attained more, been happier in another body, in another era, in another place? These are questions impossible to answer without acknowledging what human hubris it is to call one thing accident and another luck in a universe insentient to any of our hopes and fears, to our categories of good and bad. The human mind seems unwilling to wrap itself and its prosthetic of language around the notion of pure impartial probability. We imbue even the word *chance* with a constellation of subjective meanings—chance as serendipity's accomplice, chance as free will's counterpoint, chance as love's other name or a dog's only.

Even Maria Mitchell's basic unit of identity errs on the side of the improbable: Her first name, spelled like my own—for centuries the most common female name in the Christian world—follows not the Spanish pronunciation currently used in English but the traditional Latin one: Mariah / məˈrīʹə/. She is named for her mother's favorite writer, Maria Edgeworth—the pioneering Anglo-Irish author of realist children's literature with progressive political undercurrents and an edge of science. Edgeworth was one of a handful of women, alongside Joan of Arc, Sappho, and several saints, whom Auguste Comte included in his *Calendar of Great Men*—a landmark cultural biography of 559 world-changing minds, "worthiest of all ages & nations," spanning from Euclid and Pythagoras to Kepler and Galileo to Beethoven and Milton. It was part of Comte's proposal for a "positivist" solar calendar to replace the Gregorian, comprising thirteen months of twenty-eight days, each day named not for a religious saint but for a hero of secular culture—a scientist, poet, philosopher, painter, inventor, explorer.

To name her daughter for Maria Edgeworth was a choice hardly surprising given the self-taught Lydia Mitchell's immense erudition. She was the only person to have read every book that could be read on Nantucket—from the holdings of the island's two public libraries, at each of which she had worked as a librarian in order to devour their books, to the private collections of the families wealthy enough to afford such a luxury.

Lydia found an intellectual peer in the self-taught astronomer William Mitchell, who had fallen in love with the rings of Saturn at the age of eight, but she also found something rather uncommon for the time—a marriage not of convenience and domestic practicality, but of deep and passionate devotion. William relinquished his admission to Harvard because he couldn't bear to be away from his beloved. Unlike most Nantucket men, who spent the majority of their time on sailing trips, he rarely left his ever-growing family's side for the remainder of their long and loving marriage, taking on a series of odd jobs—schoolmaster, insurance broker, executor of wills, bank clerk, candlemaker—in order to avoid going to sea.

Like Lydia, William had a dual streak of integrity and insurgency. He embraced certain values of the Quaker faith—abolition, education, and equal intellectual opportunities for the sexes. He insisted that his daughters receive the same basic education as his sons, and when one of his girls began exhibiting an aptitude for science greater than that of any of the others, he met her superior natural gifts with commensurate encouragement and opportunity for scholarship. He turned his house into a stop on the Underground Railroad, in which astronomy played a key role—traveling at night, slaves were told to keep the river on one side and follow the Drinking Gourd, an African name for the Big Dipper, for if they kept after the pole star, they would keep themselves moving north.

He boycotted slave-harvested cotton by ensuring that, despite the family's meager means, his wife and daughters wore dresses of silk. (Decades later, when Maria became one of America's first scientific celebrities, many would remark on her "humble black dress," which was in fact made of silk—a vestige of her family's quiet activism. I have wondered whether Marie Curie, famed for her insistence on owning no more than her one black dress, which she wore both on her wedding day and daily at the lab, was aware of this slender thread of lineage to the cultural progenitor who paved the way for women in science.)

When Maria was eight, her father and his cousin Walter Folger—also a cousin of Benjamin Franklin's, and considered the Benjamin Franklin of Nantucket—cofounded the Nantucket Philosophical Institution, one of the first scientific associations in America. At the end of 1831, ten months after Maria's formative eclipse observation, the Institution began admitting women. Most of Europe's scientific institutions were still decades away from such inclusion. London's Royal Society, the Old World's pantheon of science, admitted its first two female members in 1835. Meanwhile, within a year of its founding, the Nantucket Philosophical Institution had as many women members as men. Thirteen-year-old Maria, her sisters, and their mother were among its first female members.

A year after the Philosophical Institution was founded, Nantucket established its first public school. William Mitchell—who had grown up without a formal school on the island, in an era when Quakers were heavily persecuted and excluded from America's handful of existing colleges—was appointed its first principal. Over the next three years, he hired a number of women teachers. When Maria was ten, an article appeared in the *Nantucket Inquirer* praising her father's insistence on educational equality. With an eye to the answer William Mitchell had modeled, the author asked:

If widening the sphere of knowledge has a direct tendency to enhance the happiness of the recipient, why not have the fountain flow as liberally for the female part of our species as for the "rougher sex"? . . . Are the imaginations of women less vivid than men? If not, why should their minds be denied the privilege of contemplating the countless orbs of argent light that roll in silent magnificence through the deep illimitable expanse?

Then, several months before his daughter beheld the eclipse that illuminated her life path, William resigned to found his own private school "for fifty scholars, half of each sex."

But as much as his Quaker faith informed his values of equality, he refused blind dogma and sculpted other Quaker tenets around his own moral sensibilities. Although Quakers considered music morally corrosive, when his daughters smuggled a piano into the house during one of his brief trips, William didn't have the heart to expel it—the instrument stayed. His boldest insurgency was the water-filled glass bowl that sprinkled the front parlor with rainbows whenever it caught a ray of sun—a scandalous sight given the Quaker ban on color. When asked about the bowl, William declared that he used it to study the bipolarity of light—something he made up on the spot in order to render the inventive kaleidoscope acceptable as a scientific instrument rather than an object whose sole purpose was the delight in beauty. He saw the hunger for beauty as inseparable from the search for truth, both indelible pillars of the human spirit. Many years later, Maria would write in her journal:

I am just learning to notice the different colors of the stars, and already begin to have a new enjoyment. Betelgeuse is strikingly red, while Rigel is yellow. There is something of the same pleasure in noticing the hues that there is in looking at a collection of precious stones, or at a flower-garden in autumn.

She would marvel at the celestial kaleidoscope while sweeping the sky for comets:

I wonder that I have so long been insensible to this charm in the skies, the tints of the different stars are so delicate in their variety.

More than a century after Mitchell's childhood, another star-struck little girl would peer out her bedroom window in Washing-

ton, D.C., night after night. One day, after reading about Maria
Mitchell in a children's book, she would be seized with a life-altering
realization: Not only could one become a professional stargazer,
but astronomy was open to women. Moved to follow Mitchell, she
would apply to and graduate from Vassar College, then grow up to
become Vera Rubin—the astronomer who confirmed the existence
of dark matter.

In 1965, exactly a hundred years after Maria Mitchell was
appointed the first professor of astronomy at Vassar, Rubin would
become the first woman permitted to use the Palomar Observatory,
home to the world's most powerful telescopes at the time. Rubin
would later reflect on the same indivisibility of beauty's enchantment and the search for truth that had prompted William Mitchell
to defend his glass bowl:

> I sometimes ask myself whether I would be studying galaxies if they
> were ugly . . . I think it may not be irrelevant that galaxies are really
> very attractive.

The adolescent Maria Mitchell accelerated her immersion in
higher mathematics and punctuated it with poetry. She attended her
father's schools—first the public, then the private—until she was
fifteen. By that point, Maria had mastered higher mathematics, and
no institution—not on the island, not on the globe—had anything
further to offer her in the way of higher education for a woman. At
seventeen, she founded a small school of her own. The first children who approached the teenage teacher for enrollment were three
"Portuguese" girls—local slang for the island's small, sequestered
population of dark-skinned immigrants. Having just witnessed a
vehement outcry when the Nantucket's public school had attempted
integration the previous year, Mitchell knew that admitting students
of color would cost her the support of many parents, particularly
the wealthy. But when the little girl representing the trio implored
for a chance to learn, Mitchell made a decision with a clarity of conviction that would come to mark her life. The three "Portuguese"
children became her first scholars, soon joined by others ranging in
age from six to fourteen.

In a single large classroom, Mitchell stretched her students' minds from Shakespeare to spherical geometry. But before she could savor the success of her school, she was offered the head librarianship of the Nantucket Atheneum. She was eighteen.

In 1798, Liverpool had modeled for the world a new kind of cultural institution—the athenaeum, named after the ancient Greek goddess of wisdom, learning, and the arts, designed as a secular gathering place to discover and discuss ideas. Within two decades, New England and the mid-Atlantic coast were populated with these temples of intellectual refinement, many built to mimic ancient Greek architecture. Unlike public libraries, athenaeums were privately owned by local shareholders. Each established its own policy of exclusivity or inclusivity. The one in Philadelphia flatly prohibited women from even entering the building. The one in Boston, America's first and largest athenaeum, admitted the writer and abolitionist Lydia Maria Child in 1824 after the success of her first novel, but later expelled her for supporting interracial marriage. The Nantucket Atheneum, built on the values of the Nantucket Philosophical Institution, was different—in how it chose to spell its name, in being open to people of all races and income levels, in not only admitting women but appointing one as its guiding intellect.

A few months after her comet discovery, eleven years into her Atheneum tenure, Mitchell was offered the prestigious job of "computer of Venus" for the United States Navy's nascent *Nautical Almanac*—one of only eleven such positions for mathematical astronomers—at the annual salary of $500, fivefold what she earned at the Atheneum. Accepting only on the condition that she could keep her Atheneum librarianship, she went on to hold the Navy position for twenty years.

The Atheneum reference desk was located at the very back of the former Unitarian church housing the institution—Maria Mitchell practically sat at the altar as she helped students find scientific references, recommended good novels to young people, and curated the books to be ordered for the library's holdings. In unpeopled hours, the Atheneum became her private Alexandria as she read the latest works by Europe's most prominent astronomers, taught herself German, and devoured poetry—from Milton to Elizabeth Barrett Browning, whom she would come to admire more than any other living poet. I can picture her tall figure crescented over the Atheneum desk, large brown eyes streaming down a verse, full lips pressed into focus, parting unconsciously every once in a while to mouth a particularly beautiful line.

These were fertile, formative hours—the woman who spent her mornings with Newton and her evenings with Milton would later grow compelled to contemplate the intersection of astronomy and poetry in an essay titled "The Astronomical Science of Milton as Shown in 'Paradise Lost.'" Never published in her lifetime, the piece appeared in 1894 in the sixth volume of *Poet-Lore*—the oldest continuously running poetry journal in the United States, founded in the year of Mitchell's death by two self-described "progressive young Shakespeare scholars who believed in the evolutionary nature of literature": the couple Charlotte Porter and Helen Archibald Clarke. (The latter signed her literary work H.C.P., effectively adopting her partner's last name long before marriage equality.) *Poet-Lore*'s early years saw the publication of works by Rainer Maria Rilke, Hermann Hesse, and Rabindranath Tagore, as well as the first English translation of Chekhov's *The Seagull*. Mitchell's piece appeared alongside a letter by George Eliot on the loneliness of her chosen path.

Mitchell, who at the end of her life would confide in one of her Vassar students that she would rather have authored a great poem than discovered a comet, wrote:

Milton, when read in childhood, fastens his Heaven and Hell upon us; we cannot forget them,—we know no other. We see no sunrise without thinking of his lines:—

"Now morn her rosy steps in th' eastern clime
Advancing, sowed the Earth with orient pearl."
[. . .]

Read astronomically, Milton may be taken as the poetical historian of the astronomy of his day. The telescope had been known for sixteen years when he was born. Seven planets had been observed. Galileo had made known the existence of the satellites of Jupiter, the belts of Saturn, the inequalities of the moon's surface, and had declared with fear and trembling, which time showed to be well-grounded, the motion of the earth.

At a time when blood was being shed over the heliocentricity that dislodged man from the center of the universe, a time when the notion of galaxies was still far away, Milton championed the Copernican model and imagined "every star perhaps a world." Long before the composition of the sun was discovered, he accurately described its physical structure, "made porous to receive and drink the liquid light." Having visited the aged, totally blind, Inquisition-imprisoned Galileo, Milton made references to him and allusions to his discoveries throughout *Paradise Lost*. Line 650 of Book I—"Space may produce new Worlds; whereof so rife"—is considered the very first use of the English word *space* to connote the cosmic expanse. Having seen several comets as a boy, Milton— himself entirely blind by the time he composed *Paradise Lost* with the scribal assistance of his daughters—dramatizes his era's superstitions about these astronomical events:

> Satan stood
> Unterrifi'd, and like a comet burn'd,
> That fires the length of Orphiuchus huge,
> In th' Arctic sky, and from his horrid hair
> Shakes pestilence and war.

Mitchell astutely observed:

> If Milton was vastly beyond his age in most respects, he yielded at times to the superstition of the period; or perhaps he did not do so seriously, but only employed it as poetic imagery.

Walt Whitman, born within months of Mitchell, might have preferred to be an astronomer, unburdened by the artifice of poetry and free to revel in the natural poetics of the universe. Late in life, he would wonder in his notebooks: "Is there not something about the moon, some relation or reminder, which no poem or literature has yet caught?" Just as Mitchell was incubating her Milton essay, Whitman wrote in the preface to *Leaves of Grass*:

> The sky of heaven and the orbs, the forests, mountains, and rivers, are not small themes . . . but folks expect of the poet to indicate more than the beauty and dignity which always attach to dumb real objects . . . they expect him to indicate the path between reality and their souls.

Mitchell tempered her praise for Milton's poetic gift and astronomical prescience by condemning his bifurcation of the soul along gender lines—the poet, she laments, had "failed to make Eve as intelligent and learned as we require that a woman should be in these days." She writes:

> I felt, even when a child, indignant that Milton should represent Eve as so careless of the angel's discourse that she must tend her flowers just at that juncture. The poet thus shows an ignorant and a manoeuvring woman. It seems to me that the childlike Eve should have remained and listened, asked questions, and kept up the dramatic interest.

Mitchell's precocious vision for who Eve could and should be wasn't the function of her parents alone. Growing up, the Mitchell children had learned to echo their father's enthusiastic response to the question of who the greatest scientist of all time was: "Herschel!" To William Mitchell, this meant William Herschel—the great German-English astronomer, discoverer of Uranus, inaugural president of the Royal Astronomical Society. But to Maria, the surname so routinely exclaimed with such veneration is as likely to have meant William's sister, Caroline Herschel—the world's first professional woman astronomer.

Having barely survived typhus fever at the age of eleven, which damaged her left eye and stunted her growth, Caroline Herschel spent the bulk of her ninety-eight years on Earth sweeping the skies

with her one good eye—a tiny figure of four feet three inches stationed at the base of a twenty-foot telescope. She arrived at this
unexampled post via a path originating at the meeting point of circumstance and choice.

When political unrest seized the Herschel family's native Hanover,
Mr. Herschel sent his two sons abroad to England, hoping to save
them from being drafted for war. There, Wilhelm changed his name
to William. A prodigy at the oboe and violin since the age of fourteen and now a budding composer, he tried his hand at making a living as a musician. Meanwhile, at home, Caroline's mother deemed
her too ugly for marriage and began training her for the life of a
domestic servant. The only surviving daughter in a large brood of
boys, Caroline would later describe herself as the Cinderella of the
family. "I could not bear the idea of being turned into an Abigail
or housemaid," she would recall in her memoirs. When her father,
to whom Caroline was deeply attached, suffered a fatal stroke just
before her seventeenth birthday, she saw no reason to remain in a
cold home preparing her for a bleak future. But her mother refused
to let her join William in England. William, twelve years older than
Caroline and a second father figure, beseeched on her behalf—to no
avail. Caroline persisted for months, years. Finally, in a bout of desperation, she knitted two years' worth of stockings for the family to
tide them over in her absence—an act of such stubborn determination that her mother relented at last.

Caroline set out for Bath, where she arrived speaking only the
few English words she had picked up on the journey, and joined
William with the intention of training as a singer so that she could
accompany him in concerts. But although she became an accomplished vocalist, her loyalty to William—at that point and ever
after—was so great that when she was invited to perform at a prestigious festival, she declined on the grounds that she never wanted
to sing in concerts where her brother was not the conductor.

Meanwhile, William had been falling in love with astronomy,
and he decided to abandon his career in music. Too poor to afford
instruments and too proud to ask for loans, he taught himself to
make mirrors and build telescopes. Caroline became his stead-

fast assistant—for forty-one years. An excellent observer and a poor mathematician, William came to rely on his sister not only for recording his observations but for making the more complex mathematical calculations. During long nights at the telescope, she brought him food and coffee, kept the fire going, and read him *The Arabian Nights* and *Don Quixote* to pass the time. A century later, Elizabeth Barrett Browning would write:

> The world's male chivalry has perished out,
> But women are knights-errant to the last;
> And, if Cervantes had been greater still,
> He had made his Don a Donna.

William enlisted Caroline's assistance "to run the clocks, write down a memorandum, fetch and carry instruments, or measure the ground with poles"—a line from Caroline's memoirs, which Adrienne Rich would weave into her poem "Planetarium," paying tribute to Herschel and other unheralded heroines of astronomy. When one of William's telescope mirrors had to be cast in a mold of loam made from horse dung, Caroline faithfully pounded vast quantities of manure in a mortar and spent hours sifting it through a fine sieve. A typical entry from her diary of the time reads "I spent the whole day in ruling paper for the register; except that at breakfast I cut out ruffles for shirts."

Between grids and stitches, Caroline was incubating her own love of astronomy—a love undergirded by growing technical acumen and the impulse "to spend the star-lit nights on a grass-plot covered with dew or hoar frost, without a human being near enough to be within call." When she learned to copy star catalogs—painstaking work that consumed countless days—she began noticing gaps in the data. She labored for years over the famous star catalog by John Flamsteed—the first Astronomer Royal and the first to theorize, opposing Newton, that comets orbit the sun in large closed ellipses as planets do. The three thousand stars Flamsteed had spent forty years cataloging tripled the records in Tycho Brahe's sky atlas, the premier astronomical reference of the day. But Caroline Herschel

found two crucial problems with the Flamsteed catalog: It was organized by constellation without a proper index, and it was plagued
by numerous star omissions and calculating errors. First, she composed a meticulous index of the catalog, reconfiguring the sky by
zones of North Polar Distance and magnitude of stellar brightness.
Then—a century before Charles Darwin proclaimed that "to kill an
error is as good a service as, and sometimes even better than, the
establishing of a new truth or fact"—she set out to remedy Flamsteed's errors and began making her own observations.

In the summer of 1782, at the age of thirty-two, Herschel
embarked on her own catalog. The following year, she made her first
independent discoveries—a nebula missing from the famous Messier catalog and, crucially, the dwarf elliptical galaxy now known
as Messier 110, a companion to the Andromeda Galaxy. Six years
after her brother's death, Herschel would become the first woman
awarded the gold medal from the Royal Astronomical Society—the
era's most respected scientific establishment. It would be another
168 years before another woman received it: Vera Rubin.

While Maria Mitchell had a powerful model in Caroline Herschel, Caroline Herschel had none. As I leaf through her memoirs
and letters—the unsentimental log of a trying life governed by tenacity so untrumpeting as to border on the saintly—I am reminded of
Lucille Clifton's lines:

> won't you celebrate with me
> what i have shaped into
> a kind of life? i had no model.
> [. . .]
> i made it up
> here on this bridge between
> starshine and clay

For Herschel, who died nine weeks after Mitchell's comet discovery and didn't live to see the young American astronomer pave
the path she herself had scythed, self-invention between starshine
and clay was no metaphor—literally and frequently, her long skirts
dragged through the mud as she trekked across a soggy English

lawn to catalog the stars through her telescope. In one particularly telling incident Herschel recorded in her diary on New Year's Eve 1783, she rushed out after a cloudy evening to take advantage of a brief window of visibility. Running through the foot-deep melting snow, she slipped and fell on the mechanism employed for rotating the telescope—two butcher's hooks, one of which pierced her leg above the knee, through the fourteen pairs of stockings she wore during winter observation, to the bone. She recounted the incident:

> My brother's call, "Make haste!" I could only answer by a pitiful cry, "I am hooked!" He and the workmen were instantly with me, but they could not lift me without leaving nearly two ounces of my flesh behind.

Herschel bandaged her own wound until a doctor could see her several days later. When he did, he remarked that "if a soldier had met with such a hurt he would have been entitled to six weeks' nursing in a hospital." She concludes the diary entry with matter-of-factness that bespeaks her superhuman devotion to science:

> To make observations with such large machinery, where all around is in darkness, is not unattended with danger, especially when personal safety is the last thing with which the mind is occupied.

Looking back on her life from the fortunate platform of old age, Herschel wrote, "I undertook with pleasure what others might have thought a hardship." In her lifetime, she calculated the locations of some 2,510 nebulae and discovered eight comets—a staggering number for any individual observer.

Comets have transfixed humanity since ancient times. With their unpredictable apparitions tickling our pattern-seeking propensity, our hunger for casual correlations, our primal tendency toward equating unpredictability and randomness with evil, they came to be seen as omens of drought, famine, and bloodshed. Long after astronomy stripped them of such superstitious enchantment, they have continued to exert a pull on the popular imagination. Like holidays, comets—icy clumps of soot and stardust shed by the eternal as emissaries of the ephemeral—serve as anchors of periodicity by which to moor ourselves to the uncertain flow of existence and space out segments of being along the fleeting interlude of life.

As Mary Wollstonecraft lies dying at the age of thirty-eight, having authored the foundational feminist text *A Vindication of the Rights of Woman* five years earlier, one of Caroline Herschel's comets looms overhead. The year Herschel's comet discoveries earn her admission into the Royal Astronomical Society, a baby is born in Missouri. "I came in with Halley's Comet in 1835," the grown man would write in his 1909 autobiography. "It is coming again next year, and I expect to go out with it." And so he does—Halley's comet, which blazes across Earth's skies once every seventy-five to seventy-six years, is visible on November 30, 1835, when Samuel Clemens is born, and again on April 21, 1910, when he dies as Mark Twain. As birthdays temper the delicious illusion of our own inevitability with the hard fact that we were once inconceivable, so comets remind us that the life of the universe operates on cycles independent of and far grander than our own lifespans.

3

WHAT IS LOST AND WHAT IS GAINED

While Maria Mitchell's mathematical calling became apparent when she was still a child and never left her, she slowly matured into another—a thoroughly different calling complementary to the cosmic in its earthliness and its humanistic concern, which she approached with the same rigor and devotion: social reform.

During her tenure at the Atheneum, Mitchell hosted the institution's regular public lectures by itinerant speakers. Among them was Frederick Douglass, who delivered his very first public speech at the island's temple of learning. One August day in 1841, three years after his escape from slavery, a nervous twenty-three-year-old Douglass—the same age as Mitchell—took the podium at the Atheneum and addressed the mixed-race audience of five hundred gathered there for the first Nantucket Anti-Slavery Convention. He proceeded to deliver a speech so electrifying that at its conclusion, the abolitionist William Lloyd Garrison, who was waiting to take the platform next, leapt to his feet, turned to the audience, and exclaimed: "Have we been listening to a thing, a piece of property, or a man?" The chamber of the Great Hall bellowed with a resounding "A man! A man!"

Four years later, Douglass—whose friendship Mitchell would cherish for the remainder of her life, exerting herself in her final year to travel to a reception given in his honor—would write in his autobiography:

I prefer to be true to myself, even at the hazard of incurring the ridi-
cule of others, rather than to be false, and incur my own abhorrence.
From my earliest recollection, I date the entertainment of a deep
conviction that slavery would not always be able to hold me within
its foul embrace.

Maria Mitchell echoed this sentiment in her own diary a decade
later, as she was doing for women what Douglass was doing for
African Americans:

The best that can be said of my life so far is that it has been industri-
ous, and the best that can be said of me is that I have not pretended
to what I was not.

Another formidable mind to take the Atheneum pulpit was
Ralph Waldo Emerson. The Sage of Concord had scandalized New
England fifteen years earlier by resigning his prestigious position
in the Unitarian church over the practice of communion, which he
considered idolatrous and uncivilized. A quarter millennium before
Emerson, Kepler's doubts about the same ritual had made him refuse
to sign the central Lutheran tenet of faith, known as the Formula of
Concord. Since his dramatic exit from the clergy, Emerson had been
making his living as a public speaker. When he visited Nantucket
for a lecture a few months before Maria Mitchell's historic comet
discovery, she taught him how to use a telescope. He was awed at
the sight of a nebula in the constellation Cassiopeia and a double
star in Ursa Minor. "The moon comes here as if it was at home, but
there is no shade," he wrote in his diary of Nantucket—a "place of
winds bleak & shelterless & when it blows a large part of the island
is suspended in the air & comes into your face & eyes as if it were
glad to see you."

Eight years later, Mitchell attended another lecture by Emerson
addressing the subject of beauty. That evening, she exulted in her
own diary:

It was like a beam of light moving in the undulatory waves, meeting
with occasional meteors in its path; it was exceedingly captivating.

It surprised me that there was not only no commonplace thought, but there was no commonplace expression. If he quoted, he quoted from what we had not read; if he told an anecdote, it was one that had not reached us.

In his meteoric lecture, Emerson argued that "beauty is the form under which the intellect prefers to study the world" and quoted Goethe: "The beautiful is a manifestation of secret laws of Nature, which, but for this appearance, had been forever concealed from us."

This notion of beauty as a focal lens for intellectual curiosity was how Mitchell herself saw the universe, and perhaps how every person of genius does. Beauty magnetizes curiosity and wonder, beckoning us to discover—in the literal sense, to uncover and unconceal—what lies beneath the surface of the human label. What we recognize as beauty may be a language for encoding truth, a memetic mechanism for transmitting it, as native to the universe as mathematics—the one perceived by the optical eye, the other by the mind's eye. "Do not wonder at the fair landscape," Emerson exhorted himself in his journal, "but at the necessity of Beauty under which the universe is." In the preface to her translation of *Prometheus Bound,* the twenty-seven-year-old Elizabeth Barrett Browning wrote:

> All beauties, whether in nature or art, in physics or morals, in composition or abstract reasoning, are multiplied reflections, visible in different distances under different positions, of one archetypal beauty.

Frederick Douglass, too, saw in beauty a deeper motive power, but of a different kind—not one that mobilizes the contemplative intellect alone but one that adrenalizes action in the service of exposing truth. A quarter century after his Nantucket debut, Douglass would deliver a visionary lecture titled "Pictures and Progress." Linking figurative art to political reform, he argues that the nascent medium of photography would help upend inequality, for it allows us to externalize our inner nature, "giving it form, color, space, and all the attributes of distinct personality, so that it becomes the subject of distinct observation and contemplation." By making visceral the rift between our reality and our ideals, Douglass asserts, photography invites us to rise to our own highest aspirations:

> It is the picture of life contrasted with the fact of life, the ideal contrasted with the real, which makes criticism possible. Where there is no criticism there is no progress, for the want of progress is not felt where such want is not made visible by criticism. It is by looking upon this picture and upon that which enables us to point out the defects of the one and the perfections of the other.
>
> Poets, prophets, and reformers are all picture-makers—and this ability is the secret of their power and of their achievements. They see what ought to be by the reflection of what is, and endeavor to remove the contradiction.

When Galileo beheld the phases of Venus through his telescope, he saw the first picture that directly contradicted the geocentric model of the universe, which held that Venus could never be fully illuminated from the vantage point of Earth, for that would place it on the far side of the sun. And yet there was Venus, aglow before his eyes—poetic, prophetic, reformatory—a picture presenting the first irreconcilable contradiction between the Ptolemaic ideal and cosmic reality, about to unsettle the universe and forever dislodge us from its center. Still, Galileo often spoke of God, and he sent his eldest daughter, whom he treated as a confidante and intellectual peer, to a convent—he was breathing the atmosphere of his era. But whatever personal version of spirituality he maintained, he resolutely shifted away from religious dogma with the fulcrum of observation and critical thinking.

Maria Mitchell was much younger than Galileo when she did the same. The combined influence of her own astronomical observations, her immersion in the scientific texts of the Atheneum, and her exposure to New England's most progressive public speakers led her to question the prescriptive tenets of religion. She never relinquished the Quaker faith's core moral values, and for the remainder of her life, even as she became one of the most famous women in the world, she dressed in simple Quaker clothing. But by 1843, she could no longer accept the dogma that crumbled in the face of her experience and critical thinking. A month after her twenty-fifth birthday, Mitchell resigned her membership in the island's Society of Friends. She would often attend Unitarian services to hear the sermons—Unitarianism, deemed heretical by the established church, had been introduced by the Reverend William Ellery Channing just before Mitchell's birth as a liberal humanistic theology that placed the divine in the human heart rather than in a mythological figure. But she never again joined a church. Later in life, she would instruct her students: "We cannot accept anything as granted beyond the first mathematical formulae. Question everything else."

A year after leaving the Quaker congregation, Mitchell cofounded a secular counterpart—a literary club devoted to "the enlargement and improvement of the mind," composed of twenty-two women and twenty-two men. Each member was required to "contribute her or his proportional share of original composition, in order to carry out one important feature of the Society: the giving of pleasure and profit to every other member." Every Monday, Mitchell herself contributed an original poem. In one, she celebrates the choice not to marry and the rewards of remaining the master of her own time and thought in an era when, still in her twenties, she was already entering spinsterhood:

> There's a deal to be learned in a midnight walk
> When you take it all alone.
> If a gentleman's with you, it's talk, talk, talk.
> You've no eyes and mind of your own.

Another poem, addressed to a bedridden young woman, begins with these lines:

> I come, my lady fair, from yon far-distant isle,
> Whose hills are ever green, whose soft skies ever smile.

It ends with these:

Take me, lady, spurn me not; this blessing grant me,
To mingle yet my life with thine, and e'en be one with thee.

Who was the fair lady who lived off the island and with whom Mitchell's poetic alter ego wished to merge her life?
Quite possibly, Ida Russell.

No record survives of how Maria and Ida first met, but the two women, born within months of each other and a world apart—Russell's father had served as the American ambassador to Sweden, where she was born in 1818—grew intensely close across the distance between Nantucket and Ida's Massachusetts hometown, named for the author of *Paradise Lost*.

In her journals, Mitchell rarely reflected on her emotions, whether because she found them uninteresting or because the beam of her intellect was aimed so far beyond the human realm that she remained rather opaque to herself. Her feelings for Ida are a rare exception. In one of the very few emotionally introspective entries in her diary, Maria writes ruefully:

> Last night I had two letters which did me good. One was from Lizzie Earle and one from Ida Russell. The love of one's own sex is precious for it is neither provoked by vanity nor retained by flattery; it is genuine and sincere. I am grateful that I have had much of this in my life. I am sometimes sorry that those who give me so much, should give it to me when it might be so well suited to the domestic station of a wife and I am humbled when I consider that they give it to me because they know me so little—that, living in the same town with me, they would know me better and love me less. I have an entirely different regard for Lizzie and for Ida. I love Lizzie as one loves a sister, I admire Ida and am jealous of her regard for others. It is something like *love* and less generous than that which I have for Lizzie, which is affection . . .

Nobody knows what goes on between two hearts—including, more often than not, the people in whose chests they beat. But my own sense—based on years of immersion in Mitchell's world and in the complex universe of other same-sex relationships between her contemporaries, and on an awareness of how puritanical conceits constrict natural human sexuality—is that Ida may have been the love of Maria's life.

Ida Russell was bright and beautiful, socially active and endowed with a kind of magnetism that attracted uncommon ardor from men and women alike. She was listed among the audience members in the famous painting *Webster Replying to Senator Hayne* by George Healy—a depiction of the landmark debate between the Massachusetts and South Carolina senators on preserving the Union on the eve of the Civil War. The artist worked on his remarkably detailed painting for seven years and populated the stately auditorium with 150 portraits of spectators. He placed the men on the floor and the women in the balcony, taking the creative liberty of filling the gallery with all the "loveliest ladies of the time," whether or not they had actually been present on the day of the debate. Ida Russell likely was not—she would have been a girl shy of twelve then—but her widely admired loveliness had induced Healy to paint her, as a young woman, into the final picture. The painting would come to be the largest piece of art in Boston's iconic Faneuil Hall. In March 2017, a bipartisan panel of five women—including the state's former governor, the first woman elected lieutenant governor in Massachusetts, and the first woman elected state treasurer and a gubernatorial nominee—would sit beneath it, reflecting on Hillary Clinton's defeat in the 2016 presidential election and issuing an old clarion call to a new generation of women leaders. One of the panelists, the former college president and lieutenant governor of Massachusetts Kerry Healey, would capture the mood of the moment: "Failure is the sinew that connects success." A century and a half earlier, Maria Mitchell had written in her diary:

He who has never failed somewhere, that man can not be great. Failure is the true test of greatness.

Barely into her twenties, Ida Russell attended the groundbreaking salons hosted by Margaret Fuller—one of Mitchell's great intellectual heroes. In 1839, well before the publication of her paradigm-unmooring treatise *Woman in the Nineteenth Century,* twenty-nine-year-old Fuller launched a series of "Conversations for Women" in Boston. In a circular quoted by Emerson, Fuller framed the spirit of her project:

> Could a circle be assembled in earnest, desirous to answer the ques-
> tions, "What were we born to do?" and "How shall we do it?" I
> should think the undertaking a noble one.

For five years, until she left Boston for New York, Fuller convened the area's most intellectually wakeful women to use Greek mythology and its inevitable astronomical dimensions as a springboard into conversations about beauty, truth, and life's grand questions.

Electrified by Fuller's "Conversations," Ida and her half sister Amelia applied to be among the few permanent residents at Brook Farm—a utopian community nine miles outside Boston, founded two years earlier upon the ideals of Transcendentalism by the former Unitarian minister George Ripley and his wife, Sophia. Part intellectual commune and part joint stock agricultural company, funded largely by tuitions to the school the Ripleys ran on the property, Brook Farm promised a gender-blind distribution of profits among its residents in proportion to their share of work on the farm—an arrangement intended to provide them with leisure for discussing ideas and cultivating the life of the mind. The novelist Nathaniel Hawthorne was one of the founding investors. Although Margaret Fuller never formally joined, she polished Brook Farm's image as an intellectual haven with her frequent visits. "At Brook Farm one man ploughed all day, & one looked out of the window all day & drew his picture, and both received the same wages," Emerson—whom the Ripleys tried to entice into joining—wrote in his journal. "I wished to be convinced, to be thawed, to be made nobly mad by the kindlings before my eyes of a new dawn of human piety." He was not.

By the time Ida and her sister joined in the autumn of 1842, Brook Farm had suffered an unhandsome collision between the ideal and the real. Its financial model had proven unviable, and the elated idealism that animated its founding ethos had devolved into what Ida's sister would later describe as a life of "bare and cheerless routine." Hawthorne had just made a dramatic exit, demanding that his initial investment be refunded. "Even my Custom House experience," he roiled with indignation, "was not such a thraldom and weariness; my mind and heart were freer . . . Thank God, my soul is not utterly buried under a dung-heap."

Polarized by her own conflicting ideals, Ida Russell stood uneasy in the space between the possible and the permissible, shipwrecked by the tides of convention that delimit each era's horizon of possibility. At only twenty-one, she had invited Emerson to deliver one of his politically wakeful lectures in her hometown of Milton, but her name also appears as one of 24 nays on an antislavery resolution, against 250 yeas, including Frederick Douglass, William Garrison's wife, and Henry David Thoreau's mother and sister. While Ida commended Maria's scientific achievements as victories for her country and her sex, she beseeched Maria not to become a "platform woman"—a public advocate for the era's two great directions of social reform, African American and women's rights. In a diary entry from 1854, when both women were thirty-six and Ida had fallen ill, Mitchell relays an exchange that bespeaks her own good-natured idealism and sunny wit with an edge of storm:

I went down to see Ida Russell ten days ago. I was curious to see for myself whether sickness had changed her in body and spirit. I found her much the same Ida . . . strong in her dislike of the "platform women" as she calls the Antislavery and woman's rights people. I told her not to speak of them with such contempt as I had always felt that when I was pushed for money I could write some astronomical lectures and go into the cities and deliver them. "Don't Maria," she said, "do anything else. Take a husband even!"

(I) What! The weak minded man such as would happen to fall in love with me?

(Ida) Well, then there's the river.

(I) Yes, as the bowl or the dagger but I don't fancy any of these things!

But then Maria adds another of her rare emotional reflections:

> Ida is always very expressive to me, she seems really to be much attracted to me and I suppose it is the evil of my own nature which makes me ask "can it be real," but I hope it is only, that setting so high a value as I do upon any one's affection and giving it so charily to others as I do myself, I cannot believe that I have really won so much of any one's heart.

Alarmed at the intensity of her attachment to Ida, Maria reasoned that rather than turning a single person into the center of gravity in our emotional universe, our attachments should be distributed among many people, each fulfilling a different need—one providing intellectual stimulation, another rendering us "more elastic and buoyant, more happy and radiating more happiness, because we know him," another inspiring in us such "warmth of affection" that "our hearts grow as if in a summer feeling." In a diary entry from the first day of 1855, she resolves for greater independence of heart and diagrams a more centripetal distribution of attachments:

> A friend is not to be found in the world such as one can conceive of, such as one needs, for no human being unites so many of the attributes of God as we feel our nature requires. . . . We have therefore a circle whom we call friends, giving a name to the whole, which perhaps in its singular occupation might be used for the combination. Out of the whole circle we may make up a single friend. We love them all but we love the union of all better.

Absolute independence of spirit is an illusion. We are porous to the ideas and judgments of those we elect into our inner circle—a recognition of interdependence that springs from the same elemental humility that shielded her, even at the height of her celebrity, from the delusions of ego:

> Whatever our degree of friends may be, we come more under their influence than we are aware.

Who of us acts and speaks without an eye to the approbations of those he loves? Is not the assent of another a sort of second conscience? . . . We prop ourselves up with accomplices, we surround ourselves with those who can down for us the uprisings of conscience. . . . It is not a weakness to be deplored. We were more than conceited did we rate ourselves so much above the rest of the world that we needed no outward aids to judgment. We were born dependent, our happiness is in the hands of others. Our character is molded by them and receives its coloring from them as much as our feeling relates the parental impress.

The following month, just before her thirty-seventh birthday, Ida died unexpectedly. "Disease of heart" was listed as the cause of death in the Milton newspaper. Maria was devastated at the fatal dissolution of so irreplaceable a bond—a loss she experienced as a "blow, sudden and severe." I can picture her at the telescope, an aching testament to Whitman's words: "To soothe and spiritualize, and, as far as may be, solve the mysteries of death and genius, consider them under the stars at midnight."

A small square of blankness now occupies the diary page onto which this woman ungiven to sentimentality had pinned a scrap since gone missing—likely the obituary from the Milton newspaper, or a daguerreotype of Ida. Framing the lost record of loss is Mitchell's swirling handwriting. Above it, she writes: "Loftier minds to burn clear with furious force . . . and Ida was my superior." Along the side, she observed that for Ida, "to do and to dare came as a birth-right." Sideways at the bottom corner: "She was many-sided but crystal-like, every side gave a gleam of light"—a metaphor evocative of the kaleidoscopic water bowl that hung above the brass telescope in Mitchell's childhood home. Though consumed with grief, she steps beyond the lacerating news of Ida's death to record a sorrowful meditation on life:

As our circle of friends narrows, they naturally seem to clasp us in a closer embrace. It is the sad mercy of growing old, that we outlive one and another of those we love.

For years, Mitchell had been dreaming of and saving for a trip to Europe—the homeland of her many long-gone heroes. Her greatest American idol had framed visiting Europe as nothing less than a moral imperative for intellectually and politically wakeful Americans. "What was but a picture to us becomes reality," Margaret Fuller had written from Rome months after Mitchell's comet discovery, "remote allusions and derivations trouble no more: we see the pattern of the stuff and understand the whole tapestry." In the year following Ida's death, Mitchell's European dream began taking shape as a reality from which she could no longer abstain. She turned in her resignation from the Atheneum after a two-decade tenure and began making arrangements, planning routes, dreaming up visits with the intellectual idols and kindred spirits she yearned to meet: Europe's leading astronomers, including the polymathic astronomer and Royal Astronomical Society cofounder Sir John Herschel—son of William and nephew of Caroline Herschel, who had introduced him to astronomy—as well as the poet Elizabeth Barrett Browning, the mathematician Mary Somerville, the naturalist Alexander von Humboldt, and the young expatriate American sculptor Harriet Hosmer, who was living in Rome and breaking ground for women in art as Mitchell was doing in science. "Figures are a common language," she would soon write while traveling through foreign lands and listening to foreign tongues. Nearly a century later, at the apogee of the Second World War's violent divisiveness, Albert Einstein's soft, heavily accented voice would stream through London's airwaves to deliver a conciliatory speech titled "The Common Language of Science."

In July 1857, Mitchell boarded a steamship in New York. Having narrowly avoided a collision with another ship, it arrived in Liverpool ten days later—on her thirty-ninth birthday. She was soon introduced to the improbable American consul at Liverpool—Nathaniel Hawthorne. Four years earlier, the novelist had been awarded America's most lucrative foreign post by his college friend Franklin Pierce, newly elected the fourteenth president of the United States—a victory Pierce attributed to the highly idealized biography of him that Hawthorne had written during the campaign. The author was now living the high life in Liverpool with his wife, the unrealized artist Sophia Peabody, and their three children.

Sophia's elder sister Elizabeth—an education reformer, founder of the first English-language kindergarten in America, and translator of the first American edition of Buddhist scripture—had once extolled Hawthorne as "handsomer than Lord Byron." But Mitchell, unimpressed with the man said to have it all, recorded in her diary:

> He is not handsome, but looks as the author of his books should look: a little strange and odd, as if not of this earth. He has large, bluish-gray eyes; his hair stands out on each side, so much so that one's thoughts naturally turn to combs and hair-brushes and toilet ceremonies as one looks at him.

Perhaps Mitchell found the dour, incurious, perennially dissatisfied Hawthorne unhandsome because her ideas about beauty were rooted in a deeper stratum of truth, a wonderment at the nature of reality.

In the following century, the poet Edna St. Vincent Millay would enroll in Vassar. Immersed in the comprehensive science curriculum Mitchell had established, she would write in one of her early sonnets: "Euclid alone has looked on Beauty bare."

Euclid, whose work Kepler part built upon and part refuted, fathered geometry and provided the first foothold of scientific certitude. In perfect Euclidean geometry, the angles inside a triangle always add up to 180 degrees—the very first mathematical proof, a validation of truth unmoored from human judgment and opinion. It was the lightning bolt that sundered the tree of knowledge into philosophy and pure science.

Euclid's Elements remains one of the most influential scientific texts of all time, on a par with Newton's *Principia*. For centuries after Euclid's death, his geometry remained our only model of understanding space. This breakthrough in science shaped art through the development of perspective—a technique originally called *geometric figuring,* which invited architecture and the figurative arts into the three-dimensional world for the first time, then through them gave back to science. Galileo's Moon drawings were so revolutionary in large part because, trained in perspective, he depicted the topography of its mountains and craters, emanating the radical suggestion that our satellite is not a perfectly smooth orb of ethereal matter but as solid and rugged as the earth—not a heavenly body but a material one. Mere months earlier, the English mathematician and astronomer Thomas Harriot had become the first person known to make a drawing of the Moon seen through a telescope. Untrained in perspective and ignorant of the Euclid-informed projective geometries that had made their way to Florence but not yet to England, he depicted the Moon as a dappled disc resembling an engraved medal. The genius that led Galileo to see what Harriot could not was indelibly *genius loci,* as much a function of his mind as of his time and place.

Still, Euclid's geometry of space seemed at first too unreal, too intangible—an abstraction, an illusionist trick. It wasn't until Galileo and Descartes—whose visionary Cartesian plane married geometric shape and algebraic equation—upheld it as the mathematical poetics of the real world that it gained traction as truth incarnate. It was reality bare, and it was beautiful.

The question of beauty's purpose and significance had arisen as one of the animating inquiries at Margaret Fuller's "Conversations," when during an 1841 session devoted to Minerva, the Roman goddess of wisdom, many of the women insisted that "the principle of Beauty" ought to be factored into any definition of wisdom. Fuller then ruled that a definition of beauty must be devised first. She asked each woman in attendance to provide her own. One defined it as "the Infinite apprehended." Another argued that beauty is "the central unifying power" of existence. Brook Farm cofounder Sophia Ripley pointed to it as an embodiment of "the All" and defined it as "the mode in which truth appears." But Fuller, in her role as sybil-arbiter, observed that these definitions could be applied equally to love and truth. Challenging the women to reflect further, she tasked them with composing short essays of more precise definition for the next gathering.

That year, Emerson wrote in his journal:

> The presence or absence of Milton will very sensibly affect the result of human history. . . . Tomorrow, a new man may be born, not indebted like Milton to the Old, & more entirely dedicated than he to the New, yet clothed like him with beauty.

The debate about beauty impressed itself upon the mind of the young Sophia Peabody, who was in awed attendance at Fuller's gathering. Seventeen years later, while traveling through Europe with Maria Mitchell, Sophia—by then Sophia Hawthorne—would gaze up at the fan vaulting over Queen Catharine's tomb and reflect:

> Take one of the divisions by itself and it looks like a rocket falling in stars or flowers, the motion in rest everywhere suggested. In comparing Gothic with the Greek architecture, one is the clear, logical understanding, coming at truth mathematically by the way of reason; and all this range of truth stands beautiful and sure, on lovely, even pillars, surmounted with square pediments, symmetrical and perfect to the eye.

Contrasting this with the Gothic, which traffics in "baffling geometric conclusions, setting known, established rules at defiance, wild beyond reach of recognized art, flaming like fire, glowing like flowers and rainbows, soaring like birds, struggling for freedom, and like the soul, never satisfied," she concludes:

> A cathedral is really an image of the whole soul of man; and a Greek temple, of his understanding only—of just decisions, serene, finished postulates, settled axioms. We need both.

Standing beneath the Euclidean dome, Sophia is renouncing the forced, limiting polarity of truth versus beauty, calling instead for a union—truth *and* beauty, the purifying clarity of mathematics married with the swirling wildness of contemplation that belongs to philosophy and art.

As her ever-gloomy husband sits out the Sistine Chapel and bemoans "this cold, rainy, filthy, stinking, rotten, rascally city"— "I hate it worse than any other place in the whole world," Nathaniel Hawthorne repines in his journal—Sophia visits the Tribune of Galileo at the Museum of Natural History—"a sort of temple erected to Galileo by the present Grand Duke Leopold—Galileo's heart being long ago thoroughly broken." In her journal, she reflects on how truth confers beauty—and how it can also confer tragedy:

> How little [Galileo] dreamed, when he sat in prison, that even his fingers would become precious relics for posterity! But I wish he had kept firm, and not denied the truth he had discovered. That is an endless grief to me.

Maria Mitchell, traveling with the Hawthornes, commits a parallel reflection to her own journal, complemented by a perpendicular sentiment—having long considered Galileo "not a mere observer and discoverer, but a philosopher," she sees not only the tragedy of his truth but also its triumph:

> I knew of no sadder picture in the history of science than that of the old man, Galileo, worn by a long life of scientific research, weak and feeble, trembling before that tribunal whose frown was torture, and declaring that to be false which he knew to be true. And I know of no picture in the history of religion more weakly pitiable than that of the Holy Church trembling before Galileo, and denouncing him because he found in the Book of Nature truths not stated in their own Book of God—forgetting that the Book of Nature is also a Book of God.
>
> It seems to be difficult for anyone to take in the idea that two truths cannot conflict.

4

OF THE INFINITE IN THE FINITE

I have wondered whether Maria Mitchell would have liked Nathaniel Hawthorne more—or even less—had she known that they were two points in the same time-warped triangle of conflicted loves.

A decade and a half earlier, Hawthorne had met Sophia Peabody. She was a tremulous aspiring artist of uncommon talent and scant self-assurance, and a lifelong invalid bedridden by long stretches of debilitating spinal headaches. He was the orphaned son of a ship captain and an obscure struggling writer who would soon become one of the era's most celebrated authors, much thanks to Margaret Fuller. "No one of all our imaginative writers has indicated a genius at once so fine and so rich," Fuller—by then one of America's most trusted cultural tastemakers—would write of the practically unknown Hawthorne after reading his first collection of short stories, recording in her diary the initial impression that the book was written by "somebody in Salem" who she assumed was a woman.

Just after her engagement to the dark, moody Hawthorne, the thirtysomething Sophia met the twentysomething Ida Russell at one of Fuller's "Conversations," convened in Elizabeth Peabody's bookshop. In addition to possessing the intellectual curiosity requisite for attending Fuller's salons, Ida Russell was almost unbearably beautiful. The relationship that blossomed between the two women was so intimate that Hawthorne soon fumed with jealousy. In a letter from the autumn of 1841, he beseeches Sophia to fall into his arms instead of Ida's:

> Dearest, I write of nothing; for I had nothing to write when I began, save to make thee aware that I loved thee infinitely; and now that thou knowest it, there is no need of saying a word more. On Monday evening, please God, I shall see thee. How would I have borne it, if thy visit to Ida Russel [sic] were to commence before my return to thine arms?

Sophia did eventually choose Nathaniel over Ida—they were married the following July and rode off into the sunset in a downpour, besieged by what she described in her diary as the "celestial artillery" of low thunder.

Not long after, Hawthorne himself would be magnetized into a friendship of similar romantic intensity. On August 5, 1850, he met Herman Melville at a literary gathering in the Berkshires. Hawthorne was forty-six and Melville, born on Maria Mitchell's first birthday, had just turned thirty-one. A potent intellectual infatuation ignited between the two men—one that, at least for Melville, seems to have grown from the cerebral to the corporeal. Within days, the young author reviewed Hawthorne's short story collection *Mosses from an Old Manse in Literary World* under the impersonal byline "a Virginian Spending July in Vermont." No claim of this intentional ambiguity was true—Melville was a New Yorker, the month was August, and he was spending it in Massachusetts.

The review, nearing seven thousand words, was nothing less than an editorial serenade. "A man of a deep and noble nature has seized me in this seclusion. . . . His wild, witch voice rings through me," Melville wrote of reading Hawthorne's stories in a remote farmhouse nestled in the summer foliage of the New England countryside. "The soft ravishments of the man spun me round in a web of dreams." Melville couldn't have known that his allusions to witchcraft, intended as compliment, had disquieting connotations for Hawthorne. Born Nathaniel Hathorne, he had added a *w* to the family name in order to distance himself from his ancestor John

Hathorne—a leading judge involved in the Salem witch trials, who, unlike the other culpable judges, never repented of his role in the murders. Unwitting of the dark family history, Melville found himself under "this Hawthorne's spell"—a spell cast first by his writing, then by the constellation of personal qualities from which the writing radiated. Who hasn't fallen in love with an author in the pages of a beautiful book? And if that author, when befriended in the real world, proves to be endowed with the splendor of personhood that the writing intimates, who could resist falling in love with the whole person? Melville presaged as much:

> No man can read a fine author, and relish him to his very bones, while he reads, without subsequently fancying to himself some ideal image of the man and his mind. . . . There is no man in whom humor and love are developed in that high form called genius; no such man can exist without also possessing, as the indispensable complement of these, a great, deep intellect, which drops down into the universe like a plummet. Or, love and humor are only the eyes, through which such an intellect views this world. The great beauty in such a mind is but the product of its strength.

After comparing Hawthorne to Shakespeare, he writes:

> In this world of lies, Truth is forced to fly like a scared white doe in the woodlands; and only by cunning glimpses will she reveal herself, as in Shakespeare and other masters of the great Art of Telling the Truth,—even though it be covertly, and by snatches.

Could it be that the young Emily Dickinson, then nineteen and a voracious reader, absorbed Melville's sentiment and later transmuted it into her iconic line "Tell all the truth but tell it slant"? But while creative work arises from the combinatorial process of transfiguring existing fragments of thought and image into new combinations, Melville himself admonished in this very piece, "Mark it well, imitation is often the first charge brought against real originality."

"I am Posterity speaking by proxy," Melville bellows from the page, "when I declare—that the American, who up to the present day, has evinced, in Literature, the largest brain with the largest heart, that man is Nathaniel Hawthorne." In an aside on the process of composing his review, he notes that twenty-four hours into writing, he found himself "charged more and more with love and admiration of Hawthorne." Quoting an especially beguiling line of Hawthorne's, he insists that "such touches . . . can not proceed from any common heart." No, they bespeak "such a depth of tenderness, such a boundless sympathy with all forms of being, such an omnipresent love" that they render their author singular in his generation—as singular as the place he would come to occupy in Melville's heart.

Fervid correspondence and frequent visits followed over the next few months. Only ten of Melville's letters to Hawthorne survive, but their houses were just six miles apart and they saw each other quite often—"discussing the Universe with a bottle of brandy & cigars," as Melville put it in one invitation, and talking deep into the night about "time and eternity, things of this world and of the next, and books, and publishers, and all possible and impossible matters," as Hawthorne recounted in his diary. Punctuating the invisible log of all that was written but destroyed is all that was spoken but unwritten, all that was felt but unspoken.

Melville's ardor was most acute during the period of writing *Moby-Dick*, which he dedicated to Hawthorne. Printed immediately after the title page was "In Token of My Admiration for his Genius, This Book is Inscribed to Nathanial [*sic*] Hawthorne."

One November evening over dinner, a restlessly excited Herman presented Nathaniel with a lovingly inscribed copy of the novel whose now-legendary protagonist sails from Nantucket into the existential unknown. I can picture the brooding Hawthorne turning the leaf and suppressing a beam of delight upon discovering the printed dedication. In the following century, Virginia Woolf would perform a similar gesture with her groundbreaking, gender-bending novel *Orlando*, inspired by her lover Vita Sackville-West and later described by Vita's son as "the longest and most charming love letter in literature." On the day of *Orlando*'s publication, Vita would receive a package containing not only the printed book, but also Virginia's original manuscript, bound specially for her in Niger leather and stamped with her initials on the spine.

But after the elated private presentation, a very different public fate awaited *Moby-Dick*. Its 1851 publication was met with a damning review in New York's *Literary World*, which set the tone for its American reception and precipitated its decades-long plunge into obscurity. The reviewer's chief complaint was that the novel "violated and defaced" "the most sacred associations of life"—an indictment aimed at the homoeroticism of Melville's choice to depict Ishmael and Queequeg as sharing a "marriage bed" in which they awaken with their arms around each other. Ten days later, Hawthorne lamented the obtuseness of the review and praised *Moby-Dick* as Melville's best work yet. Touched to the point of delirium by this "exultation-breeding letter," Melville hastened to reply:

> Your heart beat in my ribs and mine in yours, and both in God's. . . . It is a strange feeling—no hopefulness is in it, no despair. Content—that is it; and irresponsibility; but without licentious inclination. I speak now of my profoundest sense of being, not of an incidental feeling.
>
> Whence come you, Hawthorne? By what right do you drink from my flagon of life? And when I put it to my lips—lo, they are yours and not mine. I feel that the Godhead is broken up like the bread at the Supper, and that we are the pieces.

Aware of how his intemperate fervor might incinerate his relationship with the cooler-tempered Hawthorne, Melville reasons with himself for a moment, then chooses to abandon reason:

> My dear Hawthorne, the atmospheric skepticisms steal into me now, and make me doubtful of my sanity in writing you thus. But, believe me, I am not mad, most noble Festus! But truth is ever incoherent, and when the big hearts strike together, the concussion is a little stunning.

After signing, he adds a feverish postscript:

I can't stop yet. If the world was entirely made up of [magicians], I'll tell you what I should do. I should have a paper-mill established at one end of the house, and so have an endless riband of foolscap rolling in upon my desk; and upon that endless riband I should write a thousand—a million—billion thoughts, all under the form of a letter to you. The divine magnet is in you, and my magnet responds. Which is the biggest? A foolish question—they are One.

The intensity proved too concussing for Hawthorne—he pulled away from the divine magnet. Melville seems to have presaged the eclipse of their relationship in the review in which the magnetism had begun:

It is that blackness in Hawthorne . . . that so fixes and fascinates me. It may be, nevertheless, that it is too largely developed in him. Perhaps he does not give us a ray of his light for every shade of his dark.

As Hawthorne retreated into his cool darkness, Melville suffered with the singular anguish of unreturned ardor—anguish that stayed with him for the remaining four decades of his life, for he eulogized it in one of his last poems, "Monody," penned in his final year:

To have known him, to have loved him,
After loneness long;
And then to be estranged in life,
And neither in the wrong;
And now for death to set his seal—
Ease me, a little ease, my song!

By wintry hills his hermit-mound
The sheeted snow-drifts drape,
And houseless there the snow-bird flits
Beneath the fir-tree's crape:
Glazed now with ice the cloistral vine
That hid the shyest grape.

In a letter from August 1852, shortly before Hawthorne withdrew into iciness, Melville told him of his recent visit to Nantucket, remarking on "the great patience, & endurance, & resignedness of the women of the island." He had gone to a party at Maria Mitchell's house and looked through her telescope.

After Melville's death, among his papers was found an unpublished poem modeled on Mitchell, titled "After the Pleasure Party, Lines Traced under an Image of Amor Threatening." He writes of the "American Urania," describing her as "Vesta struck with Sappho's smart"—the virgin goddess of domesticity "struck with" the defiant intellect of the poet laureate of same-sex love. But while casting Mitchell as the American embodiment of the Greek muse of astronomy was unambiguously complimentary during her ascent to scientific celebrity, by the end of her life and of Melville's—their lifetimes coincided almost exactly—Urania had taken on a different meaning. As sociology and medicine sought to classify identities that diverged from heteronormative sexuality, "Uranian," coined before "homosexual," came to signify a person of a third sex—first "a female psyche in a male body," then more generally those whose attractions differed from the normative standards of their anatomy, or what we today might call queer people. As early as 1845, in *Woman in the Nineteenth Century*, Margaret Fuller celebrated the army of unmarried aunts and uncles—spinsters and bachelors who had opted out of heteronormative existence—as society's "mental and moral Ishmaelites," describing the archetypal spinster as "the Urania of a half-formed world's twilight." Oscar Wilde would soon write in a letter: "To have altered my life would have been to have admitted that Uranian love is ignoble. I hold it to be noble—more noble than other forms."

Melville was far more conflicted about Uranian love than Wilde. At the heart of his Mitchell-inspired poem is an elegy for frustrated attraction and unconsummated desire, which "nothing may help or heal," exploring the sorrow of being "bound in sex"—this, after all, was an era in which the aperture of possibility for such loves was contracted to a pinhole. Melville's American Urania is sundered by the polar pull of science and a possible lover encountered during her Mediterranean travels. Melville is giving voice to what he may have wondered about Mitchell—did she sublimate her erotic passion to her intellectual passion?

One knows not if Urania yet
The pleasure-party may forget;
Or whether she lived down the strain
Of turbulent heart and rebel brain . . .

Mitchell so admired Margaret Fuller not only for her bold inter-leaving of heart and mind, but for her pioneering condemnation of what she called "the great radical dualism" of gender and her insistence that "there is no wholly masculine man, no purely femi-nine woman." In the poem modeled on Mitchell and most probably inspired by Fuller, Melville voices Urania's lament at the violence of that artificial, limiting divide:

Why hast thou made us but in halves—
Co-relatives? This makes us slaves.
If these co-relatives never meet
Self-hood itself seems incomplete.
And such the dicing of blind fate
Few matching halves here meet and mate.
What Cosmic jest or Anarch blunder
The human integral clove asunder
And shied the fractions through life's gate?

By the time Mitchell encountered the Hawthornes in Europe and traveled with them to Italy, Nathaniel would have been as unlikely to bring up his turbid relationship with Herman Melville as Maria hers with Ida Russell. They had each met the other's Uranian coun-terpart, but under the veil of the unspoken and the unspeakable, this dual intersection of their frustrated fates would have remained invisible to both.

The isolation and alienation of experiencing oneself as "other" stems from precisely these veils of visibility, eclipsing from view the many others who are also sorrowing with kindred sorrows and con-flicted with kindred conflicts, also refugees from their own nature. Such otherness unclenches its hold only when the veils are lifted. "That visibility which makes us most vulnerable is that which also is the source of our greatest strength," Audre Lorde would write a century after Mitchell and Melville.

Meanwhile, the gaps of the invisible and the unspoken are filled with posterity's questions about specifics that vibrate with the universal: How were Maria Mitchell and Ida Russell first drawn together? What happened between them? Why did Nathaniel Hawthorne ultimately repel the divine magnet of Melville's love? Most probably, we'll never know. Possibly, they themselves never fully did. It is almost banal to say, yet it needs to be said: No one ever knows, nor therefore has grounds to judge, what goes on between two people, often not even the people themselves, half-opaque as we are to ourselves. One thing is certain: The quotient of intimacy cannot be contained in a label like "Uranian"—or "queer," or whatever comes next. The human heart is an ancient beast that roars and purrs with the same passions, whatever labels we may give them. We are so anxious to classify and categorize, both nature and human nature. It is a beautiful impulse—to contain the infinite in the finite, to wrest order from the chaos, to construct a foothold so we may climb toward higher truth. It is also a limiting one, for in naming things we often come to mistake the names for the things themselves. The labels we give to the loves of which we are capable—varied and vigorously transfigured from one kind into another and back again—can't begin to contain the complexity of feeling that can flow between two hearts and the bodies that contain them.

"It is hard to be finite upon an infinite subject, and all subjects are infinite," Melville had written at the end of his amorous review of Hawthorne—a profound sentiment rooted in the legacy of ancient Greek mathematics, harking back to Archimedes. A pioneer of illuminating physical reality through mathematics, Archimedes derived the first accurate approximation of pi. In setting out to estimate the grains of sand the universe could hold, he was arguably the first to propose that the universe is finite rather than infinite—a notion that has remained radical for two millennia, even as the astrophysicist Janna Levin reminded us at the dawn of the twenty-first century that although infinity is a thrilling plaything of abstract mathematics, no infinity has ever been observed in nature. "We're all intrinsically of the same substance," she writes. "The fabric of the universe is just a coherent weave from the same threads that make our bodies. How much more absurd it becomes to believe that the universe, space and time could possibly be infinite when all of us are finite."

Maria Mitchell contemplates this discomfiting gap between the notion of infinity and our own finitude in the pages of her journal: "We reach forth and strain every nerve, but we seize only a bit of the curtain that hides the infinite from us." A hundred miles northward, Thoreau, a year older than Mitchell and drunk on Transcendentalist grandiosity, writes in his own journal: "My life partakes of infinity."

It takes a great sobriety of spirit to fathom one's depths—and one's limits.

5

TO FIGURE AND TRANSFIGURE

A middle-aged Scottish mathematician rises ahead of the sun to spend a couple of hours with Newton before the day punctuates her thinking with the constant interruptions of mothering four children and managing a bustling household. "A man can always command his time under the plea of business," Mary Somerville would later write in her memoir; "a woman is not allowed any such excuse."

Growing up, Somerville had spent the daylight hours painting and playing piano. When her parents realized that the household candle supply had thinned because Mary had been staying up at night to read Euclid, they promptly confiscated her candles. "Peg," she recalled her father telling her mother, "we must put a stop to this, or we shall have Mary in a strait jacket one of these days." Mary was undeterred. Having already committed the first six books of Euclid to memory, she spent her nights adventuring in mathematics in the bright private chamber of her mind.

Somerville was one of Maria Mitchell's few living heroes, and the person whom Mitchell was most eager to meet during her European travels. The two scientists shared a singular distinction—since Caroline Herschel's death a decade earlier, Somerville was the only female member of Britain's esteemed Royal Astronomical Society, and Mitchell was the first and so far only female member of the American Academy of Arts and Sciences. They spent three afternoons together in Scotland, where Mitchell arrived with a prized benediction—a letter of introduction from Sir John Herschel's wife—and left feeling that "no one can make the acquaintance of this remarkable woman without increased admiration for her." In her journal, she described Somerville as "small, very," with bright blue eyes and strong features, looking twenty years younger than her seventy-seven years, her diminished hearing the only giveaway of her age. "Mrs. Somerville talks with all the readiness and clearness of a man, but with no other masculine characteristic," Mitchell wrote. "She is very gentle and womanly . . . chatty and sociable, without the least pretence, or the least coldness."

These sketches would become the backbone of Mitchell's first article in the popular press—an *Atlantic Monthly* profile of the Scottish scientist, published two years later, in which Mitchell would hold up Somerville, alongside Elizabeth Barrett Browning and Caroline Herschel, as an example of the era's "few women of genius who have become the successful rivals of man in the paths which they have severally chosen." Mitchell would later draw on the lives of women like Mary Somerville and Harriet Hosmer to incite the ambitions of her astronomy students at Vassar. In one class lecture, she contemplated the responsibility we have to our gifts and the necessity of bolstering our native aptitudes with a fiery and unrelenting work ethic:

> I am far from thinking that every woman should be an astronomer or a mathematician or an artist, but I do think that every woman should strive for perfection in everything she undertakes.
>
> If it be art, literature or science, let her work be incessant, continuous, life-long. If she be gifted above the average, by just so much is the demand upon her for higher labor, by just that amount is the pressure of duty increased. . . . Think of the steady effort, the continuous labor of those whom the world calls "geniuses." Believe me, the poet who is "born and not made" works hard for what you consider his birthright. Newton said his whole power lay in "patient thought," and patient thought, patient labor, and firmness of purpose are almost omnipotent. . . .
>
> Are we women using all the rights we have? We have the right to steady and continuous effort after knowledge, after truth. Who

denies our right to life-long study? . . . We have another right, which I am afraid we do not use, the right to do our work well, *as well as men do theirs.* . . .

The woman who does her work better than ever woman did before helps all woman kind, not only now, but in all the future, she moves the race no matter if it is only a differential movement, it is growth.

Three decades before Mitchell's visit to Scotland, the forty-six-year-old Somerville published her first scientific paper—a study of the magnetic properties of violet rays—which earned her praise from the inventor of the kaleidoscope, Sir David Brewster, as "the most extraordinary woman in Europe—a mathematician of the very first rank with all the gentleness of a woman." Lord Brougham, the influential founder of the newly established Society for the Diffusion of Useful Knowledge—with which Thoreau would take issue thirty-some years later by making a case for "the diffusion of useful ignorance," comprising "knowledge useful in a higher sense"—was so impressed that he asked Somerville to translate a mathematical treatise by Pierre-Simon Laplace, "the Newton of France." She delivered something evocative of the Nobel Prize–winning Polish poet Wisława Szymborska's wonderful notion of "that rare miracle when a translation stops being a translation and becomes . . . a second original"—Somerville didn't merely translate the math, but expanded upon it and made it comprehensible to lay readers. She had popularized Laplace's esoteric ideas. A century earlier, the same thing had happened to the real Newton in France, where the mathematical prodigy Émilie du Châtelet popularized his then-controversial ideas with her masterly more-than-translation of the *Principia Mathematica*. Voltaire, her collaborator and lover, jocularly referred to her as "Madame Newton du Châtelet" and seriously considered her to be in possession of "a genius worthy of Horace and Newton." Du Châtelet's translation of Newton, annotated with a great deal of original thought, conveyed to the popular imagination the ideas that would come to shape the modern world. It became a centerpiece of the Scientific Revolution in Europe and remains the standard French text to this day. In the course of translating and elaborating on the *Principia*, she performed pioneering research on what would later be known as the conservation of energy. Her insights into the nature of light paved the way for the invention of photography. In the preface to her translation of the philosopher, economist, and satirist Bernard Mandeville's 1714 social allegory *The Fable of the Bees*, Du Châtelet wrote:

> If I were king, I would wish to make this scientific experiment. I would reform an abuse that cuts out, so to speak, half of humanity. I would allow women to share in all the rights of humanity, and most of all those of the mind.

In 1831, after years of work, Somerville published her Laplace book as *The Mechanism of the Heavens*. It was an instant success, drawing attention from the titans of European science. John Herschel, whom she considered the greatest scientist of their time, wrote her a warm letter she treasured for the rest of her days:

> Dear Mrs. Somerville,
>   I have read your manuscript with the greatest pleasure, and will not hesitate to add, (because I am sure you will believe it sincere,) with the highest admiration. Go on thus, and you will leave a memorial of no common kind to posterity; and, what you will value far more than fame, you will have accomplished a most useful work. What a pity that La Place has not lived to see this illustration of his great work! You will only, I fear, give too strong a stimulus to the study of abstract science by this performance.

Somerville received another radiant fan letter from Maria Edgeworth—the author for whom Maria Mitchell was named—who wrote after reading *The Mechanism of the Heavens*:

> I was long in the state of the boa constrictor after a full meal—and I am but just recovering the powers of motion. My mind was so distended by the magnitude, the immensity, of what you put into it! . . . I can only assure you that you have given me a great deal of plea-

sure; that you have enlarged my conception of the sublimity of the universe, beyond any ideas I had ever before been enabled to form.

Edgeworth was particularly taken with a "a beautiful sentence, as well as a sublime idea" from Somerville's section on the propagation of sound waves:

At a very small height above the surface of the earth, the noise of the tempest ceases and the thunder is heard no more in those boundless regions, where the heavenly bodies accomplish their periods in eternal and sublime silence.

Years later, Edgeworth would write admiringly of Somerville that "while her head is up among the stars, her feet are firm upon the earth."

Like Mitchell, Somerville was troubled by the dogma and divisiveness of religion. She recounted that as religious controversies swirled about her, she had "too high a regard for liberty of conscience to interfere with any one's opinions." She chose instead to live "on terms of sincere friendship and love with people who differed essentially" in their religious views. In her memoir, she encapsulated her philosophy of creed: "In all the books which I have written I have confined myself strictly and entirely to scientific subjects, although my religious opinions are very decided."

Above all, Somerville possessed the defining mark of the great scientist and the great human being—the ability to hold one's opinions with firm but unfisted fingers, remaining receptive to novel theories and willing to change one's mind in light of new evidence. Her daughter recounted:

It is not uncommon to see persons who hold in youth opinions in advance of the age in which they live, but who at a certain period seem to crystallise, and lose the faculty of comprehending and accepting new ideas and theories; thus remaining at last as far behind, as they were once in advance of public opinion. Not so my mother, who was ever ready to hail joyfully any new idea or theory, and to give it honest attention, even if it were at variance with her former convictions. This quality she never lost, and it enabled her to sympathise with the younger generation of philosophers, as she had done with their predecessors, her own contemporaries.

That the book catapulted Somerville into scientific celebrity was some recompense for the unglamorous necessities of its creation. While working on it, she had been supporting herself as a mathematics tutor to the children of the wealthy. One of her students was a little girl named Ada, daughter of the baroness Annabella Milbanke and the only legitimate child of the poet Lord Byron. Byron had fallen in love with the mathematically brilliant baroness, but when their short-lived and tempestuous marriage imploded, the very qualities that had first attracted him to her became a nuisance—the woman he had once reverenced as a "Princess of Parallelograms" he now mocked as a coolly calculating "Mathematical Medea," immortalizing the derision in his epic poem *Don Juan*: "Her favourite science was the mathematical. . . . She was a walking calculation."

What Byron found so calculating was Annabella's motion for divorce when she began to suspect, shortly after their daughter's conception, that her husband was having an incestuous relationship with his half sister, Augusta, after whom the child had already been named. Five weeks after Augusta Ada was born, Annabella's attorneys sent Byron a notice of her request for separation, intimating that if he did not comply, evidence of his philandering would be made public.

Byron took the ultimatum seriously and left England, never to return. He vagabonded around Europe and settled for a time in Italy, where he lived for seven years with the struggling poet Percy Shelley. All along, Byron carried a small portrait of Ada and was visibly gladdened whenever visitors remarked on their resemblance, but he was also clearly conflicted about his daughter's heritage. After one such remark on his daughter's likeness, Byron picked up the picture in his hand and, his visitor recounts, sighed:

I am told she is clever—I hope not; and, above all, I hope she is not poetical: the price paid for such advantages, if advantages they be, is such as to make me pray that my child may escape them.

In raising the little girl alone, Annabella was determined to eradicate the delinquent father's "poetical" influences with the mightiest antidote at her disposal. She immersed Ada in mathematics and other sciences from the time she was four, then hired Somerville—the finest mathematician she knew—as the girl's tutor.

Meanwhile, Byron moved to Greece, where he joined the nation's war for independence from the Ottoman Empire—the same Islamic yoke that terrorized Bulgaria, my own homeland and Greece's northern neighbor, for five centuries. He died in Greece at the age of thirty-six. Ada was eight. Shortly before his death, he confided in a friend who preserved their conversations in writing:

I often, in imagination, pass over a long lapse of years and console myself for present privations, in anticipating the time when my daughter will know me by reading my works.

By the time she was a teenager, Ada excelled in mathematics and had already devised a plan for engineering a flying apparatus. But she was as animated by her father's spirit as he hoped she would be and rebelled against the suppression of what she felt was a vital part of her, of life itself: the romance of the poetic. In a bout of teenage defiance, she wrote to her mother:

You will not concede me philosophical poetry. Invert the order! Will you give me poetical philosophy, poetical science?

Ada had turned out, much to both of her parents' ambivalent blend of discontentment and pride, to be both "clever" and "poetical." The wellspring of the genius for which she would later be lauded might well be precisely this early refusal to relinquish any of her passions and aptitudes, however contradictory and even counteractory they were believed to be.

When Ada was nineteen—just before her mother married William King, who would soon be knighted Earl of Lovelace, making Ada Byron Ada Lovelace—Somerville began taking the young woman to the salons hosted by her old friend, the eccentric mathematician Charles Babbage. Twenty-three years later, Maria Mitchell would bump into the elderly Babbage, whom she had hoped to meet, as they crossed the threshold of a London drawing-room party going in opposite directions at eleven o'clock at night—Mitchell leaving, Babbage arriving.

Shortly after Somerville introduced Lovelace to Babbage, the two began working together on what is widely considered the world's first computer: their Analytical Engine. In the course of the collaboration, Lovelace would translate a scientific paper by an Italian military engineer titled *Sketch of an Analytical Engine,* adding to it seven footnotes comprising sixty-five pages—two and a half times the length of the paper itself. One of her footnotes contains what is in essence the earliest complete computer program, rendering Lovelace the world's first computer programmer. The year was 1843, and she was twenty-seven.

In 1834, the year she introduced Lovelace and Babbage, Somerville published her next major treatise, *On the Connexion of the Physical Sciences*—an elegant and erudite weaving together of the previously fragmented fields of astronomy, mathematics, physics, geology, and chemistry. It quickly became one of the scientific best sellers of the nineteenth century and occasioned the pathbreaking first that Somerville shared with Caroline Herschel when the two women were admitted into the Royal Astronomical Society the following year.

Eighteen years later, Maria Mitchell's first mention in *The New York Times* would place her in the ranks of Somerville, Lovelace, and Herschel—a report on the 1852 elections in Britain, during which one candidate advocating for women's rights had cited "Miss Mitchell" (erroneously identifying her as "of New York," with which the *New York Times* reporter took issue as a sign of ignorance in lumping all of America into one city) along with the other three pioneering women scientists. In reporting on the mismention of Mitchell's origin, the reporter took the opportunity to educate the public about her rise to prominence via her comet discovery five years earlier.

Months after the publication of Somerville's *Connexion*, the English polymath William Whewell—then master of Trinity College, where Newton had once been a fellow, and previously pivotal in making Somerville's Laplace book a requirement of the university's higher mathematics curriculum—wrote a laudatory review of her work, in which he coined the word "scientist" to refer to her. The commonly used term up to that point—"man of science"— clearly couldn't apply to a woman, nor to what Whewell considered "the peculiar illumination" of the female mind: the ability to synthesize ideas and connect seemingly disparate disciplines into a clear lens on reality. Because he couldn't call her a physicist, a geologist, or a chemist—she had written with deep knowledge of all these disciplines and more—Whewell unified them all into "scientist." Some scholars have suggested that he coined the term a year earlier in his correspondence with Coleridge, but no clear evidence survives. What does survive is his incontrovertible regard for Somerville, which remains printed in plain sight—in his review, he praises her as a "person of true science."

Whewell, an award-winning poet himself, ended his review of Somerville's work with a reimagining of John Dryden's "Lines on Milton," which crowns Homer, Virgil, and Milton as the triumvirate of poetry across epochs and civilizations in a gradation toward perfection of the form:

Three poets, in three distant ages born,
Greece, Italy, and England did adorn.
The first in loftiness of thought surpassed,
The next in majesty, in both the last.
The force of Nature could no farther go;
To make a third she joined the former two.

Whewell revises the verse to crown Hypatia of Alexandria, Maria Agnesi of Bologna, and Mary Somerville as the triumvirate of women in science, with Somerville serving as the pinnacle of this lineage of genius:

> Three women in three different ages born,
> Greece, Italy and England did adorn;
> Rare as poetic minds of master flights,
> Three only rose to science's loftiest heights.
> The first a crown in brutal pieces tore,
> Envious of fame, bewildered at the lore;
> The next through tints of darkening shadow passed,
> Lost in the azure sisterhood at last;
> Equal to these the third and happier far,
> Cheerful though wise, though learned, popular,
> Liked by the many, valued by the few,
> Instructs the world, yet dubbed by none a Blue.

But even in his praise, Whewell obliquely condones the era's stereotypes—"a Blue" refers to "bluestocking," the derogatory term for intellectual women, who were seen as having sacrificed their femininity and domesticity to the life of the mind. To point out that Mary Somerville wasn't one implies that most women of genius were.

Ironically, the term was originally inspired by the oddities not of a woman but of a man.

A century before Margaret Fuller's Boston "Conversations," the Irish intellectual Elizabeth Vesey and the British social reformer Elizabeth Montagu joined forces to host a pioneering series of salons, inviting women to discuss literary and political subjects. Men occasionally attended. When the coxcombish botanist Benjamin Stillingfleet showed up at one of the salons clad in outrageous blue knit stockings, the women saw in his outfit a caricature of intellectual posturing as a form of vanity rather than a genuine passion for learning—they themselves were far too interested in substantive conversation to care for being seen as fashionable at these gatherings. And yet somehow—for our language reflects our power structures—the term "bluestocking" came to be applied to the women at the salons. In a letter penned half a century later, Caroline Herschel would capture the double standard perfectly in her thoroughly unsarcastic style of matter-of-fact observation: "Was there ever a woman without vanity? or a man either? only with this difference, that among gentlemen the commodity is generally styled ambition."

But despite Whewell's adhesion to such flat societal archetypes, he saw the full dimension of Somerville's singular genius as a connector and cross-pollinator of ideas across disciplines. "Everything is naturally related and interconnected," Ada Lovelace would write a decade later, in the year Margaret Fuller composed *Woman in the Nineteenth Century*. In her literary debut—a poem on the nature of the mind, published the same year as Somerville's first book—twenty-year-old Elizabeth Barrett would point to the "bold Association" that "the links of fact, unites, with links of thought" as a centerpiece of genius. A quarter century after Somerville's *Connexion* was published, Maria Mitchell would celebrate it as a masterwork containing "vast collections of facts in all branches of Physical Science, connected together by the delicate web of Mrs. Somerville's own thought, showing an amount and variety of learning to be compared only to that of Humboldt."

At the time of its release, however, not everyone could see the genius of Somerville's contribution to science in her synthesis and cross-pollination of information, effecting integrated wisdom greater than the sum total of bits of fact—a skill that becomes exponentially more valuable as the existing pool of knowledge swells. One obtuse malediction came from the Scottish philosopher Thomas Carlyle, who proclaimed that Somerville had never done anything original—a remark that the young sculptor Harriet Hosmer, herself a pathbreaker who opened up the figurative arts for women in the nineteenth century, would tear to shreds. In a letter defending Somerville, she scoffs:

To the Carlyle mind, wherein women never played any conspicuous part, perhaps not, but no one, man or woman, ever possessed a clearer insight into complicated problems, or possessed a greater gift of rendering such problems clear to the mind of the student, one phase of originality, surely.

Whewell was able to see the originality to which Carlyle was blind. A poet who relished the lyrical art at least as much as he did science, the Cambridge don recognized in Somerville the uncommon achievement of the finest science writers of every generation—first explaining the abstract ideas of the science at hand, then elucidating their connection to other abstract ideas and to the real world, and finally enchanting the reader with truth of a higher order illuminated by this kaleidoscopic perspective, truth that radiates not mere information but a poetry of understanding, Thoreau's "knowledge useful in a higher sense."

But when Maria Mitchell visited Trinity College twenty-three years later, she met a different Whewell—a quarter century of absorbing the pomposity of Cambridge academia through every pore had taken a toll on a man who once saw with fresh eyes beyond his time and convention.

Mitchell was put off by the pretensions of the Cambridge lifestyle Whewell had so thoroughly bought into, from the red velvet curtains draping the windows of his mansion to the six-person uniformed waitstaff ceremoniously serving dinner. "An Englishman is proud; a Cambridge man is the proudest of Englishmen; and Dr. Whewell, the proudest of Cambridge men," Mitchell wrote in her diary. "In the opinion of a Cambridge man, to be master of Trinity is to be master of the world!" She notes that despite his gray hair, he would look "extraordinarily handsome if it were not for an expression of ill-temper around the mouth"—an ill-temper that permeated their interaction.

The wife of the director of the Greenwich Observatory, who had introduced the two scientists, observed that Mitchell and Whewell instantly "riled" each other. But why? Perhaps Whewell had a certain Pygmalion complex and enjoyed the grandiose sense that he was wielding his power to make Somerville famous, to make her brilliance come alive in the popular imagination; there was no room for this with Mitchell, who was already a scientific celebrity. It is also possible that they misaligned on scientific grounds. Four years earlier, Whewell had published a creationist treatise dismissing the possibility of extraterrestrial life. After reading it, the poet Lord Tennyson would famously proclaim: "It is inconceivable that the whole universe was merely created for us who live in this third-rate planet of a third-rate sun."

Mitchell disliked Whewell's blanket tone of sarcasm and felt that his "self-respect and immense self-esteem led him to imperiousness of manner which touches the border of discourtesy." While she admired his work, she found it impossible to reconcile the person before her with his creative persona: "He writes verses that are touchingly beautiful, but it is difficult to believe, in his presence, that he writes them." She found him to be "very severe upon Americans" and was appalled that he criticized Emerson. Never one to swallow dissent, she made her admiration for the Sage of Concord clear. I can picture her eyelids lowering coolly over her large brown eyes as she seethed within—a curtain that half-hides, half-reveals her infinite scorn. Whewell, in turn, seemed to scorn Mitchell's taste in poetry, particularly her love of Elizabeth Barrett Browning's recently published *Aurora Leigh*—an epic novel in blank verse about a young woman caught in the tension between the life of love and the life of genius, who finds her powerful voice as an artist in a society that seeks to silence it by sublimation to convention. Whewell couldn't have known that Mitchell's admiration for its author exceeded her regard for any of Europe's learned scientists—admiration so intense that it bordered on the paralytic, for when a friend attempted an informal introduction by handing Mitchell a book that belonged to Barrett Browning and sending her to return it, Mitchell couldn't bring herself to knock on the poet's door. Having traversed an ocean, she halted starstruck at the hinged plank of wood between her and her hero, left the book on the doorstep, and walked away.

Ba—as Elizabeth Barrett was known in childhood—had begun writing poetry before the age of eight, her first known poem protesting compulsory military service. It was in childhood, too, that Ba—

the eldest of twelve children—started suffering from the intense spinal headaches and muscle pain that would bedevil her for the remaining four decades of her life, now believed to have been hypokalemic periodic paralysis—a rare disorder that depletes muscles of potassium, effecting extreme weakness and bouts of acute pain. By seventeen, she had published—anonymously—*Essay on Mind, and Other Poems,* in the preface to which she defined poetry as "the enthusiasm of the understanding," argued that "thought catches the light reflected from the object of her contemplation," and divided "the productions of the mind" into two classes: the philosophical and the poetical. Her body of work would rise to the pinnacle of both, rendering her one of the most influential writers of the century and her *Aurora Leigh* a sensation best described today as viral.

In the poem, the protagonist—a poet who rejects marriage and sets out to make a life for herself as a working artist, only to discover that art is no less impoverished by the denial of love than love by the denial of art—defends poets from the cynics who may dismiss them as "virtuous liars, dreamers after dark, exaggerators of the sun and moon." Aurora paints them, rather, as "the only truth-tellers"— "the only speakers of essential truth, posed to relative, comparative, and temporal truths." A century later, James Baldwin—himself a poet in the largest sense and of the highest order—would echo Barrett Browning:

> The poets (by which I mean all artists) are finally the only people who know the truth about us. Soldiers don't. Statesmen don't. Priests don't. Union leaders don't. Only poets.

Barrett Browning was to surmount an uncommon share of adversity before becoming a titan of her time. A close succession of tragedies compounded a particularly painful episode of her disease. Just before her thirty-fourth birthday, one of Elizabeth's brothers died of fever and another, her most beloved sibling, in a sailing accident for which she blamed herself. "That was a very near escape from madness, absolute hopeless madness," she would later recount. The following year, as her physical symptoms inflicted new heights of anguish, her father took her to London in an invalid carriage. She spent seven years almost continuously bedridden in a darkened upstairs room on Wimpole Street alongside her beloved spaniel Flush, communicating with the outside world only via letters, "as people shut up in dungeons take up with scrawling mottoes on the walls." In a passage Fuller had quoted in a laudatory *Tribune* piece, the poet recounted:

> Poetry has been as serious a thing for me as life itself; and life has been a very serious thing; there has been no playing at skittles for me at either. I never mistook pleasure as the final cause of poetry; nor leisure, for the hour of the poet. I have done my work, so far, as work; not as mere hand and head work apart from the personal being, but as the completest expression of that being to which I could attain; and, as work, I offer it to the public, feeling its faultiness more deeply than any of my readers, because measured from the height of my aspiration, but feeling also the reverence and sincerity with which the work was done should protect it in the thoughts of the reverent and sincere.

Secluded in her sickroom, Barrett counterbalanced her stillness with a ferocious pace of composition that led to her first major literary success and invited the courtship of Robert Browning. "I love your verses with all my heart, Dear Miss Barrett," Browning—an obscure poet six years her junior—wrote to the stranger whose 1844 poetry collection had enchanted him beyond words. "I love these books with all my heart—and I love you too."

So began an epistolary courtship—carried out in secret, as Barrett knew her father would condemn the union—that produced some of the most exquisite love letters ever written. Within two years, Barrett and Browning eloped to marry in a small ceremony at a London church around the corner from her sickroom. After Elizabeth's punitively possessive father disinherited her, the Brownings moved to Florence, where Mary Somerville had recently settled. When the Scottish mathematician met the couple, she was instantly taken by their devotion not only to each other but to each other's art. "I can imagine no happier or more fascinating life than theirs; two kindred spirits united in the highest and noblest aspirations," Somerville wrote. The Brownings would become so famous that their personal lives would eclipse their work in the eyes of the adoring public. A century later, Virginia Woolf would see in their fate a tragic testimony to how celebrity culture hollows creative culture:

> Passionate lovers, in curls and side-whiskers, oppressed, defiant, eloping—in this guise thousands of people must know and love the Brownings who have never read a line of their poetry. They have become two of the most conspicuous figures in that bright and animated company of authors who, thanks to our modern habit of writing memoirs and printing letters and sitting to be photographed, live in the flesh, not merely as of old in the word; are known by their hats, not merely by their poems. What damage the art of photography has inflicted upon the art of literature has yet to be reckoned.

Aurora Leigh catapulted Elizabeth Barrett Browning into unexampled celebrity, lifting Robert along with her. And yet her masterwork stood as an antipode to the myth of the overnight success—she had been incubating it for more than a decade. In one of her stunning love letters to Robert, she outlines her vision eleven years before the book's publication:

> My chief *intention* just now is the writing of a sort of novel-poem—a poem . . . running into the midst of our conventions, and rushing into drawing-rooms and the like, "where angels fear to tread"; and so, meeting face to face and without mask the Humanity of the age, and speaking the truth as I conceive of it out plainly.

Browning responded with electric enthusiasm:

> The poem you propose to make, for the times; the fearless fresh living work you describe, is the only Poem to be undertaken now by you or anyone that is a Poet at all; the only reality, only effective piece of service to be rendered God and man; it is what I have been

all my life intending to do, and now shall be much, much nearer doing, since you will be along with me.

As Elizabeth rose to celebrity, Robert's pride in her work was so great that he sublimated his own ego, readily recounting that there was a period during which he could get publishers interested in his own work only if he also sent them something of his wife's. Although far more remembered today than Elizabeth, Robert spent most of his career in her shadow—always ungrudgingly, always in admiration. In 1855, he published *Men and Women*—a two-volume collection of his poems, for which both Brownings had high hopes. It fell on unenchanted ears, dismissed by critics and ignored by the public. Several months later, *Aurora Leigh* stationed Elizabeth atop a new stratum of celebrity. Robert was jubilant. "I am surprised, I own, at the amount of success," a disbelieving Elizabeth wrote to her sister-in-law. "Golden-hearted Robert is in ecstasies about it— far more than if it all related to a book of his own." Perhaps she was thinking of Robert's obscurity and the public's painful indifference to his books when she had her Aurora proclaim:

> We get no good
> By being ungenerous, even to a book
> And calculating profits—so much help
> By so much rending. It is rather when
> We gloriously forget ourselves, and plunge
> Soul-forward, headlong, into a book's profound,
> Impassioned for its beauty and salt of truth—
> 'Tis then we get the right good from a book.

And yet posterity would deal its recognition with uneven hands. "Fate has not been kind to Mrs. Browning as a writer," Virginia Woolf would observe across the breach of time and selective erasure we call history. "Nobody reads her, nobody discusses her, nobody troubles to put her in her place."

In 1856, everybody read her, everybody discussed her, though the patriarchy and the traditionalists set out to put her in her place.

Barrett Browning proudly reported that mothers wouldn't let their daughters read *Aurora Leigh*, but young women devoured it in secret. It stunned, it shocked, it unsettled the status quo with more than its central claim of women's intellectual and artistic autonomy, of the right to choose the public sphere and the life of creative work over the domestic sphere and the life of deadening dependence.

The novel-poem's narrator and protagonist begins life as the daughter of an English father and a Florentine mother, who dies when Aurora is still a small child. When her father also dies, the young Aurora is shipped off to England and raised by a cold, unloving aunt who sees her as a living record of her father's transgression with a foreigner. As Aurora buries herself in books and gives herself an education, her only companion is her cousin Romney Leigh—a young, idealistic social reformer, who scoffs at Aurora's aspiration to become a poet, seeing art as too feeble a tool in the campaign of transfiguring the world. Art, he tells her, is inferior to activism, to the hard work of improving life by social reform. At the heart of Aurora's retort is Elizabeth Barrett Browning's meta-manifesto for how art both reflects life and raises it, for its power to transform and redeem:

> What is art,
> But life upon the larger scale, the higher,
> When, graduating up in a spiral line
> Of still expanding and ascending gyres,
> It pushes toward the intense significance
> Of all things, hungry for the Infinite?
> Art's life,—and where we live, we suffer and toil.

When Romney proposes marriage, Aurora is vexed that a man who sees her calling as unfit for the task of bettering the world should see her instead as fit for wifehood. To his shock, she rejects him and moves to London to become a working writer—a bold experiment to prove her credo with her own life. Romney, both heartbroken and awed by Aurora's courageous conviction, bids her farewell with a parting admonition that art must never unmoor itself from life:

> Reflect, if Art be, in truth, the higher life,
> You need the lower life to stand upon,
> In order to reach up into that higher:
> And none can stand a-tiptoe in the place
> He cannot stand in with two stable feet.
> Remember then!—for art's sake, hold your life.

In London, Aurora spends three years in poverty, "happy and unafraid of solitude," working "with patience which means almost power," honing her art as a poet while supporting herself with the craft of commercial prose:

> I had to live, that therefore I might work.
> And, being but poor, I was constrained, for life,
> To work with one hand for the booksellers,
> While working with the other for myself
> And art. You swim with feet as well as hands
> Or make small way. I apprehended this,—
> In England, no one lives by verse that lives;
> And, apprehending, I resolved by prose
> To make a space to sphere my living verse.

Once she establishes herself as a journalist and essayist, Aurora publishes a book of poetry, which is welcomed as a triumph of originality and renders her a literary celebrity. One day, Aurora receives a visit from Lady Waldemar—an upperclass heiress who professes to have fallen in love with Romney and informs Aurora that he is about to marry a poor maiden by the name of Marian Erle. Lady Waldemar beseeches Aurora to stop the wedding—Romney must not abase himself by binding his high life to such lowliness.

Aurora—who immediately mistrusts Lady Waldemar and her "silver laugh," the way she lifts up her eyelids "with a real grave queenly look, which ruled, and would not spare, not even herself"—

sets out to find her cousin's bride-to-be and assess the fitness of the match for herself. When she meets Marian Erle—a destitute young woman who had escaped from an abusive home to live a humble working-class life—she is taken by her sweetness, her kindness, the sincerity of her life and her love for Romney. Aurora can do nothing but be glad for their marriage.

This was one of Elizabeth Barrett Browning's most subversive plot lines—a radical case for love across the dehumanizing boundaries of class. Scandalous as the notion of trespassing socioeconomic borders was in the middle of the nineteenth century, *Aurora Leigh* was well ahead of its time—not gender, not race, not orientation, but class has endured as the most divisive factor in society. The delta of change in public attitudes toward interracial and same-sex marriage between Barrett Browning's time and our own is tremendous, but eyebrows are as likely to be raised at interclass marriage—in surprise, in judgment—now as they were then.

The element in *Aurora Leigh* that most jolted convention and propriety, however, was Barrett Browning's unprecedented and uncottoned discussion of rape. On the day of the wedding, as the church bustles with spectators already abuzz with cynical whispers about the match, Marian Erle vanishes, leaving Romney confounded and bereft. Aurora is heartbroken herself by so incomprehensible an act, for she had taken a great liking to the decent, kindhearted maiden. Time passes. Having found success but not contentment in London, Aurora decides to return to her native Italy—that "magic circle" of mountains, where water leaps in rivers "like a white soul tossed out to eternity with thrills of time upon it."

Wandering through Paris on her way to Florence, she is arrested by a glimpse of Marian amid the raging human rapids of the street, with an infant at her breast. Prey to the elemental human tendency to fill the unknown with stories, Aurora immediately assumes that the young woman has betrayed her beloved cousin by taking a secret lover, for whom she left Romney at the altar. But when she finally catches up to Marian and confronts her, the truth Aurora hears is a thousandfold more heartbreaking than the seduction story she had imagined.

Before the wedding, the manipulative Lady Waldemar, determined to conquer Romney for herself, had convinced Marian that she was unworthy of him, and that he regarded her as a mere charity case for his noble reformist ideals. Disheartened and affirmed in the self-doubt that had dogged her all along, Marian saw no choice but to leave London. She took "the blank, blind, weary way, which led . . where'er it led . . away at least," not caring if the ship she boarded took her "to Sydney or to France."

In a foreign tenement, she was drugged and gang-raped. Her life was not altered by seduction, as Aurora had assumed, but severed by a living death:

> Do wolves seduce a wandering fawn in France?
> Do eagles, who have pinched a lamb with claws,
> Seduce it into carrion? So with me.
> I was not ever as you say, seduced,
> But simply murdered.

As Marian lays before Aurora the leaden truth—"Man's violence, not man's seduction, made me what I am"—Barrett Browning paints an unsparing description of how rape disfigures its survivors, leaving them

> Half gibbering and half raving on the floor,
> And wondering what had happened up in heaven,
> That suns should dare to shine when God Himself
> Was certainly abolished.

The men held Marian captive and violated her for weeks, plunging her into a spiral of madness. She tells Aurora of her release and harrowing escape:

> They feared my eyes and loosed me, as boys might
> A mad dog which they had tortured.
> Up and down I went, by road and village, over tracts
> Of open foreign country, large and strange,
> Crossed everywhere by long thin poplar-lines

Like fingers of some ghastly skeleton hand
Through sunlight and through moonlight evermore
Pushed out from hell itself to pluck me back,
And resolute to get me, slow and sure . . .

But her getaway is incomplete—Marian finds herself pregnant. Deadened by the violence to her body and spirit, she decides to keep the child as her sole umbilical cord to life—"some coin of price" embedded in her flesh as recompense for the gruesome crime that had left her "half-dead, whole mangled."

In a shattering soliloquy, Marian limns the razing of soul that rape inflicts on a being:

That little stone, called Marian Erle. . . .
Was ground and tortured by the incessant sea
And bruised from what she was,—changed! death's a change,
And she, I said, was murdered; Marian's dead.
What can you do with people when they are dead,
But, if you are pious, sing a hymn and go;
Or, if you are tender, heave a sigh and go,
But go by all means,—and permit the grass
To keep its green feud up 'twixt them and you?
Then leave me,—let me rest. I'm dead, I say.
And if, to save the child from death as well,
The mother in me has survived the rest,
Why, that's God's miracle you must not tax,—
I'm not less dead for that: I'm nothing more
But just a mother. Only for the child,
I'm warm, and cold, and hungry, and afraid,
And smell the flowers a little, and see the sun,
And speak still, and am silent,—just for him!
I pray you therefore to mistake me not
And treat me haply, as I were alive;
For though you ran a pin into my soul,
I think it would not hurt nor trouble me.

Aurora, "convicted, broken utterly" by the story and shamed at her initial presumption, insists that Marian join her in Tuscany, where they would make a home and "live on toward the truer life" together, raising the boy so that he doesn't miss a father, "since two mothers shall make that up to him." In Florence, they settle into a peaceable life of shared sweetness as Marian mothers her child and Aurora, breadwinner by her art, works on her poetry and learns the names of the birds and the insects, of the snakes and the frogs, of nature in her many-splendored tessellations.

One evening, an astonishing presence slices through the golden Tuscan moonlight—Romney Leigh has gotten word of Marian's fate and, propelled by his high moral code, has come to offer marriage, guardianship, paternity for the fatherless child.

But the rape—this murder—has made of Marian a ghost incapable of loving anything and anyone except her child. With time and distance, she has also realized that what she had felt for Romney in the first place was not love but worship—of his noble character, of his kindness to her—and worship is only a simulacrum of love. She rejects his proposal—not indignantly, but through grateful tears, governed by the conviction that she alone can be the bearer of her own redemption, that she is content and complete as a single mother.

In his bewilderment, Romney realizes that he has always loved Aurora only, whose book of poetry he has read in the intervening years and come to see as awesome proof of the ideals for which she had rejected him in their youth. Aurora, too, realizes that beneath her youthful indignation at Romney's long-ago proposal and his haughty dismissal of art, she had indeed loved him deeply for his noble character, and had never ceased loving him.

> He mistook the world:
> but I mistook my own heart.

But she also perceives that he had been right to question her immature ideals—art cannot be some lofty chandelier dangling above life but must draw its light from the plane of living. Their wrongness had been evenly divided, and now they were to join their half-rightnesses into a whole.

There were words
That broke in utterance . . melted, in the fire;
Embrace, that was convulsion, . . then a kiss . .
As long and silent as the ecstatic night,—
And deep, deep, shuddering breaths, which meant beyond
Whatever could be told by word or kiss.
[. . .]
O dark, O moon and stars, O ecstasy
Of darkness! O great mystery of love,—
In which absorbed, loss, anguish, treason's self
Enlarges rapture,—as a pebble dropt
In some full wine-cup, over-brims the wine!

Under the Tuscan moon, love prevails—love not as life's supreme
end, before which all else must subvert and prostrate itself, but love
as art's twin and equal, neither a sacrificial offering to the other,
each a pillar of what is highest in the human spirit.

Beloved, let us love so well,
Our work shall still be better for our love,
And still our love be sweeter for our work,
And both, commended, for the sake of each,
By all true workers and true lovers, born.

Art, Barrett Browning concludes in the final scene of redemption,
is an instrument of truth and transformation—for the human heart
and, through it, for the body of the world:

The world's old;
But the old world waits the hour to be renewed:
Toward which, new hearts in individual growth
Must quicken, and increase to multitude
In new dynasties of the race of men,—
Developed whence, shall grow spontaneously
New churches, new economies, new laws
Admitting freedom, new societies
Excluding falsehood.

. . .

As *Aurora Leigh* lived up to Barrett Browning's germinal vision for a work "running into the midst of our conventions, and rushing into drawing-rooms," her public success was wormed by her private sorrow at her father's rejection. She had always known that he would not condone her independence—in art or in love—but somehow she stoked an embering hope that the living proof of her self-actualization would melt his icy obstinacy. In January 1857, as *Aurora Leigh* went into a second edition, Elizabeth beseeched her sister for news that their father had made a mention of it, any mention at all. He had not. She concluded in heartbroken resignation: "I dare say he is absolutely indifferent to me and my writings." What difference does the admiration of millions make when love one longs for remains withheld? Like worship, admiration is only counterfeit love.

And yet *Aurora Leigh* would move the world, profoundly influencing the young Emily Dickinson and enchanting Maria Mitchell as no other piece of literature ever had, save perhaps Milton's *Paradise Lost*. Perhaps Mitchell saw in Barrett Browning's words a double vindication of poetry and science as "cognizant of life beyond this blood-beat,—passionate for truth beyond these senses." In a diary entry from the ferocious first months of 1857, penned in a notebook Mitchell titled "Journal of the Hard Winter"—a winter so harsh that, a hundred miles north, Thoreau's ink froze and he had to break the ice in his pail with a hammer as the mercury refused to leave the bulb of his thermometer below negative 20°F—Mitchell writes:

> I bought a copy of *Aurora Leigh* just before the freezing up and I have been careful, as it is the only copy on the Island, to circulate it freely.

She may not have known that Aurora Leigh was modeled in large part on Margaret Fuller. In the final months of Fuller's short life, having long esteemed her work, Barrett Browning had befriended the American writer, who in turn considered the poet the greatest "female writer the world has yet known." Mitchell admired *Aurora Leigh* for the selfsame reasons she admired Fuller—here was a brilliant young woman who gives herself an education by reading Shakespeare and studying the classics, then lets her genius roam in a powerful coming of age as an artist and an instrument of change.

The poem's deepest enchantment, for Dickinson as well as Mitchell, is its unapologetic insistence on the impossibility of disentwining art and life—an impossibility that was the wellspring of Margaret Fuller's public triumph and her private ferment.

6

THE MUCH THAT CALLS FOR MORE

"I am determined on distinction," Margaret Fuller writes to her former teacher. She is fifteen. The year is 1825 and she is ineligible for any formal education, so she has taken the reins of her character into her own hands, with resolute guidance from her father—a man who has tempered his disappointment that his firstborn child was not a son with the choice to treat his eldest daughter like a creature with a mind. When the first ringlets were snipped from her hair, he composed an ode to her head as a temple of divine intellect. At six, Margaret was reading in Latin. At twelve, she was conversing with her father in philosophy and pure mathematics. She would come to describe herself as "the much that calls for more." At fifteen, this is her daily routine:

> I rise a little before five, walk an hour, and then practise on the piano till seven, when we breakfast. Next, I read French—Sismondi's Literature of the South of Europe—till eight; then two or three lectures in Brown's Philosophy. About half past nine I go to Mr. Perkins's school, and study Greek till twelve, when, the school being dismissed, I recite, go home, and practise again till dinner, at two. Then, when I can, I read two hours in Italian.

Many years later, she would write in response to the frequent criticism of her uncommon drive, often mistaken for arrogance, as women's confident resolve tends to be:

In an environment like mine, what may have seemed too lofty or ambitious in my character was absolutely needed to keep the heart from breaking and enthusiasm from extinction.

From the platform of her precocious girlhood, Margaret undertakes an inquiry into the building blocks of character. "Nothing more widely distinguishes man from man than energy of will," she writes in a six-page essay, positing that a conquering will is composed of imagination, perseverance, and "enthusiastic confidence in the future." But these elements are not weighted equally—she prizes above all perseverance, which fuels the "unwearied climbing and scrambling" toward achievement. "The truly strong of will," she writes, having lived just over a decade, "returns invigorated by the contest, calmed, not saddened by failure and wiser from its nature."

Over the next twenty-five years, this teenager animated by what she calls "the all-powerful motive of ambition" would persevere to write the foundational treatise of the women's emancipation movement, author the most trusted literary and art criticism in the nation, work as the first female editor for a major New York newspaper and the only woman in the newsroom, advocate for prison reform and Negro voting rights, and become America's first foreign war correspondent. All of this she would accomplish while bedeviled by debilitating chronic pain at the base of her neck—the result of a congenital spinal deformity that made it difficult to tilt her head down in order to write and was often accompanied by acute depression.

Again and again, she would rise to reach for "incessant acts of vigorous beauty," signing her influential editorials not with her name but with a single star—at first a symbol imbued with deliberate anonymity, designed to disguise the author's gender and thus avoid any bias as to the article's credibility, but soon the widely recognized seal of Fuller's authoritative voice. Literature would be her weapon of choice—"a medium for viewing all humanity, a core around which all knowledge, all experience, all science, all the ideal as well as all the practical in our nature could gather." Behind the public face of unprecedented distinction, Fuller would sorrow and struggle for private contentment—the same cerebral tidal force that swept away the barriers of prejudice and convention would end up drowning out her heart. Over and over, she would entangle herself in intellectual infatuations and half-requited loves that fell short of what she most fervently desired: "fulness of being"—the sublime integration of emotion, the intellect, and, as she would come to realize only at the end of her short life, the body. And yet she was as intent on having an examined inner life as she was on engaging with the life of the world, of the earth, of cosmic existence. "I cannot live without mine own particular star," Fuller wrote at the age Maria Mitchell was when she discovered her comet, "but my foot is on the earth and I wish to walk over it until my wings be grown. I will use my microscope as well as my telescope."

Months after the solar eclipse that revealed to twelve-year-old Maria Mitchell her astral calling, twenty-one-year-old Margaret Fuller arrived at her "own particular star" through a transcendent experience she later described as one of eclipsing "the extreme of passionate sorrow"—a revelation that stripped all sense of self and, in that nakedness of being, made her all the more herself. In her journal, Fuller recounts being forced to go to church on Thanksgiving Day while feeling "wearied out by mental conflicts, and in a mood of most childish, child-like sadness"—the sorrow of her symphonic potential muted by those tasked with directing her life. She would later recall:

> I felt within myself great power, and generosity, and tenderness, but it seemed to me as if they were all unrecognized, and as if it was impossible that they should be used in life. I was only one-and-twenty; the past was worthless, the future hopeless; yet . . . my aspiration seemed very high.

Looking around the pews, this young woman who would later describe herself as having had "no natural childhood" now finds herself envying all the little children. Once liberated from the service, she heads into the fields and walks—almost runs—for hours, under "slow processions of sad clouds . . . passing over a cold blue sky." She is unable to contain the thoughts that have seethed for years and have now erupted to the surface. "It seemed I could never return to a world in which I had no place . . . I could not act a part, nor seem to live any longer." So she ceases to think and instead observes nature in its irrepressible aliveness—the trees "dark and silent"; the little stream "shrunken, voiceless, choked with withered leaves," and yet "it did not quite lose itself in the earth."

> Suddenly the sun shone out with that transparent sweetness, like the last smile of a dying lover, which it will use when it has been unkind all a cold autumn day. And, even then, passed into my thought a beam from its true sun, from its native sphere, which has never since departed me.

The beam illuminates her memory of herself as a little girl, stopping midstep on the stairs to wonder how she came into being:

> How is it that I seem to be this Margaret Fuller? What does it mean? What shall I do about it? I remembered all the times and ways in which the same thought had returned. I saw how long it must be before the soul can learn to act under these limitations of time and space, and human nature; but I saw, also, that it must do it,—that it must make all this false true. . . . I saw there was no self; that selfishness was all folly, and the result of circumstance; that it was only because I thought self real that I suffered; that I had only to live in the idea of the all, and all was mine.

Fuller borrows this final sentiment from her greatest literary hero, Goethe, whose work she had read passionately after teaching herself German and becoming a fluent translator in three months. The spring after Fuller's death, Goethe's notion of "the all" would make its way into Melville's romantic letters to Hawthorne. As he is finishing *Moby-Dick,* a disenchanted Melville tempers Goethe's exultation:

In reading some of Goethe's sayings, so worshipped by his votaries, I came across this, "Live in the all." That is to say, your separate identity is but a wretched one,—good; but get out of yourself, spread and expand yourself, and bring to yourself the tinglings of life that are felt in the flowers and the woods, that are felt in the planets Saturn and Venus, and the Fixed Stars. What nonsense! Here is a fellow with a raging toothache. "My dear boy," Goethe says to him, "you are sorely afflicted with that tooth; but you must live in the all, and then you will be happy!" As with all great genius, there is an immense deal of flummery in Goethe, and in proportion to my own contact with him, a monstrous deal of it in me.

Fuller's devotion to Goethe was not the blind idolatry Melville mocked, but a deeply reasoned admiration that would impel her to become the polymathic German poet's first English biographer. "It seems to me as if the mind of Goethe had embraced the universe," Fuller wrote to her romantic friend James Freeman Clarke. "He comprehends every feeling I have ever had so perfectly, expresses it so beautifully."

Born within months of each other, Fuller and Clarke met while both were recovering from the anguishing end of asymmetrical affections. Fuller had fallen for one of Clarke's classmates at Harvard, whom she saw as her sole intellectual equal in their group of friends, only to find unmet her longing for a union of intellect and passion. Perhaps she had turned the suitor off with her answer to his inquiry about her faith—she considered herself "singularly barren of illusions" and had no patience for the mindless piousness her era demanded of women and men alike. "I have determined not to form settled opinions at present," the nineteen-year-old Margaret told the young man. "Feeble natures need a positive religion, a visible refuge, a protection . . . but mine is not such." And how could she feel otherwise? "My first experience of life was one of death," she would later write, recalling the abrupt loss of her younger sister.

With death so prevalent in the nineteenth century and loss an elemental experience of every life, religion's rhetoric of immortality offered a crutch of consolation—the promise of reunion with loved

ones after death. Elizabeth Barrett Browning captured the allure of
the crutch in *Aurora Leigh*:

The incoherencies of change and death
Are represented fully, mixed and merged,
In the smooth fair mystery of perpetual Life.

To dismiss this longing for unremitting life as mere foolishness
would be to take for granted the privileges of our own era—a privilege afforded by the men and women who have labored in labs to
make our flesh a little more impervious, but only a little, to the ceaseless forces of decay that drive the universe. Weeks after the twelve-
year-old Maria Mitchell marveled at the spectacle of the eclipse, the
eighty-one-year-old Caroline Herschel, "not free from pain for one
hour out of the twenty-four," wrote to her niece: "My complaint is
incurable, for it is a *decay* of nature. . . . What a shocking idea it is
to be decaying! *decaying!*"

Our psychology has remained just as vulnerable to the shock of
our mortality, the emotional upheaval of which endures unpalliated
by reason. No one is immune to it, not even the sharpest scientific
intellect.

When James Gleick was composing his masterly biography of
Richard Feynman shortly after the physicist's death in 1988, he discovered something of arresting strangeness and splendor, which discomposed his most central understanding of Feynman's character as
an apostle of science and reason. Among a mass of unread papers
Feynman's widow gave him, Gleick found a remarkable letter to
a physical nonentity that was, for the future Nobel Prize–winning
physicist, the locus of an irrepressible metaphysical reality.

More than half a century earlier, the teenage Richard had fallen
in love with a girl on the beach at his native Far Rockaway, where
Walt Whitman had once swum naked under "the milk-white crests
curling over." The beautiful and intellectually daring Arline had
an ardor for philosophy and art that complemented young Richard's passion for science. With the eyes of young love, the couple
peered into a shared future of infinite possibility for bliss. But they

were abruptly grounded when a mysterious malady began afflict-ing Arline with strange symptoms—a lump would appear and dis-appear on her neck, fevers would roil over her with no apparent cause. Eventually, she was hospitalized for what was believed to be typhoid. To Feynman's shock, medicine—a branch of the scien-tific enterprise in which he so firmly believed—was impotent against Arline's illness. As he bombarded the doctors with questions to steer them toward a closer approximation of the scientific method, Arline recovered just as inexplicably as she had fallen ill.

The respite was only temporary. The symptoms returned, still lacking a concrete explanation, but now unambiguously pointing toward the terminal—a prognosis Arline's doctors kept from her. The secret didn't last long—Arline overheard her mother crying and confronted Richard—they had made a pact to always give each other the truth, no matter how difficult. He confirmed the prognosis and asked her to marry him.

Princeton, where he was now pursuing a Ph.D., threatened to withdraw his fellowship—the university considered the emotional and practical responsibilities of marriage a grave threat to academic discipline.

Just as Feynman began considering leaving Princeton, a conclu-sive diagnosis detonated the situation—Arline had contracted a rare form of tuberculosis, most likely from unpasteurized milk. The year was 1941—immunology was in its infancy, the antibiotic treatment of bacterial infections was practically nonexistent, and the first suc-cessful medical application of penicillin was a year away. Tubercu-losis was a death sentence, even if it was a slow death with intervals of remission—a fact Richard and Arline faced with an ambivalent mix of brave lucidity and hope against hope.

His parents, aghast, tried to intercede in their plans. "I was sur-prised to learn such a marriage is not unlawful. It ought to be," his mother scoffed unfeelingly as she worried about how the stigma of tuberculosis would impact her brilliant young son's prospects.

In the spring of 1942, Richard cushioned the back of a bor-rowed station wagon with mattresses for Arline's comfort before picking her up from her father's house, aglow in her ghostly white dress. They drove to the ferry dock in New York Harbor. Under the fluorescent lights of a government office on Staten Island, with two strangers summoned from the adjoining room as witnesses, Richard and Arline promised each other eternity. Fearful of contagion, Richard did not kiss her on the lips. After the ceremony, he helped her slowly down the stairs, and onward they drove to Arline's new home—a charity hospital in Browns Mills, New Jersey.

As World War II was reaching its crescendo of destruction, Feynman—by then one of the nation's most promising physicists—was recruited to work on the Manhattan Project at a secret laboratory in Los Alamos. Arline entered the nearby Albuquerque sanatorium, from which she wrote him letters in code—for the sheer fun of it, because she knew how he cherished puzzles, but the correspondence alarmed the military censors at the laboratory's Intelligence Office. Tasked with preventing any breaches to the secrecy of the operation, they cautioned Feynman that coded messages were against the rules and demanded that his wife include a key in each letter to help them decipher it.

While Arline was merely having fun, all across the country thousands of women were working as cryptographers for the government. Vassar, where Maria Mitchell's legacy had made the strong science curriculum known nationwide, was one of the primary recruitment grounds for gifted women with a flair for languages and mathematics—women who would come to constitute more than half of America's code-breaking force during the war.

The discomfiture of the Manhattan Project Intelligence Office only amplified Arline's sense of fun—she began cutting holes into her letters and covering passages with ink. She even mail-ordered a jigsaw puzzle kit with which to cut up the pages and completely confound the agents. But the levity masked the underlying darkness that Richard and Arline were trying so desperately to evade—Arline was dying.

The letters went back and forth daily. In every single one of his, Richard told Arline that he loved her. "I have a serious affliction: loving you forever," he wrote.

In early 1945, two and a half years into their marriage, Richard
and Arline made love for the first time. He had been too afraid of
harming her frail health, she too afraid of infecting him with the
deadly bacterium consuming her. Finally, Arline insisted that this
pent-up desire could no longer be contained and assured Richard
that consummation would only bring them closer—to each other,
and to the life they had so lovingly dreamt up for themselves. But
heightened as their hopes were by this new dimension of shared
experience, Arline's health continued to plummet. Her weight
dropped to eighty-four pounds. Exasperated by the helplessness of
medicine, which Feynman had come to see not as a manifestation
but as a mutilation of the scientific method, he invested all hope in
an experimental drug made of mold growths. "Keep hanging on,"
he exhorted Arline. "Nothing is certain. We lead a charmed life."

She began spitting blood.

He, on the precipice of a brilliant scientific career at twenty-
seven, was terminally in love.

On June 16, 1945, while working at the computing room at Los
Alamos, Feynman received a call from the sanatorium that Arline
was on the brink of death. He borrowed a colleague's car and sped
to the hospital, where he found her immobile, her eyes barely tracing his movement. A fascination with the nature of time had set
his scientific career into motion. Now the hours stretched and contracted as he sat at Arline's deathbed, until one last small breath
tolled the end at 9:21 p.m.

The wake of loss has a way of tranquilizing grief with the pressing demands of practical arrangements—a tranquilizer we take willingly, almost gratefully. The following morning, Feynman arranged
for his beloved's cremation, methodically collected her personal
belongings. On the final page of the small spiral notebook in which
she recorded her symptoms, he logged with scientific remove: "June
16—Death."

And so we arrive at Gleick's improbable discovery in that box of
letters—improbable because of the extreme rationality with which
Feynman hedged against even the slightest intimation of metaphysi-

cal conjecture untestable by science and unprovable by reason. While courting Arline, he had been vexed by her enthusiasm for Descartes, whose "proof" of God's perfection he saw as an intellectually lazy antipode to Descartes's reputation as a champion of reason. He had impishly countered Arline's insistence that there are two sides to everything by cutting a piece of paper and half-twisting it into a Möbius strip, the ends pasted together to render a surface with just one side. Everything that appeared mystical, Feynman believed, was simply an insufficiently explained mystery with a physical answer not yet found. Even Arline's dying hour had offered testing ground for his conviction: Puzzlingly, the clock in the room had stopped at exactly 9:21 p.m.—the time of death. Aware of how this bizarre occurrence could foment the mystical imagination in unscientific minds, Feynman reasoned for an explanation. Remembering that he had repaired the clock multiple times over the course of Arline's stay at the sanatorium, he realized that the instrument's unwieldy mechanism must have choked when the nurse picked it up in the dim light for a closer look at the time she had to inscribe on the medical record.

How astonishing and how touchingly human, then, that Feynman penned the letter Gleick found in the box forty-two years later—a letter to Arline dated October 1946, four hundred eighty-eight days after her death:

D'Arline,

I adore you, sweetheart.

I know how much you like to hear that—but I don't only write it because you like it—I write it because it makes me warm all over inside to write it to you.

It is such a terribly long time since I last wrote to you—almost two years but I know you'll excuse me because you understand how I am, stubborn and realistic; and I thought there was no sense to writing.

But now I know my darling wife that it is right to do what I have delayed in doing, and that I have done so much in the past. I want to tell you I love you. I want to love you. I always will love you.

I find it hard to understand in my mind what it means to love you after you are dead—but I still want to comfort and take care of you—and I want you to love me and care for me. I want to have problems to discuss with you—I want to do little projects with you. I never thought until just now that we can do that. What should we do. We started to learn to make clothes together—or learn Chinese—or getting a movie projector. Can't I do something now? No. I am alone without you and you were the "idea-woman" and general instigator of all our wild adventures.

When you were sick you worried because you could not give me something that you wanted to and thought I needed. You needn't have worried. Just as I told you then there was no real need because I loved you in so many ways so much. And now it is clearly even more true—you can give me nothing now yet I love you so that you stand in my way of loving anyone else—but I want you to stand there. You, dead, are so much better than anyone else alive.

I know you will assure me that I am foolish and that you want me to have full happiness and don't want to be in my way. I'll bet you are surprised that I don't even have a girlfriend (except you, sweetheart) after two years. But you can't help it, darling, nor can I—I don't understand it, for I have met many girls and very nice ones and I don't want to remain alone—but in two or three meetings they all seem ashes. You only are left to me. You are real.

My darling wife, I do adore you.

I love my wife. My wife is dead.

Rich.

One of the greatest scientists who ever lived, reaching for immortality, unriven by reason—an irrepressible human impulse that had survived the cultural outpacing of its use much as our wisdom teeth survived evolution.

In *Aurora Leigh*, Elizabeth Barrett Browning had captured the disorientation of loss and the impulse to commune with the dead that impelled Feynman to write to no-longer-Arline:

Death quite unfellows us,
Sets dreadful odds betwixt the live and dead,
And makes us part as those at Babel did,
Through sudden ignorance of a common tongue.

For our ancestors, a belief in immortality was a vital coping mechanism—a sole life-straw amid the deluge of untimely deaths and the acute awareness of decay. And yet Margaret Fuller, with her critical intellect and her formative confrontation with life's ultimate fact, could not accept the fictions of immortality. Emerson, too, would contend with the shift in his journal: "I regard it as the irresistible effect of the Copernican astronomy to have made the theological scheme of redemption absolutely impossible." Years later, in her epoch-making *Woman in the Nineteenth Century*, Fuller would define religion as "the thirst for truth and good, not the love of sect and dogma." Now she yearned for a counterpart who would embrace her fiery intellect and strong-willed sovereignty of spirit. Instead, despite his previous declarations of love, the Harvard suitor withdrew without explanation—an unholy ghosting that disoriented her with sorrow.

James Freeman Clarke and Margaret Fuller were magnetized by the combination of their well-attuned minds, their analogously wounded hearts, and his unintimidated regard for what he considered to be her superior intellect—first as two young people longing for romance and trying earnestly to fall in love with each other, then, upon failing, as study partners during Clarke's first year at the Harvard Divinity School, and finally as dear lifelong friends.

It was to James that Margaret would articulate her most acute fear—that she would "die and leave no trace." But only in the privacy of her own journal would she acknowledge her most deeply felt terror—that she would live and not know love. She would torment herself with the suspicion that she is "not fitted to be loved." Three years after her death, when James Freeman Clarke visits Nantucket to meet Maria Mitchell, the astronomer would be unable to suppress an uncharacteristic inquiry into the emotional life of the intellect she so admired—she would ask him whether Fuller "was a lovable person."

Young James and Margaret's first project of shared scholarship was to teach themselves German in order to read the works of the great Romantic poets and philosophers—a fitting marriage of heart and mind. Her "much" soared to meet its "more" in an astonishing pace of progress that stunned James, who struggled to keep up. Within weeks, she was fluent in German and enamored of Goethe, who swiftly replaced Byron as the poet laureate of her interior life.

During this initial immersion in Goethe's romanticism, Margaret fell in love with someone thoroughly different from the Harvard bachelor, someone for whom she came to feel an entirely different kind of love—"the same love we shall feel when we are angels."

Anna Barker was a slender, dark-haired New Yorker descended from freethinking Quakers, three years younger than Margaret. Emerson would be smitten into describing her as "a vision of grace & beauty—a natural queen." Hiram Powers, the era's most successful sculptor, would immortalize her rare loveliness in a marble bust. "I loved Anna for a time with as much passion as I was then strong enough to feel," Fuller would later recall. "Her face was always gleaming before me, her voice was echoing in my ear, all poetic thoughts clustered round the dear image." In our attractions, we are so often driven to possess what we wish to be—Margaret sought in Anna both a counterpart and counterpoint, seeing their connection as one between "the most gentle Anna and the most ungentle Margaret." To James she wrote, "Have I ever told you how much I love her?"

This attraction was no one-sided fantasy. Anna enveloped Margaret in adoration approaching the infinite. Even James, to whom Margaret had bragged about her "magnetic power over young women," was struck: "How happy it must make you to be loved by her so much," he marveled. In editing her posthumously published journals, he would later write: "Her friendships, as a girl with girls, as a woman with women, were not unmingled with passion, and had passages of romantic sacrifice and of ecstatic fusion, which I have heard with the ear, but could not trust my profane pen to report."

Margaret and Anna grew intensely close and sometimes shared a bed. What ecstatic fusion happened in that bed, between those bodies and the minds that commanded them into action or abstinence? Again we collide with the impulse to classify and label, with the tempting anachronism of containing in present labels things of a past in which such labels would be entirely foreign, things which are uncontainable in any label at all. "It is so true that a woman may be in love with a woman, and a man with a man," Margaret would later write, "for it is the same love which angels feel [and] is regulated by the same law as that of love between persons of different sexes."

Turning to poetry—that most spacious and porous container of the uncontainable—Margaret channeled her love for Anna into a series of six sonnets. In one, she imagines whisking Anna away to "some isle far apart from the haunts of men"—most likely, given her voracious appetite for Greek mythology, an allusion to the isle of Lesbos. In another, she writes:

When with soft eyes, beaming the tenderest love,
I see thy dear face, Anna! Far above,—
By magnet drawn up to thee I seem.

There it is again, the divine magnet that charged Melville's impassioned letters to Hawthorne. It is neither coincidence nor imitation, but a function of how poetry and science have long fomented one another's imagination: Magnetism was one of the era's most thrilling scientific subjects. Fuller's beloved Goethe, in fact, was the supreme cross-pollinator of nineteenth-century science and poetry.

Although he had grown to be Europe's most revered poet, Goethe saw himself equally as a scientist. He is responsible for the cloud names we use today—the invention of a young amateur astronomer by the name of Luke Howard, whose self-published cloud classification system was met with severe criticism by the scientific establishment for using Latin names instead of common English words. Goethe, who followed science closely through the era's major journals and his extensive correspondence with Europe's leading scientists, rose in solidarity with Howard—the clouds, he argued, were common to humanity and deserved to have names "accepted in all languages" rather than local translations. Goethe sent Howard—the only Englishman he would ever address as "Master"—an effusive fan letter, then enlisted his mightiest instrument in the classification's public defense. He adapted Howard's original essay into a suite of short musical poems for the different cloud types, titled with Howard's Latin names. He even celebrated the young scientist himself:

> To find yourself in the infinite,
> You must distinguish and then combine;
> Therefore my winged song thanks
> The man who distinguished cloud from cloud.

A decade earlier, Goethe had invented morphology—the study of organic forms and structures—and now his poems sealed the morphological fate of the skies.

But Goethe was the kind of scientist that Einstein was a violinist—passionate and mediocre. His greatest contribution lies not in original scientific discoveries but in synthesizing and popularizing science, in wresting from it powerful metaphors that would lodge themselves in the popular imagination for centuries. His widely circulated theory of color and emotion, written as a refutation of Newton, turned out to have no scientific validity. But it brimmed with prescient insight into aspects of perception that wouldn't be studied until long after his death: synesthesia, optical illusions, and the psychological effects of color. It was his literary work that had the greatest impact on science as a catalytic force on generations of imaginations—nowhere more famously than in the fabled case of Nikola Tesla's invention of the self-starting alternating current motor, the vision for which arrived to him almost as a hallucination. An enchanting sunset in Budapest Park inspired Tesla to recite a Goethe stanza, which suddenly gave him the vision of a rotating magnetic field:

> The glow retreats, done is our day of toil;
> It yonder hastes, new fields of life exploring;
> Ah, that no wing can lift me from this soil,
> Upon its track to follow, follow soaring . . .

The relationship was symbiotic—poets intentionally mined the golden age of nineteenth-century science for material. Coleridge famously attended Humphry Davy's chemistry lectures in search of new metaphors. Goethe himself, in his pioneering 1817 treatise on morphology, fulminated against the artificial divide between poetry and science:

> Nowhere would anyone grant that science and poetry can be united. They forgot that science arose from poetry, and did not see that when times change the two can meet again on a higher level as friends.

One of Goethe's most imaginative cross-pollinations of art and science captivated Margaret Fuller and shaped her understanding of love.

In science as in romance, the unknown is disrobed sheath by sheath as fervid fantasies imagine the possibilities conquerable by knowledge—fantasies that far outstrip the reality eventually revealed as knowledge progresses. Where are our jet packs, our time travel, our teleportation? In the early nineteenth century, the new chemistry provided some of the most exhilarating frontiers of possibility, and it was on chemistry that Goethe drew in his novel *Elective Affinities*, which pioneered the notion of erotic chemistry by proposing that indomitable chemical "affinities" charge romantic attractions. Goethe painted these charges as so powerful that no artificial constraints imposed on them—not even marital ties—could keep apart lovers they alloyed. To Fuller, who was already coming to mistrust the traditional institution of marriage as a source of fulfillment and to mistrust even more her own capacity to tolerate it, this was a liberating notion that made her serial infatuations bearable by making them natural.

Goethe's scandalous notion must have resonated as deeply with the joylessly married Emerson, who would soon become Fuller's most complex, category-defying, and enduring "elective affinity." He would write in his journal:

Marriage should be a temporary relation, it should have its natural birth, climax, & decay, without violence of any kind—violence to bind, or violence to rend. When each of two souls had exhausted the other of that good which each held for the other, they should part in the same peace in which they met, not parting from each other, but drawn to new society. The new love is the balm to prevent a wound from forming where the old love was detached.

Margaret Fuller was twenty-five and bereaved after her father's sudden death when she met the thirty-two-year-old Emerson, whom Walt Whitman would later remember as "physically and morally magnetic, arm'd at every point, and when he chose, wielding the emotional just as well as the intellectual," and as "a just man, poised on himself, all-loving, all-inclosing, and sane and clear as the sun." Newly remarried, Emerson was still grieving for the young first wife—a poet—whom he had lost to tuberculosis six years earlier, shortly after their marriage.

After his dramatic exit from the clergy, Emerson had launched a wildly popular lecture series in Boston, offering not a sectarian but a humanist view of life's most vital aspects. Fuller longed to know personally the sage whom all of New England worshipped. But it was Emerson that made the first overture to the young woman whose reputation had rippled to Concord. The ensuing relationship would be in many ways the most influential in both of their lives, and the most conflicted.

The revolutionary education reformer and editorial entrepreneur Elizabeth Peabody made the formal introduction. Eight years earlier, Peabody had met the teenage Margaret and come away enchanted by her elevated clarity of mind. "I had seen the Universe," she would later recount of that first encounter. Well before Peabody founded America's first formal kindergarten, composed the first English translation of Buddhist scripture, launched the country's first foreign-language bookstore, and published the first American edition of Saint Augustine's *Confessions*, she coined the term "Transcendentalism." A generation earlier, the German philosopher Immanuel Kant had puzzled over his theory of mind and proposed a doctrine of "transcendental idealism," which holds that concepts like space and time are transcendental—we experience them subjectively and intuitively, as they appear to us, rather than as they are in objective physical reality. But it was Peabody who, inspired by Coleridge's use of the word "transcendental" more than by Kant's philosophy, devised "Transcendentalism" to define the philosophical current sweeping New England. "Everything in the forms of society & almost in the forms of thought is in a state of flux," she wrote of the movement. Coleridge had written of consciousness in terms similar to Kant's, but he had located the moral conscience within the individual rather than in the hands of an external divinity dispensing and dictating it. In this transcendental conscience, Peabody saw an analog of the emerging ethos of self-reliance that was riveting New England, with its core belief that personal reform is the driving force of all social reform. She would later laud Emerson as the epicenter of the age's spirit, but it was she who first gave form to that spirit in an ideological container.

In early 1835, just after Caroline Herschel and Mary Somerville received their landmark Royal Astronomical Society admission across the Atlantic, twenty-five-year-old Margaret Fuller was at last admitted into the society of New England's intellectual royalty: Peabody procured an invitation for her young friend to visit Emerson in Concord.

At first jarred by Fuller's freely expressed strong opinions and lack of deference, Emerson was eventually won over—quite possibly by a poem she had recently written and published in a Boston newspaper, under the near-anonymous byline "F," elegizing the death of Emerson's beloved younger brother; or possibly by her countercultural proclamation that "all the marriages she knew were a mutual degradation," which Waldo—as the Sage of Concord was known to his intimates—later reported to Elizabeth Peabody. He affirmed Peabody's admiration for Fuller's intellect, writing that "she has the quickest apprehension." Within two years, Fuller would become the first woman to attend Emerson's all-male Transcendental Club—an occasional gathering of like-minded liberals—in a meeting from which Peabody herself would be excluded.

But Margaret and Waldo's initial meeting of minds soon became a contact point magnetized by something beyond the intellect—something she hoped, at least for a while, would propel each toward the "fulness of being" she held up as the ultimate aim of existence, something that would prompt him to shudder in the pages of his journal: "There is no terror like that of being known."

7

TO BRAVE THE LIGHT OF THE WORLD

Several months before Fuller met Emerson, she had made her literary debut when James Freeman Clarke published some of her writing—anonymously—in his magazine, *The Western Messenger*. She was the only woman in the volume. In one piece, penned five years before Frederick Douglass's "Pictures and Progress," she contemplated beauty as a mode of exploring the unknown and a means of reaching higher meaning:

> The abandon of genius has its beauty—far more beautiful its voluntary submission to wise law.—A picture, a description has beauty, the beauty of life; these pictures, these descriptions arranged upon a plan, made subservient to a purpose, have a higher beauty, that of the mind of man acting upon life. Art is Nature, but nature, new modelled, condensed, and harmonized. We are not merely mirrors to reflect our own times to those more distant. The mind has a mind of its own, and by it illuminates what it recreates.

This notion of critical reflection as a creative act of singular radiance would become the animating ethos of Fuller's journalistic work. After her death, the prominent Unitarian minister, women's rights advocate, and abolitionist Thomas Wentworth Higginson—the first to bring Emily Dickinson's genius to light, and Fuller's eventual biographer—would write that "there is probably no American author, save Emerson, who has planted so many germs of high thought in other minds."

An early feminist and devout champion of equality, Higginson was a man who lived his convictions. At thirty, he broke down a courthouse door in an effort to free a fugitive slave. At forty, he served in the Civil War as colonel in the first federally authorized black battalion, after turning his home into a well-trodden stop on the Underground Railroad. At fifty, he was editor of the official journal of the American Woman Suffrage Association, which he had cofounded—a position he would hold for fourteen years. In his sixties, he became Margaret Fuller's biographer, after having raised her sister's maternally orphaned and paternally abandoned daughter, Margaret Fuller Channing.

Early in his career as a Unitarian minister, Higginson had scribbled into his notebook the plan for a sermon entitled "The Dreamer & worker—the day & night of the soul"—a meditation on the relationship between profit and poetry in a materialistic society where the work of artists was in danger of being discarded as devoid of utility. He insisted that the dreamer and the worker are naturally symbiotic in each of us and that it would be a mistake for society to sacrifice the poetic at the altar of the practicable and the profitable. "Do not throw up yr ideas, but realize them," he wrote in his sermon notes. "The boy who never built a castle in the air will never build one on earth." Perhaps he was drawn to Margaret Fuller's example because she had refused either side of the sacrifice and had instead twined her "fulness of being" by the equal strands of dreamer and doer. Another interplay she refused to sever was that of truth and beauty in the cocreation of meaning, which Emily Dickinson—who read and admired Fuller—would later articulate in her exquisite poem "I died for beauty," built around an allusion to Elizabeth Barrett Browning's vision of true poets as those "who died for Beauty as martyrs do / For Truth—the ends being scarcely two."

I died for beauty, but was scarce
Adjusted in the tomb,

When one who died for truth was lain
In an adjoining room.

He questioned softly why I failed?
"For beauty," I replied.
"And I for truth,—the two are one;
We brethren are," he said.

And so, as kinsmen met a night,
We talked between the rooms,
Until the moss had reached our lips,
And covered up our names.

But while Fuller enlisted beauty in the pursuit of meaning in her public work, she regarded it with an embittered disinterest in her own private person. In childhood, her father had tried to straighten Margaret's figure by marching her through the house while banging a drum strapped to her shoulders. With her slouching spine and nearsighted squint—the price she paid for her heavy childhood reading—she had grown up experiencing herself as unbeautiful. "I hate not to be beautiful when all around is so," she lamented. Higginson, a childhood friend of her brother's, remembered her as a woman "with no personal attractions, with a habit of saying things very explicitly and of using the first person singular a good deal too much"—in other words, a woman who, despite her crescent spine, stood tall in her personal conviction at a time when she was expected to be a subservient and agreeable listener.

As Fuller filled every room she walked into with a vibrancy of mind and spirit that hollowed her society of expectation and stunned all present, her image was transfigured in the eyes of her beholders, and beauty of a different order came to halo her being. Sophia Peabody saw Fuller in her element as "a Sybil on her tripod," invoking the mythic oracles of ancient Greece who channeled divine inspiration. Reverend Channing, the influential founding father of Unitarianism, extolled her "commanding charm." He found an enchantment in her squint and her peculiar posture bordering on the supernatural as he described her two most distinctive physical traits:

The first was a contraction of the eyelids almost to a point . . . and then a sudden dilation, till the iris seemed to emit flashes,—an effect, no doubt, dependent on her highly-magnetized condition. The second was a singular pliancy of the vertebrae and muscles of the neck, enabling her by a mere movement to denote each varying emotion; in moments of tenderness, or pensive feeling, its curves were swan-like in grace, but when she was scornful or indignant it contracted, and made swift turns like that of a bird of prey.

But as much as Fuller may have wished to be a disembodied intellect, her mind was housed in a body she had to sustain. The notion of earning a living by her thought and her pen was still an improbable dream, so she reached for a career as a schoolteacher—the sole profession open to both sexes, and the only remunerable path available to intellectually driven women. Although it was commonly seen as a temporary endeavor until marriage furnished a woman with the financial support of a husband, a generation earlier Elizabeth Peabody had upended convention by making education not a way station on the path to marriage but a destination in its own right.

Peabody's career as a rebel had begun at the age of twelve, when she taught herself Hebrew in order to read the original Old Testament and "find out the *truth*" after her parents discovered her "heretical tendencies" and tried to force on her a moralistic religiosity with which she did not agree. At seventeen, she spearheaded a school devoted to "educating children morally and spiritually as well as intellectually" from the youngest age. She developed innovative hands-on methods of teaching mathematics with dried beans and helped her students master grammar by seeding in them a spirited love of words, "the signs of our thoughts and feelings in all their minutest shades and variations." At eighteen, she set out to perfect her Greek, which she had begun learning as a child, by hiring a tutor—the nineteen-year-old Emerson, newly graduated from Harvard and introduced to Elizabeth by her dancing partner, his cousin. "If it is best for the minds of boys—it is best also for the minds of *girls*," she wrote to her sister Sophia at home, encouraging her to also immerse herself in the classics. When she asked for Emerson's invoice at the end of their study sessions, he told her that he had "no bill to render," for he had found that he could teach her nothing. By her early twenties, Elizabeth had given herself the equivalent of a graduate school education, then devoted her energies to revolution- izing the teaching profession. Most radical of all was her choice to teach not by lecture but by conversation. Her experimental school made Peabody a central figure in Boston's cultural landscape.

A decade after Peabody's example, twenty-four-year-old Marga- ret Fuller took her first teaching job as an assistant at the Temple School, founded by the progressive-minded philosopher and ideal- istic education reformer Bronson Alcott, father of the future author of *Little Women*. Fuller had no idea that all three Peabody sisters, who had rendered the school a popular success with their rigor- ous lessons in Latin, math, and geography, had recently quit after Alcott failed to pay them for two years of work. After four months of unpaid work, she, too, resigned—but not before thoroughly impressing Alcott, who would remain one of her greatest support- ers and admirers for the remainder of her life.

When another ambitious education reformer heard that Fuller was free, he offered her a job at his posh new Greene Street School in Providence, Rhode Island, housed in a spacious new building modeled after a Greek temple. Having learned her lesson at Alcott's school, Fuller demanded that two conditions be met if she were to take the offer: complete creative freedom in what she taught and how she taught it, and an annual salary of $1,000, equivalent to that of a Harvard professor—an impressive feat given the non- negligible grain of truth in the standard twenty-first century expla- nation that the gender wage gap is due in large part due to women's unwillingness to negotiate about salaries. Fuller's was an act of tre- mendous confidence and courage—nearly thirty years later, when Vassar begins courting Maria Mitchell for a faculty position, she would be so uncomfortable with aligning the value of her intellect with the price of her employment that she would negotiate her sal- ary down by nearly half. "I do not believe I am worth it!" she would write of the $1,500 Vassar originally offered, instead taking $800 per year, along with free room and board for herself and her father, while male Vassar professors were salaried at a fixed $2,000.

With her conditions met, Fuller took the job in Providence, seeing it as a means of putting her younger brothers—whom she had educated since childhood—through Harvard, an institution closed to her. The Panic of 1837—America's first major financial crisis—had just swept the nation and left it so dumbfounded that Emerson, mining science for his metaphor, likened all attempts to make sense of it to "learning geology the morning after an earthquake." It was Emerson who took the podium at the opening of the Greene Street School and exhorted the educators gathered there, Margaret among them, to teach the boys and girls in their charge "to aspire to be all they can," to "believe in their noble nature," not to let their existential aspirations "degenerate into the mere love of money," and never to forget "the capital secret of [the teaching] profession, namely, to convert life into truth."

Fuller chose beauty as her transmutation agent, immersing the sixty girls in her class—ages ten to eighteen—in ethics explored through poetry and science humanized by the classics, taught next to a grand piano adorned with vases of fresh-cut flowers. In world history, she highlighted the lives of powerful women. In literature, she required reading by women authors. In natural history, she drew on Greek mythology, leading the girls to overcome their terror of spiders, now clinically known as arachnophobia, by telling them the myth of Arachne—the talented and ambitious mortal woman who challenges Athena, the goddess of wisdom and the crafts, to a weaving contest, and wins with a work so superior that the furious Athena turns her into a spider.

But Fuller's greatest gift to the girls lay in drawing out their minds through the art of conversation, a faculty she lamented as atrophied in women amid a culture that required them to be receptacles of male wisdom, perennially on the receiving end of what we now call "mansplaining"—a term inspired by Rebecca Solnit, who is in many ways Fuller's twenty-first-century counterpart. Fuller recon-

figured the schoolrooms designed for lectures into spaces for conversation, participation in which had only one rule: the girls must
be willing to speak their minds freely.

To her frustration, this proved far more challenging than she
had anticipated—a challenge that distracted her from the demanding project she had undertaken alongside her teaching schedule: to
translate Johann Peter Eckermann's *Conversations with Goethe* as
part of her even more ambitious endeavor of composing the first
English biography of her German hero. Despite sleeping no more
than six hours a night, her progress was slow and painful. "I have,
maugre my best efforts, been able to do very little," she lamented to
Emerson in mid-August.

Two weeks later, Emerson charged Harvard with an ideological lightning bolt—a speech so incendiary in its call for self-culture
and independence from the establishment that it riled the Harvard
authorities, and so empowering in its appeal to self-reliance that all
five hundred copies of its print adaptation, published under the title
The American Scholar, sold out in a flash. The Boston polymath
Oliver Wendell Holmes termed it America's "intellectual Declaration of Independence." Emerson urged the young to use this time
of uncertainty as a springboard toward transformation and to leap
courageously into the intellectual future. "Whilst the world hangs
before the eye as a cloud of beauty," he exhorted, "we cannot even
see its beauty. Inaction is cowardice, but there can be no scholar
without the heroic mind." Life, he argued—and not the ivory tower
of the academy—was the best teacher:

> Character is higher than intellect. Thinking is the function. Living is
> the functionary. The stream retreats to its source. A great soul will
> be strong to live, as well as strong to think. Does he lack organ or
> medium to impart his truths? He can still fall back on this elemental
> force of living them. This is a total act. Thinking is a partial act. . . .
> The scholar loses no hour which the man lives.

The following year, Emerson returned to address the graduating
class at the Harvard Divinity School and delivered a speech even

more inflammatory—one that would cause him to be banned from Harvard's campus for thirty years. In it, Emerson argued that only by speaking the truth—even at the cost of defying convention—"is the universe made safe and habitable." This was his way of urging the nation's most promising young theologians to do away with church dogma and instead "dare to love God without mediator or veil," locating divinity in every human being. "The doors of the temple stand open, night and day, before every man," he proclaimed.

But as much as Fuller admired Emerson's ideas, she was not "every man," and she wanted entry into the temple, which was only part metaphor. Boston's Athenaeum—America's premier bastion of erudition, modeled after a Greek temple—was formally closed to women. When Elizabeth Peabody was allowed to enter it, after a special vote by the board of trustees, she took out twenty-three books in a single month. Surely, Fuller wondered what would become of women—and of society at large—if such voracious appetite for learning was given free rein. It did not escape her attention that in his visionary speeches, Emerson cast the ideal of personhood and citizenship as "Man Thinking." What would the temple—the nation, the world—look like if humanity doubled its cultivation of thought and opened the doors to "every woman," inviting "Woman Thinking" into the conversation?

Despite her disappointing experience with the girls in her class, Fuller was not ready to relinquish her conviction that conversation was indeed what best loosened the ligaments of thought and trained the mind to leap. "Words are events," Ursula K. Le Guin would write a century and a half later, "they do things, change things. They transform both speaker and hearer; they feed energy back and forth and amplify it. They feed understanding or emotion back and forth and amplify it." It was Fuller who formalized conversation as the supreme intellectual instrument of Transcendentalism and made the free-flowing exchange of words the electric current that charged the women's emancipation movement.

In the summer of 1839, Fuller conceived of a series of conversations for women, designed "to systematize thought and give a precision and clearness in which our sex is so deficient"—a deficiency she attributed to a chronic withholding of opportunity on society's behalf. She reasoned that because women's opinions were dismissed by default, they never properly learned the tools of critical thinking that would allow them to transfigure "impressions into thoughts." Instead, she believed the mind could be trained to "need no aid from rouge or candlelight to brave the light of the world." She resolved to eradicate the small talk and gossip to which society had conditioned women's conversation, instead leading the group to "review the departments of thought and knowledge, and to endeavor to place them in due relation to one another"—that is, to cultivate the capacity for relational insight and dot-connecting that transmutes mere information into illumination. The chief object would be to figure out "how we may make best use of our means for building up the life of thought upon the life of action."

When Fuller shared the idea with Bronson Alcott, he thought it to be "a hopeful fact" and enthused in his journal:

> She is the most commanding talker of the day, of her sex, and must sway society: such a position is worthy of her gifts. I trust those who shall hear her will reap a rich harvest of thought and become powers of like seed in the bosom of the Age.

But like most forces of cultural transformation, the series with which Fuller was about to revolutionize culture had deeply personal roots.

That summer, as she was preparing to launch the conversation salons that would seal her public image, her private world was in tumult. Several months earlier, Margaret had found herself in another romantic intoxication with one of her former students: Caroline Sturgis—the vivacious nineteen-year-old daughter of a China trade mogul. Their relationship had been "intensating," as Margaret wrote, in the time since they ceased to be teacher and pupil—so much so that they made a plan to live together for a few months and were crushed when Caroline's father forbade it. "Cary," like Anna, adored and admired Margaret—but her feelings would soon prove too unmuscular to withstand the force of Margaret's ardor, which demanded more than admiration, more than adoration, more than even love.

Margaret Fuller experienced friendship and romance much as she did male and female—in a nonbinary way. A century before Virginia Woolf subverted the millennia-old cultural rhetoric of gender with her assertion that "in each of us two powers preside, one male, one female," making her case for the androgynous mind as the best possible mind, "resonant and porous . . . naturally creative, incandescent and undivided," Fuller denounced the dualism of gender and insisted that "there is no wholly masculine man, no purely feminine woman." The boundary, she argued far ahead of Woolf and Simone de Beauvoir in her groundbreaking *Woman in the Nineteenth Century*, is indeed porous, so that a kind of ongoing transmutation takes place: "Fluid hardens to solid, solid rushes to fluid" as male and female "are perpetually passing into one another."

Fuller was highly discriminating about her intimate relationships, but once she admitted another into the innermost chambers of her being, she demanded of them nothing less than everything—having tasted Goethe's notion of "the All," why salivate over mere fragments of feeling? But this boundless and all-consuming emotional intensity eventually repelled its objects—a parade of brilliant and beautiful men and women, none of whom could fully understand it, much less reciprocate it. Hers was a diamagnetic being, endowed with nonbinary magnetism yet repelling by both poles.

In the spring of 1839, Margaret and Cary took a trip together to a seaside resort. Some demand for "the All" was made, some significant portion of it withheld. Caroline would later recall: "Margaret asked me if I loved her, but I could not at once say yes." Margaret, who loved wholly and unhesitatingly once she did love, was irreparably wounded by the reservation. Caroline wrote to her after the trip, trying to restore their intimacy, but Margaret replied coolly— addressing her not as "Cary" but as "Caroline"—that while she didn't doubt they could remain friends, she didn't feel they could continue to be intimate.

Instead, she swiftly transferred her longing for mutuality to another candidate: Samuel Ward, Julia Ward Howe's brilliant and charismatic older brother, seven years younger than Margaret. The two had met four years earlier, in the summer of 1835—shortly after Margaret had fallen in love with Anna Barker—on a voyage up the Hudson River to see the natural wonders of upstate New York. Both had been invited on the journey by Anna's older cousin, Eliza Farrar—another striking woman with whom the eighteen-year-old Margaret had been briefly infatuated a decade earlier, now wedded to a Harvard mathematics professor in a marriage of intellectual equals. The eighteen-year-old Sam was boarding at the Farrars' house, having just returned from Europe, where he had studied as Longfellow's classmate at Tübingen University—Kepler's alma mater—and had grown fluent in German and French. He had declined the standard commercial careers laid out before him and become an artist instead—bold idealism that moved Margaret. She had just published her first poetry and was working feverishly on her translations of Goethe. The two were so taken with each other's company that Sam offered to be her escort back to Boston, where she was eager to introduce him to Anna. She was too preoccupied with Anna then, and Sam was too young, for a romantic spark to ignite. But the trip impressed upon Margaret the strong sense that her soul and Sam's spoke a common language.

The two resumed contact three years later, after Sam returned from a trip to Europe with the Farrars—a trip on which Margaret, too, had been invited, but the shock of her father's death that year had petrified her into staying home. Sam was now twenty-one and Margaret twenty-eight. She had just published, under the unsexed byline S. M. Fuller, her translations of Goethe in a collection of his poetry, to which she was once again the only female contributor and which became the subject of one of teenage Julia Ward Howe's first literary reviews.

Perhaps Margaret saw in Sam part male alter ego of who she was, part projection of who she wanted to be but constitutionally could not. Like her, he translated Goethe; like her, he was in correspondence with Emerson. But unlike her, he had the doors to the temple swung open to him with the highest educational opportunity and cultural privilege; unlike her, he was notoriously handsome.

By 1839, a fervent correspondence had ensued between them—so much so that Margaret asked Caroline, who had given her a beautiful box to hold all of Margaret's letters, to send her another box solely for her letters from Sam. "I will keep it devoted to him while I live," she vowed. That spring, just as the drama with Caroline was unfolding, Sam and Margaret began spending more and more time together, savoring nature and Boston's art galleries. She came to call him her "Raffaello." Sweet confidences were exchanged, but once again Margaret found herself on the indigent end of an asymmetrical affinity.

Without explanation, Sam began to retreat. His letters informed her of art exhibitions but didn't invite her to see them with him. He mailed her books, but only asked her critical opinion of them. Margaret was first baffled, then hurt, and finally angry. In mid-July, with a self-assured fury, she confronted him about his pivot from romance to reserve:

> You would not be so irreverent as to dare tamper with a nature like mine, you could not treat so generous a person with levity.
>
> The kernel of affection is the same, no doubt, but it lies dormant in the husk. . . . The bitterness of checked affections, the sickness of hope deferred, the dreariness of aspirations broken from the anchorage. I know them all, and I have borne at the same time domestic unhappiness and ruined health.

Lucid about Sam's prospects, she acknowledges that he—handsome, brilliant, erudite—must be on the receiving end of ample attentions, but then she drives the spear of her singular demand, suggesting that choosing her over superficial suitors would be an act of moral superiority:

> If you are like me, you can trample upon such petty impossibilities; if you love me as I deserve to be loved, you cannot dispense with seeing me.

In French, she tells him that she will wait for him and in the meantime will bury herself in work to give him space and time to make up his mind. But then she poses the all-or-nothing ultimatum of one whose much always calls for more:

If we ceased to be intimate, we must become nothing to one another. . . . It must not be my love alone that binds us.

She doesn't sign the letter but ends it with a line from the fourth stanza of Lord Byron's piercing "Stanzas to Augusta"—a love poem to the half sister who had caused the collapse of his marriage to Ada Lovelace's mother, composed just before Byron left England for good: "Though loved, thou forborest to grieve me." Margaret assumes that Sam knows the poem—as any intellect of his caliber would—which begins with these lines:

Though the day of my destiny's over,
And the star of my fate hath declined,
Thy soft heart refused to discover
The faults which so many could find.

But her ultimatum backfires—Sam withdraws even further. By September, torn between proud resignation and disbelief at his inexplicable change of heart, she writes:

You love me no more—How did you pray me to draw near to you! What words were spoken in impatience of separation! How did you promise to me, aye, and doubtless to yourself, too, of all we might be to one another.

In a bitter lament, she tells him that before she met him, she considered herself "incapable of feeling or being content to inspire an ordinary attachment" and would break off relationships as soon as she saw a flaw. But he, she reminds him, would have none of that— "Thy soft heart refused to discover / The faults which so many could find." He had been unafraid to promise her "forever, ever."

Her letter bellows with the cry of every abandoned lover: How, how could such vows simply vanish, where have the feelings gone?

> You call me your best of friends, your dearest friend, you say that you always find yourself with me. I doubt not the depth of your attachment, doubt not that you feel my worth. But the confiding sweetness, the natural and prompt expression of attachment are gone—are they gone forever?

She impels him to honesty: "You do not wish to be with me: why try to hide it from me, from yourself?"

Adding to the pain of this confounding withdrawal of affections was Sam's sudden and equally inexplicable decision to relinquish his aspirations of being an artist and to become a banker instead. In the heat of her spurned longing, she is willing to overlook even this, willing to sublimate longing itself if that would rewind his heart. In the most unguarded letter Margaret Fuller would ever pen— unguarded to the point of self-immolation—she beseeches Sam:

> I will wait—I will not complain—I will exact nothing—I will make every allowance for the restlessness of a heart checked in its love, a mind dissatisfied with its pursuits. . . . I will wait, to me the hardest of all tasks, will wait for thee whom I have loved so well. I will never wound thy faith, nor repel thy heart, never, never! Only thyself shall have power to divorce my love from its office of ministry,—not even mine own pride shall do it. So help me God, as I keep this vow, prays.

This is the common tragedy: All attempts at coercing love— whether by the aggressive demands of jealousy or by the tearful pleadings of self-martyrdom—are as effective as coaxing a tortoise out of its shell with a stick: the more you poke, the more she retreats.

It was all over.

The following month, as the successive burns of Caroline and Sam begin to scab into a single scar, a mighty old fire is rekindled by an unexpected visit from Anna Barker—Margaret's "eldest and divinest love." During this visit, Margaret finally replies to Caroline's unanswered letters, trying to make sense of the painful asymmetry of affections. In October 1839, less than a month before the launch of her conversation salons, she writes:

> I loved you, Caroline, with truth and nobleness. I counted to love you much more. I thought there was a firm foundation for future years. In this hour when my being is more filled and answered than ever before, when my beloved has returned to transcend in every way not only my hope, but my imagination, I will tell you that I once looked forward to the time when you might hold as high a place in my life as she. I thought of all women but you two as my children, my pupils, my play things or my acquaintance. You two alone I would have held by the hand.

Margaret had been wounded, she writes, in a way Caroline could never fully comprehend—a wound unhealable by any "sacred solitary wood walk, in no hour of moonlight love." Undoubtedly it was the elation of Anna's visit and the rekindling of old hopes that had given Margaret the courage for candor. But there was one immense, devastating fact Margaret didn't know, which would soon blacken her fantasy and swallow the sincerest of her hopes: Anna was in town because she was secretly engaged to Sam.

The two young people, whom Margaret herself had wished to introduce four years earlier, had met during the European trip with the Farrars. As Margaret was mourning her father at home, Sam and Anna were falling in love in Switzerland. It was because he worried that Anna's wealthy family would not approve of the match that Sam had abandoned his artistic aspirations and surrendered to banking.

In October 1839, days after Anna's elating visit, Margaret read the engagement announcement in a Boston newspaper in sundering disbelief. Sam had betrayed her by failing to reciprocate the magnitude of her feelings. He had betrayed their shared ideals by relinquishing art in favor of commerce. But this third treason, this dual betrayal by two people Margaret had loved passionately, was a blow of a different order. (Sam would betray her one final time, even beyond life, when after her sudden death he would drop out of the shared editorship of a memorial volume of her writings.)

Emerson, who had himself developed discomfiting feelings for both Caroline and Anna, took the news of the engagement "with a certain terror." Caught in a confused fantasy, he had envisioned a pentagon as the ideal Platonic form of intimacy—he, Margaret, Caroline, Anna, and Sam, "the holy society of the best the wisest & the most beautiful"—all of whom he had tried persuading to come live near him in Concord. Lydian, his wife, didn't factor into this geometry, which was further reinforced by a visit Margaret, Caroline, and Anna paid him in Concord for three hot August days—an event the inarticulable electricity of which Emerson was only able to limn in a poem, eulogizing the near-mystical way "hearts to hearts their meaning show." But he wanted more than the flitting lambency of occasional visits. "If these all had their hearth & home here," he wrote in his diary, "we might have a solid social satisfaction, instead of the disgust & depression of visitation."

After hearing of Anna's engagement, Waldo reasoned through the dashing of his hopes in a letter to Caroline with overtones of tragicomical self-delusion:

> I thought [Anna] had looked the world through for a man as universal as herself & finding none, had said, "I will compensate myself for my great renunciation as a woman by establishing ideal relations: Not only Raphael [Sam] shall be my brother, but the Puritan at Concord [Waldo] who is reputed at some time to have seen the mighty Gods, I will elect him also."

Lamenting that Anna had relinquished "ideal relations" in favor of earthly happiness, the unelected Waldo is further dumbfounded that "there is no compunction on either of their brows"—Sam and Anna seem perfectly content with their choice, unwilling to see it as the fall from grace he deems it to be. In resignation, he concludes his letter to Cary: "I cannot mistrust them. And yet, dear sister, happiness is so vulgar."

Against the backdrop of Waldo's grudging blessing, Margaret rose above her pain to perform an act of superhuman emotional strength and magnanimity—she wrote to Sam to absolve him of all guilt for his sudden abandonment, acknowledging the impermanence of even the sincerest and most splendid of feelings:

> I never should make any claim upon the heart of any person on the score of past intercourse and those expressions of affection which were the flower and fruitage of its summer day. If autumn has come, let come also chill wind and rain like those of today.

It takes a rare courage to recognize that feelings are the most perishable of our possessions, even more so than opinions, for an opinion—that is, a real opinion, which is qualitatively different from a fleeting impression or a borrowed stance—is arrived at via a well-reasoned argument with oneself. Not so a feeling—feelings coalesce out of the vapors that escape from the deepest groundwaters of our unreasoned and unreasonable being, and whatever rainbows they may scatter for a moment when touched with the light of another, they diffuse and evaporate just as readily, just as mysteriously.

Love, Margaret implies in her letter to Sam, is never to be taken for granted—it is to be met moment by moment, on its ever-changing terms. But she would spend the remaining years of her life struggling to come to stable terms with the sentiment she is now producing for his benefit: "Truth and honor noble natures owe to one another, but love and confidence are free gifts or they are nothing."

She then climbs to the pinnacle of beneficence a wounded heart can grant its wounder and gives Sam her blessing for happiness with Anna:

> The knowledge I have of your nature has become part of mine, the love it has excited will accompany me to eternity. . . . Time, distance, different pursuits may hide you from me, yet will I never forget to be your friend or to visit your life with a daily benediction. . . . Give yourself up to the holy hour and live in the celestial ray which shines on you at present. O I could weep with joy that real life is lived.

Sam and Anna were married that month. It would take Margaret two years to make sense of this maelstrom of heartache. In a journal entry marking the second anniversary of the wedding, she would acknowledge that her feelings for Anna were indeed stronger than those for Sam, and would write of her love:

> I know not yet what to think of this event which dawned so poetically on me. From it the music has not flowed that I expected, nor is my own mind now in harmony with those that seemed so fatally bound to it, yet that heart of love which beat then could not err, only we must grow wiser every day, else the true will become false.

Perhaps the loss of Sam was so painful because it both contained and caused the loss of Anna.

Three weeks after her parting letter to Sam, on November 6, 1839, Margaret Fuller convened the first of what would become known as her "Conversations," which would seed the ideas harvested by the feminist movement of the twentieth century. Fuller was twenty-nine—the age at which Maria Mitchell discovered her comet. She held the "Conversations" at Elizabeth Peabody's house, on the mornings of Emerson's successful Wednesday night lectures, so that the women who commuted to Boston to hear the sage of self-reliance could attend both in a single trip. But her format of exploration was by design the antipode of Emerson's—not a top-down, one-to-many oration of wisdom plumbed from a single lofty intellect, but a lateral, many-to-many yet intimate conversation between equal minds. Despite her own immensely superior erudition, Fuller was intent on making the women in the room feel that their minds mattered and their private thoughts were worthy of public expression.

Twenty-five women attended the first of the season's thirteen two-hour meetings, most of them Fuller's friends and former students, including the three Peabody sisters, Lydia Maria Child, and Sophia Ripley, who was about to cofound the Brook Farm utopia.

Fuller chose Greek mythology as the lens through which the group was to examine the deep questions of existence. She modeled what she sought to encourage by determinately voicing her own opinions with eloquence that bordered on enchantment. One participant in the first gathering rhapsodized in a letter to a friend:

> I know not where to look for so much character, culture, and so much love of truth and beauty in any other circle of women and girls. . . . Margaret, beautifully dressed (don't despise that, for it made a fine picture), presided with more dignity and grace than I had thought possible. . . . There was no pretension or pedantry in a word that was said . . . and I believe everyone was gratified.

After Fuller's death, Elizabeth Peabody—who at the age of thirteen had been shocked to see adult women shrivel into silence when asked to speak their minds at Reverend Channing's gospel discussion groups, and who had herself held a series of lectures for women several years before Fuller's "Conversations"—would recall with unsentimental conviction:

> I think no one attended that course . . . who did not pronounce [Margaret's] initial statements and occasional bursts of eloquence the most splendid exhibitions of conversational talent, not only that they ever heard, but that they ever heard of.

Margaret Fuller had found the singular light of her "own particular star" that blazed a new trail for her own life and for the future of her society. Her conversation circle traced a new locus of possibility for women, and for a world finally unwilling to squander half of its intellectual and creative potential. Over the next five years, the series would establish her reputation as the most erudite woman in America. The "Conversations" would explore subjects ranging from education to ethics, with session titles like "Influence," "Mistakes," "Creeds," "The Ideal," and "Persons Who Never Awake to Life in This World."

. . .

A week after her first session, when a small group of Transcendentalists set out to do in print what she was doing in conversation, Emerson proposed Fuller for the editorship of a new periodical, promising her a share of the proceeds large enough to alleviate her ongoing financial struggles. She accepted. They called this unexampled journal *The Dial*—the title that cofounder Bronson Alcott had given to his daily log of sayings by his two young daughters, Anna and Louisa May. Nothing like it had existed before—it was America's first truly independent magazine, unaffiliated with any university or church, devoted not to a religious ideology or a single genre of literature, but to a kaleidoscope of intellectual and creative curiosity: philosophy, poetry, art, science, law, criticism. Emerson envisioned it as a publication "so broad & great in its survey that it should lead the opinion of this generation on every great interest," a sort of manual on "the whole Art of Living."

Fuller aimed even higher. On the prospectus printed on the back of the inaugural issue, published on July 4, 1840—just after her thirtieth birthday—she vowed to aim "not at leading public opinion, but at stimulating each man to judge for himself, and to think more deeply and more nobly, by letting him see how some minds are kept alive by a peculiar self-trust." It was an echo of the wakeful aliveness by self-trust she had sought to inspire in the women taking part in her "Conversations."

A magazine then was nothing like what it is now—not a slim softcover galley consisting primarily of advertisements, but a hefty tome two inches thick, replete with poems and lengthy essays, devoid of a single ad. In renouncing all commercialism and dogma, *The Dial* was free to be driven solely by the idealism of its editors—an idealism they hoped would be contagious and elevate readers. More than a century before E. B. White laid down what should have become the media establishment's animating ethos and has instead become a caricature of its failings—White insisted that a writer "should tend to lift people up, not lower them down," that writers must "not merely reflect and interpret life [but] inform and shape life"— *The Dial* set out to do precisely that.

"We invite the attention of our countrymen to a new design,"

Emerson proclaimed in the editorial note to the reader opening the first issue, the 548 pages of which contained a miscellany of creative and critical works: poems about silence, sympathy, and the aurora borealis; reviews of Nathaniel Hawthorne's new children's novel (illustrated by his wife Sophia) and a Scottish book on the Solar System; essays on beauty, Dante, and the ideal; and a remarkable piece by Fuller—one of eight she contributed to the volume—titled "A Short Essay on Critics," in which she makes the case for the most undervalued yet vital stewardship of creative culture:

> Essays, entitled critical, are epistles addressed to the public, through which the mind of the recluse relieves itself of its impressions. . . . The critic . . . should be not merely a poet, not merely a philosopher, not merely an observer, but tempered of all three. . . . He must have as good an eye and as fine a sense [as the poet]; but if he had as fine an organ for expression also, he would make the poem instead of judging it. He must be inspired by the philosopher's spirit of inquiry and need of generalization, but he must not be constrained by the hard cemented masonry of method to which philosophers are prone. And he must have the organic acuteness of the observer, with a love of ideal perfection, which forbids him to be content with mere beauty of details in the work or the comment upon the work. . . . He will be free and make free from the mechanical and distorting influences we hear complained of on every side. He will teach us to love wisely what we before loved well, for he knows the difference between censoriousness and discernment, infatuation and reverence.

Like Elizabeth Peabody's bookstore, which eventually became the journal's headquarters, *The Dial* was a labor of love. The editors never aimed at commercial success—a century and a half before the TED conference "ideas worth spreading" motto, this was *The Dial*'s sole mission. The three hundred subscribers it had at its peak barely covered production costs and left nothing for editorial salaries. When the small Boston firm that served as the magazine's publisher went bankrupt in 1841, the operation was transferred to Elizabeth Peabody's nascent publishing venture, itself a passion project that turned no profit.

Fuller was never paid a penny for the two years she labored tirelessly at the editorship of *The Dial* while authoring multiple pieces for each volume herself before eventually turning the post over to Emerson, who was only half facetious in remarking: "Let there be rotation in martyrdom!" In his journal, he wrote:

> The Dial is to be sustained or ended & I must settle the question, it seems, of its life or death. I wish it to live but do not wish to be its life. Neither do I like to put it in the hands of the Humanity & Reform Men, because they trample on letters & poetry; nor in the hands of the Scholars, for they are dead & dry.

The Dial's pages catalyzed some of the most formative ideas in American democracy, modeled a new kind of cross-disciplinary thought, blurred the line between criticism and creation, and launched the careers of obscure writers, among them a young, unemployed, disenchanted schoolteacher by the name of Henry David Thoreau. In an act of tremendous ideological insurgency and moral courage, the magazine broadened the conversation on spirituality by introducing Eastern philosophy into a dogmatically Christian nation—including works by Confucius and Omar Khayyám and Buddhist sacred texts published in America for the first time thanks to Elizabeth Peabody's translations.

James Freeman Clarke's artist sister, Sarah, remarked of the new magazine that "the spirit of many of the pieces was lonely"— perhaps she sensed the loneliness of those pioneers who task themselves with cleaving into the public conscience a new sensibility, with elevating rather than catering to existing tastes, even at the price of virulent opprobrium from the bastions of the status quo. In another metaphor drawn from science, Fuller would soon write, "Those who seem overladen with electricity frighten those around them."

Even *The Dial*'s frightened detractors recognized that it was ushering in a new aesthetic of thought—one that engendered in some the grudging envy with which the small-spirited recognize the thoroughly original and seek to emulate them, always poorly. More than a decade later, the Unitarian minister and reformer Theodore Parker, onetime member of the Transcendental Club, would launch a quarterly journal of which Thomas Wentworth Higginson would wryly recall:

> [Parker] predicted that the new periodical would be The Dial, with a beard. But the result was disappointing. It was all beard, and no Dial.

8

THAT WHICH EXHAUSTS AND EXALTS

Despite *The Dial*'s financial struggles, the final blow was dealt not by the arithmetic of accounting but by the geometry of human relations.

In the course of their professional collaboration, Margaret and Waldo's relationship swelled with complexity that strained the boundaries of friendship, of soul kinship, even of intellectual infatuation. Their regular abscondings into the woods for intercourse about philosophy, poetry, life, and—inevitably—love had sparked in Lydian Emerson a jealousy Margaret could no longer deny. She chose to cloak in logic the emotional chaos of the heart, reasoning in her journal that she didn't keep Waldo away from his family duties "any more than a book would." On one of her visits to Concord, Lydian asked her on an afternoon walk, but Margaret declined, saying she had already committed to walk with Waldo. The ordinarily contained Lydian burst into tears as the rest of the family stared awkwardly at their dinner plates. Margaret reasoned in her journal once again:

> As to my being more his companion than cannot be helped, his life is in the intellect not the affections. He has affection for me, but it is because I quicken his intellect.—I dismissed it all as a mere sick moment of L's.

Waldo bonded with Margaret in a way that he would with no one else—not even his wife and children. "Most of the persons whom I see in my own house I see across a gulf," he anguished in his own journal. "I cannot go to them nor they come to me." He and Margaret found themselves on one side of an invisible wall, the rest of the world on the other. But neither knew what to make of this uncommon bond that didn't conform to any existing template. The richest relationships are often those that don't fit neatly into the preconceived slots we have made for the archetypes we imagine would populate our lives—the friend, the lover, the parent, the sibling, the mentor, the muse. We meet people who belong to no single slot, who figure into multiple categories at different times and in different magnitudes. We then must either stretch ourselves to create new slots shaped after these singular relationships, enduring the growing pains of self-expansion, or petrify.

Falling back on his trustiest faculty, Waldo tried to reason his way out of the emotional disorientation of his complex relationship with Margaret:

> I would that I could, I know afar off that I cannot, give the lights and shades, the hopes and outlooks that come to me in these strange, cold-warm, attractive-repelling conversations with Margaret, whom I always admire, most revere when I nearest see, and sometimes love,—yet whom I freeze, and who freezes me to silence, when we seem to promise to come nearest.

To hold space for complexity, to resist the violence of containing and classifying what transcends familiar labels, takes patience and a certain kind of moral courage, which Waldo seemed unable—or unwilling—to conjure up. "O divine mermaid or fisher of men, to whom all gods have given the witch-hazel-wand . . . I am yours & yours shall be," he told Margaret in a letter in the early autumn of 1840. But the following day, he lashed out in his journal, writing at Margaret what he wouldn't write to her:

> You would have me love you. What shall I love? Your body? The supposition disgusts you. What you have thought & said? . . . I see

no possibility of loving any thing but what now is, & is becoming; your courage, your enterprize, your budding affection, your opening thought, your prayer, I can love,—but what else?

This false notion of the body as the testing ground for intimacy has long warped our understanding of what constitutes a romantic relationship. The measure of intimacy is not the quotient of friction between skin and skin, but something else entirely—something of the love and trust, the joy and ease that flow between two people as they inhabit that private world walled off from everything and everyone else.

Perhaps Waldo did recognize that he and Margaret had an undeniable intimate partnership, and it was this very recognition that made him bristle at the sense of being coerced into coupledom. He was, after all, the poet laureate of self-reliance, who believed that for the independent man "the Universe is his bride." And yet, although he experienced himself as an individual, he had somehow conceded to the union of marriage and wedded a human bride—one who had grown to depend on him for her emotional well-being, which Waldo now experienced as a dead weight. He called it a "Mezentian marriage"—a grim allusion to the Roman myth of the cruel King Mezentius, known for tying men face-to-face with corpses and leaving them to die. He raged in his journal:

> Marriage is not ideal but empirical. It is not the plan or prospect of the soul, this fast union of one to one; the soul is alone. . . . It is itself the universe & must realize its progress in ten thousand beloved forms & not in one.

Margaret, too, tried to figure the form of their relationship. Three days after Lydian's tearful outburst, she wrote to Waldo with unprecedented candor, accusing him of being unclear in his feelings for her and commanding him to clarify where he stood, with an awareness that she might be yearning for more from him than he could ever give her:

We are to be much to one another. How often have I left you despairing and forlorn. How often have I said, this light will never understand my fire; this clear eye will never discern the law by which I am filling my circle; this simple force will never interpret my need to manifold being.

She addressed the unspoken implication of Lydian's jealousy—that Margaret's place in Waldo's life was beginning to encroach upon that of a romantic partner, not just a peer. Margaret assured him, perhaps as much as she was assuring herself, that it was never her intention to usurp that role—that even if she had the power to seduce him, she would not use it:

To violate the sanctity of relations, I am as far from it as you can be. I make no claim. I have no wish which is not dictated by a feeling of truth. Could I lead the highest Angel captive by a look, that look I would not give, unless prompted by true love. I am no usurper. I ask only mine own inheritance. If it be found that I have mistaken its boundaries, I will give up the choicest vineyard, the fairest flower-garden, to its lawful owner.

Acknowledging the agitation that bedeviled them both as they tried to make sense of their relationship, she promised that "this darting motion, this restless flame shall yet be attempered and subdued." She sensed between them an infinite possibility, but "the sense of the infinite exhausts and exalts; it cannot therefore possess me wholly." The paradox, of course, is that there is always something irresistibly vitalizing about our irresolvable passions, about that which we can never fully possess nor can fully possess us— some potent antidote to the wearying monotony of our settled possessions. "People wish to be settled," Emerson would write in one of his most famous essays, published just a few months later, "[but] only as far as they are unsettled is there any hope for them." For now, he painted the dark contours of this recognition in his journal: "Between narrow walls we walk: insanity on one side, & fat dulness on the other." Margaret, sensing the bipolar pull of his desires, demanded that he choose a pole:

Did not you ask for a "foe" in your friend? Did not you ask for a "large and formidable nature"? But a beautiful foe, I am not yet, to you. Shall I ever be? I know not.

And yet she told Waldo that with him alone she felt "so at home" that she couldn't imagine finding another love as quenching: "I know not how again to wander and grope, seeking my place in another Soul."

But Emerson was not looking to be "at home" in anyone other than himself. Already feeling his independent nature stifled by his marriage to Lydian, he could not—would not—let himself be trapped in a second relationship, his soul cemented and Mezented with a second weight of expectations. That month, as he voiced his reservations about the Brook Farm utopia in his journal, he could have been writing about his relationships to Lydian and Margaret:

I do not wish to remove from my present prison to a prison a little larger. I wish to break all prisons.

After nearly a month of stupefied silence, he finally responded to Margaret in a lengthy and conflicted letter:

My dear Margaret,

I have your frank & noble & affecting letter, and yet I think I could wish it unwritten. I ought never to have suffered you to lead me into any conversation or writing on our relation, a topic from which with all my persons my Genius ever sternly warns me away. I was content & happy to meet on a human footing a woman of sense & sentiment with whom one could exchange reasonable words & go away assured that wherever she went there was light & force & honour. That is to me a solid good; it gives value to thought & the day; it redeems society from that foggy & misty aspect it wears so often seen from our retirements; it is the foundation of everlasting friendship. Touch it not—speak not of it—and this most welcome natural alliance becomes from month to month,—& the slower & with the more intervals the better,—our air & diet. A robust & total understanding grows up resembling nothing so much as the relation of brothers who are intimate & perfect friends without having ever spoken of the fact. But tell me that I am cold or unkind, and in my most flowing state I become a cake of ice. I feel the crystals shoot & drops solidify. It may do for others but it is not for me to bring the relation to speech. . . . Ask me what I think of you & me,—& I am put to confusion.

Four days earlier, he had entreated her: "Give me a look through your telescope or you one through mine;—an all explaining look." Now he argues that they can neither be fully explained to the other, nor fully seen—they are as constitutionally different as if they "had been born & bred in different nations." Inverting Margaret's accusation of his withholding, he points out her own opacity:

You say you understand me wholly. You cannot communicate your-self to me. I hear the words sometimes but remain a stranger to your state of mind.

Yet we are all the time a little nearer. I honor you for a brave & beneficent woman and mark with gladness your steadfast good will to me. I see not how we can bear each other anything else than good will.

This undulating emotional confusion runs through the entire letter as Waldo struggles to reconcile his seemingly irreconcilable desires—not to lose his uncommon and electrifying bond with Margaret, but not to be trapped in bondage. We suffer by want-ing different things often at odds with one another, but we suffer even more by wanting to want different things. He tells her that a "vast & beautiful Power" has brought them into each other's lives and likens them to two stars shining together in a single constella-tion. He urges her to let things be as they have been, to savor their uncommon connection without demanding more:

Let us live as we have always done, only ever better, I hope, & richer. Speak to me of every thing but myself & I will endeavor to make an intelligible reply. Allow me to serve you & you will do me a kindness; come & see me . . . let me visit you and I shall be cheered as ever by the spectacle of so much genius & character as you have always the gift to draw around you.

But he exhorts her not to incite any more relationship conversations:

I see very dimly in writing on this topic. It will not prosper with me. Perhaps all my words are wrong. Do not expect it of me again for a very long time.

A year earlier, at the time of Emerson's ill-fated pentagon of ideal relations, he had responded to Margaret and Caroline's charge of "a certain inhospitality of soul":

I count & weigh, but do not love.—I heard the charge, I own, with great humility & sadness. I confess to the fact of cold & impartial intercourse, but . . . not to the deficiency of my affection. If I count & weigh, I also love.

Even Whitman, who never knew Emerson on so intimate a level, intuited this selfsame constitutional limitation: "Cold and bloodless intellectuality dominates him," Whitman wrote despite his fervent admiration, but noted that Emerson exemplified the classic New Englander's cold facade, behind which "the fires, emotions, love, egotisms, glow deep, perennial."

Meanwhile across the Atlantic, Elizabeth Barrett Browning is falling in love and incubating *Aurora Leigh*, in which she would write:

Life means, be sure,
Both heart and head,—both active, both complete,
And both in earnest. . . .
And thought can never do the work of love!

In their early correspondence, Waldo had articulated to Margaret a sentiment about the problem of translation in poetry, which now seemed to perfectly capture the problem of translating their interior worlds to each other:

> We are armed all over with these subtle antagonisms which as soon as we meet begin to play, and translate all poetry into such stale prose! . . . All association must be compromise.

A decade later, the German philosopher Arthur Schopenhauer would limn this central paradox of intimacy in the philosophical allegory of the porcupine dilemma: In the cold of winter, a covenant of porcupines huddle together seeking warmth. As they draw close, they begin wounding each other with their quills. Warmed but maimed, they instinctually draw apart, only to find themselves shivering and longing for the heat of other bodies again. Eventually, they discover that unwounding warmth lies in the right span of space—close enough to share in a greater collective temperature, but not so close as to inflict the pricks of proximity.

Unable to negotiate that optimal distance directly, in their private conversations and correspondence, Margaret and Waldo were to confront it obliquely in public. In 1841, having seen not a cent from her Herculean work on *The Dial* and in need of sustenance, Fuller launched a series of ten "Conversations" open to both men and women, charging $20 admission for the ten-session season—a premium price at the time, tenfold the cost of lectures at the Boston Lyceum. Around thirty people attended each session, including Emerson, Alcott, James Freeman Clarke, and Elizabeth Peabody, who hosted the sessions in her newly launched bookstore—a visionary haven for foreign-language literature and poetry by the great Romantics, most of it impossible to find elsewhere in America.

It was at one of these sessions that Sophia Peabody was smitten with the irresistible Ida Russell, the second-youngest person in attendance.

The youngest was Caroline Healey. Several months before the launch of the coed series, the bright eighteen-year-old—who would later become the influential abolitionist and women's rights advocate Caroline Healey Dall—had sauntered into Peabody's book-store, lusting after the handsome editions of *The Arabian Nights* and the classics, lamenting that she had no money of her own by which to obtain them. Instead, Caroline began earning social capital—she befriended Peabody and was invited to join the coed season of Fuller's forum as official scribe. Her transcripts, which she published many years later, remain the only reliable record of the "Conversations"—a valuable record, but a project akin to photographing electricity, for it is inherently impossible to contain the energy of conversation in written words. A curious sentence appears in Healey's transcript of one sessions: "Ida Russell thought that when Mechanic Art was married to Beauty, it might charm even Wisdom." Although these are all references to deities from Greek mythology—mechanic art was embodied in Vulcan, beauty in Aphrodite, wisdom in Minerva—the sentiment offers an inadvertent analogue to Maria Mitchell's work, for what else is telescopic observation if not a mechanical art aimed at beauty in the service of wisdom?

Three months into Fuller's series, Emerson's world was unworlded.

Amid his domestic discontentment, Waldo had found a singular joy in fatherhood. As he walked with Margaret through the woods of Concord, immersed in conversation, he often carried in his arms his beloved son, whom he had given his own name. A parent, he believed, found in a child "the unconscious projected upon a diagram"—the parent's own unexplored self revealed in a new form. In January 1842, Emerson's diagram was disfigured: Five-year-old Waldo died suddenly of scarlet fever—a disease whose guarantee of mortality would only fade a century later when penicillin became widely available. "He gave up his little innocent breath like a bird," the disconsolate father wrote in his journal the next morning of this "boy of early wisdom, of a grave & even majestic deportment, of a perfect gentleness," who had "touched with his lively curiosity every trivial fact & circumstance in the household." He sorrowed in a letter to his aunt:

My boy, my boy is gone. . . . The world's wonderful child fled out of my arms like a dream. He adorned the world for me like a morning star. . . . Shall I ever dare to love any thing again?

Upon receiving the news of the boy's death, Margaret wrote in a letter to William Channing:

I am deeply sad at the loss of little Waldo, from whom I hoped more than from almost any living being. I cannot yet reconcile myself to the thought that the sun shines upon the grave of the beautiful blue-eyed boy, and I shall see him no more.

Emerson struggled to fathom this unnatural thwarting of time scales:

The chrysalis which he brought in with care & tenderness & gave to his Mother to keep is still alive and he the most beautiful of the children of men is not here.

I comprehend nothing of this fact but its bitterness. Explanation I have none, consolation none that rises out of the fact itself; only diversion; only oblivion of this & pursuit of new objects.

Emerson coped with his shattered heart by retreating into the life of the mind. "My life is optical not practical," he wrote in his diary. "I speculate on virtue, not burn with love." He threw himself into this arena of intellectual and moral speculation, where Fuller had become ringmaster with her "Conversations." But the coed season of her series, though a triumph of ideas, was a disaster of interpersonal dynamics. The men swiftly hijacked the conversation toward their own ideological destinations, disregarding Fuller's guidance and bulldozing over the other women's opinions with the abrasive haughtiness of unbridled mansplaining. Crowning the catastrophe were the queen and king themselves, whose private tensions burst into the public arena. Emerson and Fuller "met like Pyramus and Thisbe, a blank wall between," Caroline Healey reported, drawing on the ill-fated lovers in Ovid's *Metamorphoses* who lived in adjoining houses and were allowed to communicate only through a crack in the wall—an allusion the aptness of which Healey, unwitting of the private fissure between Margaret and Waldo, couldn't have fully appreciated.

And yet the two managed to wade through the tar of their uncommon connection with a rare tenacity of spirit and an integrity of heart even rarer. Mere weeks after their disorienting conversation about who they were to each other, Waldo borrowed the phrase Bronson Alcott had used to describe Jesus—a "being of unsettled rank in the universe"—and applied it to Margaret. Margaret was unwilling to elevate Waldo to the status of Goethe—her personal Jesus—but later admitted that he had influenced her more than any other American: "From him I first learned what is meant by an inward life. Many other springs have since fed the stream of living waters, but he first opened the fountain." She would soon confer upon him power of attorney over her life's work: "You will have a complete inventory of my emblems and trappings 'in case of death.'" Emerson would give his most direct and unreserved account of his cascading admiration for Margaret—admiration not flourished to impress, as his public commemoration of her after her death would be—in the unadorned candor of his journal:

> A pure and purifying mind, self-purifying also, full of faith in men and inspiring it. Unable to find any companion great enough to receive the rich effusions of her thought, so that her riches are still unknown and seem unknowable. . . . All natures seem poor beside one so rich, which pours a stream of amber over all objects, clean and unclean, that lie in its path. . . . Beside her friendship, other friendships seem trade, and by the firmness with which she threads her upward path, all mortals are convinced that another road exists than that which their feet have trod.

Whatever we may mean by the word "love," we earn the right to use it only by doing the hard work of knowing and being known. Margaret told Waldo that to know another's soul by love is "truer than intellectual scrutiny of the details of character." Waldo knew her as she knew herself, and he beckoned forth her best possible self, for only a year later she recorded nearly the same sentiment in her own journal:

> Mine is a great nature as yet in many regions an untrodden wild, full of wild beasts and reptiles not yet tamed and classed, but also of rare butterflies, exquisite and grand vegetations respondent to the sun and stars. Its dynamics reveal not yet their concords—as yet it energizes more than harmonizes.

With an eye to her lifelong lament that she was cursed by "a man's ambition with a woman's heart," she adds:

> The woman kneels and weeps her tender raptures, finds no echo, but snowdrops and violets spring from her tears. The man rushes forth and is baffled, but returning lame a blinded Oedipus.

In his own journal, influenced by Margaret's ideas about the nonbinary nature of gender, Waldo was wrestling with the same paradox. Trying to clarify his turbid feelings for her and figure out his own heart, he wrote:

> A highly endowed man with good intellect & good conscience is a Man-woman & does not so much need the complement of Woman to his being, as another. Hence his relations to the sex are somewhat dislocated & unsatisfactory. He asks in Woman, sometimes the Woman, sometimes the Man.

Margaret Fuller wondered whether she was "fitted to be loved"—a word choice both curious and tragic: not "worthy," bespeaking an inherent endowment, but "fitted," as if she could fit herself for love by strain and discipline. With Caroline, with Sam, and now with Waldo, she had pushed and pushed to earn the affection she longed for—a push that eventually repelled each of its objects. But she could hardly have compartmentalized her nature—the very nature by which she had reached the stratospheric heights of her achievement. Those accustomed to hard work and self-propulsion, who have risen to the zenith of accomplishment by force of will and magnitude of effort, are most susceptible to the supreme self-damnation of human life—the belief that love is something to be earned by striving rather than something that comes unbidden like a shepherd's song on a summer evening in the mountains of Bulgaria.

"I have given almost all my young energies to personal relations," Fuller would later reflect on her early thirties. But it was precisely this restlessness about relationships, this unslakable thirst for private connection in which "the voice finds a listener," that furnished her contributions to public life, leading her to orchestrate her "Conversations" as a locus of connection, to inquire into gender roles and dynamics with *Woman in the Nineteenth Century*, effectively launching the feminist movement. "One writes not with the hand but with the whole person," Virginia Woolf—who was in many ways Fuller's twentieth-century counterpart—would observe.

Puzzling over this often disentwinable thread of the tragic and the triumphant, I am reminded of the closing lines of Adrienne Rich's poem "Power"—a tribute to Marie Curie:

It seems she denied to the end
the source of the cataracts on her eyes
the cracked and suppurating skin of her finger-ends
till she could no longer hold a test-tube or a pencil

She died a famous woman denying
her wounds
denying
her wounds came from the same source as her power

Fuller's wounding preoccupation with "personal relations" can no more be separated from the political power of the revolution she started than Kepler's astrology can be separated from his astronomy or Newton's alchemy from his physics. For Emerson, too, the conflicted pentagon of personal relationships fomented his ideas as a writer and philosopher. In one of his most celebrated essays, titled

"Friendship" and penned during the maelstrom of his entanglement with Fuller, he wrote:

> What is so delicious as a just and firm encounter of two, in a thought, in a feeling? How beautiful, on their approach to this beating heart, the steps and forms of the gifted and the true! The moment we indulge our affections, the earth is metamorphosed; there is no winter, and no night; all tragedies, all ennuis vanish; all duties even; nothing fills the proceeding eternity but the forms all radiant of beloved persons.

However divided we may feel within ourselves, it is the sum total of our warring fractions that makes us who we are—fragmentary but indivisible.

9

MERELY THE BEAUTIFUL

Eighteen forty-three, Margaret Fuller's thirty-third year, is her *annus mirabilis*. That autumn, she composes for *The Dial* an anguished and impassioned letter to a "Master"—Beethoven, dead sixteen years, immortal as the supreme master of the art that holds for her eternal proof that "all truth is comprised in music and mathematics." Fuller writes:

> My only friend,
>   How shall I thank thee for once more breaking the chains of my sorrowful slumber? My heart beats. I live again, for I feel that I am worthy audience for thee, and that my being would be reason enough for thine.
>   Master, my eyes are always clear. I see that the universe is rich, if I am poor. I see the insignificance of my sorrows. In my will, I am not a captive; in my intellect, not a slave. Is it then my fault that the palsy of my affections benumbs my whole life? . . . I have no art, in which to vent the swell of a soul as deep as thine, Beethoven, and of a kindred frame. Thou wilt not think me presumptuous in this saying, as another might. I have always known that thou wouldst welcome and know me, as would no other who ever lived upon the earth since its first creation.

Through the gateway of ecstatic admiration, Fuller arrives at the disquieting question of why Beethoven's genius was actualized and hers is not:

Is it because, as a woman, I am bound by a physical law, which pre-
vents the soul from manifesting itself? Sometimes the moon seems
mockingly to say so,—to say that I, too, shall not shine, unless I can
find a sun. O, cold and barren moon, tell a different tale!

It wouldn't be the Moon that tells a different tale but Fuller
herself—one she has already begun telling. Six months earlier, Fuller
had finished her first book, *Summer on the Lakes*—a book Maria
Mitchell devoured with the same zeal she did Milton, and one that
Thomas Higginson lauded as a masterwork that "presents something which is truer than statistics,—the real aroma and spirit of
Western life." Part travelogue, part anthropological study, and part
political treatise, *Summer on the Lakes* chronicles Fuller's journey
westward from her native New England—a voyage she had taken
that spring with James Freeman Clarke and his artist sister, Sarah.
Aware of Margaret's burnout in Boston, James had extended the
trip invitation in the form of a poem and tactfully enclosed fifty dollars to make acceptance possible for Margaret, who was struggling
as the sole provider for her mother, sister, and five brothers after
their father's death. Proud as she was, she couldn't resist a proposition so thoughtful, so alluring. She could catch her breath in travel.
She could let forests and horizons and grand new vistas revitalize
her languishing spirit. She could drink in some unfathomed fragment of "the All."

The journey was transformative beyond anything she imagined. Upon returning home, eager to supplement her observations
with historical research, Fuller persuaded the Harvard library to
grant her access to its book collection—the largest in the nation.
No woman had previously been admitted for more than the tour
Elizabeth Peabody had been given years earlier. She then set about
relaying her experiences and observations from the journey, ranging
from a stunning portrait of Niagara Falls to a poignant account of
the fate of the displaced Native American tribes with whom Fuller
sympathized and spent time. At the heart of the book was her search
for truth of a higher order:

Amid the manifold infatuations and illusions of this world of emotion, a being capable of clear intelligence can do no better service than to hold himself upright, avoid nonsense, and do what chores lie in his way, acknowledging every moment that primal truth, which no fact exhibits, nor, if pressed by too warm a hope, will even indicate.

Punctuating Fuller's lyrical prose are sentiments worn all the truer by time. In a passage that should be emblazoned on every voting ballot, she observes:

This country . . . needs . . . no thin Idealist, no coarse Realist, but a man whose eye reads the heavens, while his feet step firmly on the ground, and his hands are strong and dexterous for the use of human implements . . . a man of universal sympathies, but self-possessed; a man who knows the region of emotion, though he is not its slave; a man to whom this world is no mere spectacle or fleeting shadow, but a great, solemn game, to be played with good heed, for its stakes are of eternal value, yet who, if his play be true, heeds not what he loses by the falsehood of others; a man who hives from the past, yet knows that its honey can but moderately avail him; whose comprehensive eye scans the present, neither infatuated by its golden lures, nor chilled by its many ventures; who possesses prescience, the gift which discerns tomorrow—when there is such a man for America, the thought which urges her on will be expressed.

And yet, in further testament to how bounded by the era's horizons are the gazes of even its farthest seers, Fuller paints this ideal leader again and again as "a man"—how stunned she would have been, and gladdened, to know that a little more than a century and a half later, her nation's popular vote would choose a woman for the role.

Fuller composed the last sentence of *Summer on the Lakes* on her thirty-third birthday, May 23. The young Henry David Thoreau, clinging with blind zeal to the Emersonian ethos of self-reliance, recommended that she self-publish the book using *Dial* revenues to cover printing costs. But Fuller, aware of the magazine's dismal finances, decided to go with the new Boston firm Little and Brown, accepting royalties of 10 percent. To protect the perceived authority of her writing from prejudice, she obscured her gender by publishing the book under the initials S. M. Fuller—a choice common among the few women writing nonfiction and literary journalism well into the twentieth century, when the marine biologist Rachel Carson would publish her first works as R. L. Carson before catalyzing the modern environmental movement under her full name.

The publication of Fuller's first book rushed to the surface all the resentments that had been bubbling since the success of her daring "Conversations." Attacks were launched at her by the patriarchy, by religious dogmatists, and by all the other convention-appointed bastions of the status quo whom her ideas had challenged without reserve.

One reviewer, noting the acclaim of Fuller's conversational abilities, scoffs in the first-person plural, that editorial presumption of speaking for everyone: "Her writings we do not like. We dislike them exceedingly. They are . . . wholly deficient in a pure, correct taste, and especially in that tidiness we always look for in women." He hurls at her the insult—which Fuller must have taken for a compliment—that "she is German, heart and soul," that she bears Byron's skepticism and "the cold indifferentism of Goethe dashed on the warm woman's heart of Bettina Brentano." Unwittingly echoing the indictment launched at Socrates two millennia earlier, the reviewer then zeroes in on Fuller's chief offense:

> No person has appeared among us whose conversation and morals have done more to corrupt the minds and hearts of our Boston community. For religion she substitutes art; for the Divinity . . . she would give us merely the Beautiful.

Perhaps precisely for these reasons, *Summer on the Lakes* was an instant success when it was published in 1844. It was soon issued in a special luxury edition illustrated by James Freeman Clarke's artist sister, Sarah, seven hundred copies of which sold in the first year— a public appetite far surpassing that for Emerson's first book.

Summer on the Lakes greatly impressed Horace Greeley, the founder of the *New-York Tribune,* launched in the same year as *The Dial.* Fuller was already on Greeley's radar, thanks to his wife's enthusiastic praise for the "Conversations." He had come to see in her a kindred-spirited idealist during her tenure at *The Dial,* which he had praised as "the very best Magazine published in this country," and he had reprinted some of her pieces in his own publication, which had manyfold the reach of *The Dial.* Now Greeley was eager for an even closer editorial alliance—he offered Fuller a job as literary critic and editor of the *New-York Tribune,* which would make her America's first female editor of a major paper and the only woman in the *Tribune*'s all-male newsroom. Her experience in New York would become a model for Elizabeth Barrett Browning's Aurora Leigh, who also moves to the big city to make a name and a life for herself by her pen:

> I wrote for cyclopædias, magazines,
> And weekly papers, holding up my name
> To keep it from the mud. I learnt the use
> Of the editorial "we" in a review . . .

It was more than the promise of professional advancement that drove Fuller to New York. Exasperated by the growing rift between what she wanted from Waldo and what he was willing—or constitutionally able—to give, Margaret felt she must tear away from his magnetic pull if she were to cease wounding herself on her own unmet and unmeetable desire. Two centuries ago, moving from Boston to New York was the equivalent of moving from New York to New Zealand today. Who hasn't contemplated placing a state, a continent, half the world between oneself and the locus of continual disappointment in an impossible love? Margaret acknowledged as much in a letter to Waldo penned just before she left for New York, on the eighth anniversary of their first meeting:

> [My] disappointments have come but from a youthful ignorance in
> me which asked of you what was not in your nature to give.

But though she had moved two hundred miles away from Waldo, she had not inched from herself. His letter was the first to greet her upon arrival in New York, yet once again he had failed to provide what she needed of him. The missive was short—"indolent," she called it. Even his handwriting was disappointing. "Your pen wandered somewhat wildly and lazily over the paper," she scolded him in reply. In the very act of remembering her, she felt he was forgetting her: "I consent to be forgotten and neglected as long as shall be necessary," she wrote in regal, passive-aggressive resignation.

Shortly after her arrival, she penned a revelatory reply to a letter from Elizabeth Peabody, who had held up a sort of mirror to her. Addressing more her own reflection than Elizabeth, she writes the day after Christmas:

> Probably, I have, as you say, a large share of prudence by nature. It has not, however, been large enough to save me from being much disappointed, in various relations, by a want of delicacy and tenderness from those who had seemed capable of it. But, perceiving similar faults in me, and yet knowing my heart capable of pure and intelligent love, I believe them so, too, that we shall all be better, and do better as we grow.

She then proceeds to offer a striking character evaluation, which Elizabeth appears to have requested, at least to some degree. Perhaps Margaret gave herself permission to be this blunt and almost blameful because she saw much of herself—both her strengths and her struggles of character—in the elder woman who had once given her a launchpad; who had modeled the conversation salons that Margaret had later made her signature; who also toiled to reconcile a wildness of heart with a formidable intellect, also succumbed to intense intellectual infatuations with people who could never be her lovers, also thought and felt and lived in the extreme. We are always harshest upon those foibles we see in others that we know bedevil our own natures—the ones that most gravely misbecome our self-image—for blame is always easier than shame. In evaluating Elizabeth, Margaret could well be evaluating herself:

Your tendency to extremes, as to personal attachments, is so strong, I am afraid you will not wholly rise above it.

The persons whom you have idolized can never, in the end, be ungrateful, and, probably, at the time of retreat they will do justice to your heart. But, so long as you must draw persons too near you, a temporary recoil is sure to follow. It is the character striving to defend itself from a heating and suffocating action upon it.—

A little, only a little less of this in you would give your powers the degree of fresh air they need. Could you be as generous and sympathetic, yet never infatuated; then the blur, the haste, the tangle would disappear, and neither I nor any one could refuse to understand you. I admit that I have never done you justice. There is so much in you that is hostile to my wishes, as to character, and especially as to the character of woman. How could I be quite candid? Yet where I have looked at you, truly, I have also looked steadily, and always feel myself in your debt that you cordially pardon all that must be to you repressing—and unpleasant in me.

It was urgent time for a new chapter—away from Waldo, away from the intellectual universe Elizabeth had assembled, away from the old self that haunted her, that she wished to transcend.

When Fuller joined the *Tribune,* one of the most widely read papers in the country, she brought to it an attention to the arts unprecedented in a mainstream publication. Speaking to a body of fifteen thousand subscribers—sixtyfold what *The Dial* reached at its peak—she composed lyrical critiques of literature, reports on exhibitions at major museums and tiny galleries, sweeping reviews of Beethoven's symphonies performed at the New York Philharmonic. Governed by her conviction that "a great work of Art demands a great thought, or a thought of beauty adequately expressed," she championed a literary aesthetic that rose above the era's morass of moralistic storytelling and Puritan poetry—a great writer, Fuller believed, ought not to assault the reader with artificial pontifications, but must instead reveal truth and meaning via fine thought channeled through beauty that invites "a natural surrender to the charm of facts." Edgar Allan Poe, the era's other influential literary tastemaker, was unsparing in his praise for her writing: "I know of no style which surpasses it. It is singularly piquant, vivid, terse, bold, luminous."

Fuller awakened the American heart and mind to the works of Goethe, Schiller, George Sand, and other European literary giants— works she believed "might give the young, who are soon to constitute the state, a higher standard in thought and action than would be demanded of them by their own time." Seeing literature as a powerful fulcrum for raising standards not only personally but politically, she had no qualms about using it as a tool of reform and social justice. In the pages of the *Tribune*, she wrote:

> Literature may be regarded as the great mutual system of interpretation between all kinds and classes of men. It is an epistolary correspondence between brethren of one family, subject to many and wide separations, and anxious to remain in spiritual presence one of another.

In an enthusiastic review of an 1845 anthology benefiting the Massachusetts Anti-Slavery Fair, Fuller called attention to the work of a talented young writer—the recently self-liberated slave Frederick Douglass, who twenty years later would make his own famous case for art as a tool of reform in "Pictures and Progress." Nearly two decades before abolition came to pass, she advocated for Negro voting rights in the pages of the *Tribune*. She demanded prison reform and, after visiting the women's prison at Sing Sing on the Hudson River, demolished a colossal taboo by discussing in print how the complex economics of marriage and the punitive moralism of monogamy conspired to give rise to prostitution—the crime for which most of the Sing Sing inmates had been incarcerated. She descended into the mouth of a coal mine in a bucket and emerged with outrage at the inhumane conditions not only of the miners but of their "poor horses," permanently interned away from daylight in the "gloomy recesses" of their cramped underground stables. At a time devoid of any notion of animal rights, she extended her compassionate impulse for justice beyond the inequities of human gender, race, and class and toward other beings—she imagined with horror that the horses must "pass their days in dragging cars along the rails of narrow passages, and their nights in eating hay and dreaming of grass!!" She visited homeless shelters on the outskirts of New York and exposed the deplorable conditions in asylums for the insane—investigative reporting that would inspire, fifty years later, Nellie Bly's formidable exposé *Ten Days at the Mad-House*, which led to landmark policy changes in the treatment of the mentally ill. In a piece titled "Darkness Visible"—a title William Styron would borrow more than a century later for his classic memoir of depression—Fuller used her razor blade of rhetoric to cut open the abscess of the argument for capital punishment, which she—against the era's prevailing sentiment—condemned as monstrous.

Pacing the periphery of Walden Pond while philosophizing about the life of the mind is not quite the same thing as marching into prisons, asylums, and orphanages to uncover abuse and incite the public to demand change. Of the Transcendentalists, Fuller was the only one who left the sanctuary of nature and tested her ideas against the real world, using her pen to bring life as it was being lived a little closer to life as she believed it ought to be lived in a just society. And yet, like Rachel Carson a century later, she never saw human life as separate from the life of the earth—the world of ideas and the world of nature were one to her. In a love letter, she would write of the green fields and the flowers:

> I live in their life and am nourished by it, as the infant from the mother's breast. . . . It does me so much good, the soft warm life close to the earth.

Over the course of eighteen months, Fuller published two hundred fifty articles in the *Tribune*. With her reach, her prolific output, and her ferocity of thought that both elevated her readers toward a higher aesthetic of mind and grounded them in critical thinking, Fuller planted more seeds of truth and beauty in other minds than any other journalist before her, and possibly since.

But her greatest feat came in the summer of her *annus mirabilis,* a year before she moved to New York. Drawing on the ideas about women's stature in society, which she had explored in her "Conversations," and on her conflicted intercourses with Emerson about marriage, she composed an extraordinary essay she titled "The Great Lawsuit. Man *versus* Men. Woman *versus* Women." Published at the front of *The Dial*'s fourth issue in July 1843, it ran nearly fifty pages and caused such a shock of attention that the volume swiftly sold out. Greeley enthusiastically reprinted excerpts in his *Tribune.*

The young Thoreau—who, as Emerson reported, "never likes anything"—held nothing back in praising this masterpiece by the woman who had shaped his own writing as his editor at *The Dial.* Celebrating Fuller's essay as "a noble piece, rich, extempore writing, talking with pen in hand," he saw it as an epitome of great art's threefold aim:

> In writing, conversation should be folded many times thick. It is the height of art that, on the first perusal, plain common sense should appear; on the second, severe truth; and on a third, beauty; and, having these warrants for its depth and reality, we may then enjoy the beauty for evermore.

In the summer of 1844, before she moved to New York City, Fuller spent seven weeks in the Hudson Valley with Caroline Sturgis—the old flame who had embered into a lifelong friend. It was a period intended as a recuperative sabbatical from her Boston bustle. Instead, intellectual restlessness impelled her to expand the *Dial* essay into *Woman in the Nineteenth Century*—an epoch-making book that exposed with explosive eloquence and rhetorical rigor the disconnect between the ideals of American democracy and the realities of inequality tightly woven into the culture's social fabric.

In what would become American women's Declaration of Independence, Fuller sets out to "ascertain the true nature of woman;

give her legitimate hopes, and a standard within herself." Arguing for single women's self-reliance—or "self-dependence," as she called it, perhaps intentionally avoiding the Emersonian term—as one of the most transformative forces in propelling society toward progress, she writes:

> Man and woman . . . are the two halves of one thought. I lay no especial stress on the welfare of either. I believe that the development of the one cannot be effected without that of the other. My highest wish is that this truth should be distinctly and rationally apprehended, and the conditions of life and freedom recognized as the same for the daughters and the sons of time. . . . Woman . . . needs now take her turn in the full pulsation, and that improvement in the daughters will best aid in the reformation of the sons of this age.

Forty-three years later, the scratchy voice of an aged Walt Whitman would pour out of a wax-cylinder phonograph—the only surviving recording of the poet—and proclaim America to be the "centre of equal daughters, equal sons," a claim staked on Fuller's formative ground. Whitman so admired Fuller that clippings of her *Tribune* columns were found among his papers after his death. At twenty-seven, he had devoured her collection of essays on literature and art, tearing out the chapter on American literature with greedy gladness to save among his most precious possessions. He welcomed the book "right heartily" on the pages of the *Brooklyn Daily Eagle*, insisting that "the female mind has peculiarly the capacity, and ought to have the privilege, to enter the discussion of high questions of morals, taste, &c." In the final years of his life, Whitman extolled the "deep, deep cut" Fuller's intellect had made in the ego of the country by challenging America to find its original literary voice. He was as deeply influenced by her ideas about equality of the genders and races. Whitman envisioned the birth of a nation dappled with a glorious diversity of human specimens—"superb, large-sized, emotional and physically perfect individualities, of one sex just as much as the other." Fuller's legacy of literature as a force of social change reverberates through his words, penned decades after her *Woman*:

For the first time in history, a great, aggregated, real PEOPLE, worthy the name, and made of develop'd heroic individuals, both sexes—is America's principal, perhaps only, reason for being. If ever accomplish'd, it will be at least as much, (I lately think, doubly as much,) the result of fitting and democratic sociologies, literatures and arts—if we ever get them—as of our democratic politics.

Advancing a raging recalibration of the meaning of liberty and human dignity, Fuller observed in *Woman* that "there exists, in the world of men, a tone of feeling towards women as towards slaves." If America is to live up to its democratic ideals, she argued, freedom from bondage—of the body as much as of the mind and the spirit—must be granted to every human being:

The tree cannot come to flower till its root be free from the cankering worm, and its whole growth open to air and light. While any one is base, none can be entirely free and noble.

While composing and revising *Woman*, Fuller often used her journal as a workbook for fleshing out ideas. On one page, she drew a curious figure: a snake with tail in mouth—the ancient Greek symbol for eternity—encircling two equilateral triangles mirrored and overlapped to form a six-point star. She sealed the symbolism in verse:

Patient serpent, circle round
Till in death thy life is found,
Double form of godly prime
Holding the whole thought of time,
When the perfect two embrace,
Male and female, black and white
Soul is justified in space,
Dark made fruitful by the light,
And centred in the diamond Sun
Time, eternity, are one.

.   .   .

Lydia Maria Child—who had attended Fuller's "Conversations" in Boston and had withstood many attacks herself as one of abolition's leading voices and an early advocate for Native American rights— was humbled by Fuller's "bold book," a book full of ideas she herself would "not have dared to have written." Maria Child—who, like Sarah Margaret Fuller, went by her middle name—was one of the era's most successful writers. She had published numerous novels, stories, and historical texts, and founded America's first children's magazine. She was also the nineteenth century's champion par excellence of other women's genius—wherever she found courage, talent, or intelligence superior to her own, she became their zealous and unjealous celebrator, enacting in her public writings the sentiment Elizabeth Barrett had articulated to Robert Browning in the privacy of their courtship letters: "Beauty is beauty, and, whether it comes by our own hand or another's, blessed be the coming of it!" Having risen to prominence with her mobilizing abolitionist writings, Child used her position of power and visibility to shine the spotlight of public attention on others who battled bigotry and convention with intelligent bravery. Now she lauded Fuller in the *Broadway Journal* as "a woman of more powerful intellect, comprehensive thought, and thorough education" than any other in America.

More than half a century after Fuller's untimely death, Julia Ward Howe would applaud her as a woman who "dared to recognise her own mental and moral power," and would write:

> As in a vision she walked, inspired, little sensitive to praise or blame, with a message to deliver, whose full import she could not know. [Since then] the new order has asserted and established itself, and, though time has swept away most of those who held converse with her while in the flesh, the number is greatly multiplied of those who claim fellowship with her in the spirit. . . . Neither difficulty nor disappointment [had] the power to darken the glowing interpretation of life and its conditions, which was her best gift to the men and women of her time, and of our own as well.

When *Woman in the Nineteenth Century* was published, Howe was twenty-five—the same age as Whitman and Melville, a year

younger than Maria Mitchell—and newly wed to a man eighteen years her senior. The book must have been catalytic for her,
empowering her to survive an unhappy and uncommonly constricting marriage—her despotic husband, infatuated with one of his students and threatened by Julia's ambition, did his best to quash her
literary aspirations. Four years after she rose to renown by authoring "The Battle Hymn of the Republic" and twenty-two years into
the marriage, she would reflect:

> In the course of this time I have never known my husband to approve
> of any act of mine which I myself valued. Books—poems—essays—
> everything has been contemptible or contraband in his eyes.

In the spring of Fuller's *annus mirabilis,* as she was composing
what would become *Woman in the Nineteenth Century,* the newlywed Howe had boarded a steamship from Boston to Liverpool—the
same route Margaret Fuller and Maria Mitchell would eventually
take. She was headed for Europe on a double honeymoon with
Mary Peabody, who had just gotten married, rather suddenly and
with a shock of delight, to the education reformer Horace Mann.
"When I was being married," Mary would soon write to her sister Elizabeth—the only Peabody sister who remained unmarried—
"I realised that I could not grasp the felicity that was mine, but, soon
after it seemed all natural, like the stars, & the ocean & the course
of the sun." Alongside her on the deck, Julia Ward Howe was entering into a thoroughly different marriage that within a decade would
drive her to sorrow over her fate as "a comet dire and strange"—
a line from her beautiful and harrowing autobiographical poem
"The Heart's Astronomy." Ten years into her suffocating marriage,
thirty-four-year-old Howe described herself in a letter to Auguste
Comte as "an ardent, sentimental, misunderstood, and misplaced
woman," product of "the injustices of fate." The following year,
she published anonymously her first collection of poetry, *Passion-
Flowers,* in which "The Heart's Astronomy" appeared. Although
Nathaniel Hawthorne considered it one of only two underappre-
ciated American books Europeans must know about—the other

being Thoreau's *Walden,* published several months later—he cautioned that Howe's provocative and borderline erotic poems "let out a whole history of domestic unhappiness."

Howe's Boston publisher, home to such eminent authors as Maria Child, Emerson, Twain, Thoreau, and Hawthorne himself, had previously rejected a manuscript by her husband. Enraged upon finding out that his wife had dared to exercise such agency of mind, he grasped for control of her body with an ultimatum—they must resume sexual relations or he would throw her out of the house. After enduring this Faustian form of rape, Howe wrote to her sister: "I made the greatest sacrifice I can ever be called upon to make"— a sacrifice that resulted in yet another pregnancy.

Howe gave birth to her sixth and final child at forty, in the year that Darwin published *On the Origin of Species.* She endured another seventeen years of her nightmarish marriage. "My books are all that kept me alive," she would recall of this tundra three decades wide. The day of her husband's funeral, thirty-three years into their marriage, she recorded in her diary: "Began my new life today"—a life the remainder of which she would devote to the project of equality through abolition and women's rights, hoping that her writings and lectures would transmit "the message of the good hope of humanity, despite the faults and limitations of individuals."

Several months before her husband's death, Howe had met Maria Mitchell at one of her "dome parties" at the Vassar observatory— gatherings during which Mitchell's students and occasional esteemed guests played a game of writing extemporaneous poems about astronomy on scraps of used paper. Mitchell imbued the observatory with the old spirit of the Nantucket Atheneum, hosting lectures and discussions of pressing political and cultural issues by such prominent "platform women" as Elizabeth Cady Stanton and Anna Dickinson. Howe visited in the spring of 1875 to deliver a lecture titled "Is Polite Society Polite?" In it, she issued an indictment against a society that had become so drunk on ambition and outward achievement that it had come to mistake surface polish and posturing for the "inward grace of good feeling" that constitutes true kindness. A greater understanding of this distinction, she argued, "would save us from the vulgarity of worshipping rank and wealth." What makes the American people "polite," Howe suggested to the women gathered under the dome, is a combination of democratic idealism and an unselfish impulse toward equality:

> Partly the inherited blood of men who would not submit to the rude despotism of old England and old Europe, and who thought a better state of society worth a voyage in the *Mayflower.* . . . Partly, also, the necessity of the case. As we recognize no absolute social superiority, no one of us is entirely at liberty to assume airs of importance which do not belong to him. No matter how selfish we may be, it will not do for us to act upon the supposition that the comfort of other people is of less consequence than our own.
>
> [. . .]
>
> The assumption of special merit, either by an individual or a class, is not polite. . . . But we allow classes of people to assume special merit on false grounds. It may very easily be shown that it requires more talent and merit to earn money than to spend it. Yet, by almost common consent of the fashionable world, those who inherit or marry money are allowed to place themselves above those who earn it.

Howe argued that "sincerity is the best foundation upon which to build the structure of a polite life." Perhaps this conviction is what drew her to Mitchell, a woman devoid of all insincerity, uninterested in any pretense. Conceived the month Maria Mitchell was born, Howe would eventually become, a year before the astronomer's death, her first official biographer and would celebrate her as a "sister planet." Both women would look back on their lives and recognize the pathbreaking influence of Margaret Fuller and her *Woman.*

10

DIVIDED, INDIVISIBLE

It is almost impossible to grasp the furor Fuller's now-forgotten masterwork engendered when it made its debut in early 1845, or the far-reaching aftershocks of its impact. Sales of the book soared as it traversed the country to the farthest frontiers of the West. Copies pirated in London began circulating across Europe. New York and Boston, America's centers of intellectual life and political reform, were ablaze with polarized debates about the taboos and daring questions Fuller had raised—questions revolving around the economic inequalities hardwired into marriage by the collusion of social convention and the law.

Fuller condemned women's ineligibility to own property on a par with men as a legal relegation of women to the status of children. Exposing the millennia-deep roots of this sublimation, she rose above her love of ancient Greek culture to point out that even Plato, "the man of intellect," treated woman as property in his political writings and wrote in one of his allegorical dialogues "that Man, if he misuse the privileges of one life, shall be degraded into the form of Woman; and then, if he do not redeem himself, into that of a bird." Holding up Mary Somerville as a model of possibility, Fuller argued that when unblinded by the "narrowness or partial views of a home circle" and granted equal access to education, "women are better aware how great and rich the universe is." Only with a full view of this richness, she asserted, would women be able to carve out their own path, rather than seeing all the endeavors of their youth as preparation for marriage. Marriage should be one of many options, chosen freely by those who prefer it over other courses, not forced upon all as the sole means to a fulfilling life:

> A being of infinite scope must not be treated with an exclusive view to any one relation. Give the soul free course, let the organization, both of body and mind, be freely developed, and the being will be fit for any and every relation to which it may be called.

A frequent refrain of the complaint-choir of Fuller's critics would be that "no unmarried woman has any right to say anything on the subject"—an argument of logical sophistication comparable to contending that Maurice Sendak had no right to compose his body of work because he never had children, or that no white person has the right to reflect critically on race and no man on feminism.

Decrying the sublimation of women's minds to domesticity, Fuller asserts that "a house is no home unless it contain food and fire for the mind as well as for the body" and admonishes that "human beings are not so constituted that they can live without expansion." Underpinning the book is precisely this insistence on expansion of possibility as the path to empowerment. Fuller must have known, given her mastery of the classics, that the words "possibility" and "power" share a common root in the Latin *posse*. Paradoxically, one of the most short-sighted criticisms of *Woman* was that it painted new horizons of possibility but did not outline the actionable steps to get there—a criticism with which even Horace Greeley, who was grateful for the fount of publicity now surrounding the author he employed, tempered his praise for the book: "No woman, no man, ever read it without profit; but many have closed it with but vague and dim ideas of what ought to be done." Such indictments were then, as they are now, blind to the fact that possibility itself is a generator of power—that a mobilized mind is the prerequisite and catalyst by which the body springs into informed and inspired action. Maria Mitchell recorded the perfect retort to this strain of criticism in a diary entry penned a decade after *Woman*'s publication:

Reformers are apt to forget, in their reasoning, that the world is not made up entirely of the wicked and the hungry, there are persons hungry for the food of the mind, the wants of which are as imperious as those of the body. . . . Reformers are apt to forget too, that the social chain is indomitable; that link by link it acts together, you cannot lift one man above his fellows, but you lift the race of men. Newton, Shakespeare and Milton did not directly benefit the poor and ignorant but the elevation of the whole race has been through them. They probably found it hard to get publishers, but after several centuries, the publishers have come to them and the readers have come, and the race has been lifted.

When Mitchell read *Woman,* it must have struck her with resonance not only political but personal. Fuller envisioned a day when a "female Newton" would be possible. And yet Mitchell never seems to have fully envisioned how her own life was making that possibility real for generations to come. In her beloved *Aurora Leigh,* Elizabeth Barrett Browning had written of how those who ignite the profoundest revolutions are themselves blind to their own spark:

The best men, doing their best,
Know peradventure least of what they do:
Men usefullest i' the world, are simply used. . . .

Upon returning from her travels to the land of Milton and Shakespeare and Browning, Mitchell was greeted by an extraordinary gift—a five-inch refractor telescope, on a par with the instruments of the world's greatest observatories, purchased through what may have been the world's first crowdfunding campaign for science.

Elizabeth Peabody had envisioned the project and spent years raising the $3,000 for the telescope through a subscription paper, rallying Boston's women to contribute. Just as Mitchell was departing for her European journey, Emerson had lent his voice to the fund-raising effort in the pages of his popular magazine:

In Europe, Maria Mitchell would command the interest and receive the homage of the learned and polite, while in America so little prestige is attached to genius or learning that she is relatively unknown. This is a great fault in our social aspect, one which excites the animadversion of foreigners at once. "Where are your distinguished women—where your learned men?" they ask, as they are invited into our ostentatiously furnished houses to find a group of giggling girls and boys, or commonplace men and women, who do nothing but dance, or yawn about till supper is announced. We need a reform here, most especially if we would not see American society utterly contemptible.

While touring Europe's iconic astronomical institutions, Mitchell had been dreaming up an observatory of her own. The crowd-funded telescope came as a wondrous surprise after a particularly difficult stretch for her, marked by Ida's death and her once-brilliant mother's terrifying descent into dementia. The instrument became the first physical building block of her dream. Behind the school resembling a Greek temple where her father had once served as founding schoolmaster, she erected a simple eleven-foot dome that rotated on a mechanism made of cannonballs. A month before Darwin published *On the Origin of Species,* the observatory opened its doors and Mitchell, now the Newton of Nantucket, began welcoming boys and girls.

During her time in Italy the previous year, she had hungered to visit the Observatory of Rome, mecca of the latest research on spectroscopy, but was jarred to learn that the observatory was closed to women. Mary Somerville, by then celebrated as Europe's most learned woman, had been denied entrance, as had Sir John Herschel's daughter. Mitchell recorded wryly in her diary:

I was ignorant enough of the ways of papal institutions, and, indeed, of all Italy, to ask if I might visit the Roman Observatory. I remembered that the days of Galileo were days of two centuries since. I did not know that my heretic feet must not enter the sanctuary,—that my woman's robe must not brush the seats of learning.

She was eventually allowed to enter with special permission from the Pope, obtained after American diplomats pressed on her behalf.

An hour and a half before sunset, she was led through the church into the observatory, where she marveled at the expensive instruments the papal government employed in studying the very motions for which they had tried Galileo two centuries earlier. Mitchell had hoped to see nebulae through the observatory's powerful telescope, but she was informed that her permission did not extend past nightfall and was hastily sent away. She must have resolved, as soon as the back door spat her out into the narrow alley behind Collegio Romano, that when she built her own observatory, it would welcome any and all who hungered to commune with the cosmos.

Exactly twenty years after Fuller's *Woman* lit a Promethean fire of possibility for women, Maria Mitchell took a job as the first professor of astronomy at the newly founded Vassar Female College—an institution powered by Matthew Vassar's conviction that the intellectual emancipation of women was as vital to the nation's flourishing as the liberation of slaves. Although a number of higher education options had become available to women over the previous three decades, Vassar was groundbreaking not only in aspiring to the standards of Harvard and Yale but in far exceeding those venerated colleges in its rigorous focus on science, practically nonexistent in the leading universities that prepared men for careers in theology and the law. But for all its progressive idealism, Vassar was still a product of its era: The original college handbook stated that women were not permitted to go outside after dark—a preposterous problem for the study of astronomy, which Mitchell had to overturn.

In a testament to the power and ever-shifting provisions of language, controversy erupted over the word nestled between the institution's namesake and its function. Since Darwin had ignited the dawn of evolutionary theory several years earlier, the term "female" had taken on animalistic undertones associated with sexual reproduction—connotations some women saw as dehumanizing and some men used deliberately to dehumanize, particularly in referring to slave women as "females." One woman, who had previously lauded Matthew Vassar's plans for the college, charged at him in a spirited letter condemning the name:

> Female! What female do you mean? Not a female donkey? Must not your reply be "I mean a female male woman"? Then . . . why degrade the feminine sex to the level of animals?

She amplified the argument in print, proposing a renaming in a popular magazine:

> Does it seem suitable that the term female, which is not a synonym for woman and never signifies lady, should have a place in the title of this noble institution? The generous founder intended it for young women. The Bible and the Anglo-Saxon language mark, as the best and highest style, VASSAR COLLEGE FOR YOUNG WOMEN.

Language is not the content of thought but the vessel into which we pour the ambivalences and contradictions of our thinking, afloat on the current of time. The article appeared in *Godey's Lady's Book*—a magazine whose title is syntactically analogous to "Vassar Female College," its own middle word just as objectionable to the modern ear as "female" was to those of our ancestors, bounded by the very chains of convention and limiting possibility that Margaret Fuller had set out to break.

Within a year, Vassar College had scrubbed the word "female" from the inscription above its stately entrance.

Maria Mitchell didn't concern herself with the naming controversy, for she believed that a "solid phalanx of figures is a formidable opponent to a flourish of rhetoric." She spoke the purest language of the universe, and it was with mathematics that she set out to empower women. When she began teaching her first class of students—seventeen young women between the ages of sixteen and twenty-two—she estimated that there weren't as many men studying mathematical astronomy at Harvard, which had long ago dropped its mathematics requirement beyond the freshman year. By

1851, only two students in the entire Harvard class elected higher mathematics. Both later dropped it.

During the twenty-three years of Mitchell's reign, Vassar would graduate more students in astronomy and higher mathematics than Harvard. Her students were the first generation of Americans trained in what we now know as astrophysics, a product of Mitchell's insistence on marrying rigorous mathematical physics with observational astronomy—something Harvard would replicate by reinstating the mathematics requirement. Mitchell was the first university professor to turn her observatory into an exploratorium for hands-on learning, arming her students with instruments and encouraging them to use the observatory's meridian circle, transit devices, and telescopes at their leisure. Like Margaret Fuller, she conducted her lectures not as a top-down delivery of answers for rote memorization but as conversations encouraging questions and critical thinking. Near the sculpture of Mary Somerville that graced her observatory-classroom lay a notebook titled "Book of Questions," in which her pupils recorded their unanswered questions—those knowable unknowns that stretch science forward. The final exams of her advanced students challenged them to make computational predictions of solar eclipses, but Mitchell detested the grading that the college required and refused to do it. "I cannot express the intellect in numbers," she wrote defiantly. For all her faith in figures, she knew their limitations—more than a century before IQ tests became the battleground for psychologists who exposed the fool's gold of quantifying general intelligence, Mitchell boldly asserted that "there is no intellectual unit."

For the first three years of her tenure, Mitchell labored to reconcile the conflicting demands of original research and teaching while still performing her mathematically rigorous work for the *Nautical Almanac* and caring for her ailing father. Exhausted to the bone and battling severe sleep deprivation, she eventually cautioned herself in her diary: "I dare not repeat the brain struggle of last year—it is suicidal to attempt." In 1868, seven weeks after her fiftieth birthday, she finally relinquished her Navy job after twenty years as computer of Venus. Shortly after her resignation, she wrote in her journal:

RESOLVED: In case of my outliving father and being in good health, to give my efforts to the intellectual culture of women, without regard to salary.

Her self-sacrifice to a higher sense of purpose was far from an abstraction: Since the moment she arrived at Vassar, and for the next ten years, Mitchell slept on a small cot in the clock room atop her observatory, which also served as her office and classroom— the college had failed to provide her with a bedroom, apparently assuming that a woman of genius is a disembodied intellect with no need for basic creaturely comforts. A makeshift bedroom was fashioned for her father in the observatory basement. For ten years, she lived with great autonomy—there were only two buildings on Vassar's campus: the main college, nine hundred feet away, and the observatory, of which Mitchell and her father were the only residents. But she had no privacy—an arrangement that was the polar opposite of the closet she had claimed for a calculating room of her own as a child. Now she had not even a door on which to hang the notecard inscribed "Miss Mitchell is busy. Do not knock." After she rose each morning, she spread a velvet throw over her cot and neatly arranged several pillows to conceal any trace of the only private life she had—her sleep.

All the while, her male colleagues' salaries rose from the initial $2,000 to $2,500, while Mitchell's remained fixed at $800. But she recognized that just as the intellect can't be quantified in grades, the measure of a life's worth and purpose isn't to be found in remuneration figures. A decade and a half earlier, the young Henry David Thoreau had written in *Walden*:

If the day and the night are such that you greet them with joy, and life emits a fragrance like flowers and sweet-scented herbs, is more elastic, more starry, more immortal—that is your success.

Several months after *Walden* was published, Thoreau took the podium at Mitchell's Atheneum in Nantucket and asked in a lecture titled after a line from the Bible: "What shall it profit a man, if he shall gain the whole world, and lose his own soul?"

Whatever constellation of beliefs, values, and fragments of personhood we may mean by "soul," Maria Mitchell lived with unwavering fidelity to hers. The people she elevated to the stature of heroes—poets, scientists, or sculptors—had two things in common: genius and fidelity to their own souls. This combination is what she had intuited in Margaret Fuller and why she revered her so.

On Mitchell's twenty-eighth birthday, a decade before she journeyed to the Old World, Margaret Fuller boarded a steamer in Boston and headed for England with a family she had befriended—the Quaker social reformers Rebecca and Marcus Spring, who had offered to take her on the tour of Europe she had always dreamt of if she would tutor their nine-year-old son. Before her departure, she wrote to Anna and Sam Ward of the trip to Europe the two had taken a decade earlier while she mourned her father—the trip during which they had dealt her the dual heartbreak of falling in love with each other and out of love with her:

> I felt that in not going with you . . . I lost what life could never replace. I feel so still. . . . It was what I wanted after my painful youth, and what I was ready to use and be nourished by. It would have given my genius wings and I should have been, not in idea indeed, but in achievement far superior to what I can be now.

It is not cowardice but courage to acknowledge the superior role chance plays in steering the course of life, and at the same time to take responsibility for the margin of difference our personal choices do make within the parameters of chance. It is with such dignified recognition that Fuller adds:

> Fate or Heaven, or whatever we may call it, did not will it so, and in entering other and less congenital paths, I do feel that I have tried to make the best of life in every sense I could. . . . I do not look to seeing Europe now as so very important to me. My mind and character are too much formed. I shall not modify them much but only add to my stores of knowledge. Still, even in this sense, I wish much to go. It is important to me, almost needful in the career I am now engaged in I feel that, if I persevere, there is nothing to hinder my having an

important career even now. But it must be in the capacity of a journalist, and for that I need this new field of observation.

Fuller persuaded Horace Greeley to see the trip as a journalistic
opportunity and to let her serve as foreign correspondent for the
Tribune—the first American journalist to hold such a position for
a major publication. In her farewell column from New York, she
promised readers that she would transmit to them "packages of
seed for life" across the Atlantic—ideas on art, politics, and culture
from the Old World that would enrich the fertile but uncultivated
intellectual soil of her own new nation.

One other major motive for Fuller's flight from New York—"the
busy mart amid the falsehoods"—was that she had just suffered her
most devastating heartbreak.

On the last day of 1844, just as *Woman* was about to enter the
world and five days after she penned her blunt letter to Elizabeth
Peabody, Fuller met at a New Year's Eve party the charismatic,
blue-eyed, guitar-playing German Jewish textile merchant turned
Wall Street banker James Nathan—a man she found to have "so
much of feminine sweetness and sensibility" that she was instantly
enchanted. Within a month, they entered a "nameless relation" that
led them to escape on romantic excursions to art galleries in the
middle of the workday, stroll the shores of the East River on weekends with Nathan's enormous Newfoundland puppy, and fill their
nights with composing passionate love letters. "The native poetry
of your soul, its boldness, simplicity and fervor charmed mine, of
kindred frame," she wrote to him. "I do not think any human being
ever felt a lovelier confidence in the pure tenderness of another."
Margaret was finally giving herself over to a relationship of unam-
ibivalently and mutually romantic intent. "I am with you as never
with any other one." Her love letters to Nathan were a rare and
delicate interlacing of passion and intellect: "There is no time for
books and no poem like the poem we can make for ourselves."

But what Margaret didn't know was that while she was pouring her poetic passions onto paper, James was having a carnal relationship with a poor "English maiden" secretly living with him. It would take Margaret some time to confront the cold fact that James had been more interested in getting his travel writing published in her paper than in making a life-poem with her. For now, she demanded of him an explanation of the rumor. Exploiting her devotion to social justice, he told her that he had simply taken the impecunious immigrant under his protection. With the willful blindness of the besotted, she believed him and decided to press forward: "We will act, as if these clouds were not in the sky." A stubborn and misplaced dignity permeates her thoughts on how the rumor of her almost-lover's lover might affect her public image:

> Now that . . . I have made up my own mind, I have no fear nor care. I am myself exposed to misconstruction constantly from what I write. Blame cannot hurt me, for I have not done wrong, and have too much real weight of character to be sunk, unless by real stones of offence being attached to me.

Perhaps because she feared having to compete with the "English maiden" on level ground, or perhaps because she felt for Nathan a carnal passion completely novel to her, Margaret allowed the relationship to approach the erotic boundary she had never before permitted herself to go near. But she was far from ready to cross it. James was insensitive, if not entirely unsentient, to the seemingly subtle yet monumental difference between curiosity and consent. One late spring day, he cornered her and pressed his body against hers with unambiguous intent. Margaret repelled him in shock: "I could not." The next morning, she wrote to him of "what was to every worldly and womanly feeling so insulting":

> Yesterday was, perhaps, a sadder day than I have had in all my life. . . . Neither could I reconcile myself to your having such thoughts, and just when you had induced me to trust you so absolutely. I know you could not help it, but why had fate drawn me so near you?

She walked the streets of New York that day sundered by the irreconcilable desires of body and mind, by an unshakable sense that the passionate union she longed to experience would abrade the sovereignty of mind and spirit she had placed at the center of her personhood. She coped by engaging in a heartbreaking Stockholm syndrome of the psyche. "I know you could not help it," she reasoned with James, then took the blame for his attempted assault: "It is then, indeed, myself who have caused all the ill." Perhaps she thought of Milton's *Paradise Lost*:

> The mind is its own place, and in itself
> Can make a Heav'n of Hell, a Hell of Heav'n.

But no amount of sublimation could compensate for the asymmetry of affections. By late spring, five months into their asymmetrical entanglement, James Nathan set sail for Europe—with his "English maiden." Margaret's beseeching letters continued to stream behind him, unreturned. "Hast though ceased to cherish me, O Israel!" she cried out almost a year after his departure. "I have felt, these last four days, a desire for you that amounted almost to anguish." Grasping for meaning amid the disorientation of her abandonment, she sorrowed:

> So many things have happened, such a crowd of objects come between us! Alas! There is too much to be said we cannot say rightly in letters. . . . I do not know what has been or is in your mind. How unnatural! for such ignorance and darkness to follow on such close communion, such cold eclipse on so sweet a morning.

When he finally did write in June 1846, two months before Margaret's own departure for Europe, it was to ask her for copies of the *Tribune* in which his travelogues had been published—professional exposure she had procured for him in the heat of her infatuation. In her reply, she stressed twice that she was hoping to see him or at least hear from him in London that autumn.

Long ago, in what feels like a past life, I journeyed across a continent to spend time in a city that was not yet my own, home to a lover who had just dealt me my first great heartbreak. I would ride the subway idly in this swirling hive of eight million, going nowhere in particular, hoping against reason and probability to run into her. I imagine that while Margaret Fuller traversed the ocean, she was buoyed by the same unreasonable hope of running into James Nathan in a faraway city of multitudes. Probability, after all, is not for those fain to follow the imprecise instrument of the affections.

In what is perhaps her most insightful feat of retrospective introspection, Fuller would later reflect on her lifelong shorelessness of heart:

> From a very early age I have felt that I was not born to the common womanly lot. I knew I should never find a being who could keep the key to my character; that there would be none on whom I could always lean, from whom I could always learn; that I should be a pilgrim and sojourner on earth, and that the birds and foxes would be surer of a place to lay the head than I. . . . Such beings [as I] can only find their homes in hearts. . . .
>
> This thought . . . affected me sometimes with sadness, sometimes with pride. I mourned that I never should have a thorough experience of life, never know the full riches of my being; I was proud that I was to test myself in the sternest way, that I was always to return to myself, to be my own priest, pupil, parent, child, husband, and wife. . . . A sister I have truly been to many,—a brother to more,—a fostering nurse to, oh how many! The bridal hour of many a spirit, when first it was wed, I have shared, but said adieu before the wine was poured out at the banquet. And there is one I always love in my poetic hour, as the lily looks up to the star from amid the waters; and another whom I visit as the bee visits the flower, when I crave sympathy. Yet . . . all is well; all has helped me to decipher the great poem of the universe.

Twelve days before her departure to Europe, Margaret wrote to Caroline Sturgis, fearing they might not see each other again before the trip:

I go with a great pain in my heart, but that is nothing new, and nothing that I could hope to evade by staying. . . . Dear Cary, if it is farewell, (I hope not) know me more than ever yours in love.

One of the greatest betrayals of our illusion of permanence, one
of the sharpest daggers of loss, is the retroactive recognition of
lasts—the last time you sat across from a person you now know you
will never see again, the last touch of a hand, the last carefree laugh
over something spoken in the secret language that binds two people
in intimacy—lasts the finality of which we can never comprehend in
the moment, lasts we experience with sundering shock in hindsight.
Emily Dickinson, the poet laureate of loss, knew this well:

We never know we go—when we are going
We jest and shut the door—
Fate following behind us bolts it
And we accost no more.

Margaret and Caroline were never to see each other again.

After ten days and sixteen hours aboard a grand vessel that "looked
like a great winged creature darting across the apparently measure-
less expanse," Fuller arrived in Liverpool—the fastest passage across
the Atlantic yet made. In Liverpool, she was delighted to discover a
new system of schools that offered, for a very low fee, a thorough
education to working-class men as well as women—from English,
French, and German to mathematics, architecture, and fine art. She
was gladdened to learn that the founder of the initiative had quoted
The Dial in framing the educational philosophy of his schools.

By late September, Fuller had reached London, where a collection of her essays on literature and art had just been released to
great acclaim. Emerson had given her a letter of introduction to the
incorrigibly misogynistic Carlyle, who found her "a strange, lilting,
lean old maid," then added: "Not nearly such a bore as I expected."
From the philosopher laureate of the patriarchy, who had dismissed

Mary Somerville as unoriginal, this was high praise. Fuller, in turn, bifurcated her sentiments along a parallel axis of ambivalence. She was unreservedly taken by "his Scotch, his way of signing his great, full sentences, so that each one was like a stanza of a narrative ballad." But she found him afflicted with the worst pathology of the patriarchy—he was even more taken than she was with the sound of his own speech and the content of his own mind:

> The worst of hearing Carlyle is that you cannot interrupt him. . . . You are a perfect prisoner when he has once got a hold of you. To interrupt him is a physical impossibility. If you get a chance to remonstrate for a moment, he raises his voice and bears you down.

In Carlyle's "Titanic" and "anti-celestial" tirades—"he does not converse; only harangues"—Fuller saw the personal manifestation of a larger cultural epidemic—an aesthetic of haughtiness that has only intensified in the century and a half since, as we have increasingly come to mistake the magnitude of a person's arrogance and self-assertion for the measure of their merit:

> It is the usual misfortune of such marked men,—happily not one invariable or inevitable,—that they cannot allow other minds room to breathe, and show themselves in their atmosphere, and thus miss the refreshment and instruction which the greatest never cease to need from the experience of the humblest. Carlyle allows no one a chance, but bears down all opposition, not only by his wit and onset of words, resistless in their sharpness as so many bayonets, but by actual physical superiority,—raising his voice, and rushing on his opponent with a torrent of sound. This is not in the least from unwillingness to allow freedom to others. On the contrary, no man would more enjoy a manly resistance to his thought. But it is the habit of a mind accustomed to follow out its own impulse, as the hawk its prey, and which knows not how to stop in the chase.

But in the spirit of celebration that animated her literary journalism, Fuller didn't let her personal revulsion at this side of his character eclipse her full view of Carlyle as creator. Geniuses, after all, are rarely without a tragic flaw, their tragedy and triumph often springing from a shared source. In her *Tribune* column, she wrote generously:

> He is indeed arrogant and overbearing, but in his arrogance there is no trace of littleness or self-love. It is in his nature, in the untamable energy that has given him the power to crush the dragons.

Such are the simple mechanics of human psychology's feedback loop: The great determinant of how much we like another person is how much we believe they like us. As generosity of interpretation begets generosity of interpretation, Carlyle wrote to Emerson after reading Fuller's newly published *Woman*:

> Margaret is an excellent soul . . . a true heroic mind;—altogether unique, so far as I know, among the Writing Women of this genera-tion; rare enough too, God knows, among the writing Men. She is very narrow, sometimes; but she is truly high; honor to Margaret, and more and more good-speed to her.

From England, Fuller headed for France, eager to meet the person whose acquaintance she most longed to make in all of Europe: George Sand. In *Woman*, she had held Sand up as a person "whose existence better proved the need of some new interpretation of Woman's Rights than anything she wrote." Sand had attracted great controversy with her outspoken advocacy of women's freedom and "fulness of being," her habit of wearing men's clothes and smoking large cigars, and her passionate convention-defying relationships with both men and women, most famously with the composer Frédéric Chopin. (Fuller would have appreciated Chopin's remark that "Bach is an astrono-mer, discovering the most marvellous stars, [whereas] Beethoven challenges the universe.") In a *Tribune* column penned before she left New York, Fuller had lauded Sand's writings "which system-atically assailed the present institution of marriage, and the social bonds which are connected with it," and had admired that Sand's work sprang from the ethos of her personal life—a life in which she had "not only broken the marriage-bond [but] formed other connections, independent of the civil and ecclesiastical sanction."

After fruitless attempts at securing a formal letter of introduction, Fuller gathered the courage to show up on Sand's doorstep in Paris. Unlike Maria Mitchell at Elizabeth Barrett Browning's doorstep, she rang and waited. Some confusion ensued—Sand didn't initially recognize Fuller's name as repeated by her servant and was about to send the stranger away before she suddenly realized that this was the American writer she herself had wanted to meet for some time and rushed to greet her visitor. The doorway framed Sand's figure in a mental daguerreotype of a moment Fuller would never forget. She found Sand's face quite unlike her depiction in portraits—much finer, "the upper part of the forehead and eyes are beautiful, the lower strong and masculine, expressive of a hardy temperament and strong passions, but not in the least coarse." These physical details gave way to a larger impression of Sand's "goodness, nobleness, and power that pervaded the whole—the truly human heart and nature that shone in the eyes." Fuller wrote in a letter to a friend:

It made me very happy to see such a woman, so large and so developed a character, and everything that is good in it so really good. I loved, shall always love her.

She saw in Sand—in her bold idealism, in her distributed affections, in the baseline benevolence that underpinned her defiance of convention—a mirror of how she herself wanted to be seen. In a passage permeated by a subconscious self-defense, Fuller adds:

She needs no defence, but only to be understood, for she has bravely acted out her nature, and always with good intentions. She might have loved one man permanently, if she could have found one contemporary with her who could interest and command her throughout her range; but there was hardly any possibility of that, for such a person. Thus she has naturally changed the object of her affections several times . . . and I am sure her generous heart has not failed to draw some rich drops from every kind of wine-press.

She left feeling about George Sand the way Maria Mitchell had felt about Mary Somerville—filled with affectionate admiration greater than she had felt for any other woman, tethered to a sister planet by a shared sun.

But Fuller's most momentous encounter in Paris was with the revolutionary Adam Mickiewicz—Poland's greatest poet, exiled in France, revered by his compatriots as a prophet of a new age of liberty. Mickiewicz, eleven years her senior, had introduced Emerson's writing in Paris with the same ardor with which Fuller had introduced Goethe in New England. He had just been fired from the Parisian university where he taught for challenging the authority of the Church. When they met, she immediately felt "a deeper-founded mental connection," but also recognized an aliveness beyond the cerebral—the very thing she had accused Emerson of lacking. In Mickiewicz, she found "the intellect and passions in due proportion for a full and healthy human being." He further impressed her with his devotion to women's emancipation—he had read *Woman* and invited Fuller to a gathering of his young acolytes, to whom he proclaimed that the era of women's liberation had arrived and Margaret Fuller was its chief action-prophet. He would describe her as "the only one to whom it has been given to touch that which is most decisive in today's world and to comprehend in advance the world to come."

Most magnetizing of all, however, was the way he spoke to her—with the respect of a kindred intellect and an embodied candor uncottoned in the artifice of propriety. Mickiewicz urged Fuller to confront the parts of life and of herself that she had left unexplored behind pretexts of moral rectitude—the disembodied "lonely position" she had lauded in *Woman* as the choice of "saints and geniuses" who had risen above life "undisturbed by the pressure of near ties." After their momentous first meeting, he wrote to her:

> You have acquired the right to know and maintain the rights and obligations, the hopes and exigencies of virginity. For you, the first step in your deliverance and in the deliverance of your sex . . . is to know if it is permitted to you to remain a virgin.

There is a curious logical parallel between Mickiewicz's sentiment and the question Albert Camus would pose a century later in one of the most piercing and profound opening passages in literature:

> There is but one truly serious philosophical problem, and that is suicide. Judging whether life is or is not worth living amounts to answering the fundamental question of philosophy. All the rest—whether or not the world has three dimensions, whether the mind has nine or twelve categories—comes afterwards.

A disembodied life, Mickiewicz seems to suggest, is no life at all—Fuller must decide whether an embodied life is worth living.

With her chronic conflation of admiration and attraction, Fuller felt for a time that she might be falling in love with this impassioned intellect. Whether he would become the object of her awakening to the sensual dimensions of love was yet to be seen, but he certainly became its catalyst. In a twenty-four-page letter to her American travel companion, Rebecca Spring, Fuller articulated the first glimmers of that awakening:

> You ask me whether I love [Mickiewicz]. I answer, he affected me like music or the richest landscape; my heart beat with joy that he at once felt beauty in me. . . . Still, I do not know but I might love still better to-morrow. I have never yet loved any human being so well as the music of Beethoven, yet at present I am indifferent to it. There has been a time when I thought of nothing but Michael Angelo, yet the other day I felt hardly inclined to look on the forms his living hand had traced on the roof of the Sistine. But when I loved either of these great souls I abandoned myself wholly to it; I did not calculate. I shall do so in life if I love enough.

Fuller soon left Paris for Rome. "Those have not lived who have not seen Rome," she would later write to Emerson from the city that became her final home. Within months of her fiery correspondence with Mickiewicz, she would come to see him not as love object but as guru and confidant who guides her to the version of herself that learns to "love still better"—love that another would reap.

This is the paradox of transformative experience: Because our imagination is bounded by our existing templates of how the world as we know it works, we fail to anticipate the greatest transformations—the events and encounters so unmoored from the familiar that they transfigure our map of reality and propel us into a wholly novel mode of being. This is as true of civilizations—the ancient Greeks could never have fathomed the miraculous cascade of inventions that let me read Plato on a digital tablet via wireless Internet aboard an airplane—as it is of our individual imaginations.

All her life, Margaret Fuller had encountered those who would be of consequence to her—her intellectual heroes, her collaborators and champions, the objects of her infatuations—either through formal letters of introduction by existing friends or through informal circles of acquaintanceship. Our choices shape our circumstances, which in turn further cement the foundation from which we make our choices. What Fuller imagined she wanted in an ideal partner was a composite of the traits she most cherished in the various people she knew—Emerson's independence of thought, the sweetness of Anna Barker's adoration, Sam Ward's worldliness and intellectual curiosity, Mickiewicz's impassioned candor. No one person contained all she yearned for, nor was she able to imagine being fulfilled by anything different—different not by degree but by kind—from these familiar incomplete satisfactions.

We navigate the unknown frontiers of the social universe through a sextant of existing relationships—nearly every new person we meet is within only a few degrees of separation from someone we already know. But every once in a while, pure chance intercedes to remind us that whatever structures of control we may put into place, however much we may mistake the illusion of choice for the fact of choice, randomness is the reigning monarch of the universe.

11

BETWEEN SINEW AND SPIRIT

On the evening of April 1, 1847, Holy Thursday, as Maria Mitchell's comet is hurtling toward Earth, Margaret Fuller meets by chance the man with whom she would spend the remainder of her days—a man with no direct link to anyone in her cosmos of connections, unlike anyone she ever thought she desired. "The Heart has many Doors," Emily Dickinson would write. We bolt most of them with our preconceptions.

Fuller would keep their relationship a secret until just before her death, so the exact circumstances of their first encounter are shrouded in the haze of her self-protective perfidy. Here are the most probable facts gleaned from her carefully controlled revelations to a handful of close friends:

Margaret had lost her way in Saint Peter's Cathedral—perhaps the only person in the crowd of thousands more enchanted by Michelangelo's art on the ceiling of the Sistine Chapel than by the Holy Week services. Swallowed by the chaos of worshippers, she wandered in agitated disorientation, looking for her American traveling companions. Across the grand vault, a tall, slender young Italian espied the visibly flustered foreigner and offered his aid.

Giovanni Angelo Ossoli peers out of the sole surviving daguerreotype of him with calm, dark, deep-set eyes anchored by a stately Grecian nose, the femininity of his delicate features offset by a trim mustache and thick, level eyebrows that face each other with the subtle upfurrow of questioning alertness. Something about his air of benevolent composure and quiet self-possession with an edge of melancholy must have spoken to Fuller, for she took his arm in the middle of the crowded cathedral. The two proceeded to look for her friends—in vain. By the time they relinquished the search, the evening had spilled into night. Ossoli—as Margaret would call him from that day to her last—offered to escort her home, even though his own abode lay in the opposite direction. He spoke no English and she had only a rudimentary grasp of Italian, so whatever animated the forty-five-minute walk, it wasn't the familiar intellectual repartee of her walks with Waldo or the emotional effusions of her travels with Caroline. Ossoli, eleven years younger than Fuller and motherless since the age of six, had no sense of her cultural stature and couldn't admire her for her work, of which he could not have read a single word. Something else magnetized his nature to hers and hers to his—something as uncerebral and ineffable as the effect of a Beethoven sonata.

Nine days after the encounter at St. Peter's, in a letter to Rebecca and Marcus Spring, she penned her most succinct and self-aware romantic history:

> I have never sought love as a passion—it has always come to me as an angel bearing some good tidings. I have wished to welcome the messenger noble, but never to detain it, or cling with a weak personality to a tie which had ceased to bind the soul. I believe I should always do the same, however I might suffer from loss or void in the intervals of love. . . . I do not know whether I have loved at all in the sense of oneness, but I have loved enough to feel the joys of presence, the pangs of absence, the sweetness of hope, and the chill of disappointment. More than once my heart has bled, and my health has suffered from these things but mentally I have always found myself the gainer, always younger and more noble.

Disappointment itself can become the drug that perpetuates the addictive cycle of ill-fated obsessions. These elated intellectual infatuations with persons of genius, followed by abysses of despair at the lack of reciprocity, were Fuller's single most consistent emotional experience. Not yet ready to relinquish this familiar pattern, she was eager to fill the "void in the intervals of love" once more.

"I have not yet formed any friendship of the mind," she reported of her time in Rome in a letter to her brother penned two weeks after she met Ossoli, who was a poor candidate for the patterned part. Fuller had already cast another actor in it: the young American painter Thomas Hicks, whom she met through that degrees-of-separation swing of her social sextant—Mickiewicz made the introduction. In the twenty-three-year-old artist, who had left America for Europe the year she published *Woman*, the thirty-six-year-old Fuller found a ready screen onto which to project her templated fantasy. But the cycle contracted faster than any previous, and she was soon contending with the "chilling disappointment" she knew so well. In a letter from April 23, addressing him as "Dear youth," she indicted Hicks with a fickleness of heart for failing to make time for her—"I can always find time to see any one I wish to; it seems to me it is the same with every one." In that part-blameful, part-beseeching way of the jilted, she appealed to him to see the meeting of souls she felt they shared:

> You are the only one whom I have seen here in whose eye I recognized one of my own kindred. I want to know and to love you and to have you love me; you said you had no friendliness of nature but that is not true; you are precisely one to need the music, the recognition of kindred minds. How can you let me pass you by, without full and free communication. I do not understand it, unless you are occupied by some other strong feeling. Very soon I must go from here, do not let me go without giving me some of your life. . . . I wanted to speak to you with frank affection, and I could not. Something prevents— what is it? Answer.

Taking nearly two weeks to answer, Hicks pronounced himself unfit for Margaret's ardor in a sorrowful and self-pitying letter:

> I would like to tell you all about myself, you would then see that there is but little fire in the hut and that could you enter you would find but a few embers on the hearth of a lonely ambitious man. . . .

You speak of my youth; is it by years then that *life* is measured? Do you not perceive that my heart has grown grey?

Blackened by disappointment in the young artist, Fuller—whose boundary between her personal and professional passions was as porous as that between the intellectual and the erotic—renounced art itself. In a despondent letter to William Channing back home, she declared for the first time her shifting focus from literature and the arts to politics and social reform:

Art is not important to me now. I like only what little I find that is transcendentally good. . . . I take interest in the state of the people, their manners, the state of the race in them. I see the future dawning. . . . I must be born again.

This shift in foci may have been what drew her thoughts back to the young Ossoli, who lacked both intellectual and artistic refinement but was passionately devoted to the cause of Italian unification and independence from Austrian rule—a cause in the noble ideals of which Fuller saw "the most striking contrast to our own country." They began spending time together, first because Ossoli provided an invaluable inside perspective for Fuller's journalistic work, and then because she sensed while with him something arrestingly novel: an attentive presence that seemed to cherish her company not for her mind or accomplishments but simply for who she was. He appeared to have the answer to the question she had asked of the open sky all those years ago: "How is it that I seem to be this Margaret Fuller? What does it mean?"

The seven weeks that followed were filled with the private mystery of early love. But two facts do survive: that one midspring day, Ossoli proposed marriage to Margaret; and that she declined it. In her public writings, she had dismissed marriage as "a contract of convenience and utility"; in her private letters, she had escalated the indictment to a "corrupt social contract." Quite apart from her reservations about marriage and any qualms she may have had about their age difference, she was unable to let whatever feelings Ossoli awakened eclipse her cerebral unease at the fact that, despite being governed by a native sweetness and an unfaltering moral compass, he was unschooled and unlettered. Nearly two years later, just before her death, Fuller would finally confide in her sister:

> Our meeting was singular, fateful I may say. Very soon he offered me his hand through life, but I never dreamed I should take it. I loved him, and felt very unhappy to leave him; but the connection seemed so every way unfit, I did not hesitate a moment.

With this conflicted but unhesitating conclusiveness, Fuller left Rome in the late spring of 1847 and set out to travel through northern Italy. But this "exceedingly delicate person," as she would describe Ossoli, had impressed himself upon her soul—this man "so sweet in his disposition . . . so harmonious [in] his whole nature," who had "not the slightest tinge of self-love," who was not self-satisfied or encrusted with the shell of narcissism that encases insecurity but simply "happy in himself," buoyed by "the purity and simple strength of his character." She would later write to a friend in America:

> My relation to Ossoli has been like retiring to one of those gentle, lovely places in the woods—something of the violet has been breathed into my life, and will never pass away.

In his theory of color and emotion, published the year of Fuller's birth, Goethe had limned violet as a hue that, though of an "active character" and "unquiet feeling," one can "find a point to rest in."

Two years after the chance encounter that brought her and Ossoli together, Fuller would capture the uncharted connection at the heart of their bond:

> My love for Ossoli is most pure and tender, nor has any one, except my mother or little children, loved me so genuinely as he does. To some, I have been obliged to make myself known; others have loved me with a mixture of fancy and enthusiasm, excited by my talent at embellishing life. But Ossoli loves me from simple affinity;—he loves to be with me, and to serve and soothe me.

Years earlier, just after her thirty-fourth birthday and midway through writing *Woman*, Fuller had despaired in her journal:

> With the intellect I always have, always shall, overcome; but that is not half of the work. The life, the life! O, my God! shall the life never be sweet?

In Ossoli's sweetness, she saw an invitation to "the life, the life!" In a letter to one of her few Italian intimates, Fuller painted him as a simple man of confident constancy and unambivalent affinities:

> He has very little of what is called intellectual development, but unspoiled instincts, affections pure and constant, and a quiet sense of duty, which, to me, who have seen much of the great faults in characters of enthusiasm and genius, seems of highest value.

She was beginning to realize that no amount of genius ever compensates for, nor excuses, a paucity of kindness, integrity, and unconflicted devotion.

Meanwhile, Waldo, unwitting of Margaret's transformation of heart, beckoned to her from England, where he had just returned on a lecture tour: "O Sappho, Sappho, friend of mine"—an allusion to the ancient Greek poet laureate of love, exiled to Italy.

What Emerson didn't know, Mickiewicz did. The Polish poet encouraged Fuller to embrace every aspect of her being—to enact and embody the very rights and freedoms she had so spiritedly advocated in *Woman*. In a benevolent bomb of a letter, he exhorted her:

> You have pleaded the liberty of woman in a masculine and frank style. Live and act, as you write. . . . I saw you, with all your knowledge and your imagination and all your literary reputation, living in bondage worse than a servant. You have persuaded yourself that all you need is to express your feelings and ideas in books. You existed like a ghost that whispers to the living its plans and desires, no longer able to realize them itself. Do not forget that even in your private life as a woman you have rights to maintain. Emerson says rightly: give all for love, but this love must not be that of the shepherds of Florian nor

that of schoolboys and German ladies. The relationships which suit you are those which develop and free your spirit, responding to the legitimate needs of your organism and leaving you free at all times.

Mickiewicz misquotes the line from Emerson's debut poetry collection, published the year Maria Mitchell discovered her comet—the poem he invokes contains the lines "give all to love" and "leave all for love," but Mickewicz's subtle syntactic revision in "give all *for* love" yields an entirely different semantic overtone. It is highly probable that Emerson's poem was influenced by Rumi. "Gamble everything for love if you are a true human being," the Persian poet and Sufi mystic had written six centuries earlier. Emerson had discovered Rumi and Hafiz through German translations—including, notably, those by Goethe, who had introduced Persian poetry into the literary consciousness of the European Romantics. *The Dial* was the first American journal to publish the work of the great Persian poets and Emerson the first American to give public lectures on Persian poetry.

Fuller responded defensively, telling Mickiewicz that she had found his letter "harsh." But he persisted in his sentiment, which sprang from a wish for her to flourish as a complete human being:

Try to get this inner life lodged and established in your body. . . . You still live spiritually in the society of Shakespeare, Schiller, and Byron. Literature is not the whole of life.

No one had spoken to Fuller with such candor before, nor had she ever allowed that her sinews might be as worthy of life as her cerebrations. The questions Mickiewicz raised echoed her own with a bellowing urgency—questions about what love necessitates as a lived reality rather than a mental abstraction, about how rigid ideals can trammel the delicious fluidity of real life, about what a "fulness of being" really means. These questions began to erode her veneration of intellectual achievement as the only ground of self-actualization. For years, she had nurtured the discomfiting suspicion that the life of the mind might be inseparable from the life of the body, the cerebral inseparable from the sensual. Now she had the chance to confront it directly. Perhaps she reread an old letter from Sam Ward, which had so unsettled her that she had copied it into her journal—a letter that had admonished her that only those who don't know the fullness of sexual love could dismiss it as inferior to Platonic love. Sam had written to Margaret just after he and Anna Barker had fused the passions of the heart with those of the body:

> I, too, once knew and recognized the possibility of Platonic affection. It is possible to those who have never passed the line. Before that, all the higher class of emotion all the nobler views of life exist; but in a shape that seems sublimated and idealized to the more experienced: to those who *have* passed that line X X X X, the higher emotions and the passions are apt to be always afterward inextricably commingled.

In October 1847, with Maria Mitchell's comet blazing across the sky, Margaret Fuller returned to Rome—and to Ossoli—with "a flood of joy," surrendering to "a kind of passive, childlike well-being." With revolution in the air, they "passed the line" and became lovers.

Fuller chose to keep their metamorphic relationship a secret. She worried that it would cast a shadow on her public image as a champion of emancipation, but the primary reason was Ossoli's family—a long lineage of fallen nobility employed by the Catholic Church. His elderly father and all three of his older brothers were in the service of the Pope. The youngest son's radical leftist politics were already a point of combustible friction within the family, on whose financial support the vocationless Ossoli relied, but entering a public relationship with a Protestant foreigner thirteen years his senior would have meant expulsion from the family.

Fuller did, however, give clues to the transformative electricity of their union in her letters to a handful of intimate friends. The way she described Rome on the cusp of revolution in a letter to Caroline Sturgis could double as a description of her union with Ossoli:

It must be inhaled wholly, with the yielding of the whole heart. It is really something transcendent, both spirit and body.

Days before Christmas, Margaret suspected with a shock that she might be pregnant. Nearly thirty-eight and in chronically frail health, she doubted her body would survive childbirth. Abortion, legal in America and often resorted to by married women who couldn't endure another pregnancy, was a capital crime in papal Rome. What she wished her brother on the first day of the new year contained her wish for herself—"a year that may heal the wounds of the past and ripen seed for better joys." But her uncertain future and her precarious condition filled her with premonitions of doom. With her pregnancy a closely guarded secret, she punctuated her letters home with glimmers of her dread but withheld its cause. Margaret shared with her brother an ominous dream in which he visited her grave. "My health will never be good for any thing to sustain me in any work of value," she told him cryptically, not specifying the reason she had been "not well at all" for the past two weeks.

Accustomed to sharing the full expanse of her experience with her nearest correspondents, she now painted only rough outlines. "The air presses with such a weight as to destroy the appetite," she told one friend, "and everything I do eat hurts me." She couldn't reveal that acute morning sickness, rather than atmospheric pressure, was the cause of her infirmity. In another veiled allusion to her pregnancy, she wrote to Emerson of her gloomy "incubus of the future."

Adding to the weight of her worries was the sinking sense of being severed from those who had once constellated her universe most brightly. She hadn't heard from William Channing since her departure for Europe and hadn't received a single line from Caroline Sturgis in more than a year—a silence that particularly troubled her, for she knew Caroline had married and was composing a new life-chapter herself. Margaret sorrowed at being written out. "It will be very strange to me to call you by another name," she wrote to her, "but I suppose it will be necessary," then signed her letter "Ever dear Carrie yours in love."

When she finally did hear from Caroline, three weeks into the secret pregnancy, Margaret replied with a bittersweet reflection on their parted yet parallel fates, part chosen and part chanced into, imbued with the abiding question of love's constancy and durability that had preoccupied Margaret since her first infatuation:

> The friendships I had paid for with so much heart's blood, so many thoughts in the long past, seemed to flee from me, and I lost courage for the ties at present. Now comes your letter and gives me the dear certainty that there is love, is realization, hope and faith in your life. At present you have really cast your lot with another person, live in a house I suppose; sleep and wake in unison with humanity; an island flowers in the river of your life.
>
> I cannot say anything about it from my present self. Yet permanent love for the same object does not seem to me impossible, though once I thought, I felt it and have ceased to feel. At any rate the union of two natures for a time is so great.

Are we to despair or rejoice over the fact that even the greatest loves exist only "for a time"? The time scales are elastic, contracting and expanding with the depth and magnitude of each love, but they are always finite—like books, like lives, like the universe itself. The triumph of love is in the courage and integrity with which we inhabit the transcendent transience that binds two people for the time it binds them, before letting go with equal courage and integrity. Fuller's exclamation upon seeing the paintings of Correggio for the first time, overcome with beauty she had not known before, radiates a larger truth about the human heart: "Sweet soul of love! I should weary of you, too; but it was glorious that day." And yet some fragment of the magnet that once pulled two people together always lodges itself in each of their hearts. Fuller knew this, for she wrote to James Freeman Clarke in the final year of her life:

> Spirits that have once been sincerely united and tended together a sacred flame, never become entirely stranger to one another's life.

When the attention of one is turned upon the other, a responsive thrill is felt.

Margaret must have wondered whether all the ways in which Ossoli was unlike her former fixations added up to an assurance that their bond would outlast the fleeting affections of yore. With Caroline, newlywed and on the conventional track to motherhood herself, she could share the anguishing ambivalence that colored her view of the future, at once full of dread and of obstinate, dignified optimism:

> I enter upon a sphere of my destiny so difficult that I at present see no way out, except through the gate of death. It is useless to write of it; you are at a distance and cannot help me—whether accident or angel will, I have no intimation. I have no reason to hope that I shall not reap what I have sown, and do not. Yet how I shall endure it I cannot guess; it is all a dark and sad enigma.

At watershed moments of upheaval and transformation, we anticipate with terror the absence of the familiar parts of life and of ourselves that are being washed away by the current of change. But we fail to envision the unfamiliar gladnesses and gratifications the new tide would bring, the unfathomed presences, for our imaginations are bounded by our experience. The unknown awakens in us a reptilian dread that plays out with the same ferocity on scales personal, societal, and civilizational, whether triggered by a new life-chapter or a new political regime or a new world order. It is the same dread to which the Inquisition gave shape and sinew in punishing all who dared to consider that the universe might be far vaster and more mysterious than the consolations of mythology had preached for millennia. To be a revolutionary is to be in possession of an imagination capable of leaping across the frontier of the familiar to envision a new order in which what is gained eclipses the ill-serving comforts of what is lost.

12

BETWEEN ART AND LIFE

As Margaret Fuller is dreading the prospects of her future, the air of revolution is swarming around her, saturated with intoxicating optimism at the prospect of religious freedom, independence from the Austrian Empire, and a democratic government. Already deeply invested in the Risorgimento, she took up Rome's republican cause as her own, perhaps because it provided such a buoyant counterpoint to her personal despair. "*My* Italy," she would soon write, envisioning her part in the country's liberation "either as an actor or historian." On the pages of the *Tribune*, she held up the revolution's idealism as a model for America, failing in her own democratic ideals, to rise to. In a letter whose searing prescience stuns a century and a half later, she wrote to Emerson:

> My own country is at present spoiled by prosperity, stupid with the lust of gain, soiled by crime in its willing perpetration of slavery, shamed by an unjust war [the Mexican-American War over the proposed annexation of Texas as a slave state]. . . . In Europe, amid the teachings of adversity, a nobler spirit is struggling—a spirit which cheers and animates mine.

Bedeviled by constant headaches and nausea during the first trimester of her pregnancy, she was able to keep down only boiled rice. "I am tired and woe-worn; often, in the bed, I wish I could weep my life away." She could take no exercise as unremitting rain poured from the wintry skies for forty days. To Fuller, trapped threadbare in body and spirit inside a small apartment that received almost no light in the shadow of the tall neighboring houses, the downpour may have felt like the primordial rains that began teeming down when the infant Earth cooled and the saturated clouds above it cracked open—torrential floods that spanned months, years, centuries, filling the depressions in Earth's crust with the primeval oceans in whose womb life emerged from nonlife.

Many years earlier, Fuller had shone a hopeful sidewise gleam at motherhood in the pages of her journal: "Surely a being born wholly of my being, would not let me lie so still and cold in lonely sadness." Now, with her surety shaken, she steadied herself with work and continued to report in her *Tribune* columns on the upheaval she believed would lead "not merely to revolution but to radical reform." Fuller chose to remain in Rome, pregnant and unprotected by citizenship. She was soon the last American journalist remaining in the conflict-torn Eternal City, watching through her small handheld telescope "the smoke of every discharge, the flash of the bayonets" fired between the papal government's guard and the freedom fighters, listening to the leaders of the revolution give electric speeches aglow with "celestial fire."

Emerson gleaned little from the shadowy outlines she had painted for him in her letters. He must have sensed that she was on the cusp of a profound transformation—one he feared would take her permanently away from him. Only with Margaret far away, perched on the precipice of a new life that would render her irretrievable, was Waldo finally able to consider the union from which he had once shrunk—perhaps precisely because, in no longer being a viable possibility, it was a safe fantasy. But even now, his latent answer was in the form of an elegiac question:

> Shall we not yet—you, you, also,—as we used to talk, build up a reasonable society in that naked unatmospheric land [of Concord] and effectually serve one another?

But Margaret had floated too far into the improbable atmosphere of her new life—a life she came to inhabit, sometime in the spring of 1848, as Margaret Fuller Ossoli.

No marriage certificate has ever been unearthed. If Fuller and Ossoli did in fact marry, oblique evidence from her letters suggests that it would have taken place in April 1848, when she was five months pregnant, a year after their chance encounter at St. Peter's Cathedral. The document she began using to traverse the gates of revolution-ravaged Rome identified her as Margherita Ossoli, an Italian citizen born in 1820. Ten years were scraped from her real age and her nationality was altered. Why should her married name be any more factual? Half a century earlier, after renouncing sexual passion as complicit in women's oppression, Mary Wollstonecraft had become pregnant by the American expatriate George Imlay— her first lover—and given birth to a daughter while living in war-torn Paris. She, too, had left her homeland to join another country's national cause. Despite her opposition to marriage, Wollstonecraft consented to being registered as the father's wife in order for her and the baby to have the safeguard of American citizenship—many of her compatriots in Paris had no such protection and were either arrested or guillotined. Imlay authorized her to conduct business on his behalf and referred to her in letters as "Mrs. Mary Imlay, my best friend and wife," but no legal marriage had actually taken place.

Fuller's father had greatly admired the political and intellectual daring of Wollstonecraft's foundational treatise, *A Vindication of the Rights of Woman,* but his admiration was sullied by his disdain for how "discountenanced" the author had been for losing her virginity and becoming pregnant out of wedlock. Perhaps Margaret inherited his ambivalent admiration for Wollstonecraft and saw in it a cautionary foreboding of her own public image if she remained unmarried while pregnant. Or perhaps she simply followed Wollstonecraft's practical lead and sought the civic protection of marriage amid a revolution to which she belonged in spirit but not in citizenship. Whether or not Fuller and Ossoli ever actually married, for the short remainder of her life Margaret Fuller would sign every document, letter, and byline as Margaret Fuller Ossoli.

Margaret confided at first only in Mickiewicz and eventually in Thomas Hicks, but she couldn't help coding revelations into her letters home. Upon receiving news of the birth of Emerson's second son, she wrote back: "Children, with all their faults, seem to me the best thing we have."

Meanwhile, the skies over the revolution in which Fuller was now so invested darkened. Only a year earlier, Italians had celebrated Pope Pius IX as the prophet of liberty after his decision to free political prisoners. Fuller herself had lauded him to her readers as a noble man with "his heart upon doing something solid for the benefit of Man." Now, Pius thundered treason from the Vatican, retracting his support for the Risorgimento and urging the Roman people to abide by the authority of the Austrian Empire. Unrest by a betrayed populace flooded into Rome as a tide of revolution swept across all of Europe, beginning in France and now culminating in Italy.

Fuller resolved to remain in the Eternal City. "I shall return possessed of a great history," she told William Channing. "Perhaps I shall be called to act." Declining the touring Emerson's invitation to journey with him back to America, she hinted at the human motives coeval with the political ideals in her decision to stay: "Imperfect as love is, I want human beings to love, as I suffocate without." As the seasons turned, Fuller exulted in the combined force of transformation in another letter home:

> The Gods walk on earth, here in the Italian Spring. . . . Such beauty is irresistible. But ah dearest, the drama of my fate is very deep, and the ship plunges deeper as it rises higher. You would be amazed, I believe, could you know how different is my present phase of life, from that in which you knew me; but you would love me no less; for it is still the same planet that shews such different climes. . . . I am enlarging the circle of my experiences. . . . I have done, and may still do, things that may invoke censure; but in the foundation of character, in my aims, I am always the same.

What makes a person "the same" person across life's tectonic upheavals of circumstance and character? Amid the chaos and decay toward which the universe inclines, we grasp for stability and permanence by trying to carve out a solid sense of self in our blink of existence. But there is no solidity. Every quark of every atom of every cell in your body had been replaced since the time of your first conscious memory, your first word, your first kiss. In the act of living, you come to dream different dreams, value different values, love different loves. In a sense, you are reborn with each new experience. What, then, made Margaret "the same" person as the girl who long ago had asked into the stormy skies: "How is it that I seem to be this Margaret Fuller? What does it mean?"

Questions of meaning are a function of human life, but they are not native to the universe itself—meaning is not what we find, but what we create with the lives we live and the seeds we plant and the organizing principles according to which we sculpt our personhood. Margaret Fuller's constancy of selfhood sprang from her willingness to accept all of her former selves and exclude none. The Russian nesting doll of her character included the child prodigy with the demanding father whose withheld affections she sought to earn through intellectual achievement, the resolute idealist who held humanity accountable to its highest potential, the perennially dissatisfied romantic cycling through half-requited loves, the writer who with the lone star of her byline beckoned the reader to think and feel unthought thoughts and unfelt feelings, the American who thought in German and wrote love letters in Italian, and now the mother-to-be uncowering before the competing probabilities of death and wholly novel happiness.

At the end of May, as she entered her final trimester, Fuller decided to take respite from the dangerous tensions of Rome. Before leaving, she had Thomas Hicks paint a portrait of her before he headed back to America. Seated on a red velvet bench in a Venetian portico with the dusky ocean behind her, a pale Fuller swelling with new life gazes into some invisible world of her own with melancholy strength. "Say to those I leave behind that I was willing to die," she instructed Hicks in a letter of last wishes as she weighed the possibility of perishing by childbirth or war. "I have wished to be natural and true, but the world was not in harmony with me." Then, while Ossoli remained in Rome as part of the freedom fighters' Civic Guard, she made the trying three-day journey to a small mountain village, where she was to rest her body and apply her mind to the project she would later call "what is most valuable to me if I live of any thing"—her chronicle of the Italian revolution.

On September 5, 1848, in a willow-hedged cottage by a rapid river in the mountains of Italy, with her maybe-husband by her side, Margaret Fuller Ossoli gave birth to Angelo Eugene Philip Ossoli— baby Nino, as the new parents would come to call him, short for Angelino. That she survived the birth at all was miracle enough for Margaret, so she was hardly surprised when her body reached its limit and failed to produce milk. As Ossoli returned to Rome to resume his duties in the Risorgimento, she hired a local wet nurse. Throughout her time in Europe, Fuller had struggled to make ends meet, writing tirelessly for the *Tribune* for only $10 per column and constantly negotiating various loans and literary advances. Now she was once again the sole breadwinner for a family—for the baby, for the wet nurse and her own infant, and for Ossoli, who remained unemployed and had relinquished support from his father on account of their political differences. She wrote to William Channing:

> I have these two terrible drawbacks, frequent failure of health and want of money, but the first I should not mind, if it were not for the latter. Ah! my dear William, what a vast good would money be to me now, and I cannot get it. This is too hard, so many people have it to whom it is of no use, and to me it would give happiness, days and months for real life. I may complain to you, as you have none to give me; it is some relief to mourn.

Fuller had long relinquished the Transcendentalist disdain for material means, having poked fun at it five years earlier in a letter to her dependent brother, in which she enclosed some of her meager literary earnings:

> Even your frugality does not enable you wholly to dispense with the circulating medium you so much despise and whose use, when you have thought more deeply on these subjects, you will find to have been indispensable to the production of the arts, of literature and all that distinguishes civilized man. It is abused like all good things, but without it you would not have had your Horace and Virgil stimulated by whose society you read the woods and fields. . . .

In the mountain cottage, which she rented for nine dollars a month, she could feast on "a great basket of grapes" for one cent and a day's worth of figs and peaches for five. She didn't hesitate to let her brother know, at the end of a three-page letter, that getting a single page to him cost her eighty cents. In another letter to him penned in the first months of her pregnancy, as she was facing the reality of providing for her new makeshift family, Fuller crystallized her sober philosophy of making a living in a life of purpose:

> It is not reasonable to expect the world should pay us in money for what *we are* but for what we can do *for* it. Society pays in money for the practical talent exerted for its benefit, to the thinker, as such, only the tribute of materials for thought. . . . We cannot have every thing; we cannot have even many things; the choice is only between a better and worser.

Fuller was now convinced that the most she could do for society lay in her chronicle of the revolution she saw as an exalted reach for better over worse, with implications not only for Italy but for the whole of humanity in upholding the ideals of liberty and equality she had long considered vital to human flourishing. In early November, not without ambivalence, Fuller decided to leave the newborn Nino with his wet nurse and return to Rome—a journey on which she narrowly escaped death in crossing a river raging with the floods of the rainy season.

Despite the gloomy weather and the political tumult, Margaret was overjoyed to return to the Eternal City. She took a sunny new apartment atop a house with direct view of the Pope's palace, occupied on the stories below by "a frightful Russian princess with moustaches, and a footman who ties her bonnet for her," and "a fat English lady, with a fine carriage, who gives all her money to the church" and who tends on her balcony a flower garden with many birds and has "an immense black cat," addressed by both husband and wife as "Amoretto"—Little Love.

From Rome, Margaret sent her mother a long, cryptic message designed to alleviate anxiety but likely to only perturb any parent:

> Of other circumstances which complicate my position I cannot write. Were you here, I would confide in you fully, and have more than once, in the silence of the night, recited to you those most strange and romantic chapters in the story of my sad life. . . . In earlier days, I dreamed of doing and being much, but now am content with the Magdalen to rest my pleas hereon, *"She has loved much."*

Margaret was ordinarily unsentimental about and with her mother, having since her girlhood considered her intellectually incurious and meek. Now, perhaps seized with the kindred tenderness of motherhood herself, she adds:

> The thought of you, the knowledge of your angelic nature, is always one of my greatest supports. Happy those who have such a mother!

Shortly after her return to Rome, the Pope's gate was nearly burned down, his newly appointed prime minister stabbed in the back before entering the papal palace, and his confessor shot after firing from a window at the crowd of protesters below. Fuller heard the gunfire from her apartment. The following morning, she wrote to her mother:

> Never feel any apprehension for my safety from such causes . . . I am on the conquering side. These events have, to me, the deepest interest. These days are what I always longed for,—were I only free from private care!

She illustrates her devotion to Italy with a line from Byron: "O Rome, *my* country, city of the soul!" She would repeat and amplify the sentiment over many letters, always underlining the possessive pronoun with a proud sense of ownership. In one, she writes:

> O Rome, *my* country, bad as the winter damp is, lazy as the climate makes me, I would rather live here than anywhere else in the world.

To her mother, she writes:

> Of course, I wish to see America again; but in my own time, when I am ready, and not to weep over hopes destroyed and projects unfulfilled. . . . If I came home at this moment, I should feel as if forced to leave my own house, my own people, and the hour which I had always longed for. If I do come in this way. . . . Do not feel anxious about me. Some higher power leads me through strange, dark, thorny paths, broken at times by glades opening down into prospects of sunny beauty, into which I am not permitted to enter. If God disposes for us, it is not for nothing. This I can say, my heart is in some respects better, it is kinder and more humble. Also, my mental acquisitions have certainly been great, however inadequate to my desires.

Like any keen observer of character, Fuller was intensely interested in the conditions that bring forth the dormant potentialities of human nature. In her literary writings, Fuller afforded a generosity of interpretation that encouraged her readers to rise above the impetuousness of instant condemnation, inviting a tolerance for the flaws—even in the extreme ancient Greek notion of the tragic flaw—that inhere in the character of every creator, every human being. Now she was forced to confront a former hero's failure of character inexcusable by any generosity of interpretation. The Pope whom Rome had once celebrated as the prophet of liberty and justice had become "the Demon with his cohort of traitors." He had revealed himself to be a softhearted but morally spineless man—at the moment of truth, when he was called upon to uphold the rights and values of his people against the tyrannical regime of the Austrian Empire, he had acquiesced to authority. A week after the prime

minister's assassination, the Pope fled the city through a secret pas-
sageway, disguised as a priest. Fuller was bitterly disappointed in
this man "now abandoned and despised by both parties"—a man
who "shrinks from the danger, and shuts the door to pray quietly in
his closet, whilst he knows the cardinals are misusing his name to
violate his pledges." The task of moral courage now fell wholly on
the revolutionaries, who awakened in Fuller some of her own dormant nature: "It is a time such as I always dreamed of; and that fire
burns in the hearts of men around me which can keep me warm."

Meanwhile, accustomed to sharing the innermost truths of her
life with those she loved, she struggled to keep her son and her
maybe-husband a secret, making ominous admissions that her "private fortunes are dark and tangled" but not saying how or why. She
told William Channing: "I do not write you of myself because there
is too much to tell. There are things I long for you to know but in
the right way." The letter she wrote to her brother, finally revealing the facts of her new life, she destroyed before mailing. Instead,
she sent him a sealed envelope to pass on to Caroline, whose new
address she did not have, confessing to her instead. Without shading in the details, she painted her reticulated reality in a letter to
William Channing:

> I have lived in a much more full and true way than was possible in our
> country, and each day has been so rich in joys and pains, actions and
> sufferings, to say nothing of themes of observation, I have never yet
> had time to know the sum total—to reflect. My strength has been
> taxed to the uttermost to live.

Over the next few months, Fuller made several trips to be with
her son in the mountains. But she kept returning to Rome, now
wholly vacated by foreigners, to complete her chronicle of the liberation yet to be won. Meanwhile, nearly every other revolution in
Europe had either been defeated or had lost momentum under the
scattered pull of disorganized, competing internal forces.

There was hope, though, for Rome's Risorgimento. For the first
time in history, a local government was established in the city and a

procession took to the streets under a new *tricolore* flag. The Pope threatened that anyone in support of the new Constitutional Assembly, which included Garibaldi and Napoleon's nephew, would be excommunicated from the Church—an ultimatum that only further incensed the populace. At one o'clock in the morning of February 8, 1849, the Assembly proclaimed the inception of a new sovereign nation-state. Fuller was elated as she listened to a deputy read aloud the constitution of the new republic, with the capitol's grand bell ringing and the crowd roaring *"Viva la Repubblica, viva Italia!"* after each decree. The first stated:

> The Papacy has fallen in fact and in right from the temporal government of the Roman State.

The third, most resonant with Fuller's lifelong ideals, proclaimed:

> The form of government of the Roman State shall be a pure democracy, and will take the glorious name of the Roman Republic.

With Ossoli now promoted to captain in the Civic Guard and all her foreign friends fled, Fuller witnessed, cheered for, and chronicled the transformation she saw as a triumph not only of the Italian republican cause but of all that is best in the human spirit. In the spring, as accelerating violence thrust the city into a state of siege, she was appointed to head the nursing staff at a hospital on Tiber Island, which Princess Belgioioso—one of the revolution's leading benefactors—had newly allocated to the care of the wounded. Many objected to the presence of women in hospitals, but the princess persevered. Fuller was summoned to report for duty on April 30 "at twelve, if the alarm bell has not rung before," and was tasked with directing and scheduling the team of nurses. It would be years before the social reformer and statistician Florence Nightingale, whom Emily Dickinson would describe as "holy," would do the work that established her as the founder of modern nursing.

Nightingale, like Maria Mitchell and Margaret Fuller, had been raised by a father with the countercultural impulse to give his daughter the same education as he would have given a son. He taught his two daughters—his only children—history, philosophy, mathematics, and statistics from an early age. But it was Florence, named for the Italian city where she was born during her parents' extended honeymoon, who took to this immersion in intellectual life, adamantly defying her mother's attempts to initiate her instead in the domestic work young women were expected to master. "She has taken to mathematics," her sister reported. "She is deep in them and working very hard." Florence was still a young girl when she began engaging in serious political and philosophical debates with her father. By age seventeen, a moral conscience had awakened in her that made the upperclass life expected of her unthinkable. When she announced that she planned to become a nurse, her horrified parents forbade it. But Nightingale pressed on. "I do not expect that love passages will be frequent in her life," her mother wrote with mournful acceptance as she watched her daughter choose the life of service. "No more childish things. No more love. No more marriage," Nightingale herself would resolve in her diary on her thirtieth birthday as she set out to live her values: "Voluntarily to put it out of my power ever to be able to seize the chance of forming for myself a true and rich life would seem to me like suicide." Seven years later, when Julia Ward Howe's husband gave her his diabolical ultimatum, she asked him how he could be so admiring of Florence Nightingale yet so demanding that his own wife surrender to the "extremes distraught and rent" of deadening domesticity. He replied that if Nightingale had been his wife, he would have demanded that she, too, abandon her calling and become a housewife—a *goody*, in the era's colloquialism, short for "goodwife."

"Who would be a goody that could be a genius?" Margaret Fuller had asked in *Woman* the year she left for Europe on the steamship alongside the newlywed Howes.

On a clear starlit night in early November 1847, just after Maria Mitchell discovered her comet, Florence Nightingale arrived in

Rome and took lodging within a stone's throw of where Fuller and Ossoli were becoming lovers. There, she met a honeymooning English politician who had just finished a term as secretary of war. He would soon become a lifelong friend and would procure Nightingale's appointment as head of the volunteer nursing staff during the Crimean War. With her team of thirty-eight women, Nightingale would revolutionize nursing by using hard data to demonstrate the lifesaving power of codified hygiene.

After arriving at a Crimean hospital with floors carpeted with an inch of fecal matter, she undertook a sanitation effort that she instituted, measured, and recorded with equal rigor. Meanwhile, she pressed the disengaged Sanitary Commission for accountability. Nightingale's efforts effected a decline in death rates by 99 percent, from 42 percent to 2 percent—a triumph she knew would save thousands, perhaps millions of lives if replicated across other hospitals. But confident as she was in her data, she questioned their power of persuasion among a public illiterate of statistics and a popular press uninterested in them.

To figure the hopeful facts of an ugly subject, Nightingale devised a new type of pie chart, known today as the Nightingale rose diagram. It compared mortality rates across time in a simple, elegant histogram. Blue, red, and black wedges fan centrifugally in what Nightingale called a "coxcomb," rendering unambiguous the effectiveness of her sanitation strategy. She sent the diagram to Queen Victoria. "It should affect through the eyes what we fail to convey to the brains of the public through their word-proof ears," she wrote. Her pioneering data visualization was an instant sensation and soon made her the first female member of the Royal Statistical Society.

Having effected major policy change, Nightingale returned from Crimea as one of Britain's most prominent figures, nicknamed "the Lady with the Lamp" after a laudatory article in the *London Times*:

> She is a "ministering angel" without any exaggeration in these hospitals, and as her slender form glides quietly along each corridor, every poor fellow's face softens with gratitude at the sight of her. When all the medical officers have retired for the night and silence

and darkness have settled down upon those miles of prostrate sick, she may be observed alone, with a little lamp in her hand, making her solitary rounds.

Four years before Nightingale arrived in Crimea, at the same age at which Margaret Fuller arrived in Rome, Fuller walked through a different hospital haloed by the flickering light of her own whale oil lamp, visiting wounded man after wounded man—many barely out of adolescence, having joined the Risorgimento with no military training; many badly maimed; many dying. She watched a young man kiss his amputated arm goodbye. "I forget the great ideas," she wrote ruefully with baby Nino on her mind, "to sympathize with the poor mothers, who had nursed their precious forms, only to see them all lopped and gashed." How she must have braced upon approaching each bunk for the possibility that it might contain Ossoli, who was fighting on the front lines of the revolution.

Fuller brought books and flowers to the wounded, read to them, talked with them. The convalescents leaned on her with their slings and crutches as she took them for walks in the hospital's beautiful garden while cannons boomed across the piazza. Fifteen years later, Walt Whitman would reflect on his service as a volunteer nurse in the Civil War:

> There is something in personal love, caresses, and the magnetic flood of sympathy and friendship, that does, in its way, more good than all the medicine in the world.

Every afternoon under the burning sun, Fuller marched through the raging revolution to the post office, past a blood-splattered wall near where Ossoli served, hoping for news of Nino. Nino was "perfectly well," the wet nurse finally assured.

On the first day of June, a week after Fuller's thirty-ninth birthday and eight months after Nino's birth, a deadly siege engulfed Rome—a "terrible, real battle" she could see from her balcony, fought "from the first till the last light of day." Fuller estimated that three hundred Italians were killed and wounded that day, many more of the enemy. In clearheaded view of the possibility that her son might be orphaned, she sent his birth certificate to the American ambassador for safekeeping, designating her friend Emelyn Story—her closest confidante during her time in Rome—as Nino's guardian should his parents perish in the civil war. Writing in Italian, by now fluent, she exhorted Ossoli with morbid selflessness:

> If you live and I die, be always very devoted to Nino. If you ever love another woman, always think first of him, I beg you, beg you, love—*io preggio, preggio, amore.*

One small word rekindles the supposition that their marriage may have indeed been a necessary legal fiction:

> Should I by any chance die, you can take back this paper from me, if you want, as from your wife.

As from your wife.

But Fuller's greatest fear wasn't the potential loss of her own life—"I have never yet felt afraid when really in the presence of danger," she had written to her mother at the outset of the revolution. She dreaded most of all the potential loss of that to which she had devoted her life—the hallmarks of humanity's impulse for truth and beauty that Rome, more than any other city in history, had preserved for millennia. With the Austrian army no more than three days away, Fuller anguished over the impending bombardment of the Eternal City:

> It seems incredible that any nation should be willing to incur the infamy of such an act,—an act that may rob posterity of the most precarious part of its inheritance,—only so many incredible things have happened of late.

A year earlier, in the intoxicating atmosphere of a revolution that was still all ideals and no sacrifices, she had renounced art for politics. Now she was maturing into the realization that the violence of war, however necessary for progress it may appear in the short term, is never in the service of "the state of the race"; that at the altar of no future may we make a bloody sacrificial offering of the past, with its hard-won triumphs of the intellect and the imagination; that art and beauty are humanity's lifeblood and the most enduring truth we have. Watching the villa of Raphael demolished in the siege, Fuller sorrowed to Emerson:

> Rome is being destroyed; her glorious oaks; her villas, haunts of sacred beauty, that seemed the possession of the world forever,— the villa of Raphael . . . and so many other sanctuaries of beauty—all must perish, lest a foe should level his musket from their shelter. *I could not, could not!*
>
> I know not, dear friend, whether I ever shall get home across that great ocean, but here in Rome I shall no longer wish to live. O, Rome, *my* country! could I imagine that the triumph of what I held dear was to heap such desolation on thy head!

Margaret longed for a haven of permanence. "Those whom I have once loved," she would soon write, "have rarely failed me, and I hope to love them eternally." Now she beckoned to Waldo:

> Should I never return,—and sometimes I despair of doing so, it seems so far off, so difficult, I am caught in such a net of ties here—if ever you know of my life here, I think you will only wonder at the constancy with which I have sustained myself; the degree of profit to which, amid great difficulties, I have put the time, at least in the way of observation. Meanwhile, love me all you can; let me feel, that amid the fearful agitations of the world, there are pure hands, with healthful, even pulse, stretched out toward me, if I claim their grasp.

Amid the chaos and heartbreak of a revolution that had pivoted from creation to destruction, Fuller found herself "perplexed with doubts" about remaining in Rome. She began considering, for the first time since she had set foot on Italian soil, returning to America. This would mean revealing her secret, but its consequences for her public image no longer troubled her. She assured Caroline, who feared for her friend's reputation:

> I pity those who are inclined to think ill, when they might as well have inclined the other way. However, let them go; there are many in the world who stand the test, enough to keep us from shivering to death.

Fuller was beginning to question her most elemental beliefs about humanity as she watched the collapse of ancient ideals all around her. Dispirited, she was buoyed by thoughts of her baby boy safe from bloodshed and tumult in his tranquil mountain nest. But thoughts alone no longer sufficed—Margaret couldn't bear being away from Nino any longer and decided to make once again the dangerous journey to the mountains through the war-ravaged country. She wrote to her brother before departing:

> Private hopes of mine are fallen with the hopes of Italy. I have played for a new stake and lost it. Life looks too difficult. But, for the present, I shall try to waive all thoughts of self, and renew my strength.

Upon arrival, Fuller found only more shock and sorrow—Nino, whose angelic blue eyes and flushed cheeks had been her guiding light through the darkness of the failing revolution, was "worn to a skeleton, all his sweet childish graces fled," an apparition that "wanders feebly on the surface between two worlds, inclining . . . most over the abyss." The wet nurse had greedily used Fuller's allowance to feed her own child, starving Nino nearly to death and pacifying his hungry cries with wine instead of breastmilk.

To Fuller, the thought that her boy might not live seemed unsurvivable: "I was too fatigued before, and this last shipwreck of hopes would be more than I could bear." As she nursed Nino back to life, she received news that Horace Greeley's beloved son had died at the same age as Emerson's, of the same disease that had taken Kepler's beloved hyacinth of a son. There was no more time to waste in fear of censure—she was ready to share the truth of her new life with the loves of her old. To William Channing, she announced:

> I am a mother now, and the spirit of my little one embellishes more and more its frail temple, so frail it requires great care from me to keep it fixed here on earth. His smiles are an exceeding rich reward, and often give my heart amid the cries of carnage and oppression an even bird-like joy. Yet for his possession also, whether given or lent, a great price is exacted.

Describing Nino's father as her "gentle friend, ignorant of great ideas, ignorant of books, enlightened as to his duties by pure sentiment and an unspoiled nature," Fuller once again contemplated the countercultural idea that the richness of a bond need not correlate with its permanence, that permanence is a self-defeating measure of any real love that slakes a particular thirst at a particular time. Aware of how discordant with her romantic past Channing would find her choice to be with Ossoli, she observed unselfconsciously that she would not have chosen him for eternity, but she chose him for that particular moment in her life and its particular needs of the soul:

> If earthly union be meant for the beginning of one permanent and full we ought not to be united, for the time was gone by when I could more than *prefer* any man. Yet I shall never regret the step which has given me the experience of a mother and satisfied domestic wants in a most sincere and sweet companion.

A century and a half before polyamory began loosening the residual grip of Puritanism, Fuller added:

> The tie leaves me mentally free, as I wish him also to remain. I trust in the midst of a false world, we may be able to sustain some degree of truth, though indeed children involve too deeply, in this corrupt social contract and truth is easier to those who have not them. I however pined too much and my heart was too suffocated without a child of my own.

Five days before Nino's first birthday, Margaret shared with her mother all she had been obscuring from view. More than a page into her lengthy letter, she announces the "piece of intelligence" that would, she acknowledges, bring her mother "a pang" at first but, she hopes, "pleasure" in the grand view. In curiously removed and almost hypothetical language, she writes: "Your eldest child might long ago have been addressed by another name than yours, and has a little son a year old." Even more curious is the fact that although she calls Ossoli her "husband"—one of only two instances in which she refers to him by this word in her hundreds of surviving letters—nowhere in the multipage missive to her mother does she mention him by name. Once again Fuller issues the assurance that had become the dominant refrain of how she broadcast the relationship to the world and perhaps how she made sense of it within her own conflicted psychic factions: He lacks education and intellectual ambition, but has an unfailing sense of duty and a "very sweet temper" that nurtures her soul in a new way. She tells her mother:

> His love for me has been unswerving and most tender. I have never suffered a pain that he could [not] relieve. His devotion, when I am ill, is to be compared only with yours. . . . In him I have found a home, and one that interferes with no tie. Amid many ills and cares, we have had much joy together, in the sympathy with natural beauty,—with our child,—with all that is innocent and sweet.

In trying to justify to others her choice to be with a partner so unlike her previous infatuations, Fuller is continually revising her own understanding of love, of character, of herself. "You are intellect. I am life," she had stormed at Waldo on the eighth anniversary of their meeting. Bruised again and again in the hesitant hands of almost-lovers who met her longing for "fulness of being" with only half of themselves, people whose hearts thrashed about in the self-erected cages of intellectual ambition, she at last comes to recognize that the most exalted qualities of character—those that make for "the life, the life!"—are not of the mind but of the heart and spirit: integrity, unaffected kindness, constancy of affection.

But as much as Fuller has come to cherish the qualities of character at the center of her love for Ossoli, she is unsentimental about
the temporal reality of human relations. Once again she acknowledges with a countercultural sobriety the impermanence of all
things, which only sharpens the urgency of relishing them in the
resplendent, fleeting present:

> I do not know whether he will always love me so well, for I am the
> elder, and the difference will become, in a few years, more percep-
> tible than now. But life is so uncertain, and it is so necessary to take
> good things with their limitations, that I have not thought it worth
> while to calculate too curiously.

What solidity of sentiment it takes not to let an awareness of the
moment's impermanence dilute its richness, its sweetness, but purify
it and saturate it with the utmost "fulness of being."

With an eye to the most inescapable confrontation with
impermanence—the specter of mortality that had accompanied her
since childhood, now realer than ever—she writes of the child who
had barely survived illness and starvation:

> I find satisfaction, for the first time, to the deep wants of my heart.
> Yet, thinking of those other sweet ones fled, I must look upon him as
> a treasure only lent.

With Fuller's journalistic work halted by her effort to revive
Nino, and with all prospects of Ossoli's slim inheritance demolished by the divisive war that had placed him on the opposite side
of his family's papal loyalties, they were now thoroughly destitute.
Fuller continued to write to friends and acquaintances for loans and
advances, scraping funds together to move her new family to the
safer regime and gentler clime of Tuscany. At the end of September,
they arrived in Florence, where Nino set his tiny foot back into the
realm of the living—first gently, then with playful firmness. Each
morning, he would wake up and patter into his parents' bedroom,
open the curtains with a dimpled hand, and show his four teeth as

he laughed and danced. In the simple, unassailable jubilation of her child—"my ever growing mystery"—Fuller found a new dimension of contentment:

> He is to me a source of ineffable joys, far purer, deeper than any thing I ever felt before, like what Nature had sometimes given, but more intimate, more sweet. He loves me very much, his little heart clings to mine. I trust, if he lives, to sow there no seeds which are not good, to be always growing better for his sake.

Few things elate more than the discovery of new chambers of one's own heart. Motherhood had unlatched something entirely new within Fuller—"the first unalloyed quiet joy I have ever known"— and she marveled at it with unmitigated astonishment:

> Before . . . I had felt so much love that seemed so holy and soft, that longed to purify, to protect, to solace *infinitely*; but it was nothing to what I feel now, and that sense of pure nature, for the eager, spontaneous life of childhood, was very partial in me before.

And yet every novel love only enriches the existing by broadening the spectrum of the heart. With an eye to "the mixture of solemn feeling" and sweet joy she felt for and with Nino, Fuller wrote to her brother:

> Yet this is only different in degree, not in kind, from what we should feel in other relations; the destiny of all we come in contact we may more or less impede or brighten.

From this strange platform of her new life, Fuller peered through a reflective telescope at her old life. In a letter to Sam and Anna, now married and with a child of their own, she wrote:

> Pardon dear Anna, so great has been my passion for life since you knew me, it is difficult to speak. My friends remain in their place. I seem to have more clue to their state than they to mine. Across the

stream I see them; they look fair and tall, but I must go to them; they cannot come to me. Farewell.

Reluctantly, feeling "home-sick for Rome" but unable to return to the war-ravaged remnants of the ancient "ideal beauty," Fuller began seriously considering a return to America.

At this very moment, America seemed to return to her, a strand of her past life intersecting her present in an uncanny encounter one midautumn evening as she was walking home with Ossoli at sunset. Midstride, Fuller froze at the sight of "a pale, erect, narrow little figure" she immediately recognized as an old friend from the failed utopia of her youth. "Imagine Brook Farm walking the street of Florence," she wrote in disbelief a century and a half before modern travel and the forces of globalization shuffled space and culture to make such intersections far more probable. As she conversed with her Brook Farm friend, "listening with a sort of pleasure to the echo of the old pastoral masquerade," her two lives met like the tendrils of the grapevines that reached across the narrow Florentine street from opposite terraces.

Fuller's most momentous encounter in Florence was with the literary power couple Robert and Elizabeth Barrett Browning, whom she had been trying to track down via various failed attempts to obtain letters of introduction since her arrival in Italy. Fuller had been one of the Brownings' earliest and most enthusiastic American reviewers. "Byron could only paint women as they were to him," she had written in the *Tribune*, "[Robert] Browning can show what they are in themselves." Elizabeth she ranked "in vigor and nobleness of conception, depth of spiritual experience, and command of classic allusion, above any female writer the world has yet known."

When Fuller met the Brownings, Elizabeth had just given birth to the couple's first child after a series of miscarriages—a son named Pen, a few months younger than Nino. Against the backdrop of Elizabeth's severe chronic illness and the fact that the forty-three-year-old poet was of an age when most women in those days became grandmothers, Pen's birth was nothing short of miraculous. When

Fuller saw the child, she marveled at a miracle not merely physical but almost metaphysical:

> [The Brownings] have the prettiest little baby; it is so fat and laugh-
> ing and violet eyed; it looks as if was created fresh after a flood, and
> could not be the child of two people who had written books and
> such thoughtful sad books too.

Elizabeth Barrett Browning, who had read Mary Wollstonecraft by the age of twenty-one and had spent the two decades since as an ardent champion of women's rights, had been aware of Fuller's work and took an equally instant liking to her. But she, too, was astonished by Fuller's choice of partner in the unlettered Ossoli. Margaret herself continued to struggle with the mismatch of sensibilities. "Ossoli is forming some taste for books," she reported home hopefully, "which I never expected." He was also beginning to take lessons in English from Fuller's Brook Farm friend, in exchange for teaching him Italian. "How I wish that you would dismiss the past," she had once exhorted William Channing, "except as the birthplace of the future!"

Before Fuller could journey across the ocean of ambivalence, she had a far more pressing practical concern: She was now destitute beyond any poverty she had previously known. The milk and bread she needed to feed her baby were within reach only with severe strain. No longer able to afford carriages, she walked long distances for every minor errand. Whatever meager means she had, she earned by writing, but the only room in their unheated apartment where she could write undisturbed was "quite uninhabitable" during a February spell of "a cold unknown before to Italy." The very letters to friends in which she lamented the crushing load of poverty and intimated that she could use financial help only piled up a postal bill she couldn't pay. The steamer she had taken on her way to Europe three years earlier, paid for by the family that had taken her on as a caretaker for their child, was a luxury far out of the question. Even the cheapest transatlantic journey by wind and sail cost more than what she had. And yet she imagined that a life of humble contentment was possible on the other side:

> If we had a little money and could live in obscure quiet, I should not be sorry to leave Italy till she has strength to rise again, and stay several years in America. I should like to refresh my sympathy with her great interests and great hopes. I should like to do anything I could for people there.

As for how "people there" would receive her, Fuller grew increasingly unperturbed by "the social inquisition" likely to ensue as her New England coterie and her readers found out about the surprising turn in her life, united in secret with that of a man who appeared to any outside observer as intellectually incurious but who grew in her eyes "more lovely and good every day." She would never live to read Emily Dickinson's proclamation that "the Heart is the Capital of the Mind," but she was living its sovereign truth.

Fuller expected that those who loved her in any real sense would accept her choices, understanding that she had not only lived by her own ideals but evolved them. She dismissed those inclined to judge her private life ungenerously: "The lower persons everywhere are sure to think that whatever is mysterious must be bad." Perhaps it was with such "lower persons" of harsh and hasty judgment in mind that she wrote to Elizabeth Barrett Browning of their infant sons meeting:

> Babies seem amazed at one another, they are not in haste to make acquaintance, probably they still feel what a world lies hidden in each person, they are not yet made callous by those habits of hasty unfeeling intercourse soon formed by what is called society.

To William Channing, she wrote with equal parts defensiveness and dignity:

> If my life be not wholly right, (as it is so difficult to keep a life true in a world full of falsities,) it is not wholly wrong nor fruitless.

Still, Margaret ached at not having heard a word from Elizabeth Peabody and Waldo, who by now must have received the news. "I suppose they don't know what to say," she reasoned in a letter to her sister. "Tell them there is no need to say anything about these affairs if they don't want to. I am just the same for them I was before."

She wasn't, of course, "the same" at all. She was transformed beyond her own recognition—by war, by motherhood, by the collapse of her political ideals and the discovery of new frontiers of personal contentment. The inner workings of such profound personal transformation parallel the proof of relativity, which Einstein envisioned in what he would later call the "happiest thought" of his life—a thought experiment that would radicalize physics with a landmark revision of Newton's laws.

According to an apocryphal story circulated by early newspapers and refashioned in numerous variations by later biographers, one day in 1907, Einstein found himself peering out the window of the Zurich patent office where he worked. He was puzzling over how his theory of special relativity, published two years earlier, could be reconciled with Newtonian gravity, when his gaze was arrested by the sight of a construction worker plummeting from the rooftop of a nearby building. The man was fortunate—he landed on a supple pile of garbage below. Einstein, the story goes, seized the opportunity to test his theory and rushed out to ask the startled man an odd question: During his unexpected fall, did he feel that some invisible force was pulling him violently toward the ground? Einstein reasoned that from the hyperlocal vantage point of the free-falling observer, gravity would be imperceptible and would therefore appear nonexistent. The puzzled, shaken workman confirmed this—he had felt no forceful pull during his fall. Einstein went on to develop this insight into his now-famous elevator thought experiment, demonstrating that any measurement of the laws of physics within a small contained space such as an elevator could not discern whether the elevator is static, cradled in a strong gravitational field, or rapidly accelerating upward across space—when the frames of reference are mutually accelerating, any general theory of relativity would implicitly also be a theory of gravity.

To the person undergoing it, any rapid ascent to new heights of experience can feel equally imperceptible from the interiority of the transformation. Fuller was both aware and unaware of how profoundly she had changed as life had lived itself through her. She reflected on the transfiguration that seemed at once to have befallen her from the chance-governed outside and to have been chosen from the inside, with the full agency and integrity of her character:

> I acted upon a strange impulse. I could not analyze at all what passed in my mind. I neither rejoice nor grieve, for bad or for good I acted out my character. . . . As to marriage I think the intercourse of heart and mind may be fully enjoyed without entering in this particular partnership of daily life, still I do not find it burdensome.

In response to an acquaintance who, on receiving news of her new life, supposed that she must be happier "because the position of an unmarried woman in our time is not desirable," she wrote defiantly:

> To me on the contrary it had seemed that in a state of society where marriage brings so much of trifling business arrangements and various soporifics the liberty of the single life was most precious. I liked to see those I loved only in the best way. With Ossoli I liked when no one knew of our relation, and we passed our days together in the mountains, or walking beautiful nights amid the ruins of Rome.

What made their union so joyous, she pointed out, was not the social contract she had so rigorously criticized in *Woman*, but that they met as equal partners in domestic life, "of mutual solace and aid about the dish and spoon part," while continuing to enjoy each other's company beyond domestic duties "as much as ever." And yet, as singular and strong as their love was, Fuller once again weighted the longing for permanence against the impermanence she knew to govern life:

Should he continue to love me as he has done, his companionship will be an inestimable blessing to me. I say *if*, because all human affections are frail, and I have experienced too great revulsions in my own, not to know it.

Did Emerson's long-ago admonition—"the soul knows nothing of marriage, in the sense of a permanent union between two personal existences"—reverberate through her mind as she counterargued herself in envisioning a permanence of affections with Ossoli?

Yet I feel great confidence in the permanence of his love. It has been unblemished so far, under many trials; especially as I have been more desponding and unreasonable, in many ways, than I ever was before, and more so, I hope, than I ever shall be again. But at all such times, he never had a thought except to sustain and cheer me. He is capable of the sacred love,—the love passing that of woman.

In a letter to Caroline, she reconciled her conflicting awarenesses by choosing to dwell in the sanctuary of the present moment:

Ossoli diffuses such a peace and sweetness over every day, that I cannot endure to think yet of our future.

By the spring of 1850, Margaret Fuller was wide awake to the dark side of the Italian revolution. It had delivered "much fruit of noble sentiment, noble act." But it was at bottom a war—like any war, whatever its ideals, it "breeds vice too, drunkenness, mental dissipation, tears asunder the tenderest ties." The time had come to return to America, to save from severance her tender ties to Ossoli and their child. "Happy the prodigal son who *returns*!" she had written to Anna Barker what seemed like a lifetime ago. Now, she lamented in her final *Tribune* column from Rome: "Go where I may, a large part of my heart will ever remain in Italy."

Destitute and in debt, Fuller could not afford the extravagant steamship that had long ago brought her to Europe in a record ten days. When she heard that a cargo ship sailing to New York was willing to take a few passengers for a fraction of the steamship cost, she was riven by hesitancy—the journey would take two months, maybe more, on a merchantman at the mercy of wind and sea, bereft of the sturdy engineering and superior navigation instruments of a packet ship or steamship. Years earlier, she had recorded in her diary the statistic that "more than five hundred British *vessels alone* are wrecked and sink to the bottom *annually*."

After meeting with the assuringly named Captain Hasty, finding him to be a kind man "among the best and most highminded" of her compatriots, and seeing that the ship was in fine condition, Fuller sublimated her dread and decided that her small clan would make the passage aboard the *Elizabeth,* departing just before her fortieth birthday in mid-May. They would be living cargo on a vessel shared with 150 tons of Carrara marble, rolls of silk, fine paintings, and Hiram Powers's sculpture of a pro-slavery South California senator who had died that March, before the Compromise of 1850 was passed in an effort to alleviate the deadly tension between slave and free states.

Just before the departure, Margaret wrote to her mother in a short, dark letter deliberately sent via a different vessel:

> Should anything hinder our meeting on earth, think of your daughter as one who always wished at least to do her duty, and who always cherished you, according as her mind opened to discover excellence.

To William Channing, whom she had always entrusted with her innermost turbulence, she named her fears more concretely:

> I shall embark . . . praying fervently, indeed, that it may not be my lot to lose my boy at sea, either by unsolaced illness or amid the howling waves; or if so, that Ossoli, Angelo, and I may go together.

The three spent their last night in Italy with the Brownings. Nervously, Fuller obscured her terror of the journey and her "trembling solicitude on account of the child" with the remark, only half facetious, that a ship sharing a name with the great poet could only be a good omen. A great disquietude had been reverberating through her being. "I am absurdly fearful," she had written to her closest Italian friend a month before the departure, "and various omens have combined to give me a dark feeling."

Here was a woman who had predicated her entire life on the refusal to abdicate personal agency to convention or luck, who had labored to rise far above the ceiling that biology and culture had placed on her self-actualization, who had conceded that chance governs the universe and resolved to do within its governance what Beethoven had done when fortune dealt him its deafening blow— "take fate by the throat." That this woman should give superstition even half a thought, the other half so self-aware of its absurdity, attests to how fear works us over—how it strips us of our evolved responses and debases us to our most primitive reactions.

Fuller's odd parting gift to the Brownings bespoke a further testament: Despite her lifelong resistance to religious doctrine, she presented the poets with a handsome Bible, intended as a present from Nino to their own young son. Stranger still was her word choice for the inscription: "In Memory of Angelo Eugene Ossoli."

Just before Fuller left Florence, Emerson mailed a letter entreating her to "stay in Italy, for now." He, too, had grown worried about how New England would receive its prodigal daughter when she brought home the shock of a child and a young lover, the nature of their union shrouded in mystery and speculation. Emerson offered to publish, distribute, and popularize her prized book on the revolution, as he had done for Thomas Carlyle's first major work a quarter century earlier. He wrote:

I can see plainly . . . the very important advantages which continued residence in Italy will give to your factors at home, not only as adding solidity to your testimony, but new rays of reputation & wonder to you as a star.

The letter never reached America's wandering star before she drifted homeward in the umbra of doubt.

On May 17—six days before Fuller's fortieth birthday—the trio boarded the *Elizabeth* along with the ship's crew and four other mammals: the captain's young wife; Fuller's old Brook Farm friend, homebound at last; a young Italian woman determined to make a life for herself in New York; and a goat. Unable to pay for the wet nurse's travel, Fuller had instead acquired the goat to provide milk for the newly weaned Nino, who quickly became the sailors' beloved mascot. Captain Hasty grew especially fond of the child—so fond that when the commander succumbed to a sudden attack of what he took for "nervous fever," which began with violent headache and back pain, Fuller took Nino into his cabin to cheer him up. But by the next day, inflamed pustules began colonizing the captain's body, constricting his throat until he could no longer swallow and could hardly breathe. Soon, the pustules began turning black. The convulsing cough crescendoed into full-body agony.

It was smallpox.

Captain Hasty was dead within days, three weeks into the voyage, the morning after the *Elizabeth* arrived in the port of Gibraltar. The ship was immediately quarantined, not even a physician allowed to go aboard. The British authorities, unwilling to allow the captain's unliving flesh to carry the deadly disease ashore, ordered that he be buried in deep water. Margaret held his weeping widow as his blistered remains were lowered into the abysmic blue of the Mediterranean, the flag of every ship in the harbor raised in solemn solidarity under the early evening Sunday sun.

Back in the mountains of Italy, Fuller had paid a local doctor to inoculate Nino against smallpox—the disease that had bereaved a litany of parents over the centuries, among them Kepler and Emerson. But two days after the *Elizabeth* sailed into the open ocean under the command of the inexperienced first mate, Margaret watched in horror as dimpled bumps engulfed Nino's small body and swelled his eyes shut, until the boy named for an angel came to resemble a reptilian demon shrieking in agony. The crude vaccine administered by the village doctor had not worked. It would be another 130 years before advances in vaccination would culminate in the global eradication of smallpox.

The child whose first experience of life had been near-death was once again circling the event horizon of the ultimate abyss. Two months earlier, upon receiving word of the death of a friend's young child, Margaret had written:

> These things make me tremble with selfish sympathy. I could not, I think, survive the loss of *my* child. I wonder daily how it can be done.

Watching helplessly as the disease raged in Nino's system, Margaret did the only thing she could—she sang to him. And when he began waving his blistered little hands to the music, a ferocious new species of hope surged through her being. By the ninth day, Nino could see again. Within a fortnight, he had made another miraculous recovery—so miraculous that even his pockmarks soon faded, a fact in which Margaret rejoiced somewhat self-consciously, not wishing to present her mother with an unbeautiful grandchild. Long ago, in her own childhood, she had made up her mind "to be bright and ugly." And yet she couldn't but wish beauty upon the being she most loved—no, not vanity but the humanest humanity, where all is one: love, truth, beauty.

With the elation of one who has been narrowly spared the unsurvivable, Margaret drank in the splendor of the open ocean. Under the light of what she had once called in a love letter "that best fact, the Moon," she reverenced the shimmering undulance as nothing less than "holy." What consonance she would have found in Rachel Carson's words: "There is something deeply impressive about the night sea as one experiences it from a small vessel far from land."

The elation only escalated when, after weeks of exasperating near-stillness, a sudden gust of wind picked up the *Elizabeth* and carried her, small and buoyant, toward her destination. On July 14, the ship entered the jubilant home stretch after sailing past Bermuda—an unusual route, and not one Captain Hasty would have followed. But the first mate who had taken over captain duties was not a seasoned sailor, nor sufficiently educated in the basic science necessary for navigation, unable to make calculations Maria Mitchell was making before she was ten. When he couldn't compute the ship's longitude—a complex mathematical problem that had dogged scholars since ancient times—he instead navigated the *Elizabeth* solely by latitude, a simple calculation drawing on the time of day and the height of the sun or any other star visible above the horizon.

Whereas the zero-degree parallel of latitude—the equator—stands as an immutable feature of our planet fixed by the physical forces that made the universe, the zero-degree meridian of longitude has been drawn across different points over the millennia—Rome, Paris, London, Philadelphia, St. Petersburg, Jerusalem—based on geopolitics and various other fickle human discretions. The actual measurement of meridians further unwields the problem of longitude, for it must factor in not only place but time: To determine a ship's longitude, the navigator must simultaneously know the precise local time at that particular slice of sea and the time at one other known coordinate, typically the home port. Given the earth's revolution of 360 degrees every twenty-four hours, each hour would indicate fifteen degrees of lateral rotation of the earth, and each degree four minutes of time. It is a simple computation of time, a basic arithmetic. But not so with the equivalent distance—while one degree of longitude equals the same four minutes of time all over the globe, its measure of 109 kilometers at the equator shrinks to zero at the poles. Because of this elasticity, even a slight error in the calculation could steer a ship wildly off its charted course.

Over the centuries, this high-stakes quest for a standardized and reliable measure of longitude had taken on mythic proportions, as alluring as the dream of perpetual motion, as lucrative as the alchemical scheme of transmuting copper into gold. It was a puzzlement that drove countless scholars to figurative madness and countless sailors to literal death, a problem that occupied every natural philosopher between Kepler and Herschel. Even Galileo was enticed by its dual seduction of science and ego. When the king of Spain offered an opulent life pension to "the discoverer of longitude," Galileo set about devising a system of calculating longitude based on the orbits and eclipses of the four moons of Jupiter, which he himself had discovered and named, after Kepler's suggestion, Io,

Europa, Ganymede, and Callisto, mythological paramours of Zeus, or Jupiter. But when Galileo submitted his solution twenty years after the prize announcement, the king's committee rejected it, pointing out that simply seeing the faint Jovian moons against the firmament from a small seafaring vessel was so difficult that it rendered the technique impracticable.

Galileo was undaunted. To enhance his elaborate scheme, he invented an elaborate contraption—a knightlike brass navigation helmet, which sailors could don to find the elusive satellites, one eye peering naked through the left eyehole to locate Jupiter's bright light in the night sky, the other eye searching for the moons through the small telescope affixed to the right eyehole. The helmet never took off. Galileo walked away from his attempts at solving longitude, which he pitched all over Europe, with a gold chain for effort from the Dutch government. Eight years after his death, and exactly two hundred years before Margaret Fuller boarded the *Elizabeth*, his Jovian method gained wide acceptance for calculating longitude—on land, but not at sea. Longitude remained a complex mathematical computation.

The novice captain of the *Elizabeth* could do none of it. But when the ship breezed past Bermuda on the wings of unexpected winds, he took heart that nature had compensated for his mathematical inadequacy and chance had interceded in his favor. When the distant pulsar of the New Jersey lighthouse appeared on the horizon, it seemed like nothing less than divine intervention. He ordered the passengers to pack their trunks and ready their salutes.

13

THE BANALITY OF SURVIVAL

In the spring of 1849, as Margaret Fuller was weighing her return to America, the polymathic astronomer John Herschel—Caroline Herschel's nephew—invited Charles Darwin to contribute the section on geology to an ambitious manual on ten major branches of science, commissioned by the Royal Navy. (Building on Kepler's legacy, Whewell contributed the section on tides. Astronomer Royal Dr. Airy—Maria Mitchell's favorite host and greatest kindred spirit in England—composed the chapter on astronomy.) Darwin produced a primer that promised to make good geologists even of readers with no prior knowledge of the discipline, so that they might "enjoy the high satisfaction of contributing to the perfection of the history of this wonderful world."

In submitting his manuscript, Darwin wrote to Herschel:

> I much fear, from what you say of size of type that it will be too long; but I do not see how I could shorten it, except by rewriting it, & that is a labour which would make me groan. I do not much like it, but I have in vain thought how to make it better. I should be grateful for any corrections or erasures on your part.

A perfectionist prone to extreme anxiety, Darwin was vexed by the editorial process. But in the autumn of 1850, just as the manual was about to go to press, trouble of a wholly different order eclipsed the professional irritation: The Darwins' beloved nine-year-old daughter, Annie—the second of their ten children and Charles's favorite, fount of curiosity, sunshine of the household—fell ill with a mysterious ailment. When Charles and Emma first realized that their daughter's condition was more than a fleeting sickness, they turned to what the era's medical authorities prescribe for sickly children: sea-bathing, believed to be a reliable cure-all for symptoms ranging from "languor and weakness of circulation," per one medical encyclopedia, to cases of "listless and indolent state of the mind." A natural history and travel guide from the era describes the craze for sea-bathing at Ramsgate, a coastal resort in Kent: "A sudden plunge into the ocean causes the blood to circulate briskly, and promotes the heat of the body." It was to Ramsgate that the Darwins first sent Annie, hoping for maritime recovery. But her illness only escalated into fever and headaches.

A year earlier, the Darwins had traveled to the spa village of Malvern, where Charles was to try a new "cold water cure" devised by a Dr. James Gully. Darwin's chronic illness at times manifested as insomnia, at other times as "dreadful vomiting every week." It was never accurately diagnosed nor treated, and he was desperate for relief. One contemporary theory holds that he suffered from an acute anxiety disorder. Having read Dr. Gully's *The Water Cure in Chronic Disease,* Darwin set his scientific skepticism aside and wrote to the physician, willing to try his treatment—he worried that the constant vomiting was getting in the way of his work. "If once half-well," he wrote to his best friend, "I could do more in six months than I now do in two years."

Dr. Gully's treatment, developed in response to his two-year-old daughter's death, included the vehement disavowal of medication. The little girl had been treated with every known drug at the time—including heavy metals like mercury, lead, and arsenic—and had died convulsed with harrowing pain. The bereaved father had set out to devise a course of alternative medicine. His hydropathy drew such famous patients as Lord Tennyson and Florence Nightingale—and now Charles Darwin.

In Darwin's defense, this was a time when medical science was so rudimentary that it bled into the same metaphysical manipulation techniques that religious rhetoric used to keep belief systems and power structures in place. Such manipulation was only possible because the line between science and pseudoscience was blurred again and again as modern medicine was finding its footing. Because the body—especially woman's body—was so poorly understood and the paradigm of clinical trials was generations away, most medical treatments in Darwin's day were based on some combination of speculation, common lore, and anecdotal trial and error. When twenty-one-year-old Margaret Fuller experienced the first attack of the incapacitating headaches that would haunt the remainder of her life, she sought relief in bloodletting—a cure applied to a vast array of sicknesses. This was an era when the majority of early childhood illnesses—from diarrhea and colic to fever and restlessness—were attributed to teething, also the most commonly listed cause of infant death in local registers. The all-inclusive malady was treated with a litany of allegedly curative barbarisms—blistering, bloodletting, and massive doses of dubious medication. Parents would lance the inflamed gums of their infants using unsterilized kitchen utensils, which often inflicted infections that ended up as the true cause of fatality. One of the most common medications was a solution of calomel powder—mercury—given to the child until he or she began to salivate, now a recognized symptom of acute mercury poisoning. With their tongues swollen to manyfold the usual size, children often died of dehydration following calomel treatment, but neither parents nor physicians implicated the drug in causality for half a century. It took many more decades to uncover the permanent neurological damage—from seizures to tremors to chronic fatigue—on those who survived the treatment, with mercury lodged in their bodies for life.

Sophia Peabody's history illustrates the limits of nineteenth-century medicine's promise. Treated with mercury as an agitated infant, she was bedeviled by paralyzing headaches from childhood, which rendered her so sensitive to noise that she often remained in her bedroom during family meals, for the clatter of utensils furnished "excruciating torture." These extreme headaches left her in a state of out-of-body confusion, syncopating pain, and occasional delirium. Her father, a Harvard-trained physician, set about treating Sophia by blistering her skin with hot poultices intended to siphon out the "humors"—the bodily fluids at the basis of ancient Greek and Roman systems of medicine—believed to be causing the malady. She was not yet seventeen when leeches were applied to the "humors." So desperate was Sophia for a cure, and so hopeful in her desperation—for hope is how we only ever survive despair—that she wrote fondly of her leeches as "incomparable, lovely, gentle, delicate, tender, considerate, generous, fine, disinterested, excellent, dear, elegant, knowing, graceful, active, lively, animated, beautiful" creatures, providers of "the very quietest, easiest way of freeing oneself from pain that can be thought of." When the temporary relief, likely owing much to the placebo effect of her high hopes, gave way to the bleak reality of the unsolved medical mystery and the headaches returned, the leeches became to her "little vile imps of darkness."

In her journal, Sophia wrote of how pain clung to her "like a good friend" and detailed the physical symptoms of the headache attacks, which lasted from a few hours to a few days. But she also limned in vivid detail the interplay of the physical and psychoemotional aspects of these all-consuming headaches, which she experienced as coursing through her with a "supernatural force." She captured the mind-body electricity of the onset:

> Tonight I felt like the embodied spirit of pain. What are these agonizing twinges coming to? It seems as if my veins were finer than a cambric needle and that through them a deluge of fiery metal was struggling to wend, all but bursting the narrow pass. And what a singular elation of mind it brings with it. I could study Hebrew or hieroglyphics or solve to abstrusest problems better now than ever if my eyes would keep steady and could see. Am I and my body one? What a mystery!

Sophia often harnessed this initial period of elation in her work as an artist, painting feverishly until "excessive agitation" and "tumultuous heaving and palpitation" foreboded the next phase: the onslaught of the pain itself with its "blinding and annihilating fury," which rendered her in a state of "utter prostration" as "a coronet of thongs" seemed to slice through her brain. Once the storm of extreme pain swept out of her body, it left an almost unnatural stillness, "a vacuum within," which eventually transformed into a clearing for a temporary resurgence of elated energy. These cycles repeated with such frequency that throughout her life, Sophia was never free from "the silent ministry of pain" for more than a few days or, in a respite of rare duration surrounding her marriage to Nathaniel Hawthorne, a few weeks. "My duty seems plainly," Sophia would write, "to become a saint through rejoicing instead of through suffering." A century later, the French philosopher, political activist, and radical reformer Simone Weil would write with her life a testament to this redemptive power of suffering. After having placed first in France's competitive national university entrance exam—Simone de Beauvoir placed second—Weil would go on to advocate for worker rights, laboring incognito in a car factory for more than a year to better understand the reality of her working-class compatriots, and would serve in the anarchist militia during the Spanish Civil War—all the while plagued by a rare neuropathy that gave her frequent debilitating headaches. She would die of starvation during World War II while being treated for tuberculosis in an English sanatorium, where despite the doctor's orders to eat heartily, Weil refused to consume more than what was rationed to her compatriots under the German occupation. "To make use," Weil wrote, "of the sufferings that chance inflicts upon us is better than inflicting discipline upon oneself."

What Sophia Peabody suffered from was an acute case of migraine, though the term wouldn't come into popular use until after her death. Perhaps the first serious exploration of this confounding malady came from John Herschel, who was afflicted by what he termed "ocular spectra"—visual migraines that had also tormented Newton, would accompany Virginia Woolf's mental illness, and accounted for the visions that fueled Sophia's painting spells during the elation phase of her attacks. Shortly after Maria

Mitchell visited Herschel's home during her European travels, he began working on a paper titled "On Sensorial Vision" to be presented at the Literary Society of Leeds in the autumn of 1858, while Darwin was finalizing *On the Origin of Species*. In it, Herschel described these curious attacks of "ocular spectra," which flood not only the mind's eye but the actual organ of vision with gyrating geometrical patterns of "perfect regularity" and "exceedingly delicate lines," emanating "a sort of kaleidoscopic power." These visual migraines, Herschel found, furnished a singular lens on the interweaving of the mind and the body, of the psychology and the physiology of perception. They offered an experience of which one is acutely aware but which lies beyond one's willful control, thus illuminating the invisible thread linking the conscious and the unconscious mind. Herschel wrote:

Now the question at once presents itself—What are these Geometrical Spectra? and how, and in what department of the bodily or mental economy do they originate? They are evidently not dreams. The mind is not dormant, but active and conscious of the direction of its thoughts; while these things obtrude themselves on notice, and, by calling attention to them, direct the train of thought into a channel it would not have taken of itself.

Herschel went on to extrapolate from this conundrum larger questions about consciousness, unaddressed until the dawn of modern neuroscience long after his death. His groundbreaking insight into the phenomenon of visual migraines, far ahead of a medical culture unripe for its reception, would lie dormant for more than a century, until the young immigrant neurologist Oliver Sacks, newly appointed at a headache clinic, would pick up the subject and lift it into the limelight with his groundbreaking 1970 book *Migraine*. In it, Sacks examines multiple varieties of migraines and uncovers the delicate mind-body dance that hints at the answer to the question Sophia Peabody had asked in her journal about the mystery of whether the body and the "I"—that is, the complex ecosystem of our conscious experience comprising our sense of self—are one.

Sacks, a Goethe of medicine, reflects on his approach to the understanding and treatment of these debilitating mind-body headaches, completely radical at the time:

> Some patients I could help with drugs, and some with the magic of attention and interest. The most severely-afflicted patients defeated my therapeutic endeavours until I started to enquire minutely and persistently into their emotional lives. It now became apparent to me that many migraine attacks were drenched in emotional significance, and could not be usefully considered, let alone treated, unless their emotional antecedents and effects were exposed in detail.
>
> I thus found it necessary to employ a sort of continuous double-vision, simultaneously envisaging migraine as a *structure* whose forms were implicit in the repertoire of the nervous system, and as a *strategy* which might be employed to any emotional, or indeed biological, end.

Such integrated understanding of illness was alien to Sophia Peabody's era. Maladies like hers were being treated with mercury, arsenic, and, most commonly, opium. Elizabeth Barrett Browning had been taking large doses of opium since the age of fourteen for her debilitating lifelong ailment, which had a discernible psychoemotional correlate—the young poet's health had deteriorated significantly when her family lost its fortune and had to move out of their mansion and into lodgings, then all but collapsed after her brother's death, which sent her into her seven-year sickroom seclusion.

In his foundational treatise on migraines, Sacks argued for a Darwinian basis of the interplay between emotions and the body in chronic headaches. Darwin had described an alternative reaction some organisms have to the classic fight-flight instinct—a response of immobilization and paralysis in the face of threat—and had contrasted these two modes as "active fear (terror)" and "passive fear (dread)." Migraines, Sacks argued, evolved from the latter response mechanism and "have become, with the elaboration of human nervous systems and human needs, progressively differentiated and refined."

But a century and a half earlier, at the time of his daughter's mysterious illness, Darwin himself was still trapped between the medical lore of his day and the ineradicable human hope for miracles. Although Dr. Gully's belief in clairvoyance and general susceptibility to unscientific thought sat uncomfortably with Darwin, he came to like the hydropath a great deal and readily submitted to his methods—which included "cold feet baths and compress on the stomach," as well as a proprietary "sweating process."

The Darwins left Malvern after three months. In a letter to John Herschel penned in June 1849, Charles set aside his discontentment over the editorial tensions with the manual and instead enthused about the treatment's "astonishingly renovating action" on his health:

> Before coming here I was almost quite broken down, head swimming, hands tremulous & never a week without violent vomiting, all this is gone, & I can now walk between two & three miles. Physiologically it is most curious how the violent excitement of the skin, produced by simple water, has acted on all my internal organs.
>
> I mention all this out of gratitude to a process which I thought quackery a year since, but which now I most deeply lament I had not heard of some few years ago.

Despite Darwin's elation over the effect of the "cold water treatment" on his own health, when Annie fell gravely ill, he couldn't set aside his scientific doubts about Dr. Gully's dubious beliefs in clairvoyance, homeopathy, and other pseudoscience. "Homœopathy," he scoffed in a letter,

> is a subject which makes me more wroth, even than does Clairvoyance: clairvoyance so transcends belief, that one's ordinary faculties are put out of question, but in Homœopathy common sense & common observation come into play, & both these must go to the Dogs, if the infinetesimal doses have any effect whatever. . . . No one knows in disease what is the simple result of nothing being done, as a standard with which to compare Homœopathy & all other such things.

Meanwhile across the Atlantic, the aging father of the Peabody sisters, having failed to provide for his family as a physician and a farmer, would finally try his hand at homeopathy in retirement, selling his medicines at Elizabeth Peabody's bookstore, where Margaret Fuller had held her "Conversations" a decade earlier.

Such approaches were out of the question when it came to Darwin's most beloved child—he entrusted her health to traditional medicine. In November 1850, the Darwins took their daughter to London to be seen by the prominent physician who had supervised her birth. After a second futile visit the following month—Annie had added a barking cough to her swelling chest of symptoms—Darwin was once again desperate, betrayed by medical science. He finally gave in and wrote to Dr. Gully for advice, then commenced a water treatment at home under the doctor's instruction, planning to take Annie back to Malvern in the spring for a proper "water cure." But even this home remedy Darwin approached with scientific rigor. In a medical diary of sorts, he meticulously recorded Annie's changing condition as he applied the six-part method, which included Dr. Gully's proprietary "spinal wash" (a towel repeatedly drenched in icy water is swept up and down the patient's spine) and "sweating by the lamp" (the patient is draped with a tent of sheets, under which a lamp containing alcohol is lit, producing nearly unbearable heat).

Although Annie would show intermittent signs of improvement— enough to give the anxious parents hope that what they were doing was effective—her health declined over the longer span of weeks. In the first days of spring, Darwin gave up on his home treatment, ended the medical diary, and braved the two-day passage to Malvern with Annie and two of her siblings, leaving Emma at home, seven months pregnant with the ninth of their ten children.

During their time in Malvern, Darwin picked up a handful of books to read to Annie, a favorite among them being *The Flower People*—a botany guide for children by Mary Peabody, published by her sister Elizabeth and composed before Mary fell in love with the dashing idealist Horace Mann, who had previously courted Elizabeth and gleaned his ideals from her. Ten years into her improbable marriage to Mann, Mary would reflect on what she had learned of life:

> Never be afraid to love. Surrender yourself to its sway, & even if it tears your earthly fibres to tatters, it will strengthen the heavenly ones. Such love is the only *proof* of Immortality.

In the spring of 1859, having devoted his life to advancing universal public education after Elizabeth Peabody ignited his interest in the cause, Mann delivered an electrifying commencement address in which he exhorted graduates: "Be ashamed to die until you have won some victory for humanity." (A century and a half later, the astrophysicist Neil deGrasse Tyson would choose these words of Mann's for his epitaph.) Shortly after the speech, as Darwin was finalizing *On the Origin of Species,* Mann collapsed and died. Devastated by his death, as sudden as their marriage, Mary Peabody would reach for self-salvation in reinventing herself as a writer—the vocation she had abandoned two decades earlier after composing the botany book Darwin read to Annie.

As Annie was lying mortally ill, Charles Dickens and his wife were also at Malvern, where Catherine Dickens was undergoing hydropathy to improve her shaky health. Dickens, who had just lost his father, left Kate at Malvern just after Darwin arrived with Annie and returned home, where he was given harrowing news: His youngest daughter, Dora—named after David Copperfield's child bride—had died, not yet one, after a sudden and inexplicable series of seizures. A decade later, in a letter of consolation to his sister upon the loss of her husband, Dickens would write that while grief never fully leaves, "a real earnest strenuous endeavour to recover the lost tone of spirit" is necessary if one is to go on with life— observing that in "a determined effort to settle the thoughts, to parcel out the day, to find occupation regularly or to make it, to be up and doing something, are chiefly to be found the mere mechanical means which must come to the aid of the best mental efforts." The strategy seems almost banal. But anyone who has lived through loss will recognize in it the essential banality of survival—we come unmoored, then buoy ourselves up with the flimsiest of lifeboats, cobbled together out of any plank and rope we can grasp.

On April 23, 1851, Annie Darwin dies in her father's arms.

Eight years later, *On the Origin of Species* would subvert the elemental human instinct with its argument for natural selection—the survival and improvement of the species through the demise of the individual. Death, Darwin would imply, is not unjust but inherently natural—part of the impartial laws holding the universe together, mortality unshackled from morality and metaphysics, leaving no room for charges of blame and pleas for mercy. "There is grandeur in this view of life," Darwin would write, speaking perhaps to himself. Across the Atlantic, Emily Dickinson would ponder this cycle—"circuit," she called it—of life and death:

Seed, summer, tomb.
Who's doom—
To whom?

With Annie's body still warm beside him, Darwin drags the pen across the letter paper, across the British archipelago, across his lacerated consciousness, to deliver to Emma the most undeliverable news in the universe.

"I am so thankful for the daguerreotype," he writes.

14

SHADOWING THE LIGHT OF IMMORTALITY

John Herschel coined the word *photography* in 1839, the year Margaret Fuller launched her "Conversations," in his correspondence with Henry Fox Talbot—a onetime aspiring artist turned amateur inventor and polymath.

Six years earlier, a young Talbot, newly elected to Parliament, had honeymooned on the shores of Lake Como—an Italian idyll of nature, in which Fuller would later revel and which the besotted Sophia Peabody had painted in two fantasy landscapes for Nathaniel Hawthorne during their courtship. Taken with the splendor of the Italian lakeside, Talbot took to sketching with the aid of a *camera lucida*, Latin for "light room"—an optical device first described by Kepler two centuries earlier, which uses a half-silvered mirror tilted at 45 degrees by an adjustable metal arm to refract an object onto an artist's drawing paper for accurate tracing. But the simple, ingenious contraption failed to make Talbot a better artist. In a frustrated lament, he wrote:

> When the eye was removed from the prism—in which all looked beautiful—I found that the faithless pencil had only left traces on the paper melancholy to behold.

A decade earlier, Talbot had experienced analogous disappointment with the camera obscura as a draftsmanship aid.

Although the term *camera obscura*—Latin for "dark room"—didn't come into use until the late Renaissance, versions of the device had been constructed for centuries to study light, which a tiny hole allows into a vast darkened chamber, projecting an inverted image of whatever is outside the hole onto the inside wall opposite it. By the sixteenth century, the room had become a box, a lens had been added to the hole, and the camera obscura had been turned over from the protoscientists to the artists, who used these projections to trace accurate drawings of real objects. Leonardo da Vinci was an ardent proponent of the camera obscura and used it to hone his understanding and representation of perspective. Painters like Vermeer very probably employed a camera obscura to render their supreme perfection of detail, so that, as Elizabeth Barrett Browning wrote in her 1826 poem *An Essay on Mind,* "Nature's pencil, Nature's portrait, drew."

The ineradicable human longing for permanence prevailed—resourceful minds set out to capture these ephemeral projections. As alchemy gave way to chemistry, scientists and inventors began experimenting with techniques for transmuting the impermanence of light and shadow into permanent prints on paper coated with receptive chemicals. The breakthrough came from a young potter, barely in his twenties: Thomas Wedgwood.

Shortly after Caroline Herschel's birth, a small group of freethinking intellectuals began congregating on the first Monday after every full moon. They called themselves the Lunar Men. Among the fourteen founding members were the philosopher Erasmus Darwin, Charles Darwin's grandfather. Inspired by the gathering's cross-pollination of the various sciences—astronomy, chemistry, botany, geology, natural history—he accomplished something unprecedented: In 1791, he composed a book-length poem titled *The Botanic Garden,* using scientifically accurate poetry to enchant the popular imagination with the scandalous new science of sexual reproduction in plants. The best-selling book was deemed too explicit for unmarried women to read. Three years later, in his book *Zoonomia,* he explained the anatomy of human vision by likening the eye to a camera obscura. At the same time, the young Tom Wedgwood—son of one of the original Lunar Men—imagined something no one had imagined before: that chemistry could be used to capture permanent images of camera projections. The steam engine pioneer James Watt, also a Lunar Man, described the results of Wedgwood's experiments as "silver pictures" for their use of silver nitrate—a chemical the alchemists of the previous centuries had associated with the Moon and regarded as a lunar caustic. These impressions, later known as shadowgrams, were made by laying small objects like leaves and insect wings atop paper coated with silver nitrate dissolved in water, then exposing the paper to light. But there was one major problem: These ephemeral miracles were destroyed by the very thing that made them—if left out in daylight, they would darken until the image all but vanished. Created by light, they could only be viewed in the dark.

Before he could improve on his technique, Wedgwood succumbed to the chronic illness that had bedeviled him since childhood. After he died at thirty-four, his friend Humphry Davy, who had lent his lavish laboratory in the basement of the Royal Institution to Wedgwood's chemical experiments, published a brief summary of the image-making process under the title "Account of a method of copying paintings upon Glass and of making Profiles by the agency of Light upon Nitrate of Silver"—the first published paper on the science of photography, decades before the word itself existed.

A generation later, Henry Fox Talbot—a graduate of the college where Newton had once studied—became obsessed with using chemistry to capture images of real-life objects on paper. He was the same age Wedgwood had been when he died.

In the late summer of 1835, as Caroline Herschel and Mary Somerville were receiving their landmark admission into the Royal Astronomical Society and Halley's Comet was blazing across the night sky, Talbot dreamt up his first serious experiment to perform under the bright August daylight. He created a new coated paper—first painted with an emulsion of water and sodium chloride, plain table salt, then, once dried, painted again with silver nitrate to produce the highly light-sensitive silver chloride. He commissioned a local woodworker to build him a small wooden box, outfitted it with a microscope eyepiece where the pinhole of a standard camera obscura would be, then placed a tiny scrap of his purplish paper in the back of the box opposite the eyepiece.

Talbot placed his "mousetrap"—the nickname his wife gave to the rickety contraption—on a shelf facing the lattice window in his abbey for a brief exposure. Upon opening the box, he was elated to discover the image of every one of the two hundred diamond-shaped panes of glass crisply printed onto his piece of paper. This miracle in miniature, barely larger than a thumbnail, marked the first time the projection of the camera obscura had been captured on paper—the very first photographic negative.

But pleased as he was with the feat, Talbot succumbed to the chronic malady of the polymathic mind: distraction by competing intellectual enthusiasms. Chief among them were his observations of Halley's Comet, perhaps hoping his epistolary reports would earn him the venerable John Herschel's esteem. Talbot was, after all, an "amateur," as were most inventors at the time. Although schooled at Trinity, he had no standing in the formal scientific pantheon, in which Herschel was reigning monarch—that is how blind people can be to their own brilliance and how easily susceptible even the most brilliant are to impostor syndrome.

Unbeknownst to Talbot, a twentysomething artist by the name of Louis Daguerre was conducting his own experiments across the channel in Paris and was far less reluctant to advertise his technological triumphs. Frederick Douglass would later proclaim:

> The great discoverer of modern times, to whom coming generations will award special homage, will be Daguerre. Morse has brought the ends of the earth together and Daguerre has made it a picture gallery.

By the time he was twenty-five, Daguerre had apprenticed with France's first panorama painter and had invented the Diorama theater—a spectacle of large-scale panorama painting and lighting effects, which became a commercial blockbuster attracting significant investors. Now, despite having no formal education nor even an amateur's prior interest in science as a field of intellectual curiosity, he became obsessed with making the perfect diorama and set up a series of experiments trying to capture images with a camera obscura. He begins devouring books on chemistry and builds a half-studio, half-laboratory in the basement of his wildly successful Diorama theater. For two years, he works long hours by candlelight, electrified by obsession and ambition. Even Louis's wife, Louise, is not permitted to enter his sandbox of invention. Amid his books and beakers, with an alchemist's zeal and in a state of near-madness, Daguerre is trying to transmute the ephemerality of light and shadow into the permanence of a paper image. All the while, he is required by the terms of his Diorama theater investors to keep producing several large-scale, high-quality paintings per year.

Numerous failed experiments follow. Then, after a brazen self-introduction by the young Daguerre impatient with proper etiquette, a partnership with a leading inventor—Nicéphore Niépce—who has proper technical training and has already invented the heliograph, a process by which he captured the earliest surviving photograph from nature in the year that Daguerre founded the Diorama theater. Then Niépce's sudden death. Then more solitary experiments, which, after many iterations, produce the chemical process Daguerre proudly names after himself.

Despite his business savvy, Daguerre, now in his forties, fails to attract private investors. So he lurches forth and makes a public announcement of his daguerrotype—its striking results, but not its proprietary process—on January 7, 1839, at a joint meeting of the Academy of Sciences and the Académie des Beaux Arts in Paris.

When Talbot hears of the sensational announcement, he realizes that the revolution he has spent years planning is already afoot and might have another leader. He writes to Herschel frantically in the last week of January that he must present his own findings before the Royal Society, for "no time ought to be lost, the Parisian invention having got the start of 3 weeks." He scrambles to rally excitement for his "art of photogenic drawing."

In a letter of February 28, 1839, Herschel objects to the term "photogeny" to describe Talbot's new image-making process, noting that it "recalls Van Mons's exploded theories of thermogen & photogen." This associative defect, Herschel argues, is amplified by the word's poetic deficiencies: "It also lends itself to no inflexions & is not analogous with Litho & Chalco graphy." Instead, Herschel proposes "photography" then writes in his diary that evening: "Photography. Made up a packet sent to Fox Talbot of 9 specimens."

On March 12, Herschel reads before the Royal Society a paper titled "Note on the Art of Photography or the Application of the Chemical Rays of Light to the Purposes of Pictorial Representation"—the first public utterance of the word *photography*.

Talbot patents his process as *calotype,* from *kalos,* Greek for "beautiful." But despite his pride in the aesthetic beauty and scientific usefulness of calotypes, he knows that his process of fixing images onto paper is too slow and not permanent enough. It is Herschel again who steps in with a solution, proposing to Talbot that he use sodium thiosulfate—hyposulphite of soda, known simply as hypo—which quickly proves to be a supremely effective photographic fixer. But although Talbot sets about touring his invention throughout Europe, Daguerre's primacy takes its toll across the Atlantic: Studios using the Frenchman's process begin spreading like wildfire along the East Coast.

There were two primary projects of early photography: to capture art and to liberate science. Sculpture and painting were the only major figurative arts of the nineteenth century. All else—drawing, sketching, engraving—was secondary and subservient to them, mere preparation for one or the other. Because any new art form—or even form of science, as with non-Euclidean geometry—uses as its reference frame the established paradigms of yore, some of the first subjects of daguerreotypes were sculptures.

New England's premier daguerreotype studio, Southworth & Hawes, enchanted Boston shortly after Daguerre debuted his invention in Paris. Over the following decade, luminaries like Emerson, Harriet Beecher Stowe, and Louisa May Alcott sat before their camera. The most famous portrait of Frederick Douglass is also thought to have been taken at their studio.

The two partners saw beyond the allure of a new technology, the craft of which they mastered swiftly, and envisioned its potential as a new art form—curiously, and rather brilliantly, by turning its lens onto one of the oldest forms of art: sculpture, which was experiencing a renaissance in the nineteenth century. Boston's Athenaeum had held its first exhibition of neoclassical sculpture in 1839, photography's birth year.

In statues, Albert Southworth and Josiah Hawes saw the perfect subjects to showcase the aesthetic potential of the new medium. Unlike their human sitters, even the most classically beautiful of whom were either too fidgety for the long exposure times necessary or too unnatural in their stillness, marble masterpieces emanated a seductive proximity to perfection and remained unflinching before the camera.

Southworth & Hawes made their name by selling daguerreotypes of *The Greek Slave*—a wildly popular sculpture by the neoclassical sculptor Hiram Powers, depicting with astonishing expressiveness the sorrow of a nude young woman in shackles. Elizabeth Barrett Browning would capture its nuanced might of visual eloquence in a poem that begins with the words "They say Ideal beauty cannot enter / The house of anguish" and ends with "strike and shame the strong, / By thunders of white silence, overthrown." *The Greek Slave* would go on to become the first world-famous American work of art when it was displayed at the 1851 Great Exhibition in London. When the sculpture was revealed in Boston in the summer of 1848, the *Boston Globe* reported that of all the artworks on exhibition at the time, this was "the most prominent to persons of refined taste."

The Southworth & Hawes studio was around the corner from the exhibition, so they photographed the famous sculpture—without the artist's permission. Capitalizing on the public enthusiasm for the Powers sculpture, Southworth & Hawes began selling daguerreotypes of it, which in turn popularized the notion of daguerreotyping itself as an artistic process in allegiance with the figurative arts. But the duo's most inventive cross-pollination of novelty and tradition was the decision to photograph their human subjects in the style of classical and neoclassical sculpture. In more than a hundred surviving portraits from their studio, women pose in near-identical manner, wearing evening dresses so low-cut that the closeup framing of the photographs makes them look almost nude—a striking aesthetic in an era predicated on propriety, made permissible only by the fact that the women in the portraits were emulating, on the photographers' direction, two particularly popular statues: an antique sculpture of the water nymph Clytie from Greek mythology, and a Hiram Powers bust of Proserpine, the Roman goddess of springtime.

The most famous daguerreotype to come out of Southworth & Hawes's studio is a self-portrait Albert Southworth took in 1848, as Margaret Fuller was witnessing the demolition of Rome. A pensive bearded head gazing to the left at some invisible trouble crowns his slender nude torso for a combined effect evocative of Henry Fox Talbot's famous calotype of his bust of Patroclus. (In taking the image, Talbot had envisioned how the photographic reproduction of artworks—not only statues, but manuscripts and paintings—would forever alter the course of visual culture, writing in the caption of his Patroclus calotype: "Already sundry amateurs have laid down the pencil and armed themselves with chemical solutions and with cameræ obscuræ.") Even Southworth's facial hair, in marked contrast to his other self-portraits, is deliberately styled to resemble Patroclus's likeness, inadvertently making him look like a nude version of the famous photograph of Henry David Thoreau, taken eight years later, when the author had three daguerreotype portraits made for fifty cents each to satisfy a fan's request for a likeness.

Neoclassical sculpture, with its fusion of beauty and melancholy, surface stillness and interior tumult, became the template of aesthetic and conceptual sensibility for the new medium. But it also accomplished something else, perhaps half-intended—a mirroring of marble's defiance of our mortal finitude. Southworth & Hawes bookended the promise of immortality with life and death—the daguerreotype offerings they most prominently advertised were "children's and infants' pictures" and "likenesses of the deceased."

Photography, born out of a scientific battle against the ephemerality of light and shadow, grew into an art contesting the impermanence of existence itself.

Southworth wrote a number of articles instructing sitters—primarily women—on how to pose for artful portraits. "Expression is everything in a daguerreotype," he writes in a *Lady's Almanac* article. "All else,—the hair—jewelry—lace-work—drapery or dress, and attitude, are only aids to expression. It must at least be comfortable, and ought to be amiable." He saw photographs as portraits not only of physical likeness but of state of being. "Select an hour for sitting when you may be in your best mental as well as physical condition," he counsels. His directives also offer a jarring reminder of our changing ideals of beauty—thinness, not plumpness, was a point of shame and an object of concealment: "Thin necks and projecting collar bones require high dresses with lace, whether in fashion or not. The same remarks apply to arms and hands. If not well filled out, with good outlines, let them be appropriately covered in a picture."

Southworth's article makes the first cogent case for photographic portraiture as a legitimate figurative art. He exhorts the public:

> Have confidence in the Art itself. There is far more danger of undervaluing than overrating it. It may not, like painting and sculpture, be susceptible of the expression of feelings and emotions which have been awakened in the mind of the Artist, and more nearly realized in his own conceptions. Though it be not to his inner fancy in the creation of scenes and characters and forms which might have existed in a state of higher perfection and rarer intellectual refinement, yet the genius and spirit of poetry must possess the Artist, so that he can ever elevate his characters in portraiture far above common nature.

Such a poetic disposition, he argues, would ensure that the photographer—the Artist—is "not degraded to a servile copyist, and his Art to a mere resemblance." He points out that while painters and sculptors have the liberty of working with materials and colors of their choice to bring their artistic vision to life, photographers can use light and shadow in "representing independently, action, expression, and character to a great extent . . . developing beauty in grace of motion and in repose, which is the first object and the supreme law of all Art."

Two decades later, an Indian-born Englishwoman by the name of Julia Margaret Cameron pioneered soft-focus photographic portraiture after receiving a camera as a fiftieth-birthday gift from her son. Cameron photographed some of the most prominent figures of her day, including Charles Darwin, Robert Browning, Alfred Tennyson, and John Herschel himself, and had the good sense to register copyright for each of her photographs, which ensured their survival to this day.

In 1926, Virginia Woolf—whose mother was Cameron's cousin and favorite photographic subject—published a posthumous volume of Cameron's photographs under her own independent Hogarth Press imprint. She prefaced the monograph with a biographical sketch of her great-aunt, who had died before Woolf's birth and whom she had gotten to know primarily through family anecdotes and letters. Woolf writes:

> The Victorian age killed the art of letter writing by kindness: it was only too easy to catch the post. A lady sitting down at her desk a hundred years before had not only certain ideals of logic and restraint before her, but the knowledge that a letter which cost so much money to send and excited so much interest to receive was worth time and trouble. With Ruskin and Carlyle in power, a penny post to stimulate, a gardener, a gardener's boy, and a galloping donkey to catch up the overflow of inspiration, restraint was unnecessary and emotion more to a lady's credit, perhaps, than common sense. Thus to dip into the private letters of the Victorian age is to be immersed in the joys and sorrows of enormous families, to share their whooping coughs and colds and misadventures, day by day, indeed hour by hour.

Woolf's point applies not only to letter writing but to the very medium celebrated by the book in which her essay appears, and in fact to every technology that ever was and ever will be. She couldn't have—or could she have?—envisioned what would become of photography as the technology became commonplace over the coming decades, much less what digital photography would bring. But her insight holds true—the easier it becomes to convey a message in a certain medium, the less selective we grow about what that message contains, and soon we are conveying the trifles and banalities of our day-to-day life, simply because it is effortless to fill the page (or feed, or screen, or whatever medium comes next). Letters about lunch items have been supplanted by Instagram photographs of lunch items, to which we apply the ready-made filters that have purported to supplant the artistry of light, shadow, and composition. The art of photography, too, is being killed by kindness.

But at its dawn, every medium—like every new love—is aglow only with the exhilaration of endless possibility. While Albert Southworth was busy broadening the creative horizons of the new technology by aligning it with "the supreme law of all Art," an equally alluring frontier of promise opened up in science—early photography turned to the supreme law not of all Art but of all Nature, taking to the stars and beginning a slow, steadfast revolution in astronomy.

When Maria Mitchell visited Mary Somerville in Florence nearly two decades after photography's invention, the Scottish polymath asked her new American friend to send her a daguerreotype of a star, for she had not yet seen one but believed that photography would light a new dawn for astronomy. One evening the previous October, during Mitchell's stay in Greenwich, the English astronomers attending a dinner party at the observatory had regaled her with tales of the great "Leviathan"—the enormous sixteen-ton telescope with an aperture of 72 inches housed in the castle of the Anglo-Irish astronomer William Parsons, Third Earl of Rosse, which would remain the largest telescope in the world until exactly a century after Mitchell's birth. A decade earlier, well before the discovery of other galaxies, Lord Rosse had used his Leviathan to observe and draw the spiral structures he believed to be nebulae inside the Milky Way. His engraving of the swirling spectacle M51, known today as the Whirlpool Galaxy, became one of the most reproduced astronomical images in Europe and went on to inspire *The Starry Night*, which Van Gogh painted ten days before Maria Mitchell's death and nine months before his own.

A few months after Maria Mitchell made her comet discovery with a modest telescope hardly superior in optical power to the primitive spyglass Galileo had first pointed at the sky, the Harvard College Observatory installed a colossal telescope dubbed the Great Refractor. With nearly tenfold the aperture of Mitchell's instrument, it would remain the most powerful in America for twenty years. Mitchell herself saw in telescopes more than mere mechanical behemoths—to her, they were equally triumphs of craftsmanship and of the human spirit. In a lecture to her Vassar students, she would use Alvan Clark—America's finest optician, maker of both the crowdfunded telescope she had received from the "women of America" and of the instrument at the Vassar observatory—as a breathing testament to the human ingenuity and perseverance by which we expand our frontiers of knowledge:

> The telescope maker Mr. Clark, who has just improved the glass of our telescope, stands over such a glass eight hours a day, for six months, patiently rubbing the surface with a fine powder. It is mere manual labor, you will say. But at the end of that six months he has made a glass which reveals to the world heavenly bodies which no mortal eye ever saw before.
>
> You know that Archimedes said "Give me a place to stand on and I will move the world." The man who makes a glass which penetrates into space farther than was ever before reached, moves the world in space. The step, however small, which is in advance of the world, shows the greatest of the man, whether that step be taken with brain, with heart, or with hands.

When the Great Refractor was installed at Harvard, the observatory director, William Bond—who had helped Mitchell and her father build a small observatory atop Pacific Bank in Nantucket—befriended the daguerreotypist John Adams Whipple, who thought of photography as a figurative art rather than a technical craft but applied it to the advancement of science. The two men began a series of collaborations that lit the dawn of astrophotography. Four years into it, in 1851, Whipple would awe the world with his stunning photographs of celestial objects—particularly his photographs of the Moon, evocative of the Milton verse that Maria Mitchell had lauded in her essay on *Paradise Lost* as the most elegant portrait of Earth's ancient companion: "that Globe whose hither side / With light from hence, though but reflected, shines." Daguerre himself had taken the first lunar photograph on January 2, 1839—five days before he announced his invention—but his studio and his entire archive were destroyed by a fire two months later. Whipple's remains the earliest known surviving photograph of the Moon—an image that continues to stun with its simple visual poetics even as technology has far eclipsed the primitive equipment of its photographer.

Whipple's collaboration with Bond was the beginning of what would become the world's largest collection of astrophotography plates at the Harvard College Observatory. From this vast visual library, a team of women known as the Harvard Computers—including a number of Maria Mitchell's former students—would wrest pioneering insight into the nature of the universe, patiently analyzing and annotating the glass plates that today number half a million.

The Harvard Computers came to be when Edward Charles Pickering, Bond's successor, realized that his Scottish housemaid, Williamina Fleming, had better mathematical ability than the barely qualified men he had employed to analyze his observatory data. He hired Fleming as a part-time computer and was quickly swayed by her superior skill and work ethic, firing the men and enlisting a whole team of women to do the job, which they did formidably.

Within a decade of joining the observatory, Fleming—whose father had been the first person in their Scottish hometown to try his hand at daguerreotyping—had published a four-hundred-page catalog of ten thousand stellar spectra she herself had classified. Another computer, Henrietta Swan Leavitt—whose work was so valued that she was paid thirty cents an hour, five cents more than the standard salary of the computers—furnished the calculations that later became the basis for Edwin Hubble's law demonstrating that the universe is expanding. Among the team was the deaf Annie Jump Cannon, who within three years of taking over the observatory's variable star data had added a staggering twenty thousand new index cards and transfigured the almost uselessly disorganized database into an impressive catalog. Another computer, Cecilia Payne, discovered that stars were made primarily of hydrogen, which rendered it by far the most abundant element in the universe—a landmark discovery illuminating the chemical composition of the cosmos. Ninety years earlier, the eminent French philosopher of science Auguste Comte had proclaimed of the stars: "We shall never be able to study, by any method, their chemical composition or their mineralogical structure."

Payne had become besotted with astronomy during her first year at the women's college of Cambridge University in 1919, while attending a lecture on relativity by Sir Arthur Eddington— the English Quaker astronomer who had catapulted Einstein into celebrity earlier that year by proving the most significant scientific theory since Newtonian gravity.

When World War I broke out, Eddington refused to be drafted into the army on account of his faith's commitment to pacifism. To keep the young astronomer from being jailed for treason, his boss, Britain's Astronomer Royal, arranged for him to undertake a major scientific mission—he was to lead an expedition to test Einstein's theory of general relativity, completed four years earlier. Data obtained during a total solar eclipse would be compared to Einstein's predictions for how a strong gravitational field should deflect light by bending spacetime. With the sun curtained by the Moon, Eddington could observe the light of the Hyades cluster, positioned directly behind the sun from Earth's vantage point but unblinded against the firmament darkened by the eclipse. If Einstein was right and Newton wrong, when the sun crossed the cluster during the eclipse, its massive gravitational field would warp spacetime itself and bend the Hyades starlight from its baseline nighttime position, which Eddington had recorded several months earlier. On May 29,

1919, as totality swept its otherworldly veil over the small island of Príncipe off Africa's western coast, Eddington's observations matched Einstein's theoretical model perfectly, validating the single greatest achievement in humanity's understanding of spacetime and the fabric of reality. "Dear Mother, joyous news today," Einstein wrote upon receiving word of the triumphant results.

Later that year, the nineteen-year-old Cecilia Payne would sit in the crowded Cambridge hall, enchanted by Eddington's account of the expedition. She would later recall:

> The result was a total transformation of my world picture. . . . For three nights, I think, I did not sleep. My world had been so shaken that I experienced something very like a nervous breakdown.

This revelation would send young Cecilia across the Atlantic, where she would work as a computer alongside some of Maria Mitchell's former students and become the first person to earn a Ph.D. in astronomy at Harvard University's Radcliffe College.

In her doctoral thesis, Payne challenged existing theories about the chemical composition of the universe, but her adviser dissuaded her from publishing her results and subsequently took credit for her discovery. Lest we judge Payne too harshly for not pushing forth with her data, may we not forget that Galileo, too, recanted his revolutionary findings under the pressures of his time. His era's men of the cloth were now men of Ivy League regalia, but they were still men in positions of power who bulldozed and bullied any challenge to their authority. Payne would persist and later become the first woman to chair a Harvard department.

In a telling testament to their times, Payne and the other women astronomers and mathematicians of the Harvard College Observatory were mockingly nicknamed "Pickering's harem"; in a telling testament to ours, the moniker has endured and recurs with frequency across pages analog and digital.

In the 1920s, Edwin Hubble would draw on Henrietta Swan Leavitt's data and discover that the Andromeda nebula is many times farther from Earth than are the farthest stars of the Milky Way, suggesting that there are galaxies other than our own. (Long ago, Walt Whitman had written: "Those stellar systems . . . suggestive and limitless as they are, merely edge more limitless, far more suggestive systems.") Half a century after Hubble, Vera Rubin would demonstrate that galaxies like M51 are held together by dark matter, thus confirming the existence of what was until then a purely theoretical proposition—a discovery made possible by spectrography, progeny of photography.

When the pioneering astrophotographers of John Adams Whipple's generation began pointing one end of the telescope at the cosmos and affixing the other to the camera, we could behold for the first time images of stars that lived billions of light-years away, billions of years ago, long dead by the time their light—the universe's merchant of time and conquistador of space—reached the lens. Against the backdrop of the newly and barely comprehensible sense of deep time, the blink of any human lifetime suddenly stung with its brevity of being, islanded in the cosmic river of chaos and entropy, drifting, always drifting, toward nonbeing.

We say that photographs "immortalize," and yet they do the very opposite. Every photograph razes us on our ephemeral temporality by forcing us to contemplate a moment—an unrepeatable fragment of existence—that once was and never again will be. To look at a daguerreotype is to confront the fact of your own mortality in the countenance of a person long dead, a person who once inhabited a fleeting moment—alive with dreams and desperations—just as you now inhabit this one. Rather than bringing us closer to immortality, photography humbled us before our mortal finitude. Florence Nightingale resisted it. "I wish to be forgotten," she wrote, and consented to being photographed only when Queen Victoria insisted.

I wonder about this as I stand amid the stacks of the Harvard College Observatory surrounded by half a million glass plates meticulously annotated by the hands of women long returned to stardust. I imagine the flesh of steady fingers, atoms spun into molecules throbbing with life, carefully slipping a glass plate from its paper sleeve to examine it. In a museum jar across the Atlantic, Galileo's finger, which once pointed to the Moon with flesh just as alive, shrivels like all of our certitudes.

Pinned above the main desk area at the observatory is an archival photograph of Annie Jump Cannon examining one of the photographic plates with a magnifying glass. I take out my smartphone— a disembodied computer of Venus, mundane proof of Einstein's relativity, instant access to more knowledge than Newton ever knew—and take a photograph of a photograph of a photograph.

The half million glass plates surrounding me are about to be scraped of the computers' handwriting—the last physical trace of the women's corporeality—in order to reveal the clear images that, a century and a half later, provide invaluable astronomical information about the evolution of the universe. There are no overtones of sentimentality in entropy's unceasing serenade to the cosmos.

15

TO GAZE AND TURN AWAY

A steamboat is puffing up the Mississippi River, approaching a bluff towering above the shore, not far from where a steamboat pilot named Samuel Clemens would pick up his pen name Mark Twain a decade later. Bored and brazen, the young men aboard boast that they can reach the top of the bluff. One scoffs that if women weren't such poor climbers, the ladies in the party could join them.

Harriet Hosmer thrusts her hands into her pockets and a mischievous smile lifts her chin as she proposes a foot race, wagering that she can reach the summit before any of the boys. A spectator to the scene would later remember her as "a gay, romping, athletic schoolgirl." The captain, amused, banks the boat, and off they all go. Harriet—Hatty to those who love her—slices through changing altitudinal zones of vegetation up the five hundred feet of elevation above the river, dashing through the virgin pine forest, charging through the bramble, and scrambling up the jagged rock to triumph first atop the summit, waving a victorious handkerchief.

The captain, with amusement transmuted into astonishment, christens the bluff Mount Hosmer—a name it bears to this day.

This is not Harriet Hosmer's first triumph against expectation and convention, and it is far from her last.

At twenty-one, she has given herself the Mississippi River adventure as a small summer reward for having completed her anatomical studies—a centerpiece of her plan, as confident and single of purpose as her climbing wager, to become a sculptor. Packed in her trunk is a diploma from the medical school of St. Louis University. The year is 1851. An American university attended by men is not to officially begin admitting women for decades to come. She would go on to become one of the most celebrated sculptors since ancient Greece, a neoalchemist who invents a process for transmuting cheap limestone into precious marble, a Pygmalion of her own destiny. She would break new ground for women, claim a place for American art in the Old World pantheon, model for artists a life of self-made prosperity and uncompromising creative vision, and furnish queer culture with a bold new vocabulary of being. She would also spend the last decades of her life trying to invent a perpetual motion machine, and would die bankrupt and obscure.

How can a single person be both a stratospheric success and a failure bordering on the pathetic? Why do we seek narratives that move from less to more rather than from more to less, if the sum total is the same? Why do we consider it a failure when a long and loving relationship eventually grows troubled and ends, but celebrate romances bedeviled by innumerable obstacles that the lovers overcome before settling into a comfortable love? Why do we prefer the stories of lives that begin in poverty or obscurity and end in riches or fame to the stories of those that attain achievement early and end in poverty or oblivion? We long for perpetual motion out of the same impetus—a stubborn refusal to recognize that cessation is the ultimate nature of all things, and that any dynamism, wherever in time it may fall, however briefly, is cause for celebration. "No amount of effort can save you from oblivion," Kurt Cobain would write in his journal.

Harriet Hosmer is unafraid of effort, which she exerts with indefatigable might toward the impossible—be it in the illusion of permanence so exquisitely rendered in her marble sculptures or in her obsession with perpetual motion—perhaps because death has been with her since the dawn of life.

.   .   .

Born in a small Massachusetts town in 1830, before she was six Hatty had already lost two infant brothers and her mother to tuberculosis. The only surviving sibling—her sister Helen—died when Harriet was twelve, of the same disease. Grief-stricken into desperation, her father—a man who had come from little and earned considerable wealth through his practice as a physician—took it upon himself to inoculate young Hatty against the consumption that had borne away the rest of his family. He bought her a horse, a boat, a bow and arrows, and skates, instructed her to live "all out-doors," and devised for her a regimen of rigorous physical activity—hiking, swimming, riding, rowing, hunting, skating—which Hatty embraced with a natural vitality and a zest then condoned only in boys.

Although Dr. Hosmer had invested heavily in his daughter's education, he even withdrew her from school, proclaiming that "there is a whole lifetime for the education of the *mind*, but the *body* develops in a few years; and during that time, nothing should be allowed to interfere with its free and healthy growth."

Harriet saw nature not only as an outdoor gymnasium but as a field of observation. She used clay from the banks of the Charles River to make models of wildlife encountered during her adventures. A quarter century later, upon visiting Hosmer's revered studio in Rome, Maria Mitchell would marvel in her diary: "She fashions the clay to her ideal—every little touch of her fingers in the clay is a thought; she thinks in clay." Growing up, Hatty played not with dolls but with a human skeleton that hung in her father's study, which she would dress in her cousin's clothes and pretend to feed. By the time she was eighteen, she had mounted more than five hundred species of butterflies, fixed numerous reptiles in bottles of formaldehyde, and taxidermied various birds and animals. She adopted a snake as a pet and, true to her native irreverence, named her Eve. Eve eventually ended up on Harriet's dissection table, fomenting her fascination with anatomy.

In the fall of 1847, just as Maria Mitchell was about to make her comet discovery, Dr. Hosmer decided to complement his daughter's robust physical education with its intellectual counterpart. He chose the Sedgwick School—a pioneering "female academy" in Lenox, at the heart of the Berkshires. Its founder, Elizabeth Sedgwick, wrote of her teaching philosophy with uncompromising clarity of vision:

> If you succeed in training properly [young people's] powers of mind, in forming in them habits of patient and careful study, of a concentration of their powers, bearing upon a single point, as the sun's rays are collected in a focus, and in inspiring them with a love of knowledge for its own sake, you have done inexpressibly more for them than if you had made them passive repositories of the knowledge to be got out of all the school-books that ever were printed.

A decade earlier, Elizabeth Peabody had articulated the same sentiment in a letter of advice to her younger sister Sophia:

> Do not study for the sake of having acquirements to display, for the sake of being admired, for the sake of attracting attention [but for the] pleasure . . . derived from the feeling of energy that arises in the mind from the keen exercise of its powers in metaphysical, scientific or mathematical reasoning.

When Mrs. Sedgwick was entrusted with the sharp-witted but unruly Hatty Hosmer, she welcomed her with a wink: "I have a reputation for training wild colts, and I will try this one." Rather than restricting the girl's natural wildness, she taught her how to channel it into a ferocious work ethic that would remain with Harriet for the rest of her life. Maria Child—who would become her greatest champion—would later write in her influential biographical sketch that Harriet roamed the Berkshire outdoors "gazing with a poet's eye on the evening star . . . like a true artist, observant of all the forms of things, except the conventional forms . . . cementing friendships with charming young girls, and in constant intercourse with intellects of a high order."

The Sedgwick School did more for Harriet than shape her habits of mind. It sculpted her habits of heart and provided a safe space for self-discovery as she came to know her emerging sexuality and her identity as a lesbian—a word that wouldn't come into popular use until more than a century later. We are always trapped by the lexicon of the present in narrating the past, so let it be a shorthand for the complex and confusing ecosystem of emotional and physical relations that the women-loving women of Hosmer's time navigated.

Despite her jovial and adventurous personality, an aching alienation seemed to rupture Harriet's sense of belonging in Boston—something she articulated in what had become her surest self-defense against melancholy: humor. In an anonymously published poem titled "Boston and Boston People in 1850," she offered a satirical walking tour of the city, guided by an irreverent androgynous narrator who mocks the locals' mercantile mind-set, laments the lack of support for the arts, and regards with pity the dreariness of traditional married life. Between the lines is her growing recognition of her gender identity and sexual orientation—against the dull backdrop of domesticity, she regards herself as "inclined to be friendly with woman kind" and commends the woman who dares to live as "a single miss" or "that saint on earth—a good Old Maid"—an astute recognition that the women labeled thus by their contemporaries have often been history's censored and censured lesbians.

At the Sedgwick School, Harriet met a mathematically gifted young woman from St. Louis named Cornelia Carr—her first romantic infatuation and the recipient of Hatty's youthful love poems, her most loyal lifelong friend, her eventual estate executor and biographer, and, crucially, the daughter of the man who would become Hosmer's greatest patron and second father figure.

When Hatty decided to pursue sculpture seriously as a vocation after completing her three years at Lenox, there had been no successful woman sculptor in America before, and only partial successes in Europe. After taking some modeling classes in Boston and creating her first model in wax—a head of Lord Byron—she grew convinced that in order to be not just a good sculptor but a great one, she must master human anatomy beyond what she had already absorbed from books and her father's medical practice.

She decided to go to medical school.

The nearby Harvard Medical School would have been the natural choice. They had already turned away another woman, but Harriet's reasons for applying elsewhere were more personal. Wayman Crow—her beloved Cornelia's father, whom Hatty would soon come to call Pater—arranged for her to attend the newly established medical school in St. Louis, where she would be reunited with Cornelia. Wayman Crow had dropped out of school at twelve to become a dry goods merchant, worked his way to being one of the wealthiest businessmen in St. Louis by the time he was forty, and was eventually elected to the state senate. He had just cofounded what would become Washington University with the New Englander William Greenleaf Eliot—Margaret Fuller's onetime teenage intellectual sparring partner and grandfather of the poet T. S. Eliot.

Four weeks after her twentieth birthday, Hatty enrolled in the St. Louis medical school, listing anatomy and chemistry as her majors. (Several months earlier, the English-born Elizabeth Blackwell had graduated from a small university in upstate New York as the first woman to earn a degree in medicine in America.) Every morning, Hatty trekked two muddy miles to the university in her signature brown bonnet, the hem of her dress petrified with dirt by the time she arrived, her flowing skirts rumored to have concealed a pistol.

Crow introduced her to his friend Joseph McDowell, head of the medical school at the university, who had trained Hiram Powers a generation earlier and who now took Harriet under his wing. Already far better equipped to handle the gore of dissections and cadavers than her peers, thanks to her experience with hunting and taxidermy, Hosmer became Dr. McDowell's favorite student. He would summon her to his office before lectures for private lessons and detailed study of cadavers, to which she brought, in the professor's admiring words, "an eye that beamed with pleasure at the exhibition of Nature and Nature's work." Her meticulous draftsmanship of human musculature rivaled Leonardo's.

The reputation of this unusual and unusually driven "lady student" would soon travel beyond campus. Shortly after her graduation in 1852, a *Godey's Lady's Book* article highlighted Harriet as a beacon for women across disciplines. Noting that she could reach "the highest renown" in art if she continued on her chosen course, the author remarked on Hosmer's sidewise contribution to culture:

> She has shown the superiority of the female mind in the study of anatomy, thus pointing to woman's true profession in the sciences, viz., the medical. In this science, females will excel whenever they are permitted to enter on the study.

Despite her intellectual vitality and buoyant spirit, an undercurrent of sadness coursed through Hatty. Even her trip along the Mississippi offered a counterpoint to the sunny confidence with which she had raced the boys to the top of the bluff. On the steamship, she wrestled with the awareness that everyone and everything we love is eventually swept away. She wrote to Cornelia:

> There are people enough in this great world but how few for whom we can care, in whom we can take an interest or whom we can love. The great tide of life ebbs and flows bringing hundreds on whom we are never to bestow a thought and taking in return those whose lives are as dear to us as our own and filling their places with strangers.

It is a life's work to reconcile ourselves to the fact that none of the things we gain by force of effort—admiration, awards, wealth, chiseled abs—ever make up for the unbidden gifts we are given and inevitably lose. To arrive at that realization shy of twenty-one is perhaps tragic, perhaps redemptive, perhaps both. Harriet Hosmer possessed the uncommon bend of character to hold the beauty and the tragedy of life with even hands. Upon returning to the Boston area after medical school, she met the sorrow of her separation from Cornelia with a passionate immersion in art. With the same zeal with which she had once taken to the outdoors, she now took to the cultural indoors, making frequent trips to the Boston Athenaeum—the heart of the American art world at the time—and to Tremont Temple, the music hall where the Boston Symphony

Orchestra performed and practiced. In a letter to Cornelia near the end of 1851, she writes:

> You can't imagine how delightful are the musical rehearsals in Boston every Friday afternoon[. O]nce a week, at least, I am raised to a higher humanity. There is something in fine music that makes one feel nobler and certainly happier. Fridays are my Sabbaths, really my days of rest, for I go first to the Athenaeum and fill my eyes and mind with beauty, then to Tremont Temple and fill my ears and soul with beauty of another kind, so am I not then literally "drunk with beauty"?

The quoted phrase she borrows from a Lord Byron stanza about the Venus de' Medici, the ancient Greek marble sculpture of Aphrodite in Florence:

> We gaze and turn away, and know not where,
> Dazzled and drunk with beauty, till the heart
> Reels with its fulness; there—for ever there—
> Chain'd to the chariot of triumphal Art,
> We stand as captives, and would not depart.

Poetry would aways remain a wellspring of personal exaltation and professional inspiration for Harriet. Artists, she believed, "should be students not only of human nature, but of letters." That year, she discovered in a poem—one embodying her familiar intersection of sorrow and splendor—the seed for the sculpture that would bring her first flood of acclaim. In another letter to Cornelia, she exclaims that she found "Sad Hesper"—one of 131 short elegiac poems in Tennyson's *In Memoriam*—to be "one of the most exquisite poems, containing some of the most beautiful ideas in the English language." Among them was the discomposing fact at the center of Margaret Fuller's lifelong turmoil: "We are not wholly brain, magnetic mockeries."

Tennyson had completed *In Memoriam*, originally titled *The Way of the Soul*, in 1849 to commemorate a beloved friend who had died of a stroke at twenty-two nearly two decades earlier. Inspired by the emerging science of the transmutation of species, the poem advances evolutionary ideas a decade before Darwin unsettled the world.

These are the verses that so moved Hosmer:

> Sad Hesper o'er the buried sun
> And ready, thou, to die with him,
> Thou watchest all things ever dim
> And dimmer, and a glory done:
>
> The team is loosen'd from the wain,
> The boat is drawn upon the shore;
> Thou listenest to the closing door,
> And life is darken'd in the brain.

In Greek mythology, Hesper, the evening star, is the nocturnal counterpart to Phosphor, the morning star. Pythagoras was the first to realize that the two were simply different apparitions of the same "wandering star"—the planet Venus—determined by its orbit. Two millennia later, Galileo's revolutionary observations of the phases of Venus would become the first nail in the coffin of the geocentric model of the universe.

Tennyson's elegy for the seesaw of life and death, embodied in Hesper's setting fate, spoke powerfully to Hosmer's preoccupation with impermanence. In early 1852, at twenty-one, she set out to bring to life her first ideal sculpture, which she titled *Hesper, the Evening Star*—the bust of a beautiful young woman, serene with an edge of solemnity, her lowered gaze gliding along the invisible frontier between day and night, existence and nonexistence. A star—not the typical five-point geometry, but a sunlike star of seven points—crowns her braided hair above an androgynous face as a crescent moon arches below her bare, nippleless breasts.

But *Hesper* may have meant something more to Hatty than a tribute to Tennyson—a tribute of a much more intimate order. That year, her creative elation plummeted into personal misery as she learned of Cornelia's engagement to a young anthropologist—news that gave Hatty a "spasm" of jealousy, which she concealed with her stated concern that Cornelia was too young to marry and her chosen husband too financially unstable to support her. Even if her love for Cornelia had never been fully requited, Hatty mourned its loss so acutely that she asked her beloved not to mention her engagement again in their correspondence. She beseeched Cornelia to model for her: "Bequeath to me your body and it shall be honored in history." With loss as the most formative experience of her life and marble her mightiest coping mechanism against impermanence, she envisioned the sculpture as a tribute "in death as in life"—a way to possess Cornelia permanently, to immortalize the fantasy of an idealized beloved from which she was now so pointedly departing with her choice to marry.

This request only made Cornelia retreat further. Despite her adoration of Harriet, it had become too discomfiting that while their deep love for each other was matched in magnitude, it was profoundly different in texture. Cornelia simply couldn't meet Hatty's sexual attraction.

Perhaps the bust of *Hesper* was modeled on Cornelia, depicting not the body her beloved withheld but those parts of which their incomplete bond had been composed—heart and mind. Or perhaps it was her hope for a miracle modeled after the hidden personal dimension of Tennyson's epic poem. This is the story the poet himself told: Two decades before he composed *In Memoriam*—around the time the friend eulogized in the poem died—Tennyson had fallen in love with Emma Sellwood, a young woman he'd known since childhood. He courted her and won her heart, but not her mind and moral conscience—Emma found his atheistic inclination too incompatible with her own theological bent. She declined his offer of marriage, but—so Tennyson's account goes—her heart remained faithful to him and she rejected all other suitors. After ten years of such remote mutual fidelity across the distance and the silence, the poet wrote to Emma, asking if her mind had changed. It had not. Another decade passed, the two still in each other's hearts, though apart. Then, a week after *In Memoriam* was published, Tennyson received a letter from Emma—she had been so moved by the work's sincerity and purity of sentiment that she was ready at last to join her fate to the poet's. The two were married that June and soon had two sons, naming the firstborn after the friend for whom Tennyson had composed *In Memoriam*.

But if *Hesper* was Hosmer's last, most valiant attempt to win Cornelia's heart—her very own *In Memoriam*—it produced no such miraculous turn of mind. Cornelia married the young anthropologist, but she did name her newborn daughter Harriet, and for the remainder of her life, she clipped and collected every glowing mention of Hosmer in the press.

An encounter that would become another catalyst in Hosmer's personal and professional development interrupted the heartache of Cornelia's loss.

In the fall of 1851, while John Adams Whipple was pointing Harvard's Great Refractor at the stars, Charlotte Cushman visited Boston as part of her farewell tour of the United States before settling permanently in Europe. Cushman was the most prominent American actress of her time. In the year of photography's birth, at age twenty-three, she had stunned the theatrical public by appearing as Romeo alongside her sister, who played Juliet. She was also—and this is a crude anachronistic application of a modern term, for there is no historical analog—an out lesbian. By the time Hosmer was introduced to her by a former Sedgwick School classmate, Cushman was traveling with her longtime partner, the British journalist Matilda Hays. Their union was so public and accepted that the two women appear in a traditional couple arrangement in one of Southworth & Hawes's most famous daguerreotypes—Cushman sitting, Hays standing behind her, both dressed in fitted male attire above the waist and flowing skirts below. Elizabeth Barrett Browning termed their relationship a "female marriage" in which the two women had "vowed eternal attachment to each other." EBB was only partly surprised to learn from a friend that such marriages were "by no means uncommon"—these were women true to their nature, true to their loves, and she would soon write in *Aurora Leigh* that "whoever lives true life, will love true love." (Thirty-some years later, Henry James's novel *The Bostonians* would popularize the term "Boston marriage"—a domestic partnership between two women financially independent of any man. James likely modeled this type of partnership on his sister Alice's relationship with Katharine Peabody Loring, though he had also met Hosmer and characterized her as "above all, a character, strong, fresh, and interesting.")

That fall, Hosmer met the thirty-five-year-old Cushman and an instant attraction sparked between them, though its precise nature was probably unclear to both. When we encounter a person of exceptional intellectual and creative vitality, their magnetism can disorient the compass needle of admiration and attraction—it becomes difficult, sometimes impossible, to tease apart the desire to be with from the desire to be like. For Hosmer, Cushman provided a dual model of being a successful artist and a queer woman living a public life. Cushman, who admired artistic excellence and perhaps saw a younger version of herself in the boldly eccentric young woman, encouraged Hosmer's sculpture and enthralled her with stories of life in Rome, where she had been residing for years.

For three electric weeks, Harriet accompanied Cushman to rehearsals every night and spent a good deal of time in her dressing room. After Cushman and her partner returned to Europe in December, she lamented in a letter to Cornelia, with whom she was beginning to settle into a more equitable friendship: "Isn't it strange how we meet people in this world and become attached to them in so short a time? Now I feel as if I had lost my best friend . . ."

A surge of success distracted Hosmer from her loneliness. In the summer of 1852, *Hesper* was exhibited in Boston. Maria Child— who would soon become the era's most devoted celebrator of women's genius—took notice. Child's husband was an old friend of Dr. Hosmer's, so she took the opportunity to visit Harriet's home studio. She was so taken with the work, both conceived with poetic vision and crafted with impeccable skill, that she wrote a laudatory article for the *New-York Tribune*, which Margaret Fuller had established as the country's most trusted voice in the arts. It was published, without a byline, under the title "A New Star in the Arts."

Child became Harriet Hosmer's most ardent champion—a relationship that illuminated the paradox of altruism, for while Child admired and cared for the young sculptor, she also saw in Harriet an archetype by which to advance her own cause of women's suffrage. In her later memoir of Hosmer—which she wrote by dipping her pen in an inkstand Hatty herself had made as a girl out of a seagull's egg—Child would hold up Hosmer's medical studies as a pathbreaking example that evolved the frontiers of possibility for society at large:

> These things are a matter of custom, and, in a progressive state of society, customs are always changing. Asiatics think it shamefully immodest, and even dangerous, for a woman to appear abroad with her face uncovered; but intercourse with Europeans gradually teaches them that women may be allowed to breathe God's free air, without committing or causing crime. Europeans have further steps to take in social progress. They must learn that no harm comes from allowing the souls of women to breathe free air. I feel personal gratitude to Florence Nightingale, Harriet Martineau, Rosa Bonheur, Harriet Hosmer, and all other women, who, by following noble impulses, unrestrained by mere conventional rules, prove woman's right to do whatever she can do well.

Under the enchantment of Cushman's tales of life in Rome's expat community of artists and queer women, Hosmer made another radical decision that would shape her life: She would move to Rome to apprentice with one of the great masters. A decade earlier, Margaret Fuller had written to her mother: "Those have not lived who have not seen Rome."

Four weeks before her departure, Hatty wrote to Wayman "Pater" Crow: "I feel that I am on the eve of a new life, that the earth will look larger, the sky brighter, and the world in general more grand." More than a century before the American government established a national endowment for the arts, she writes:

> You do not know how thoroughly dissatisfied I am with my present mode of life. I ought to be accomplishing thrice as much as now, and

feel that I am soul-bound and thought-bound in this land of dollars and cents. I take it there is inspiration in the very atmosphere of Italy, and that there, one intuitively becomes artistic in thought. Could the government of this country and its glorious privileges be united with the splendors of art in Italy, that union would produce terrestrial perfection. . . . My motto is going to be, "Live well, do well, and all will *be* well."

Just before her twenty-second birthday, Harriet packed the diploma of her anatomical studies and two daguerreotypes of *Hesper* and sailed for Europe with her father, who was to help her settle in.

Traveling in her party was Grace Greenwood—the literary pseudonym of Sara Jane Lippincott, a writer and social reformer who had risen to prominence at the age of twenty-one with her politically wakeful poems, then turned toward journalism with Margaret Fuller as her role model. Now the age Maria Mitchell was at the time of her comet discovery, Greenwood was writing for *The New York Times*—the first woman on the young paper's payroll. She had a new assignment to cover the arts while traveling in Europe. Already an admirer of Hosmer's work, she made her the subject of ample praise in print, ensuring that American audiences were following the beginnings of a promising career with elated excitement, in near-real time.

Upon their arrival, the large makeshift family of friends and lovers—Charlotte Cushman and Matilda Hays, Harriet and her father, and Grace Greenwood—rented a house together in central Rome. Hosmer pursued what she considered "the dearest wish" of her heart: studying with the great English sculptor John Gibson—the unofficial king of Rome's expatriate artist community, himself trained by the pioneering neoclassical sculptor Antonio Canova. Gibson had many applicants, but had accepted none when another sculptor approached him on Hosmer's behalf and showed him the daguerreotype of *Hesper*. Gibson's oft-cited response might be the ornament of early florid biographies, or it might be the simple fact of the occasion: "Send the young lady to me,—whatever I can teach her, she shall learn." Whatever Gibson said, what he did remains indisputable: He took on Harriet as his sole student, gave her the room in his studio where Canova had previously worked, and immersed her in attentive mentorship, extolling to anyone who would listen her "vast degree of native genius." He gave her books, casts, and engravings to study and assigned her sculptures to copy in perfecting her craft. Hosmer took to it all with indefatigable enthusiasm and work ethic. "He is my master," she wrote to Wayman Crow, "and I love him more every day. I work under his very eye, and nothing could be better for me in every way."

After a year of study with Gibson, Hosmer was ready to create her first original sculpture since *Hesper*—another bust of a woman drawn from ancient Greek mythology, loaded with meaning and layered with questions about women's status, rights, and fate in a male-dominated society: Medusa.

According to the version of the Greek legend Hosmer chose, the beautiful Medusa was raped by the sea god Poseidon—a crime committed in the temple of Athena, for which the goddess of wisdom decided to dispense punishment. But in a subtle reminder that the writers of these myths were men, the jealous Athena, rather than punishing the rapist, punished Medusa for having attracted Poseidon's attention—she transformed the lovely maiden into a gorgon so hideous that men turned to stone at the sight of her. In an era when statutory rape was almost impossible to prosecute in Hosmer's homeland, where wives had no legal right to refuse sex to their husbands and legions of white men were raping black women with complete legal and societal impunity, her depiction of Medusa was a bold and prescient choice commenting on the gruesome deficiencies of a justice system that had failed to protect women since antiquity and a society in which victim-blaming has endured to the present day.

Medusa was a popular subject with the great masters, but she was customarily rendered in her monstrous form following Athena's punishment. Hosmer chose to capture the moment of transfiguration—her bust, completed in 1854, depicts a proud and beautiful woman just as her hair is beginning to turn into serpents. She cast Medusa's hair from a real snake captured in the wilderness outside Rome. But she didn't have the heart to kill the serpent, so she anesthetized it with chloroform, made a cast by keeping it in plaster for three and a half hours, then released it back into the wild. Hosmer's *Medusa*—her choice of subject matter, her atypical depiction, her treatment of the live serpent—embodies the complex relationship between agency, victimhood, and mercy made tangible.

The same year, Hosmer created another original sculpture animated by a similar subject: a bust of Daphne, the beautiful nymph who ran from Apollo's lust and, in the final moment before being overtaken, was transformed into a laurel tree by her merciful father, the river god Ladon. Here was another woman who had to relinquish her womanhood and her very humanity in order to avoid the assailing ardor of unwanted male attention. In Hosmer's marmoreal rendering, a Hesper-like Daphne glances downward with a subtle smile as a laurel branch curves beneath her bare breasts.

Hosmer referred to the statue as her "first child" and sent it across the Atlantic to her patron and dear "Pater," Wayman Crow, Cornelia's father, in gratitude for his life-changing support—"as a love offering to the whole family, and as a very slight return for the many kindnesses."

That November, a *Liberator* review of Hosmer's *Daphne* and *Medusa* lauded them as "convincing proof of her genius and success," just above an op-ed urging the newly established Tufts University to open its doors to women. (The school did not—it would be another half century before the trustees voted to admit both sexes on equal terms.)

Meanwhile, the famed English actress Fanny Kemble—who had visited the Sedgwick School frequently during Hatty's studies and had taken a great liking to the energetic girl—traveled to Rome and witnessed Harriet's growing success up close. She reported to Wayman Crow:

I think she will distinguish herself greatly, for she not only is gifted with an unusual artistic capacity, but she has energy, perseverance, and industry; attributes often wanting where genius exists, and extremely seldom possessed or exercised in any effectual manner by women.

But then Kemble added:

> Hatty's peculiarities will stand in the way of her success with people of society and the world, and I wish for her own sake that some of them were less decided and singular, but it is perhaps unreasonable to expect a person to be singular in their gifts and graces alone, and not to be equally unlike people in other matters.

This was odd coming from Kemble, who was often cited as a major influence on Harriet's "peculiarities." Kemble, who sympathized with the cause of abolition, had married a wealthy American heir, but after he inherited his family's slave trade, she had found it impossible to remain in a marriage of such clashing values. She would later write to Hosmer of the outcome of the Civil War: "Surely there never was a more signal overthrow of the Devil and all his works, in the world's history since it began." How much of the acrimonious divorce was motivated by these political differences and how much by her growing impatience with heterosexuality we may never know, but by the time Kemble first met the teenaged Harriet at Lenox, she was a single woman who would spend the remainder of her life frequently clad in men's clothing, enjoying the company and courtship of women.

To Harriet, Kemble continued to be a force of loving encouragement. In one letter, she wrote with astronomical affection:

> My sweet little Hatty . . . [tell me] of what interests ever so little or much; your work, your plans, your ideas; what you are doing and what you are thinking of doing, what new shapes of beauty and of grace are haunting you, whether you have *fixed* any of your fair sisterhood of stars in clay or marble, or whether your heavens, with all those pretty creatures floating in them, are still only *planetary*?

Conscious of her own growing stardom, twenty-two-year-old Hosmer commissioned a photographer to affix her image in a portrait. But rather than making her "peculiarities" "less decided and singular," she played them up, deliberately sculpting her public image as what was fashionably, though not always flatteringly, known as "an emancipated female." In the portrait, Hosmer is wearing her daily studio outfit—another uncommon decision, for women were rarely photographed in work clothes, but especially daring since she sculpted in male attire. The intention is clearly to create the impression of being captured in the midst of creative labor during her regular workday. But salted paper—the photographic process used in the portrait, invented by Talbot in the early 1830s just before John Herschel helped him perfect the calotype—required at least an hour of exposure for a crisp image. Hosmer must have held her Puckish smile for quite some time—a living sculpture before the camera.

Her butch aesthetic—to use another anachronistic shorthand— was frequently remarked upon, but always with a warm acknowledgment of how her choice of clothing and her short curly hair seemed to emanate from her very nature. Gibson often addressed her as he would a man, by her last name—"my dear little Hosmer"—and affectionately wrote that she was a "clever fellow" no other pupil of his could match. Hosmer left an arresting first impression on Maria Mitchell. A "pretty little girl wearing a jaunty hat and a short jacket, into the pockets of which her hands were thrust" had rushed into the studio Mitchell was visiting in Rome and commenced "a rattling, all-alive talk" with another artist. The Hawthornes were there, too. "I liked her at once," Sophia wrote in her diary, "she was so frank and cheerful, independent, honest and sincere—wide awake, energetic, yet not ungentle."

Even the grouchy traditionalist Nathaniel Hawthorne, appointing himself as the voice of the patriarchy, reluctantly gave Hosmer permission to be herself. Describing her as "a small, brisk, wide-awake figure, not ungraceful; frank, simple, straightforward, and downright," he remarked on her male attire—"a shirt-front, collar, and cravat like a man's, with a brooch of Etruscan gold, and on her curly head was a picturesque little cap of black velvet"—then wrote:

She was very peculiar, but she seemed to be her actual self, and nothing affected or made up; so that, for my part, I gave her full leave to wear what may suit her best, and to behave as her inner woman prompts.

But he ultimately twists his permissive fascination into capitulation to convention, adding:

I don't quite see, however, what she is to do when she grows older, for the decorum of age will not be consistent with a costume that looks pretty and excusable enough in a young woman.

Hawthorne, who would later use Hosmer as inspiration for his characters in his final novel, *The Marble Faun*, was interpreting her dress not as a statement of identity but as youthful sartorial rebellion. But Hosmer was very much carving out her identity—Rome had become her Paradise Found, both its thriving community of artists and its expat coterie of queer women. She wrote to Cornelia:

Don't ask me if I was ever happy before, don't ask me if I am happy now, but ask me if my constant state of mind is felicitous, beatific, and I will reply "Yes." It never entered into my head that anybody could be so content on this earth, as I am here. I wouldn't live anywhere else but in Rome, if you would give me the Gates of Paradise and all the Apostles thrown in. I can learn more and do more here, in one year, than I could in America in ten. America is a grand and glorious country in some respects, but this is a better place for an artist.

Her conviction grew firmer as the months rolled by, illuminating the monumental influence of *genius loci* on what we call genius in a personal sense. That fall, she wrote to Cornelia:

If I could come out of Paradise to this place, I should think it perfect. . . . The longer I stay, the more frightful seems the idea of ever going away, and the more impossible seems to be that of being happy elsewhere. My father says that of all places in the world, Watertown is the place for him, and I say that of all places in the world, Rome is the one for me. Nothing this side of Eternity will induce me to go to America to live for the next twenty-five years.

Two weeks later, she exulted to Cornelia again:

It is a moral, physical and intellectual impossibility to live elsewhere. Everything is so utterly different here that it would seem like going into another sphere, to go back to America.

Hosmer's use of the word "sphere" is doubly significant—in the sense of celestial spheres, going back to America would be like moving to another planet; but this was also the heyday of the "separate spheres" rhetoric, which granted men the public sphere and relegated women to the domestic sphere. Harriet Hosmer was determined to live the public life of the artist, not the domestic life of the wife. There was no place for her in America—she was now a cultural refugee, blissfully encamped in the subcultural mecca of Rome's queer artists.

16

FROM ROMANCE TO REASON

Rome became Hosmer's sandbox of self-invention. It offered the strange alchemy by which we transmute our former selves—barely recognizable in their different bodies and different minds holding different ideas, values, and beliefs—into the fleeting constellation of what we so confidently claim as a solid self at this particular moment. The chain of umbilical cords by which one self gives birth to another again and again at once fetters us to our past and liberates us into a novel future. That chain is invisible, except for the rare moments when we feel it tug on the confident present self with its formidable weight. "My life is so unlike what it was then," Hosmer wrote with an eye to her teenage days at Lenox. "I think and feel so differently it seems to me I must have left my former body and found another. . . . These changes make me feel twenty years older."

In *Aurora Leigh*, Elizabeth Barrett Browning had limned the singular self-reinvention of such new beginnings amid the "perfect solitude of foreign lands," where you can

> be, as if you had not been till then,
> And were then, simply that you chose to be,

where you can "possess yourself" in

> A new world all alive with creatures new,
> New sun, new moon, new flowers, new people—ah,

And be possessed by none of them!
[. . .]
Such most surprising riddance of one's life
Comes next one's death; it's disembodiment
Without the pang.

Another letter to Cornelia escalates Harriet's elation at her rebirth:

There is something in the air of Italy, setting aside other things, which would make one feel at home in Purgatory itself. In America I never had that sense of quiet, settled content such as I now have from sunrise to sunset.

Harriet's serenity was punctuated by a lively sociality—she was beginning to meet the intellectual royalty of Europe: the Longfellows, the Thackerays, the Trollopes. She was careful, though, not to let her social life interfere with her art: "To a certain extent I suppose it is right to indulge in social gayeties," she told Cornelia, "but the difficulty is to draw the line between just enough and too much."

In her twenty-third year, she befriended Robert and Elizabeth Barrett Browning, who would remain loving parental figures for the young artist until Elizabeth's death seventeen years later. In a letter to a friend, Barrett Browning relayed her powerful first impressions of

Miss Hosmer . . . , the young American sculptress, who is a great pet of mine and of Robert's, and who emancipates the eccentric life of a perfectly "emancipated female" from all shadow of blame, by the purity of hers. She lives here all alone (at twenty-two), works from six o'clock in the morning till night, as a great artist must, and this with an absence of pretension, and simplicity of manners, which accord rather with the childish dimples in her rosy cheeks, than with her broad forehead and high aims.

Hosmer herself was so taken with the Brownings' love story and their mutual championship of each other's artistry that she asked if they would consent to her casting their hands in plaster. When they did, she honored their love in her most unusual work—a bronze sculpture of the Brownings' clasped hands. Nathaniel Hawthorne would immortalize it in *The Marble Faun* as a symbol of "the individuality and heroic union of two high, poetic lives." Both full of tenderness and resembling a handshake, Hosmer's homage to the Brownings gives physical form to the marriage of equals that Margaret Fuller had condoned in *Woman* as the only form of marriage worth entering.

Alongside such labors of love, Hosmer was beginning to support herself through commissions—an achievement almost incomprehensibly thrilling, as she wrote to Cornelia with her characteristic fusion of perceptiveness and good-natured humor:

> Now that I am supporting myself I feel so frightfully womanly that I cannot describe my venerable sensations, nor could you "realize" them, any more than dear Miss Elizabeth Peabody did the tree at Lenox, when she walked into it, and upon being asked about it, said, "Yes, I saw it, but I did not realize it."

Beneath her characteristic jocularity, Hosmer was taking a serious stance—radical at the time for a woman artist and to this day too feebly defended by all who survive by creative work—that artists ought to be paid in more than appreciation and flattery. To Wayman Crow, whose patronage had made her career possible, she wrote:

> It is time that I was paid in more glittering currency than "glory." Glory does not drive the machine, though it makes it glisten, and at this very moment I have far more of the glitter than of the precious metal.

Hosmer had taken a path not only alternative but almost entirely untrekked in a society in which marriage was women's most standard and almost only means of support. Watching her peers marry all around her, she wrote to Crow:

Everybody is being married but myself. . . . Even if so inclined, an artist has no business to marry. For a man, it may be well enough, but for a woman, on whom matrimonial duties and cares weigh more heavily, it is a moral wrong, I think, for she must either neglect her profession or her family, becoming neither a good wife and mother nor a good artist. My ambition is to become the latter, so I wage eternal feud with the consolidating knot.

It is difficult to disentwine Harriet's resentment of marriage as a trammeling of talent from her resentment of the fact that it was available only to heterosexual love. A decade later, she would meet a woman to whom she would consider herself a "hubby" and a "wedded wife" for a quarter century, until death did them part. But, for now, she was wedded solely to her art, as she intimated to Crow:

One must have great patience in matters of art, it is so very difficult, and excellence in it is only the result of long time. . . . Oh, if one knew but one-half the difficulties an artist has to surmount, the amount of different kinds of study necessary, before he can see the path even beginning to open before him, the public would be less ready to censure him for his shortcomings or slow advancement. The only remedy I know is patience with perseverance, and these are always sure, with a real honest love for art, to produce something.

Meanwhile in America, the early fruits of Hosmer's labor were garnering growing attention not only as a feat of art but as a feat for women. In a *Liberator* op-ed that opened with the words of Mary Wollstonecraft—"If the abstract rights of man will bear discussion and explanation, those of women, by a parity of reasoning, will not shrink from the same test"—Caroline Dall extolled Hosmer's *Hesper* as a masterpiece animated by the promise of "new life and light; new power to act and see," turning it into an emblem of early feminism. "It is a significant feat," she wrote, "that, during the past year, one of the most beautiful works of art, ever produced upon this continent, has been conceived and executed by a woman under twenty-one, gone now to perfect her powers in sunny Italy."

In 1857, as Maria Mitchell was packing her trunks for Europe, Hosmer received a commission for a monument from a wealthy Italian woman who had lost her young daughter, Juliet. The marmoreal elegy she composed—Juliet reclining on her deathbed, hovering serene between life and death—became the first monument by a foreign artist permitted to be displayed in an Italian temple.

While working on the private commission, Hosmer was incubating what would become her two greatest masterpieces—self-initiated works of art perfecting the intersection of beauty and tragedy, amplifying her previous commentary on women's rights in a patriarchal society.

In 1856, just as Elizabeth Barrett Browning's *Aurora Leigh* was going to press as a manifesto for women's right to art, proclaiming that "a woman . . . must prove what she can do before she does it," Hosmer had begun working on a sculpture of Beatrice Cenci—a young sixteenth-century woman, whose devastating story and the mythology that enveloped it had become an icon for antiauthoritarian Italians, fomenting the ideas of the Roman revolution.

Beatrice's father, a violent and depraved nobleman, had raped her repeatedly. When the papal authorities to whom she reported the crimes did nothing to protect her and to serve punishment, Beatrice took her salvation into her own hands. Together with her brother and stepmother, she hired two assassins to murder the abuser. They attempted to poison him, but the poison failed to kill. Beatrice saw no other recourse than to complete the task herself, which she did either by driving a spike through the rapist's eye or by bludgeoning him with a hammer—the stories vary. (Did Hosmer see analogs to the chisel and mallet she wielded daily in these tools of vengeance?) Only then did the papal authorities leap to punishment—they executed Beatrice in 1599, beheading her with a small ax in a public spectacle after extended torture. Margaret Fuller, upon visiting the prison cell where Beatrice was tortured, observed two years before Hosmer arrived in Rome: "There is, undoubtedly, foundation for the story of a curse laid on Eve."

Moved by Beatrice's story, Percy Shelley had resurrected it in 1819 in a verse drama in five acts. Although his good friend Lord Byron—a man thoroughly uninterested in women's rights—criticized it for having a subject he considered "essentially un-dramatic," Shelley's poem-play was so popular that it became his only work to reach a second edition in his lifetime. (The poet was buried in Rome.) Reproductions of a famed seventeenth-century portrait of Beatrice were as prevalent in nineteenth-century Rome as the Mona Lisa is in the Rome of today, but given Hosmer's love of poetry, it is probable that Shelley's poem is what awakened her to the human drama of Beatrice's story and planted the seed for her sculpture.

Hosmer depicts Beatrice in the final hours of her life, wearied by the torture, lying on the scaffold specially erected for her execution. Her turbaned head rests on one arm; her other hand hangs over the edge of the platform holding a rosary. Hovering between despair and dignity as she hovers between life and death, Hosmer's Beatrice arrests with the contrast between the tragedy of her fate and her final beauty—it is impossible to view this work of immense subtlety and immense intensity without being overtaken by a tidal wave of emotion.

When Hosmer completed *Beatrice Cenci*, Gibson famously exclaimed: "I can teach her nothing." Margaret Fuller, upon touring Europe's remnants of classical Greek and Roman sculpture a decade earlier, had lamented that "they will not float the heart on a boundless sea of feeling, like the starry night on our Western Prairie." Had she lived to see Hosmer's neoclassical *Beatrice,* she might have found in it the very cosmic aliveness of which the ancient world's statues were bereft.

Hosmer's masterpiece was first exhibited at London's Royal Academy of Art, where women would not be admitted as students for another three years. The first woman would not be hired as a professor at the institution until more than a century and a half later, in 2011—two hundred forty-three years after the Academy's founding.

On the wings of *Beatrice Cenci*'s success, Hosmer returned to America to take her masterpiece on tour. In Boston, Maria Child found her to be "the same frank, unaffected child" who had left five years earlier, with "no tinge of pretension to mar the beauty of her enthusiasm for art." During her American tour, anxious to return to Rome and resume work, Hosmer began sketching her vision for what would become her other major masterpiece: *Zenobia in Chains*—another homage to a woman who has taken charge of her own destiny, another poignant meditation on the relationship between victimhood and agency.

Zenobia was the third-century queen of the land that is now Syria—one of antiquity's two famous female heads of state, far more politically ferocious than Cleopatra and ultimately far more tragic. Many centuries later, Margaret Fuller would write in *Woman in the Nineteenth Century,* perhaps with Zenobia in mind: "The presence of a woman on the throne always makes its mark. Life is lived before the eyes of men, by which their imaginations are stimulated as to the possibilities of Woman."

An erudite and intellectually ambitious woman who valued conquests of the mind as much as those of land, Zenobia cultivated a welcome atmosphere for scholars in her court and espoused equality within her dominion, where people of various ethnic, cultural, and religious backgrounds mingled. In the year 270, Zenobia led an invasion of the Roman Empire. She conquered the majority of the Roman East and annexed Egypt. Over the next two years, she continued extending her empire, which nonetheless remained under the nominal jurisdiction of the Roman Emperor, until she eventually declared complete secession. In the ensuing revolution, the Roman army prevailed after a bloody fight, capturing Zenobia and exiling her to Rome.

Playing with the line between homage and refutation, Hosmer's *Zenobia* presented an aesthetic parallel and a conceptual mirror image to Hiram Powers's *The Greek Slave,* which depicted a feeble young nude about to be sold at auction. Powers's choice to eroticize and glamorize subjugation is particularly perplexing, given that the sculptor himself was part Native American. His blockbuster statue was not without critics. Chief among them were Elizabeth Barrett Browning, whose poem "The Greek Slave" offered a counterpoint to Powers's depiction of resigned passivity in the face of oppression, and John Tenniel, the original illustrator of *Alice's Adventures in Wonderland,* who published a cartoon in the famed satirical magazine *Puck,* depicting a black woman on an auction block in the posture of the Powers statue under the caption "The Virginian Slave, Intended as a Companion to Powers' Greek Slave."

Unlike Powers's helpless nude, Hosmer's larger-than-life Zenobia—"of a size with which I might be compared as a mouse to a camel," she wrote to Cornelia—depicts the captive queen, still in her regal robe and crown, as she is being paraded in the streets of Rome. One strong hand is holding up the chain hanging between her shackled wrists, as though willfully refraining from snapping the link and breaking free. Gazing down from her seven-foot stature, Zenobia's intelligent face radiates complete composure—an unassailable dignity despite defeat, bolstered by the knowledge that she has fought for her values to the hilt.

Hosmer deliberately subverted other popular depictions of the ancient queen. Five years earlier, in his romance novel fictionalizing the utopian community of Brook Farm, Nathaniel Hawthorne had created a character named Zenobia—an opinionated woman of brilliance and beauty, bedeviled by excessive pride, modeled on Margaret Fuller—a thankless portrayal of the woman who had launched his literary career with her own generous pen. His Zenobia eventually elects her own ruin and drowns herself. A more historically literal interpretation had appeared in another novel published when Hosmer was a child, the year her mother died. In it, the queen is eventually stripped of dignity and reduced to "Zenobia in ruins."

Hosmer's Zenobia, while in chains, was a woman of inextinguishable strength and moral triumph. In a widely circulated and syndicated article of praise for the masterpiece, Maria Child quoted Hosmer: "I have tried to make her too proud to exhibit passion or emotion of any kind; not subdued though a prisoner; but calm, grand, and strong within herself."

It was a choice of poignant timing. In 1857, the landmark Supreme Court ruling in the Dred Scott case declared that African slaves had no American citizenship rights and therefore no legal

standing even in free states and territories. A major blow to abolition, it sent the fight against slavery in retrograde motion. Under
the critical urgency of this human rights cause, many advocates of
women's emancipation found themselves diverting their energies
toward abolition—a cause that had been kindred all along. "While
any one is base, none can be entirely free and noble," Margaret
Fuller had written in *Woman in the Nineteenth Century*. "Let us
have one creative energy, one incessant revelation. Let it take what
form it will, and let us not bind it by the past to man or woman,
black or white." Those marginalized for one aspect of their nature
are bound to have sympathies with those marginalized for another,
but no marginalized group moves to the center solely by its own
efforts—such is the paradox of power. It takes a gravitational pull
by those kindred to the cause who are already in relative positions
of power or privilege. White women became abolition's semisecret
weapon, and Hosmer's *Zenobia in Chains* came to stand as the
missing link between the fate of women and the fate of slaves.

Hosmer worked on her masterpiece for nearly three years.
("Nobody asks you how long you have been on a thing but fools,"
Gibson had told her at the outset of her career, "and you don't care
what they think.") But the triumph of its completion was eclipsed
by a series of major life changes and personal devastations for the
young sculptor. First, Cushman and Hays separated in a tumult of
violent jealousies, effectively breaking up the household that had
become Harriet's home. The disorientation only escalated when
Cushman became involved with Cornelia's younger sister, who
eventually married Cushman's nephew, forming a highly unorthodox family unit. Then, largely on account of *Zenobia*'s enormous
size, Hosmer moved out of Gibson's studio and into a loft of her
own—a large space with a skylight and a small orange tree potted
in one corner. She was now displaced from the paradise she had so
relished.

Just as Hosmer was trying to build from scratch a new place of
her own, she received news of the unexpected death of Elizabeth
Barrett Browning, for years her maternal figure and intellectual
fairy godmother. A sorrowful Harriet wrote to Cornelia:

She lives in my heart, and in my memory, as the most perfect human being I have ever known. To have seen her, and to have been admitted to her friendship, I must always consider as one of the happiest events of my life, inasmuch as in the study of her character one saw to what a degree of beauty human nature may attain even in this unfavoring world.

The final and most violent blow came as she was readying *Zenobia* for the prestigious London Exhibition of 1862: That April, her father died. Harriet was now fully orphaned and without a home.

In the wake of Hosmer's personal disorientation, *Zenobia* had a mixed debut at the London Exhibition, dismissed by some as too traditional and recognized by others as an unprecedented masterpiece. It became a focal point of the professional jealousies that had been orbiting Hosmer's rising star. An anonymous article in a London paper alleged that *Zenobia* was created by Harriet's workmen and not by the sculptor herself. Another article insinuated that Gibson had sculpted it and let his pupil claim the credit. Hosmer didn't hesitate to sue for libel. Corrections were printed. In the course of the lawsuit, it was revealed that the author of the malicious rumor was Joseph Mozier—another expatriate American sculptor, who had long harbored jealousy for the far more successful Hosmer and who had been particularly riled by her recent winning of the commission for a major monument to Thomas Hart Benton, the nation's longest-serving senator. Later, Hosmer—a prolific lifelong writer of satirical verses—would make light of the incident in a lengthy poem titled "The Doleful Ditty of the Roman Caffe Greco," which includes these lines spoken by one of the pompous male patrons of the famed artists' café:

'Tis time, my friends, we cogitate,
And make some desperate stand.
Or else our sister artists here
Will drive us from the land.

It does seem hard that we at last
Have rivals in the clay,

When for so many happy years
We had it all our way.

At the outset of the *Zenobia* project, Gibson had sent Hosmer a prescient letter of advice on life and art, in which he counseled:

There are many obstacles in the path to fame, but to surmount them, to produce fine works, we must have tranquillity of mind. Those who are envious cannot be happy, nor can the vicious. We must have internal peace, to give birth to beautiful ideas. I am glad that you feel impatient to begin your statue; that impatience is love, the love of the art. The more you feel it, the more is the soul inflamed with ambition, the ambition of excellence.

When the dust of the artificial controversy settled, *Zenobia*'s excellence earned Hosmer admission into the Academy of Rome—the Old World's pantheon of art. Her success effected an outpouring of admiration, including praise from Mary Somerville, whom Hosmer and Cushman had visited the previous year while traveling with Gibson—an old friend of the mathematician's. "I heartily congratulate you on your brilliant success in the most difficult and refined of all the arts," wrote the Scottish mathematician in February 1863 upon receiving some photographs of Hosmer's sculptures. "I hope to live to see the author once more and to tell her I am proud of the triumph of my sex." She added jocularly: "I am still writing more 'nonsense about the sky and the stars' than ever I did, besides sinning mortally about things on earth." In her memoirs, she noted her admiration for Hosmer as a person who "has proved by her works that our sex possesses both genius and originality in the highest branches of art."

The following year, Hosmer returned to America to tour with her seven-foot queen. In Boston, nearly fifteen thousand people poured in to see *Zenobia* within the first few days, and the gallery remained crowded daily thereafter. In another laudatory article for a Boston paper, Maria Child saw a "loving study of the character" in "this marble embodiment of the Queen of the East, by a Queen of the West." Massachusetts senator Charles Sumner, one of the country's leading abolitionists, exulted: "I rejoice in such a work by an American artist, as in a new poem." *Uncle Tom's Cabin* author Harriet Beecher Stowe, taken with Hosmer's subtle and profound commentary on enslavement, eagerly attended the statue's private showing in New York. "I find you always so true hearted," Hosmer's girlhood teacher Mrs. Sedgwick wrote after her American visit, "and you are not spoiled but improved by success."

Hosmer embraced her new status with unclinging generosity and used it to help other creative women up, being keenly aware that she herself had been helped up by a team of impassioned advocates and supporters. In a letter to Wayman Crow, Hosmer gratefully acknowledged her indebtedness:

> The great thing in every profession, and most certainly so in art is to get a good "start," as we Yankees say, and then all is right. But without this good start, I want to know what a young artist is to do? . . . I never read the life of any artist who did not date the rising of his lucky star from the hand of some beneficent friend or patron.

One of the young artists Hosmer took under her wing was the sculptor Edmonia Lewis—the daughter of a Cherokee mother and a black father. After growing up among Native Americans, Lewis had attended Oberlin College—not only the first university to admit women, but the first to admit women of ethnic minorities. But the university was no unbigoted idyll—when two white classmates became ill after sharing spiced wine served by Lewis, they accused her of poisoning them, even though she herself had drunk the wine without harm. Word spread beyond the liberal Oberlin campus. One evening, as Lewis was walking home from class by herself, she was attacked and forced into an open field, where she was brutally beaten and left for dead. Having barely survived, she—rather than her assailants—was arrested, an analog across the centuries to the same warping of justice that had befallen Medusa and Beatrice Cenci. Lewis was charged with poisoning her classmates on evidence as logically consistent and factually compelling as that on which Katharina Kepler had been tried for witchcraft. A prominent black lawyer, himself an Oberlin alumnus, defended her successfully—she was exonerated and eventually moved to Boston, where she studied with a successful sculptor before following in Hosmer's footsteps and moving to Rome at the same age that Hosmer had migrated there fifteen years earlier.

From Rome, Lewis wrote to Maria Child, who—predictably, given her devotion to abolition and women's rights—had become a friend:

> A Boston lady took me to Miss Hosmer's studio. It would have done your heart good to see what a welcome I received. She took my hand cordially, and said, "Oh, Miss Lewis, I am glad to see you here!" and then, while she still held my hand, there flowed such a neat little speech from her true lips! . . . Miss Hosmer has since called on me, and we often meet.

Lewis went on to become the nineteenth century's only African American artist of mainstream recognition. In 1876, her 3,015-pound marble sculpture *The Death of Cleopatra*—a pinnacle of beauty and tragedy in a daring direct portrayal of unglamorized death—became a crowning curio at the first official World's Fair in America, lauded as the most remarkable piece in the American section of the exhibition. Reverberating through it were echoes of Hosmer's *Zenobia*.

When Maria Mitchell visited Hosmer's studio with the Hawthornes in 1858, she was most touched by Hosmer's dedication to using her success as an opportunity-broadening instrument for the success of others:

> Whatever may be the criticism of art upon her work, no one can deny that she is above the average artist. But she is herself, as a woman, very much above herself in art. If there came to any struggling artist in Rome the need of a friend,—and of the thousand artists in Rome very few are successful,—Harriet Hosmer was that friend. I knew her to stretch out a helping hand to an unfortunate artist, a poor, uneducated, unattractive American, against whom the other Americans in Rome shut their houses and their hearts. When the other Americans

turned from the unsuccessful artist, Harriet Hosmer reached forth the helping hand.

Mitchell and the Hawthornes were far from the only notable figures who clamored to visit Hosmer's studio—so did a ceaseless parade of itinerant writers, artists, and European royalty, including the Prince of Wales (who purchased some of Hosmer's statues), the queen of Holland (whom Hosmer didn't recognize as anything more than a charming and erudite stranger), the Crown Princess of Germany (who marveled at Hosmer's special "talent for toes"), and the exiled queen of Naples (who would become her lover—"the romance of my life," Hosmer would later recall—and the only living woman whom she ever sculpted).

Among her famous visitors was Hans Christian Andersen—a man of supreme storytelling genius and aching self-alienation, which Hosmer instantly intuited. In a letter to her patron-father, she described Andersen as "a tall, gaunt figure of the Lincoln type with long, straight, black hair, shading a face striking because of its sweetness and sadness," adding that "it was perhaps by reason of the very bitterness of his struggles, that he loved to dwell among the more kindly fairies in whose world he found no touch of hard humanity."

Andersen's struggles were ones of a heart unsettled, ambivalent, at war with itself. By all biographical evidence, he died a virgin. For years, he was infatuated with the Swedish opera diva Jenny Lind, but his great erotic love was reserved for Edvard Collin—a boyhood beloved who remained the single most intense emotional relationship throughout Andersen's life. "The femininity of my nature and our friendship must remain a mystery," Hans wrote to Edvard. "I languish for you as for a pretty Calabrian wench . . . my sentiments for you are those of a woman." Lind, on the other hand, was a woman of the highest caliber of femininity, and one of the most successful women artists of her time. Andersen sent her passionate, pouting letters, then wrote his classic story "The Nightingale" out of his frustrated reverence shortly before making an awkward marriage proposal in a letter handed to her on a train platform. The tale didn't earn him Lind's reciprocity, but it earned her the monicker "the Swedish Nightingale."

Jenny Lind had a special ardor for astronomy. During her American tour—which brought in more than $350,000, all of which she donated to charity, most for the endowment of free schools in Sweden—Lind visited observatories whenever she could. On the last day of September in 1850—just before her first concert at Boston's Tremont Temple, which Harriet Hosmer frequented to fill her "ears and soul" with music that left her "drunk with beauty"—Lind visited the Harvard Observatory with the intention of looking at Saturn. But as soon as she pressed her eye against the enormous telescope, she was stunned by the sight of a meteor fireball—something one reporter saw as "an omen of the brilliant reputation which is to attend the great vocalist on her travels through the United States."

Farther along on her American tour, Lind visited the Cincinnati Observatory—the first public observatory in the Western Hemisphere. Charlotte Cushman had also peered through the telescope and also visited observatories whenever she could. Cushman's niece, Florence Cushman, would become one of the Harvard Computers in the 1920s.

Cushman was in Rome as Hosmer began work on her next statue. *The Sleeping Faun* was exhibited at the Dublin Exposition of 1865. The London *Times* proclaimed that of all the statues in the show, this was the "one which at once arrests attention and extorts admiration," marveling that amid this showcase of work by artists from the European countries where classical art originated, the crowning achievement was by a young American woman. The statue was sold on the opening day. The buyer—the brewer and philanthropist Benjamin Guinness, by then the wealthiest man in all of Ireland—had seen it at the private showing the day before and, enchanted by the work, offered $5,000 to own it. When he was told that the statue was not for sale, as it was destined for other exhibitions in America, Guinness doubled his offer. When Hosmer got word of the exchange, she was so touched by Guinness's zeal for her work that she agreed to sell it to him, but she returned the extra $5,000, for she didn't think it honorable to accept it. The incident became an anecdote about Hosmer's noble character, but it conceals a darker undertone: Although Hosmer had overridden so many of her era's limitations, she—like Maria Mitchell, who down-negotiated her Vassar salary to half of what was offered—was not invulnerable to the most deeply ingrained cultural messages about women's value and the worth of their work.

The spring of 1867 brought what Hosmer would later recall as the most eventful day of her life. When Louisa, Lady Ashburton—a wealthy Scottish widow and art collector with a young daughter—walked into her studio, Harriet stood still in a seizure of enchantment, transfixed by Louisa's "square-cut and grandiose features where classic beauty was humanized by a pair of keen, dark eyes"—a face that struck her as a perfect likeness of the famous Roman statue of Juno she had seen in an Italian museum a decade earlier. Upon meeting Harriet's gaze, this striking face grew animated by "a lovely smile and then a rich musical voice of enquiry arousing me to the situation." What is it about the chemistry of voice, which can afflict with passion as readily and mysteriously as a pheromonal infusion? When Harriet heard the siren song of the striking stranger's voice, she was thirty-seven and Louisa forty. What began in patronage and friendship swirled into a romance during a trip to Perugia a year after their first meeting. "Only a week ago," Harriet wrote to her beloved, "we left Rome good friends as we have always been & nothing more. But between that hour & this, something has come into our love which is to bind us." Lady Ashburton acquired a number of Hosmer's existing statues and inspired an original piece, becoming Harriet's lover, patron, and muse, her "generous Beloved," as the sculptor herself addressed her. Soon Harriet would refer to Lady Ashburton as her "sposa" and to herself as Louisa's "hubby" or "wedded wife." Beckoning her to Rome for a spousal visit, Harriet promises: "When you are here I shall be a model wife (or husband whichever you like)." For the next twenty-five years, the two women would remain bound in what they thought of as a marriage, although both had other relationships—notably, Lady

Ashburton's disastrous courtship with the then-widowed Robert Browning.

Hosmer's momentous first encounter with Lady Ashburton came during a pivotal period in her professional ascent. In 1866, a competition was announced for a monument to the recently assassinated Abraham Lincoln, to be erected in Washington, D.C.—the culmination of a story both triumphant and tragic. A decade earlier, a slave by the name of Charlotte Scott was freed by her owner, who began paying her a salary. When Scott learned of Lincoln's assassination in 1865, she was devastated. "Mr. Lincoln was a friend to the colored people," she proclaimed, "and he was my friend!" She resolved to have a memorial built in his honor and took the task upon herself, donating her entire savings of $5 to her former owner and instructing him to start a fund for a monument to the slain friend of equality. Word of her gesture spread and, a century and a half before crowdfunding, a grassroots movement was soon afoot as other former slaves began donating their earnings to the monument fund. But a St. Louis war relief agency eventually took over the project. Well-intentioned though they may have been, its white members ended up as the final decision makers in commissioning the monument.

The design Hosmer proposed for the statue was novel and daring: Lincoln surrounded by four colossal statues of black men symbolizing the different stages of African American history—auction, enslavement, freedom, citizenship—all encircled by thirty-six female figures representing the states of the Union. Her celebrity, the recent success of *Zenobia*, and her longtime association with leading abolitionists like Maria Child were in her favor. Hosmer soon received an official letter from the head of the St. Louis agency indicating she had won the commission. Congratulatory articles began appearing in the popular press.

But in 1868, the agency announced that it didn't have the funds to execute Hosmer's ambitious design. Although she offered to help raise the funds herself, she ultimately lost the commission—it was given to Thomas Ball, whose career had begun eighteen years earlier with a widely copied bust of Jenny Lind. That Hosmer's concept was expensive is undeniable, but it was also probably too progressive for the agency's voters and too controversial for a divided nation. Here was a successful and self-sufficient queer white woman celebrating the dignity and growing cultural power of black men. Instead, the winning design—by a heterosexual white man—only affirmed the existing power dynamic, depicting a male slave kneeling at Lincoln's feet. Before the statue was completed, the Fifteenth Amendment was ratified, giving voting rights to black men—but not to women, black or white.

In the midst of her protracted Lincoln pitch, Hosmer had commissioned a peculiar photograph. In the arresting image, the diminutive Harriet stands with her mischievous smile and arms crossed at the center of a group of men—the twenty-four workers she employed at her studio in Rome, ranging in age from the adolescent to the elderly. Titled "Hosmer and Her Men" and originally intended as a joke, it ended up cementing her legacy in a visceral way and presaging the personal political awakening that her loss of the Lincoln commission effected, finally prompting her to engage with the women's rights movement directly. While visiting America to campaign for the Lincoln commission, she had gone to hear a sermon by Phebe Ann Hanaford—one of the nation's first women ministers. Moved, Hosmer wrote to Hanaford:

> I honor every woman who has strength enough to step out of the beaten path when she feels her walk lies in another; strength enough to stand up to be laughed at, if necessary. That is the bitter pill we must all swallow in the beginning, but I regard these pills as tonics quite essential to one's mental salvation.

But the changes Hosmer was living through were not all in the direction of her aspirations. The Roman revolution Margaret Fuller had lived through a generation earlier now culminated in major political and civic upheaval that changed the face of Rome before Harriet's eyes as grenades fell within yards of her. As her Italian idyll was crumbling, the tastes that had drawn American admirers to neoclassical sculpture in her youth were changing. After the

Civil War, neoclassicism plummeted out of fashion as a reflection of bygone Jeffersonian ideals. Science and technology emerged as the measure of the nation's progress, seeding a worship of exactitude that favored realism over the ideal forms of classical art. Hosmer was forced to reinvent herself. She turned from art to her early interest in science, setting out to devise a synthetic alternative to marble—something that would emulate the material dignity of marble, but would be significantly easier, faster, and less costly to work with. In 1876, after a series of chemical experiments, she succeeded, christening her invention "petrified marble." By 1879, she had a patent in both America and Italy.

During that period of recalibration, Hosmer penned *1975: A Prophetic Dream*—a science fiction drama written in a single evening. "The ghost of Shakespeare came to my aid," she joked. That year, she began what would become a two-decade-long quest to invent a perpetual motion machine—the ultimate insurance against impermanence, and an impossibility of physics. Leonardo, whose anatomical sketches Hosmer's were once said to rival, had scoffed four centuries earlier: "Oh, ye seekers after perpetual motion, how many vain chimeras have you pursued? Go and take your place with the alchemists." Yet in his notebooks, he made two sketches of self-acting pumps—another impossibility of physics.

A cross-disciplinary curiosity is vital for originality in any field of creative endeavor. But solving the major unsolved problems in any one discipline requires deep expertise in it, even if the final insight is aided by a wide lens on surrounding fields. Maria Mitchell intuited this in her essay on the astronomy of *Paradise Lost*: "Where Milton confines himself to phenomena, he is very accurate; but when he attempts to reason, he reasons as a poet, but not as an astronomer."

Hosmer was hardly a scientist—her medical studies had been a means to refining the anatomical accuracy of her art, and she had invented her artificial marble with only an elementary knowledge of chemistry. With her plans for a perpetual motion machine, she endeavored to overturn the fundamental laws of physics—a discipline in which she had no training and not even the rudimentary knowledge necessary for grasping the futility of her project. In physics, she reasoned like an artist, not like a scientist. Ambition is disfigured into arrogance when it becomes unmoored from self-awareness, from a realistic assessment of one's competences. In her quest for perpetual motion, Hosmer was no more arrogant than the archetypal entrepreneur who makes his fortune in Silicon Valley, then declares that he will solve the ancient puzzle of immortality in its modern and equally unreasonable guise, the singularity. Some portion of genius surely lies in the ability to tell apart what is presumed to be impossible by consensus or convention and what is physically impossible because the forces that made us made it so.

Emily Dickinson, born in the same year as Hosmer, would write:

We play at Paste—
Till qualified, for Pearl—
Then, drop the Paste—
And deem ourself a fool—

In 1898, the sixty-eight-year-old Harriet sent Cornelia a prototype of her perpetual motion machine in a coffin-shaped box, referring to the invention only as "it." And yet her devotion to this fool's dream is no more pathetic than Newton's devotion to alchemy or Kepler's to astrology. Rather, it is a touching testament to the common wellspring of our genius and naïveté—that resolute, sometimes transcendent, sometimes self-defeating reach for the impossible. Once again Adrienne Rich's tribute to Marie Curie springs to mind:

She died   a famous woman   denying
her wounds
denying
her wounds   came   from the same source as her power

Hosmer's virtuosity in immortalizing the most fragile emotional realities of human life in marble shares a common root with her longing for a mechanical counterpoint to the cessation of life—for what else is the idea of perpetual motion if not the dream of interceding in the inevitable cycle of growth and decay that governs physical reality?

When Lady Ashburton died of breast cancer in 1903 at the age of seventy-six, the seventy-three-year-old Harriet, whose lifetime of letters emanated exuberance and shunned melancholy almost on principle, wrote to Cornelia: "I have had the saddest week I have ever known." Two months later, her grief had only intensified: "Every day the void seems greater. . . . There is no heal to the wound—and never will be." This woman, who had known deep loss since early childhood and had devoted her life to the illusion of permanence in marble, was now living the fear she had articulated to Cornelia from the Mississippi steamboat half a century earlier: Nothing lasts, life proceeds in stops and starts of loss, and everyone we love is eventually taken away from us. Is it any wonder that she should—that we should—long for permanence, for perpetual motion?

Hosmer's legacy is not to be found in what she created or failed to invent, not in the permanence of marble or in the escapist dream of perpetual motion, but in her very being, in the way she expanded the locus of possibility for others and enlarged their lives—our lives—by how she chose to live hers. Every woman artist born in the epochs since, every creative person who has carved out a purposeful life amid a culture where they are in any way "other," every queer person who is comfortably out or benefits from living in a culture where there is hardly anything left to be "in," is indebted to Harriet Hosmer—the bedrock of our being is marbled with the ancestral genes of hers.

More than Hosmer's gender-defiant demeanor, even more than her formidable work ethic, this modeling of possibility is what most enchanted Maria Mitchell with the young sculptor when she visited her studio in Rome. The life Hosmer had made for herself cast into sharp relief the longtime unease that haunted Mitchell's admiration for Caroline Herschel—a woman whose lifelong self-negation was the very opposite of the self-possession with which Hosmer lived. Mitchell now saw her hero clearly as an astronomer of high aptitude and low fidelity to her gifts, bedeviled by what she called a "sense of subordination" to her brother William—even the scrap of Caroline's handwritten observations, which John Herschel had handed to Mitchell at the end of her visit to his home, began each line with "W.H. thinks . . . ," "W.H. says . . ." Caroline had written to John of "the great and undeserved and unexpected honour" of receiving the prestigious medal of admission to the Royal Astronomical Society. "I felt from the first more shocked than gratified by that singular distinction," she confided in her nephew, "for I know too well how dangerous it is for women to draw too much notice on themselves."

In the final years of her life, Mitchell was able to address her ambivalence about Caroline Herschel's example and to formulate in public her ideas on the modeling of opportunity as the essential catalyst for setting genius free. In an 1885 article about the legacy of the Herschels, she notes that Caroline's life was "a lesson and a stimulus to all women," but also an implicit admonition in its punishing self-denial. "Has any being a right not to be?" Mitchell asks with an eye to Herschel, but then observes that "the fault was only in part her fault." Herschel's genius was bounded by her *genius loci*—by the spirit of the place, which is always also the spirit of the time. "It is probable that the human spirit has its place in time assigned to it," Virginia Woolf would write in *Orlando*. We are who we are in large part because of where we are and when we are. But lives of courage and consequence remap the locus of spirit and possibility for generations to come. Mitchell writes:

> To discuss the question whether women have the capacity for original investigation in science is simply idle until equal opportunity is given them. We cannot overrate the consequences of such lives, whether it be Mrs. Somerville translating Laplace, Harriet Hosmer modeling her statues, Mrs. Browning writing her poems or Caroline Herschel spending nights under the open canopy; in all it is devotion to idea, the loyalty to duty which reaches to all ages.

After Mitchell died at the age of seventy, having taught at Vassar until the very end, *The New York Times* published a biographical sketch titled "The Female Astronomer," remarking on her choice to neglect common women's interests in favor of her scientific endeavors. The closing sentences of the remembrance touch on the broader choice—that "loyalty to duty"—that many persons of trailblazing contribution, including Hosmer and the other pioneers Mitchell admired, consciously or unconsciously make in configuring lives that transfigure the world:

> Those about her saw something of the disadvantages of genius. It climbs to heights, but too often climbs alone, and it hears the sounds of cheerful voices on the plains below in conversations in which it cannot join.

17

FROM TERROR TO TRANSCENDENCE

A slender teenage girl clutching a posy of silk violets is peering out of a daguerreotype with neatly parted hair and a velvet neck ribbon, the hazel of her eyes and the fire of her hair obscured in black and white. There is no inkling in her broad brow that she would become one of the world's most prolific, inventive, and mysterious poets, her image fixed in posterity's eyes by this sole authenticated photograph of her sixteen-year-old self—a crocus pressed between the pages of time. For a century and a half, her far-set eyes, wide forehead, and full lips would be a canvas for projection and interpretation onto which generations would paint a look of quiet fortitude, of intense emotion, of buoyant genius. "Genius," Emily Dickinson herself would later write, "is the ignition of affection—not intellect, as is supposed,—the exaltation of devotion, and in proportion to our capacity for that, is our experience of genius."

In her thirty-first year, Dickinson would suffer some unnamed and unnamable arson of affection. She would call it a "terror" in one of the only two direct references in her surviving letters and would recast it throughout her one thousand seven hundred eighty-nine known poems, penned onto letter paper, pieces of old envelopes, shopping lists, French chocolate wrappers, drugstore flyers, and salvaged newspaper margins, as a kind of death. This enigmatic devastation would send her into self-elected seclusion in a small and sunny southwest bedroom in the Amherst house nicknamed the

Homestead. Beneath a portrait of Elizabeth Barrett Browning, this miniaturist of meaning, who saw herself as "Vesuvius at Home," would sit dressed in white and erupt the truth—her truth, and the human truth—as she saw and understood it, encoded in a symbolic language as complex and powerful as mathematics.

"Truth is such a rare thing it is delightful to tell it," she would say. In words and dashes dealt like breaths, like blades, like bullets, she would limn the terror of abandonment in a short verse, the otherworldliness of a total solar eclipse in two perfect stanzas, the soaring fragility of hope in a single line, meticulously calibrating the gravitational pull of her words to keep the reader suspended along the event horizon of meaning, perpetually circling but never fully falling into the depths of her truth.

Emily Dickinson and her mother sat for the "Daguerrian Artist" William C. North in his Amherst House hotel room sometime between the last three weeks of 1846 and the early spring of 1847, as Maria Mitchell's comet was making its unwitnessed approach to Earth and Margaret Fuller was commencing the momentous European chapter of her life. That autumn, Emily enrolled in the Mount Holyoke Female Seminary—America's first institution of higher education for women, nicknamed a "castle of science" by its students and founded a decade earlier, in the year Caroline Herschel and Mary Somerville became the first women admitted into the Royal Astronomical Society and Fuller met Emerson. In Dickinson's freshman year, Emerson wrote in his journal:

> The problem of the poet is to do the impossible . . . to unite the wildest freedom with the hardest precision. . . . Dante was free imagination, all wings, yet he wrote like Euclid.

As Emily Dickinson began her studies at Mount Holyoke, Susan Gilbert, born nine days after her, entered the Utica Female Academy nearly two hundred miles to the west, in upstate New York. The orphaned mathematician-in-training would soon become the poet's first love and would remain her greatest.

After graduating from the Utica Female Academy, Susan settled in Amherst, to be near her elder sister. She entered the lives of the Dickinsons in the summer of 1850, a month after news of Margaret Fuller's death thundered across New England. Emily would later remember it as the summer "when love first began, on the step at the front door, and under the Evergreens." Poised and serious at twenty, dressed in black for the sister who had just died in childbirth and who had been her maternal figure since their parents' death, Susan cast a double enchantment on Emily and Austin Dickinson. Sister and brother alike were taken with her poised erudition and her Uranian handsomeness—her flat, full lips and dark eyes were not exactly masculine, her unchiseled oval face and low forehead not exactly feminine.

"Best Witchcraft is Geometry," Emily Dickinson would write. Now both she and her brother found themselves in a strange bewitchment of figures, placing Susan at one point of a triangle reminiscent of those that had stretched between Margaret Fuller, Waldo Emerson, and Caroline Sturgis, between Maria Mitchell, Nathaniel Hawthorne, and Ida Russell. But Emily's was no temporary infatuation. Nearly two decades after Susan entered her heart, she would write with unblunted desire:

To own a Susan of my own
Is of itself a Bliss—
Whatever Realm I forfeit, Lord,
Continue me in this!

A tempest of intimacy swirled over the eighteen months following Susan's arrival into the Dickinsons' lives. The two young women took long walks in the woods together, exchanged books, read poetry to each other, and commenced an intense, intimate correspondence that would evolve and permute but would last a lifetime. "We are the only poets," Emily told Susan, "and everyone else is *prose*."

By early 1852, the poet was besotted beyond words. She beckoned to Susan on a Sunday:

Come with me this morning to the church within our hearts, where
the bells are always ringing, and the preacher whose name is love—
shall intercede for us!

When Susan accepted a ten-month appointment as a math teacher
in Baltimore in the autumn of 1851, Emily was devastated at the
separation, but tried to keep a buoyant heart. "I fancy you very
often descending to the schoolroom with a plump Binomial Theorem struggling in your hand which you must dissect and exhibit to
your uncomprehending ones," she teased in a letter. Susan was science personified, capitalized—she would haunt Dickinson's poems
for decades to come as "Science." Throughout their lifelong relationship, Dickinson would punctuate her stormy devotion with
sunny wit. In one of her "letter-poems," as Susan called the missives that read like poems and the poems that conveyed concrete
messages, she writes:

Dear Susie—I send
you a little air—
The "Music of the Spheres"

The concept of the "Music of the Spheres" is attributed to Pythagoras, but Dickinson is likely teasing Susan—a mathematician—
with a joke about the "Pythagorean maxim" Herman Melville
posited in the recently published *Moby-Dick*: "Avoid eating beans,
which cause flatulence." I am not above delighting in the fact that
one of humanity's greatest poets was not above making a fart joke
to her beloved. What is love, after all, if not an affectionate acceptance of the lover's full spectrum of being, the silly along with the
solemn?

Jest aside, an allusion to Pythagoras is a notable choice. Pythagoras, whose identity is as mysterious as Shakespeare's, his persona
as adrift in the lacuna between myth and truth, set into motion
the golden age of mathematics with the development of numeri-
cal logic—the foundation of mathematical physics. His ideas went
on to influence Plato, Copernicus, Descartes, Kepler, Newton, and

Einstein. To Pythagoras, numbers were more than tools for counting and computing. He studied their properties and relational patterns, seeking to extract from them some larger revelation about the
nature of reality, the way a poet uses words not merely to denote
and describe the world but to evoke and wrest meaning via symbolic logic.

Alongside his mathematics, Pythagoras coined the word *philosopher* to describe himself as a "lover of wisdom" and invented a
whole symbolic language of mysticism. His progressive views on
social reform led him to flee the tyrannical rule of his native Samos.
When he settled in the Greek colony of Croton, he founded a philosophical school whose sect of disciples, known as the Pythagoreans, originated a novel conception of the universe—they placed at
its center a ball of fire more than a millennium before Copernicus
proffered his heliocentric model. In fact, in his letter to the Pope,
Copernicus cited the Pythagoreans as his inspiration for upending
the Ptolemaic system. In another highly unusual model for their
time, the Pythagoreans admitted women. One of them, Hypatia of
Alexandria, became the world's first known woman astronomer,
predating Caroline Herschel by fourteen centuries.

A millennium and a half before Kepler's *Harmonices Mundi,*
Pythagoras discovered the relationship between musical harmony
and the mathematical harmony of numbers. In his day, the most
widespread musical instrument was the tetracord—the Hellenic
four-string lyre. Musicians had no standardized system of tuning
their instruments and only an intuitive sense of how to produce
harmonious melodies rather than discord, with no understanding
of the underlying tonal patterns. According to the fourth-century
Syrian scholar Iamblichus, who became Pythagoras's foremost
biographer, Pythagoras took it upon himself to devise a mechanical aid for musical tuning—something that would do for the ear
what the early optical instruments had already done for the eye.
One day, Iamblichus's account goes, Pythagoras was strolling past
a blacksmith's forge and was captivated by the sound of the many
hammers pounding in a pattern that suddenly sounded harmonious.
He rushed into the forge and immediately began investigating the

cause of the harmony, testing the various hammers in various stroke combinations—some producing harmony, others discord. After analyzing the patterns and weighing the hammers, he discovered a simple mathematical relationship between those that produced harmony—their masses were exact ratios of one another's.

Although the blacksmith anecdote may belong to that murky shoreline between the apocryphal and the factual that marks a great many biographies of genius, Pythagoras did eventually test these ratios on the lyre. They proved to be perfectly predictive of harmony—the first discovery of a mathematical rule undergirding a physical phenomenon, and the basis for the Music of the Spheres concept that would stoke Kepler's astronomical imagination and inspire Melville's joke.

But Pythagoras's greatest scientific contribution was his namesake theorem, etched into the mind of every schoolchild in the millennia since—his discovery of the fundamental mathematical relationship between the three sides of a right triangle. By furnishing this elemental definition of the right angle itself and of the perpendicularity by which the dimensions of width, length, and height are measured, Pythagoras brought mathematics to our basic understanding of three-dimensional space.

More than two millennia later, the English mathematician and number theory pioneer G. H. Hardy would write with an eye to the ancient Greek mathematics that gave rise to modern science:

> Languages die and mathematical ideas do not. "Immortality" may be a silly word, but probably a mathematician has the best chance of whatever it may mean.

At Mount Holyoke, immersed in language and mathematics, Dickinson found herself having "no interest in the all-important subject" of "becom[ing] a Christian." This would be the first serious articulation of her lifelong struggle with traditional religion, which had begun in childhood as she came to doubt the immortality so resolutely promised by the Calvinist dogma of her elders. Soon, she would write to Susan: "Sermons on unbelief ever did attract me." Dickinson went on to reject the prescriptive traditional religion of her era and to write in a poem dedicated to Susan:

> To believe the final line of the Card would foreclose Faith—
> Faith is Doubt.

She would caricature the faith of the church as a flighty girl, bereft of critical thinking and giddy with delusion:

> Faith slips—and laughs, and rallies—
> Blushes, if any see—
> Plucks at a twig of Evidence—
> And asks a Vane, the way—
> Much Gesture, from the Pulpit—
> Strong Hallelujahs roll—
> Narcotics cannot still the Tooth
> That nibbles at the soul—

She eventually adopted a view of spirituality more kindred to Maria Mitchell's than to that of the church, which Dickinson, like Mitchell, never joined. "Every formula which expresses a law of nature is a hymn of praise to God," Mitchell wrote in her journal in Dickinson's thirty-fifth year. The poet turned not to formulae but to the forms of verse in wresting from nature spiritual hymns—or elegies, which comprise the bulk of her work. The elegiac form, with its dual purpose of celebration and lamentation, gave Dickinson the perfect container for how she experienced life itself—and certainly for how she experienced love, with its parallel promise of exaltation and annihilation, its tonic and its tribulation.

In a comet of a letter from the early spring of 1852, eight months into Susan's absence, she hurls a grenade of conflicted self-revelation:

> Will you be kind to me, Susie? I am naughty and cross, this morning, and nobody loves me here; nor would you love me, if you should see me frown, and hear how loud the door bangs whenever I go through; and yet it isn't anger—I don't believe it is, for when nobody sees, I brush away big tears with the corner of my apron, and then go

working on—bitter tears, Susie—so hot that they burn my cheeks, and almost scorch my eyeballs, but you have wept much, and you know they are less of anger than *sorrow*.

And I do love to run fast—and hide away from them all; here in dear Susie's bosom, I know is love and rest, and I never would go away, did not the big world call me, and beat me for not working. . . . Your precious letter, Susie, it sits here now, and smiles so kindly at me, and gives me such sweet thoughts of the dear writer. When you come home, darling, I shan't have your letters, shall I, but I shall have *yourself*, which is more—Oh more, and better, than I can even think! I sit here with my little whip, cracking the time away, till not an hour is left of it—then you are here! And *Joy* is here—joy now and forevermore!

That year, in a Prussian lab, the physician and physicist Hermann von Helmholtz measured the speed of nerve conduction at eighty feet per second. How unfathomable that sentiments this intense and emotions this explosive, launched from a mind that seems to move at light-years per second, can be reduced to mere electrical impulses. And yet that is what we are—biomechanical creatures, all of our creative force, all of our mathematical figurings, all the wildness of our loves pulsating at eighty feet per second along neural infrastructure that evolved over millennia. Even the fathoming faculty that struggles to fathom this is a series of such electrical impulses.

Although the inhospitable reality of Dickinson's time would decelerate the lightning-speed of her desire, its nucleus would be untransfigured, so that many years later she would write in a poem dedicated to Susan:

I chose this single star
From out the wide night's numbers—
Sue—forevermore!

But now, in the dawning fervor of early love, forevermore collides with the immediacy of want. Midway through her spring outpouring, Emily suddenly casts Susan in the third person, as if beseeching an omnipotent spectator to grant her desire in the drama of their impending reunion: "I need her—I must have her, Oh give her to me!"

The moment she names her longing, she tempers its thrill with the lucid terror that it might be unspeakable:

> Do I repine, is it all murmuring, or am I sad and lone, and cannot, cannot help it? Sometimes when I do feel so, I think it may be wrong, and that God will punish me by taking you away; for he is very kind to let me write to you, and to give me your sweet letters, but my heart wants *more*.

Here, as in her poetry, Dickinson's words cascade with multiple meanings beyond literal interpretation. Her invocation of "God" is not a cowering before some Puritanical punishment for deviance but an irreverent challenge to that very dogma. What kind of "God," she seems to be asking, would make wrong a love of such infinite sweetness?

Four years earlier, during her time at the "castle of science," Emily had begun giving shape to the amorphous doubt about the claims of religion that had been gnawing at her since childhood— doubt she would later immortalize in verse:

> It troubled me as once I was—
> For I was once a child—
> Deciding how an atom—fell—
> And yet the heavens—held.

Mary Lyon, Mount Holyoke's founder and first principal, divided her pupils into three categories along the spectrum of salvation— the saved, those for whom there was hope, and the "no-hopers." She placed Emily in the third. At the end of her first term, on the day of the Sabbath, she was among seventeen students—"the impenitent," as Lyon called them—who couldn't readily proclaim that "they would serve the Lord" but instead "felt an uncommon anxiety to decide." The following day, Emily reported the docility she'd observed, writing to a friend at home with removed reproof: "There is a great deal of religious interest here and many are flocking to the ark of safety."

While Emily was unwilling to flock to illusory salvation, nor did she fear punishment from "God" for her desire for Susan, she did feel that her wayward heart was its own retribution—as well as its own reward:

> Have you ever thought of it, Susie, and yet I know you have, how much these hearts claim; why I don't believe in the whole, wide world, are such hard little creditors—such real little *misers*, as you and I carry with us, in our bosom every day. I can't help thinking sometimes, when I hear about the ungenerous, Heart, keep very still—or someone will find you out! . . . I do think it's wonderful, Susie, that our hearts don't break, *every day* . . . but I guess I'm made with nothing but a hard heart of stone, for it don't break any, and dear Susie, if mine is stony, yours is stone, upon stone, for you never yield, *any*, where *I* seem quite beflown. Are we going to *ossify* always, say Susie—how will it be?

There is palpable restlessness in Emily's oscillation between resignation and demand, between love's longing to be unmasked and the fear of being found out. Later that month, she exhorts Susan: "Loved One, thou knowest!"—an allusion to Juliet's speech in *Romeo and Juliet*: "Thou knowest the mask of night is on my face."

By June, anticipating Susan's return from Baltimore in three weeks, Emily is pining with unbridled candor:

> When I look around me and find myself alone, I sigh for you again; little sigh, and vain sigh, which will not bring you home.
> I need you more and more, and the great world grows wider . . . every day you stay away—I miss my biggest heart; my own goes wandering round, and calls for Susie. . . . Susie, forgive me Darling, for every word I say—my heart is full of you . . . yet when I seek to say to you something not for the world, words fail me. . . . I shall grow more and more impatient until that dear day comes, for til now, I have only *mourned* for you; now I begin to *hope* for you.

She ends her letter with aching awareness of the dissonance between her private desire and the public norms of love:

> Now, farewell, Susie . . . I add a kiss, shyly, lest there is somebody there! Don't let them see, *will* you Susie?

Two weeks later, with Susan's return now days away, her anticipatory longing rises to a crescendo:

> Susie, will you indeed come home next Saturday, and be my own again, and kiss me as you used to? . . . I hope for you so much, and feel so eager for you, feel that I *cannot* wait, feel that now I *must* have you—that the expectation once more to see your face again makes me feel hot and feverish, and my heart beats so fast—I go to sleep at night, and the first thing I know, I am sitting there wide awake, and clasping my hands tightly, and thinking of next Saturday. . . . Why, Susie, it seems to me as if my absent Lover was coming home so soon—and my heart must be so busy, making ready for him.

Dickinson would frequently and deliberately reassign gender pronouns for herself and her beloveds, recasting her love in the acceptable male-female battery of desire. Throughout her life, she would often use the masculine in referring to herself—writing of her "boyhood," signing letters to her cousins as "Brother Emily," calling herself a "boy," "prince," "earl," or "duke" in various poems, in one of which she unsexes herself in a violent transfiguration:

> Amputate my freckled Bosom!
> Make me bearded like a Man!

Again and again, she would tell all the truth but tell it slant, unmooring the gender of her love objects from the pronouns that befit their biology. Later in life, in flirting with the idea of publication, she would masculinize the pronouns in a number of her love poems—"bearded" pronouns, she called these—to fit the heteronormative mold, so that two versions of these poems exist: the earlier addressed to a female beloved, the later to a male.

That insufferable spring, she had already declared to Susan that her "heart wants *more.*" Twenty Augusts after they met, Dickinson would write: "Enough is so vast a sweetness, I suppose it never occurs, only pathetic counterfeits." Now, she could only address that "more" through metaphor—for Dickinson, a child of her age even in her insurgency, the passion of bodies is fathomable only in figurative language. In another letter to Susan from that heated June, she confronts as directly as she can the unspoken between them—the possibility of physical passion:

> Those unions, my dear Susie, by which two lives are one, this sweet and strange adoption wherein we can but look, and are not yet admitted, how it can fill the heart, and make it gang wildly beating, how it will take us one day, and make us all it's own, and we shall not run away from it, but lie still and be happy!
>
> You and I have been strangely silent upon this subject, Susie, we have often touched upon it, and as quickly fled away, as children shut their eyes when the sun is too bright for them.
>
> [. . .]
>
> You have seen flowers at morning, satisfied with the dew, and those same sweet flowers at noon with their heads bowed in anguish before the mighty sun; think you these thirsty blossoms will now need naught but—*dew*? No, they will cry for sunlight, and pine for the burning noon, tho' it scorches them, scathes them; they have got through with peace—they know that the man of noon, is *mightier* than the morning and their life is henceforth to him. Oh, Susie, it is dangerous, and it is all too dear, these simple trusting spirits, and the spirits mightier, which we cannot resist! It does so rend me, Susie, the thought of it when it comes, that I tremble lest at sometime I, too, am yielded up. Susie, you will forgive me my amatory strain—it has been a very long one, and if this saucy page did not here bind and fetter me, I might have had no end.

Throughout Dickinson's body of work, dew is her recurring symbol of love and noon of passion. But flowers would always be her richest symbolic language. "To cower before a flower," she would write in the final years of her life, "is perhaps unwise—but Beauty is often timidity—perhaps oftener—pain."

While floral symbology had figured in literature for millennia, it wasn't until the Linnaean revolution of botany in the mid-eighteenth century that flowers came to be properly understood as sexual organisms. Amid Puritan proprieties, their pretty sensuality became a safe analogue for exploring questions of human sexuality. When Charles Darwin's grandfather, the Lunar Man Erasmus Darwin, harvested this nascent interest in the reproduction of plants in his inventive 1791 marriage of science and poetry, *The Botanic Garden,* he was planting the seed for what would become a widespread symbolic language of botanical erotica—nowhere more delicately yet fervently suggestive than in the verses and letters of Emily Dickinson. "The poet alone knows astronomy, chemistry, vegetation and animation," Emerson had written, "for he does not stop at these facts, but employs them as signs."

Long before she began writing poems, Dickinson undertook a rather different yet kindred art of contemplation and composition—the gathering, growing, classification, and pressing of flowers, which she saw as manifestations of the Muse. By the age of nine, Emily had started reading about botany. At twelve, she began assisting her mother in the garden. But it was only upon entering Mount Holyoke that she awakened to the full splendor of flowers as dual objects of aesthetic beauty and scientific significance. The school's founder was an ardent botanist herself, trained by one of the era's most famous horticulturalists. Although all Mount Holyoke pupils were encouraged to collect, study, and preserve local flowers in herbaria, Dickinson's herbarium is a masterpiece of uncommon punctiliousness and poetic beauty: four hundred twenty-four flowers from the Amherst region, arranged with a remarkable sensitivity to scale and visual cadence across sixty-six pages in a large leather-bound album. Slim paper labels punctuate the specimens like enormous dashes inscribed with the names of the plants—sometimes colloquial, sometimes Linnaean—in Dickinson's elegant early handwriting. "It has always pleased me," Charles Darwin would write in his autobiography three decades later, "to exalt plants in the scale of organised beings."

Botany was the back door through which Victorian women entered the scientific establishment formally closed to them. Around the time Dickinson was composing her herbarium, the self-taught English botanist Anna Atkins set out to overcome "the difficulty of making accurate drawings" of sea algae by applying the cyanotype imaging process John Herschel had invented less than a year earlier. Algae hunting had become a popular hobby among scientifically inclined women of the era, with such prominent practitioners as George Eliot and Queen Victoria herself. But Atkins was interested in more than the mere collecting of specimens. In rendering the algae she collected as otherworldly white forms aglow against a cobalt background, she became the first woman known to take a photograph, and her self-published volume was the world's first book illustrated with photographs.

Although Dickinson approached her herbarium with great care and rigor, something larger than scientific curiosity radiates from the pages—an elegy for time, composed with passionate patience, emanating the same wakefulness to sensuality and mortality that marks her poetry, nowhere more palpable than in her early love letters to Susan.

That same summer, Thoreau writes in his diary seventy-five miles east: "Every poet has trembled on the verge of science."

But when Susan returned from Baltimore on that long-awaited Saturday, something had shifted between them. Perhaps the ten-month absence, filled not with their customary walks in the woods but with letters of exponentially swelling intensity, had revealed to Susan that Emily's feelings for her were not of a different hue but of a wholly different color—one that she was constitutionally unable to match. Or perhaps Emily had always misdivined the contents of Susan's heart, inferring an illusory symmetry of feeling on the basis not of evidence but of willfully blind hope. In *Aurora Leigh*, Elizabeth Barrett Browning would write that in youth

The love within us and the love without
Are mixed, confounded; if we are loved or love,
We scarce distinguish.

Few things are more wounding than the confounding moment of discovering an asymmetry of affections where mutuality had been presumed. It is hard to imagine how Dickinson took the withdrawal—here was a woman who experienced the world with a euphoria of emotion atmospheres above the ordinary person's and who therefore likely plummeted to the opposite extreme in equal magnitude. But she seems to have feared it all along—feared that her immense feelings would never be wholly met, as is the curse of those who love with unguarded abandon. Five months earlier, she had written to Susan:

> I would nestle close to your warm heart. . . . Is there any room there for me, or shall I wander away all homeless and alone?

She suspected, too, that she might injure—and not only herself—with the force of her love:

> Oh, Susie, I often think that I will try to tell you how dear you are . . . but the words won't come, tho' the tears will, and I sit down disappointed. . . . In thinking of those I love, my reason is all gone from me, and I do fear sometimes that I must make a hospital for the hopelessly insane, and chain me up there such times, so I won't injure you.

Even in her ardent anticipatory letter penned before Susan's return, she questions for a moment whether the love that stands as the central truth of her daily being is real:

> Shall I indeed behold you, not "darkly, but face to face" or am I *fancying* so, and dreaming blessed dreams from which the day will wake me?

Now she had been awakened—not rudely, but unmistakably and irreversibly. In the anxious insistence of her entreaty is the sorrowful sense that Susan is slipping away from her—and toward Austin, who commenced an open courtship of her.

. . .

That summer, Emily Dickinson cut off her auburn hair.

In *Aurora Leigh*, Barrett Browning would contemplate the maturing ferment of intimate rejection, how disappointment so deep sculpts the canyons of character:

> You who keep account
> Of crisis and transition in this life,
> Set down the first time
> Nature says plain "no"
> To some "yes" in you, and walks over you
> In gorgeous sweeps of scorn. We all begin
> By singing with the birds, and running fast
> With June-days, hand in hand: but once, for all,
> The birds must sing against us, and the sun
> Strike down upon us like a friend's sword caught
> By an enemy to slay us, while we read
> The dear name on the blade which bites at us!

"She loved with all her might," a girlhood friend of Dickinson's would recall after the poet's death, "and we all knew her truth and trusted her love." No one knew that love more intimately, nor had reason to trust it more durably, than Susan. Where Austin's love washed over her with the stormy surface waves of desire, Emily's carried her with the deep currents of devotion—a love Dickinson would compare to the loves of Dante for Beatrice and Swift for Stella. Throughout the poet's life, Susan would be her muse, her mentor, her primary reader and editor, her fiercest lifelong attachment, her "Only Woman in the World." To Susan, Dickinson would write her most passionate letters and dedicate her best-beloved poems; to Susan she would steady herself, to her shore she would return again and again, writing in the final years of her life:

> Show me Eternity, and I will show you Memory—
> Both in one package lain
> And lifted back again—

Be Sue—while I am Emily—
Be next—what you have ever been—Infinity.

Something of the infinite would always remain between them. But by 1853, Sue imposed an artificial finitude. Increasingly unnerved by Emily's unslakable intensity, she put a soft but deliberate distance between them. Emily continued to pine, writing in February 1853 while Susan was once again away:

It seems to me a long while since I have seen you much—it is a long while, Susie, since we have been together—so long since we've spent a twilight, and spoken of what we loved, but you will come back again, and there's all the *future* Susie, which is as yet untouched! It is the brightest star in the firmament of God, and I look in its face the oftenest.

She painted an almost cruel parting scene:

I ran to the door, dear Susie—I ran out in the rain, with nothing but my slippers on, I called "Susie, Susie," but you didn't look at me; then I ran to the dining room window and rapped with all my might upon the pane, but you rode right on and never heeded me.

It made me feel so lonely that I couldn't help the tears. . . . And now, my absent One, I am hoping the days away, till I shall see you home—I am sewing as fast as I can, I am training the stems to my flowers, I am working with all my might, so as to pause and love you, as soon as you get home.

[. . .]

Oh, Susie, Susie, I must call out to you in the old, old way—I must say how it seems to me to hear the clock so silently tick all the hours away, and bring me not my gift—my own, my own!

Susan didn't respond. "Your absence insanes me so," Emily entreated. Seized with self-doubt over the flaming directness of her previous letter, she implored:

Why don't you write me, Darling? Did I in that quick letter say anything which grieved you, or made it hard for you to take your usual pen and trace affection for your bad, sad Emilie?

> Then Susie, you must forgive me before you sleep tonight, for I will not shut my eyes until you have kissed my cheek, and told me you would love me.

She then added a sentence of tragic prescience, remarking on how she enjoyed talking about Susan with the other two Dickinson siblings—her brother, Austin, and her sister, Lavinia, "Vinnie":

> It is pleasant . . . to find how you are living in every one of their hearts, and making it warm and bright there—as if it were a sky, and a sweet summer's noon.

She hadn't yet fathomed the noonday of Austin's ardor for Susan.

While the only union available to Emily was a fantasy marriage of hearts, interceded by "the preacher whose name is Love," her brother was in the privileged position of being aligned with the era's sole acceptable framework of love—the heteronormative pursuit of marriage. As Emily smoldered with desire for Susan that could never enflame in the open air of society—desire to be fully known, to have the edge of her darkness met and softened with the light of a love that accepts all—Austin pursued her openly. Perhaps discomfited by Emily's growing attachment, perhaps lucid about the practical prospects for two women in love in the middle of the nineteenth century, Susan herself coped by drifting away from Emily and toward her brother. Or perhaps, as a pragmatist by nature and necessity—an orphan of no privilege, who survived by teaching mathematics—Susan saw clearly the practical impossibility of Emily's romantic fantasy of their love and chose instead the nearest approximation: to remain in the Dickinson household, at Emily's side, as her brother's wife.

The thirty-three-year-old Austin would soon become a lawyer so serious and devout that he would frown upon laughter on Sundays—reproof permanently sculpted into his broad, downward-turned mouth haloed by briery auburn hair. But inside the stern mountain of his person roiled the lava of emotional intensity kindred to his sister's. He wrote to Susan with the barely repressed passion that Emily uncorked without guard. (Courtship was mostly an epistolary enterprise in Puritanical New England, where contact between the sexes was so controlled that the president of Amherst College forbade dances on the Sabbath. The youths danced in secret, codenaming their insurgency P.O.M.—"poetry in motion.")

Three days after the spring equinox in 1853, Susan made an overnight stop in Boston while traveling for work. Austin was there, having just enrolled in Harvard Law School. She stayed at Revere House—the oldest house in downtown Boston, once the home of the patriot Paul Revere, by then a boardinghouse and inn of sorts. Three decades later, an elderly Walt Whitman would journey to Revere House—I like to imagine him slumbering in the bed Susan once occupied. He would remark on the city's atmosphere saturated with "that subtle something . . . which effuses behind the whirl of animation, study, business, a happy and joyous public spirit"—an atmosphere he saw as akin to that of ancient Greek cities. "Indeed there is a good deal of the Hellenic in B[oston]," Whitman would observe, breathing in Margaret Fuller's legacy.

When Austin came to see Susan at Revere House, he proposed marriage. She accepted. The following morning, he wrote, intoxicated with the tease of desire permitted but unconsummated:

> Those hours, Sue, let us never forget—& I can never be unhappy. . . . Those sweet kisses you, leaning over me imprinted on my forehead—our parting that night—how warmly you let me press you to my heart—& how passionately you clung around my neck—and held my lips to yours let me never forget—Let me never forget it all—and I never shall doubt that the deepest, strongest love . . . has been given to me—

In a testament to Margaret Fuller's observation that the loss of letters "makes irreparable gaps in the history of feeling," Susan's letters to Emily are lost—her history of feeling survives only in fragmentary quotations in Emily's replies. A year before the engagement to Austin, Emily had written to Susan with her parallel passion articulated in strikingly similar language:

> Thank you for loving me, darling, and *will* you "love me more if ever you come home"?—it is enough, dear Susie, I know I shall be satisfied. But what can I do towards you?—*dearer* you *cannot* be, for I love you so already, that it almost breaks my heart—perhaps I can love you *anew*, every day of my life, every morning and evening—Oh if you will let me, how happy I shall be!

Now, unlet, Emily marks a line in her father's copy of a Jane Porter novel: "I feel as if love sat upon my heart, and flapped it with his wings." A quarter century later, she would write: "Love is its own rescue, for we—at our supremest, are but its trembling Emblems." And then: "Emblem is immeasurable—that is why it is better than Fulfillment, which can be drained."

With her love unfulfilled yet undrained, she reluctantly began signing her letters to Susan with the tame "Aff. Emilie," rarely included poems, and soon turned to Benjamin Newton—a law student at her father's firm, whom she came to consider her "tutor"—for thoughts on her verse. It was Newton who gave her a copy of Emerson's first volume of poetry, published in the year the teenaged Emily sat for her famous daguerreotype. Newton, already aware that he was dying of tuberculosis, told her that he was buoyed by the wish to live long enough to see her a published poet. When he died a week after this optimistic pronouncement, at the age of thirty-one, she grieved for him intensely. But it was likely a double-edged grief—for the loss of her mentor to death and for the loss of her fantasy life with Susan to distancing and domesticity as she and Austin announced their engagement over Thanksgiving dinner that year.

> We never know we go—when we are going
> We jest and shut the door—
> Fate following behind us bolts it
> And we accost no more.

This dread of a permanent parting—by death, by distancing, by abandonment—seems to be the single most powerful animating force of Dickinson's poetry. Susan's engagement to Austin occasioned it with unprecedented might.

In the summer of 1856, after a four-year courtship, Susan Gilbert and Austin Dickinson were married and moved into the Evergreens—the stylish new house Mr. Dickinson had built for them across the western hedge of the Homestead. It was an ambivalent contract for Susan, who found herself "troubled" by the thought of physical intimacy with Austin. With the unsustainable self-denial of the besotted, he dealt with her reluctance at first by telling her that he was willing to relinquish his "man's requirements" and assured her that she could remain a virgin if that was her wish. "If so you are happier," he wrote, "then I will ask nothing of you, take nothing from you—you are not the happier in giving me." This resistance to giving herself over transcended the physical—it was her complete self-possession, body and spirit, that Susan was unwilling to surrender. A year into her marriage, she inscribed a new volume of Goethe with her maiden name. Her most significant and willful bond was with the poet across the hedge, who would write a decade later:

> Title divine—is mine!
> The Wife—without the Sign!

Some loves lodge themselves in the tissue of being like mercury, pervading every synapse and sinew to remain there, sometimes dormant, sometimes tortuously restive, with a half-life that exceeds a lifetime.

18

UNMASTERING

A corridor denuded of grass formed between the Homestead and the Evergreens as Emily and Susan traversed the lawn daily to see each other or to press into the other's hand a letter unpinned from the bosom of a dress. A "little path just wide enough for two who love," Dickinson called it. Over the next quarter century, two hundred seventy-six known poems would travel between their homes—some by hand and foot, but many by post. I have often wondered what prompted the poet to head for the mailbox and not the hedge, stuffing her sentiments into an envelope addressed to a house a stone's throw from her own. And yet the heart is not a stone—it is a thing with feathers.

Four years after the marriage, in one of her many poems addressed to Dollie—her pet name for Susan—Emily continues to oscillate between the reality and unreality of their love, to suffer with the terror of abandonment:

You love me—you are sure—
I shall not fear mistake—
I shall not *cheated* wake—
Some grinning morn—
To find the Sunrise left—
And Orchards—unbereft—
And Dollie—gone!
I need not start—you're sure—

That night will never be—
When frightened—home to Thee I run—
To find the windows dark—
And no more Dollie—mark—
Quite none?
Be sure you're sure—you know—
I'll bear it better now—
If you'll just tell me so—
Than when—a little dull Balm grown—
Over this pain of mine—
You sting—again!

Dickinson's awareness of how her life and Susan's had begun to diverge only amplified this vibrating dread of desolation—while she retreated further and further into the solitude of her chamber, placing Susan at the center of her universe, Susan was actively constellating her life with sociality beyond Emily. The salons she began hosting in her drawing room, not unlike Margaret Fuller's "Conversations," made the Evergreens an intellectual epicenter of Amherst and drew such luminaries as Emerson, Thomas Wentworth Higginson, *Uncle Tom's Cabin* author Harriet Beecher Stowe, and *Springfield Republican* editor Samuel Bowles, who would become one of Dickinson's closest correspondents. The poet attended some of these gatherings but shied away from most. I like to imagine her swallowed by the forest-green velvet of the Victorian armchair by the grand piano in Sue's drawing room on the cold December evening in 1857 when Emerson stayed at the Evergreens after giving a lecture in Amherst. I like to imagine her watching him quietly, indirectly, in the giant mirror by the marble miniature of Canova's *Psyche Revived by Cupid's Kiss,* as the Sage of Concord measures his words, not like beans, not like pebbles, but like heavy polished stones, masoning the path of his thought with weighty eloquence. Several hours earlier, several time zones away, Maria Mitchell had done the same in some faraway French parlor after her visit to the Observatoire de Paris.

Most likely, however, Emily Dickinson never left her bedroom during Emerson's stay, never slipped through the glass door of her father's library stacked with two thousand books, never scuttled across the well-trodden path between the Homestead and the Evergreens as she did on less peopled nights, with lantern in hand— "I am out with lanterns, looking for myself," she had written to a friend the previous year—for she wrote of the imagined rather than witnessed scene in a letter to Susan the day after the famous guest departed: "It must have been as if he had come from where dreams are born!"

Around the time of Emerson's visit, Dickinson began dressing in white, binding her poems into small hand-stitched booklets that wouldn't be found until after her death, and evacuating into what would soon become a near-total corporeal withdrawal from the outside world. For the remaining quarter century of her life, she would write at her miniature desk, receive visitors as a disembodied presence conversing with them through the parlor door, and would rarely leave her bedroom—not even for her mother's funeral. But from the chamber of her seclusion, she would go on reaching for Susan. Nearly three decades after they met, she would once again cast their relationship in the third person, like some great Greek tragedy the plot of which she was impartially following: "Susan knows she is a Siren—and that at a word from her, Emily would forfeit Righteousness—"

The precise reason for Dickinson's deliberate withdrawal from the world has become a central point of speculation in her myth and mystery. Her biographer Lyndall Gordon has made the case that the poet may have suffered from epilepsy. Still, the theory is predicated more on intelligent inferences about the social stigma of the disease and interpretations of the symbolism of Dickinson's poems than on direct evidence, which is scant—the poet's drugstore prescriptions for arsenic, commonly used for epilepsy but also for numerous other ailments, and the documented fact that her nephew suffered from the disease, which has a hereditary component.

Whether the shame of illness or the continual disappointment of an impossible and unrequited lovesickness drove Dickinson into the inner darkness of her light-filled bedroom we may never know. But we do know that beginning in her late twenties, she came out only rarely and always reluctantly.

> Ourself behind ourself, concealed—
> Should startle most—

"Coming out" is a decidedly modern term—modern and already dated. I am fortunate to be of a generation in which I never really had to come "out," for I never felt myself to be particularly "in," thanks to the moral courage of my elders, who put their loves and their lives on the line by choosing visibility. And yet "coming out" is an apt term, for any effort toward self-unconcealment, toward disclosing one's "fulness of being," is a vulnerable-making step from the safe interiority of the self into the harsh spotlight of public attention. Today, people come out not only as queer—or whatever the modern-dated terminology of the day may be, for as Emerson observed, "language is the archives of history"—but also as atheists, or as after-hours artists. For Emily Dickinson, who drew her metaphors so directly from life as to render them only half metaphorical, "coming out" took on a literal quality. Struggling to reconcile her unusual interiority with the outward demands of her time, she chose simply not to try—she shut herself in her bedroom and came out into the world only as discarnate verses strung together with breathless dashes.

And yet, as Elizabeth Barrett Browning had written in *Aurora Leigh,* "a love that burns through veils will burn through masks."

Around the onset of her self-elected seclusion, Dickinson began composing the three letters that would become the most transfixing focal point of her mystery, known as the "Master Letters"— missives penned between 1858 and 1862, discovered after her death as drafts, addressing some real or imagined "Master" and exploding with almost violent desire, the object of which—is it desire for love?

for recognition? for artistic self-actualization?—is as enigmatic as the identity of Dickinson's "Master," as layered as the poet herself.

In the second Master Letter, Dickinson assumes the third person and writes of "a love so big it scares her, rushing among her small heart—pushing aside the blood and leaving her faint (all) and white in the gust's arm."

In the third Master Letter, she implores:

> What would you do with me if I came "in white"? Have you the little chest—to put the alive—in? I want to see you more—Sir—than all I wish for in this world—and the wish—altered a little—will be my only one.

Generations of scholars have treated the Master Letters as a cryptogram the elusive solution to which would unlock the mystery of Emily Dickinson. But hers is a mystery that grows only more impenetrable with each step of approach. All attempts to identify a concrete candidate as "Master" have so far failed, lacking logical consistency. Among the proposed candidates have been Samuel Bowles, her close friend and correspondent, whose *Springfield Republican* would print several of the eleven poems published in Dickinson's lifetime; Charles Wadsworth, a charismatic minister Emily had met while accompanying her father on a trip to Philadelphia in her early twenties, whom Martha Dickinson Bianchi—Susan's daughter and the poet's early biographer—would go to great lengths to cast as Dickinson's romantic interest, deliberately misdating letters and inventing events to substantiate the romantic fiction; and Otis Lord, the elderly judge with whom Dickinson did fall in love, but a decade after she composed the Master Letters. After her death, as speculation swirled about her personal life, Austin reportedly scoffed at such attempts to assign an identity to "Master" and insisted that his sister "had been several times in love, in her own way"—a recognition not only that her loves were multiple, but also that they deviated from the standard "way" in their nature or their intensity or both.

Beyond failing to reconcile the factual when and where of each theorized recipient with the timeline of Dickinson's own life, the various Master theories have also failed to account for the emotional reality of her relationships and her temperament. This, after all, was a woman who at only nineteen confidently mocked her brother for saying that her philosophic meditations were incomprehensible and that she should write in simpler style: "I'll be a little ninny—a little pussy catty, a little Red Riding Hood, I'll wear a Bee in my Bonnet, and a Rose bud in my hair." She didn't hesitate to poke fun at his patriarchal condescension: "Permit me to tie your shoe, to run like a dog behind you. I can bark, see here! Bow wow!" She would grow out of her teenage sarcasm but would retain the willful defense of her sensibility, consistently refusing suggested simplifications of her poems with the same quiet confidence in her style of thought and expression. After her death, her longtime editor Thomas Wentworth Higginson would bow at the self-possession with which she had upheld her peculiar style and resisted his edits over the decades: "After all, when a thought takes one's breath away, a lesson on grammar seems an impertinence."

Having so irreverently defied authority throughout her life, Dickinson is unlikely to have surrendered willingly to the patriarchy by electing any living man as her "Master." My own supposition is that her cryptic missives have more in common with Margaret Fuller's letter to Beethoven than with the impassioned love letters Dickinson wrote to the living. In her era, the practice of writing such letters to one's heroes was not at all uncommon among young people of creative ambition. At the end of his life, Walt Whitman would recollect having been afflicted with a common case of "Emerson-on-the-brain" in his youth. "I read his writings reverently, and address'd him in print as 'Master,' and for a month or so thought of him as such," Whitman recalled of his hero, then added the observation that "most young people of eager minds pass through this stage of exercise."

Dickinson was not yet thirty and endowed with an uncommon eagerness of mind when she began composing her Master Letters. Decades later, in the final years of her life, she would write to Susan:

"With the exception of Shakespeare, you have told me of more knowledge than any one living—To say that sincerely is strange praise." It is a strange sentence indeed, remarkable both in its grandeur of sentiment toward Susan's influence and in placing the bearded bard so sincerely and unselfconsciously among the living— Shakespeare was as alive to Dickinson as Beethoven was to Fuller. The parallels between their letters are striking:

Fuller:

> Master! . . . Oh, if thou wouldst take me wholly to thyself.

Dickinson:

> Master, open your life wide and take me in forever. . . .

Fuller's letter to Beethoven was included in her posthumously published *Memoirs*, which soon became a best seller across New England. Emily Dickinson, twenty-one at the time, almost certainly read it. She was well aware and admiring of Fuller—permeating her correspondence with Susan was a private lexicon derived in part from Shakespeare, in part from Fuller's translation of *Die Günderode*, Bettina Brentano's novel about an intense romantic friendship between two women.

Even if Dickinson's Master Letters were not directly inspired by Fuller's letter to Beethoven, it is still far more probable that their recipient was symbolic—whether a concrete Master-as-Muse figure like Shakespeare, or a composite figure containing fragments of the real women and men she had loved, and of imaginary beloveds blurring her longings for lover, reader, sister, mentor, muse. Indeed, a passage from her third Master Letter strongly echoes one of her early love letters to Susan, penned a decade earlier:

To Susan:

> Thank you for loving me, darling . . . —it is enough, dear Susie, I know I shall be satisfied. . . . *Dearer* you *cannot* be, for I love you so

already, that it almost breaks my heart—perhaps I can love you *anew,* every day of my life, every morning and evening—Oh if you will let me, how happy I shall be!

To Master:

Take me in forever, I will never be tired—I will never be noisy when you want to be still—I will be your best little girl—nobody else will see me, but you—but that is enough—I shall not want any more—.

This mosaic-Master hypothesis is furthered by the fact that Dickinson herself, meticulous about how she organized her manuscripts, kept the drafts of her Master Letters among her poetry and not among her correspondence. Unlike the prose of letters, pinned to the physical and emotional reality of the present, in poetry the imagination is allowed to travel between fact and fantasy, to traverse present, past, and future, so that the reader, and perhaps even the writer, is never quite sure—nor need ever ask—to what extent the images evoked correspond to the intersection of matter and moment we call reality.

Reality, for Dickinson, was unrestricted to material fact.

It is curious that in an age when death was an experience so common, which most people confronted from an early age with the premature deaths of parents, of siblings in infancy, of young spouses to tuberculosis, Emily Dickinson was almost entirely protected from it until well into adulthood, and yet she was entirely consumed with it. But shielded as she was from the nuclear immediacy of death so prevalent in families at the time, Dickinson lived for sixteen years—between the ages of nine and twenty-five, before the family moved into the Homestead—in a farmhouse overlooking the Westwood Cemetery, where every funeral in town passed beneath her bedroom window. She would later write that an early awareness of death gave her "Awe for friends" and made her hold them in her heart "in a brittle love, of more alarm, than peace." This concentrating, consecrating urgency that death confers upon life would come to undergird the vast majority of her poems and letters—death not only, and in fact not especially, of the body but of the spirit in the loss of love.

A throe upon the features—
A hurry in the breath—
An extasy of parting
Denominated "Death."

Dickinson was able to capture in exquisite and excruciating detail the emotional reality of an imagined experience, no less real to her than those which had occurred in matter. How can a person of such imaginative ability restrict it to death and not to life itself? She erected towering fantasies in that "chamber facing West," and the loves she experienced were perhaps as real to her as the deaths. Why trammel their poetic reality, which belongs to Dickinson alone, with the impossible cryptography of fragmented facts?

Shortly after she composed the final Master Letter, Dickinson wrote:

This is my letter to the World
That never wrote to Me—

What is "this"? This particular poem? The larger act of writing poetry? Her Master Letters? "In a Life that has stopped guessing, you and I should not feel at home," she would write to Susan well into their adulthood, referring perhaps to the unclassifiable nature of their bond, perhaps to the enduring enigma of her own interiority.

Beyond any human lifetime, and often even within it, what is recorded is what is remembered, the records gradually displacing the actuality of lived events. And what is recorded is a fraction of what is thought, felt, acted out, lived—a fraction at best edited by the very act of its selection, at worst warped by rationalization or fictionalized by a deliberate retelling of reality. The stories we tell about our own lives, to others but especially to ourselves, we tell in order to make our lives livable.

I am struck by this awareness whenever I reread my own diaries from earlier years, penned by past selves, rife with the wishfulness and denial by which we navigate the incomprehensible. I am struck by it doubly when I read a biography of a person long gone, for it lacks even the tenuous net of personal memory. An outsider to the temporal and psychic reality of the person has reached across time to grab a fistful of selective surviving fragments—diaries and letters, themselves already warped by the self-selection of recording—to reconstruct from them a whole existence. It is difficult to do. Often, it cannot be done. In some cases, it must not be done. In lives like Emily Dickinson's—lives of tessellated emotional complexity encrypted in a private lexicon, throbbing with intensity bloodlet in symbol and metaphor—the inevitable blind spots of biography become eclipses. Because we bring our whole selves—our beliefs and our biases, our experience-sculpted curiosity and our limited knowledge—to all we do, each biographer is less an instrument of truth than an interpreter of meaning.

And yet: Like a scientific theory, a biography is a map—one of many possible maps—to an objective external reality that may never be fully discernible or describable to the subjective observer but that is still best explored by mapping, by approximating the landscape of truth from the territories of the knowable.

19

THE HEART'S CIRCUMFERENCE

In the spring of 1862, the year Dickinson composed the last Master Letter and exactly four decades ahead of Rilke's *Letters to a Young Poet*, *The Atlantic Monthly* published a twenty-page piece titled "A Letter to a Young Contributor" by the abolitionist and women's rights advocate Thomas Wentworth Higginson—an occasional guest at Susan's salons and Margaret Fuller's eventual biographer.

Addressing young writers—primarily the many women who sent the *Atlantic* manuscripts for consideration under male pseudonyms— the thirty-nine-year-old Higginson writes: "No editor can ever afford the rejection of a good thing, and no author the publication of a bad one. The only difficulty lies in drawing the line." A good editor, Higginson asserts, has learned to draw that line by having "educated his eye till it has become microscopic, like a naturalist's, and can classify nine out of ten specimens by one glance at a scale or a feather." He chooses a strangely morbid metaphor to illustrate the editorial challenge and thrill of finding that rare undiscovered genius among "the vast range of mediocrity":

> To take the lead in bringing forward a new genius is as fascinating a privilege as that of the physician who boasted to Sir Henry Halford of having been the first man to discover the Asiatic cholera and to communicate it to the public.

He goes on to offer a bundle of advice on how an aspiring writer is to court her prospective editor: Revise amply before sending in your manuscript; write legibly with "good pens, black ink, nice white paper and plenty of it"; develop a style of expression not "polite and prosaic" but "so saturated with warm life and delicious association that every sentence shall palpitate and thrill with the mere fascination of the syllables"; counterbalance profundity of sentiment with levity of style; know that "there is no severer test of literary training than in the power to prune out your most cherished sentence, when you find that the sacrifice will help the symmetry or vigor of the whole"; don't show off your erudition but showcase its fruits; and remember that "a phrase may outweigh a library."

> There may be phrases which shall be palaces to dwell in, treasure-houses to explore; a single word may be a window from which one may perceive all the kingdoms of the earth and the glory of them. Oftentimes a word shall speak what accumulated volumes have labored in vain to utter: there may be years of crowded passion in a word, and half a life in a sentence. . . . Labor, therefore, not in thought alone, but in utterance; clothe and reclothe your grand conception twenty times, if need be, until you find some phrase that with its grandeur shall be lucid also.

In a sun-filled bedroom fifty miles to the west, a woman who had crowded lifetimes of passion into her thirty-one years and corked it up in the volcanic bosom of her being devoured the piece—a woman who would boldly defy Higginson's indictment that a writer should use dashes only in "short allowance" or else they "will lose all their proper power," a woman whose reclusive genius would become his choleric discovery.

For more than a decade, Dickinson had been welding her words to her experience with white heat in the private furnace of her being, sharing her poems only with her intimates. Now she felt beckoned to step across the threshold of the door Higginson had set ajar with his open letter inviting unknown writers into the public life of literature.

On April 16, 1862, Emily Dickinson sent Thomas Wentworth

Higginson four of her poems, along with a short, arresting note in the slanted swoop of her barely decipherable hand, stripped of the era's epistolary etiquette. "Mr. Higginson," she addressed him bluntly, with no formal salutation, "Are you too deeply occupied to say if my Verse is alive?" She was likely making an allusion, whether conscious or not, to her revered *Aurora Leigh*, in which Barrett Browning's heroine exults in her calling while struggling to become a published poet:

> I felt
> My heart's life throbbing in my verse to show
> It lived

And then Dickinson added:

> The Mind is so near itself—it cannot see, distinctly—and I have none to ask. Should you think it breathed—and had you the leisure to tell me, I should feel quick gratitude.

She didn't sign the letter, either, but instead enclosed a smaller sealed envelope with her name inscribed in pencil on a cream-colored note-card—a choice that would still puzzle Higginson thirty years later.

Struck by the directness and dignified vulnerability of his enigmatic correspondent who wrote like no one Higginson had ever read, he replied, probing about her life—who was she and how did she come to be this person? To this near-stranger, Dickinson responded with a most unusual letter of self-revelation and self-concealment commingled into a near-allegorical portrait of being—the deliberate creation of her personal myth:

> You inquire my Books—For Poets—I have Keats—and Mr and Mrs Browning. For Prose—Mr Ruskin—Sir Thomas Browne—and the Revelations. I went to school—but in your manner of the phrase—had no education. When a little Girl, I had a friend, who taught me Immortality—but venturing too near, himself—he never returned—Soon after, my Tutor, died—and for several years, my Lexicon—was my only companion. . . . You ask of my Companions Hills—Sir—and

the Sundown—and a Dog—large as myself, that my Father bought me—They are better than Beings—because they know—but do not tell. . . . I have a Brother and Sister—My Mother does not care for thought—and Father, too busy with his Briefs—to notice what we do—He buys me many Books—but begs me not to read them—because he fears they joggle the Mind. They are religious—except me—and address an Eclipse, every morning—whom they call their "Father."

This is Dickinson's Bayeux Tapestry of paradoxes. In her confessional breathlessness four decades ahead of the notion of *stream of consciousness*, she chooses her words with razing precision—words that shear the fabric of reality to expose the weft thread of autobiographical fact and the warp thread of psychological truth. Why did Dickinson declare that she had "none to ask" about her poetry, when Susan had been her steadfast reader and de facto editor for a decade, scribbling detailed revisions onto the hundreds of poems that passed between the Homestead and the Evergreens? Among the four poems she sent Higginson is one of her most famous: a mocking ode to her skepticism of religion's promise of an afterlife, on which Susan had provided feedback Dickinson ultimately dismissed—to cut out the second stanza.

Safe in their Alabaster Chambers—
Untouched by Morning—
and untouched by noon—
Sleep the meek members of the Resurrection,
Rafter of Satin and Roof of Stone—

Grand go the Years,
In the Crescent above them—
Worlds scoop their Arcs—
and Firmaments—row—
Diadems—drop—
And Doges surrender—
Soundless as Dots,
On a Disk of Snow.

Positioning herself as a demure novice author, ripe for the discovery that so exhilarated the editor, Dickinson omitted the fact that Samuel Bowles had published the poem—anonymously, without the poet's consent, and marred out of her idiosyncratic styling—in his *Springfield Republican* six weeks earlier, or that she had been writing poetry for more than half her life. But she did tell Higginson, obliquely, that two other editors had visited her the previous winter, interested in publishing her poetry. "[They] asked me for my Mind—and when I asked them 'Why,' they said I was penurious—and they, would use it for the World." But then she hurried to add, "I could not weigh myself—Myself," flattering Higginson into the desideratum of his opinion.

And why did she claim she had "no education," when the education she had received far exceeded what most women of her era attained? Even before she entered Mount Holyoke, she had benefited from the excellent free public schools of New England— a system built on the hard work of education reformers like Elizabeth Peabody and Horace Mann, who had devoted their lives to the cause of universal education a generation earlier. When Dickinson was ten, Maria Child had proclaimed in an influential essay that "there is no subject so much connected with individual happiness and national prosperity as the education of daughters." Three years earlier, Dickinson had reaped a strange mixed harvest of misfortune and fortune: When the local public school for girls was destroyed by a fire, the nearby Amherst Academy—a preparatory school for boys—opened its doors to girls to accommodate community need. Although the sexes occupied different floors in the building, the school didn't alter its curriculum—Emily received the same education that prepared local boys for Harvard.

To Higginson, she casts herself as a "little girl" at the time she met Ben Newton—she was eighteen—but this, indeed, is how she experienced herself throughout her young adulthood, writing to her brother at twenty-two: "I love so to be a child. I wish we were always children, how to grow up I don't know." She would soon sign her letters to Higginson "Your Scholar," accentuating this childlike submission to an intellectual father figure. But I hesitate to take this stance too literally—she was, after all, responding to an open letter of advice on how to court an editor, which exhorted young writers to humble themselves before their literary elders. In his *Atlantic* piece, Higginson himself had disobeyed his admonition against exclamation points to enthuse: "How few men in all the pride of culture can emulate the easy grace of a bright woman's letter!" Astronomers distinguish between the apparent brightness of a star, which is based on how far it is from the observer, and its luminosity, which measures the inherent magnitude of the star's light. Higginson must have recognized that pride presses itself against the face of the observer, but only in the grace of humility is inner radiance revealed. Dickinson, too, knew this when she presented herself to him. And yet this was a woman for whom every presentation, be it of sentiment in verse or of self in letters, was a construction as deliberate and carefully crafted as a poem.

She painted her corporeality with the same exquisite, exact strokes:

> I . . . am small, like the Wren, and my Hair is bold, like the Chestnut Bur—and my eyes, like the Sherry in the Glass, that the Guest leaves.

She ended her third letter to Higginson with the come-hither of a bespoke verse, then asked seductively: "Will you be my Preceptor, Mr. Higginson?"

He would, and he did, commencing a correspondence that would last the poet's lifetime. But as enchanted as Higginson was by the whole of the enigma who signed herself Emily Dickinson, he was unconvinced that her subversive verse, which bent form and language in its velvet fist, was fit for print and marketable to the general public. Early in their correspondence, he suggests that she hold off on publication, to which Dickinson responds with a wry renunciation of fame as her animating aim:

> I smile when you suggest that I delay "to publish"—that being foreign to my thought as Firmament to Fin—

If fame belonged to me, I could not escape her—if she did not, the longest way would pass me on the chase—and the approbation of my Dog, would forsake me—then—My Barefoot-Rank is better.

Although Dickinson had so insistently enlisted Higginson as her "Preceptor," again and again she would reject his efforts to tame and commercialize her poetry, to make it "more orderly," buoyed by a quiet confidence in the integrity of her unorthodox verse. "Could you tell me how to grow," she implored in her third letter to Higginson, "or is it unconveyed—like Melody—or Witchcraft?" When he offered criticism, then worried that he might have been too harsh, she assured him with humility and aplomb that it was all welcome: "Men do not call the surgeon, to commend—the Bone, but to set it, Sir, and fracture within, is more critical." And then she promptly sent him four more poems, unheeding of his editorial suggestions.

Over the years, Dickinson would fracture Higginson's stiff understanding of art, and through the cracks a new kind of light would flood his world. "There is always one thing to be grateful for— that one is one's self & not somebody else," she would tell him. Here stood a writer who was unassailably her own self. Between her unruly punctuation, Higginson would eventually find "flashes of wholly original and profound insight into nature and life," language ablaze with "an extraordinary vividness of descriptive and imaginative power." But he would never fully fathom the depth of being Dickinson mined for these verses that would change the landscape of literature.

The most mystifying sentence Emily Dickinson ever wrote, and to me the most beautiful—a sentence over which dust-clouds of speculation would swarm for epochs to come—came in her second letter to Higginson, just before she half-answered, half-skirted his questions about her life:

I had a terror—since September—I could tell to none, and so I sing, as the Boy does by the Burying Ground—because I am afraid.

Not a "fright," not a "shock," but a *terror*. What lay behind this enormity implied by a woman who measured her words so meticulously? Generations of biographers have filled pages with conjectures of varying persuasiveness—a death, some unrecorded heartbreak in her relationship with Susan, an ill-fated courtship by some male suitor or mysterious "Master," the first attack of epilepsy—but the most intriguing theory came nearly a century after Dickinson encrypted these words.

In 1951, after years of research and travel to various archives, the scholar Rebecca Patterson proposed a wholly novel candidate for the "terror" of 1861: Kate Scott Anthon—a newly widowed young woman Susan had befriended during their studies at the Utica Female Academy and then introduced to Emily, who fell into an intense romantic and possibly physical affair with the enticing newcomer before Kate severed the relationship without explanation, dealing a blow Dickinson would experience as deathly and furnishing the raw material for much of her mournful poetry.

This is what we do know: Like Ida Russell to Maria Mitchell, Kate was born within months of Emily, in the year of the eclipse that furnished Mitchell's first astronomical observation. In early March 1859, as Darwin's *On the Origin of Species* was going to press, Kate's fashionable black hat and widow's veil charred across the snowy driveway of the Evergreens as she descended from Austin's sleigh to pay the first of many visits to her former classmate.

This is what Patterson infers from various surviving documents, as direct as Dickinson's letters and as oblique as marginalia in Kate's favorite books: Almost immediately, Susan introduced Kate to the beloved auburn-haired friend who lived across the hedge in the brick house painted deep red and who had been hearing of her for nearly a decade. When Emily, wrapped in a merino shawl, met the tall, handsome woman with the penetrating dark eyes, musical voice, and lively passion for literature and astronomy, she was instantly entranced.

During the three weeks of Kate's first stay at the Evergreens, the two women, both twenty-eight, became inseparable. They took long walks with Emily's dog, Carlo, read *Aurora Leigh* aloud to each other, and spent evenings at the piano as Emily improvised—"weird and beautiful melodies, all from her own inspiration," Kate would remember. As Emily played, Kate towered behind her—"Goliath," the petite poet would call her. When Kate left to go home, Emily beckoned her for another visit to Amherst:

> I am pleasantly located in the deep sea, but love will row you out, if her hands are strong, and don't wait till I land, for I'm going ashore on the other side.

Emily's early letters to Kate pulsate with electricity. Writing weeks after they first met, she tries to disguise with playfulness the push-and-pull of irrepressible, frustrated longing:

> I never missed a Kate before. . . . Sweet at my door this March night another Candidate—Go Home! We don't like Katies here!—Stay! My heart votes for you, and what am I indeed to dispute her ballot—? What are your qualifications? Dare you dwell in the East where we dwell? Are you afraid of the Sun?—When you hear the new violet sucking her way among the sods, shall you be resolute? . . .
>
> Will you still come? *Then* bright I record you! Kate gathered in March!
>
> It is a small bouquet, dear—but what it lacks in size, it gains in fadelessness,—Many can boast a hollyhock, but few can bear a *rose*!
>
> And should new flower smile at limited associates, pray her remember, were there *many* they were not worn upon the breast—but tilled in the pasture! So I rise, wearing her—so I sleep, holding,—Sleep at last with her fast in my hand and wake bearing my flower.—

It is an explosive message, both direct and bewildering, abloom with the code language of flowers that populates the writings of the poet who so often referred to herself as Daisy. The summer after Kate entered her life, Dickinson once again turned to flowers to articulate the precious, hard-won awakening of heart, writing to one of her closest friends:

The gentian is a greedy flower, and overtakes us all. Indeed, this world is short, and I wish, until I tremble, to touch the ones I love before the hills are red—are gray—are white—are "born again"! If we knew how deep the crocus lay, we never should let her go. Still, crocuses stud many mounds whose gardeners till in anguish some tiny, vanished bulb.

The rich flower imagery of Dickinson's first love letter to Kate bears the elegiac undertones of the recognition that all that is beautiful is perishable—something she would capture in verses perhaps inspired by the confounding night the two women spent in Emily's bedroom in the late winter of 1860:

Her sweet Weight on my Heart a Night
Had scarcely deigned to lie—
When, stirring, for Belief's delight,
My Bride had slipped away—

If 'twas a Dream—made solid—just
The Heaven to confirm—
Or if Myself were dreamed of Her—
The power to presume—

Several weeks after that momentous night, she would articulate this precious perishability in a letter to Kate:

Finding is slow, facilities for losing so frequent, in a world like this, I hold with extreme caution. A prudence so astute may seem unnecessary, but plenty moves those most, dear, who have been in want. . . . Were you ever poor? I *have* been a Beggar. . . .

This image would recur in one of Dickinson's poems. "I never lost as much but twice," she would write. "Twice have I stood a beggar / Before the door of God!" Two great casualties of the heart—first Susan, now Kate. And yet this perceived inevitability of loss is meager counterforce against the all-consuming yearning for love. Immediately following Dickinson's cautious sentiment in

the letter to Kate is her implicit argument with the most famous
sentiment from Tennyson's *In Memoriam*: "'Tis better to have loved
and lost / Than never to have loved at all." From the cradle of her
anticipatory loss, she reaches for Kate:

> Kate, Distinctly sweet your face stands in its phantom niche—I touch
> your hand—my cheek your cheek—I stroke your vanished hair, Why
> did you enter, sister, since you must depart? Had not its heart been
> torn enough but *you* must send your shred? . . . There is a subject,
> dear, on which we never touch. Ignorance of its pageantries does not
> deter me. I too went out to meet the "Dust" early in the morning.
> I too in Daisy mounds possess hid treasure, therefore I guard you
> more.

Little is known of Kate's side of the experience. None of her letters to Dickinson survive. (The poet had instructed her sister that all
letters be burned after her death, a request which Lavinia Dickinson
promptly obliged before discovering the trove of poems that made
her realize her sister's correspondence might have immense literary
value.) But Kate did have an unambiguous and lifelong proclivity
for romantic attachment to women, culminating later in life with a
longtime relationship with a young Englishwoman. In a Thomas De
Quincey book Kate had bought just a couple of days before meeting Emily Dickinson, she had underlined this sentence: "There are
women to whom a female friendship is indispensable, and cannot
be supplied by any companion of the other sex."

She signed many of her letters "Tommy" or "Thomas"—a name
her family and friends readily took up, often referring to her in the
masculine: "Aunt Tommy" or "Aunt Thomas," then "Mr. Pump,"
as her English beloved would call her. "I have loved her ever since I
was seventeen years old," Kate would later recall of Emily's beloved
Susan, whom she considered her "dearest friend in America." But
that friendship, too, seems to have begun with an infatuation. In old
age, Kate would write:

> Dear, dear Sue, I have loved you always, since the first night you
> were "monitress," and I hardly knew you, but kissed your dear face

simply because I could not help it! Your sweet eyes looked into mine,
and I could never forget them!

It must have been a strange triangle to inhabit, in her twenty-
eighth year, when Kate found herself a moving point between the
Homestead and the Evergreens, visiting the woman she had once so
loved, now married, and exploring a new attraction to the woman
who too had loved Susan with enduring ardor and indeed still did.

This strange geometry was bound to break. In April 1861, as the
Civil War was erupting, Kate sent Emily a letter severing the relationship. There is no record of what was said, but perhaps Dickinson was thinking of Kate when she wrote

She dealt her pretty words like Blades—
How glittering they shone—
And every One unbared a Nerve
Or wantoned with a Bone—

Many years later, she would write to Higginson:

If ever you lost a friend—Master—You remember you could not
begin again because there was no world—
    A breathless Death is not so cold as a Death that breathes.

Such are the stages of affect as infatuation festers into unrequited
love, then rots into rejection: Drunk on blind devotion, we hope for
a while that our feelings will be matched. When they are not, at first
we rationalize what may be keeping the beloved from reciprocat-
ing and responding. No imagined explanation is too implausible—
busyness, undelivered mail, even death. We fill the silence with our
own symphonic fantasies. "The absence of the witch," Dickinson
would write, "does not invalidate the spell." When we eventually
acknowledge the asymmetry of feeling and the irretrievable loss of
the other's interest, we first labor to persuade ourselves that the
sweet intensity of our own love is reward enough. Then, unable to
sustain this fast and famished for reciprocity, we finally confront the
terror of rejection—for even a love partially returned is a rejection

of the wholeness hungered for—but still some part of us remains aglow with the hope of a future reunion.

Shorn of hope, Emily wrote to a friend:

> When the Best is gone—I know that other things are not of consequence—The Heart wants what it wants—or else it does not care—.

To Kate, she wrote plaintively:

> How many years, I wonder, will sow the moss upon them, before we bind again, a little altered, it may be, elder a little it *will* be, and yet the same, as suns which shine between our lives and loss, and violets. . . .

Her third Master Letter, penned months after Kate's severance of their relationship, would echo this sentiment: "I am older—tonight, Master—but the love is the same—so are the moon and the crescent—."

The following spring, from the recesses of her retreat from the world, Dickinson reached out to Thomas Wentworth Higginson.

Higginson was uniquely poised to recognize poetry in its varied guises—during his time in the Union army, he had grown enchanted by Negro spirituals and endeavored to help preserve the poetic form by writing down the verses and melodies he heard sung around the campfire. He was also uniquely poised to recognize the poetry of the unmet heart eulogizing impossible love.

As a teenager at Harvard, where he had enrolled at the age of thirteen—a fact not uncommon for an era in which university students ranged in age from the early teens to late twenties—Higginson had fallen in love with an androgynous beauty by the name of William Hurlbut. It was the anguishing and arduous love that marks the heart's awakening in adolescence. In his memoir, Higginson—who, like Sarah Margaret Fuller and Ralph Waldo Emerson, went by his middle name, Wentworth—would recount unselfconsciously:

Going through the doors of Divinity Hall I met one day a young man so handsome in his dark beauty that he seemed like a picturesque Oriental; slender, keen-eyed, raven-haired, he arrested the eye and the heart like some fascinating girl. . . . He was the breaker . . . of many hearts, the disappointer of many hopes,—and this in two continents.

Wentworth's competition for William's attention was none other than the reigning queen of the Old World: Oscar Wilde. But William, who opened his letters with such frolicsome flirtations as "The unfaithful to the unforgetting—greeting," kindled Wentworth's inner fire with enough attention to keep it going for the remainder of his life. Higginson's second wife would later recount in her biography of him that "their letters were more like those between man and woman than between two men."

It is impossible to tell at what point and why an intense mutual attraction skews toward an anguishing asymmetry of expectations, but William eventually stopped replying to Wentworth's impassioned letters. "Give too much love to the dearest and fairest and oh! what sad dissatisfaction," he anguished in his journal. But he kept writing to William for years: "Still, O changing child, out of the depths of my charity I still believe in you and out of the depths of my heart I still love you."

Decades later, with a heartache unsalved by the passage of time, he would recount: "I never loved but one male friend with passion— and for him my love had no bounds—all that my natural fastidiousness and cautious reserve kept from others I poured on him; to say that I would have died for him was nothing. I lived for him."

This love, he wrote, was his "one terrible disappointment." Could it be that Higginson sensed a kindred crushing enormity of unrequited devotion in Dickinson's poems—poems in which she died again and again at the altar of the impossible love for which she lived? Did he hear in her professed "terror" an echo of his "one terrible disappointment"?

Since so few of Dickinson's letters from that period survive, and none of Kate's, it is unsound to presume that Kate was the sole trigger of that September "terror." Three months earlier, after a five-year abstinence in her marriage to Austin followed by an attempted abortion, Susan had given birth to their first child—something that must have amplified Emily's sense of desolation. Susan certainly knew of her suffering, for she drew on an image from Hans Christian Andersen's fairy tale "The Nightingale and the Rose" in writing to apologize for turning away from Emily's kiss:

> If you have suffered this past Summer—I am sorry—I Emily bear a sorrow that I never uncover—If a nightingale sings with her brast against a thorn, why not *we*?

Susan wrote this in October. Could the "terror" of the previous month have been the jilted kiss, a climax of the loss of intimacy Emily feared as Susan finally consummated her social contract with Austin? Or is terror a cumulative state—an accretion of stabs at the spirit? When my grandmother speaks of surviving World War II as a child, she points to no individual bombing, no particular sight of soldiers or siren cry, as the source of the terror through which she lived. It was the atmosphere of dread, of losses anticipatory and actual, that fomented the bone-trembling horror of it.

Kate's abrupt abandonment, Susan's spurned kiss, the outbreak of the Civil War—losses anticipatory and actual swarmed all around Emily Dickinson in the late summer of 1861. Like her "Master," her "terror" may well have been a composite entity. She survived it by making art. The three years following it would be the most prolific of the poet's life, during which she composed more than a third of her surviving poems—a testament to "the grief we grow ourselves divine by overcoming with mere hope and most prosaic patience," of which Elizabeth Barrett Browning had written in *Aurora Leigh*, Dickinson's poetic bible.

Her niece and eventual biographer—Susan and Austin's second child, Martha, not yet born at this time of tumult—would mark that period as the precipice of the poet's ultimate withdrawal from

society. Around the time Hawthorne gloomed in the *Atlantic* that
"there is no remoteness of life and thought, no hermetically sealed
seclusion, except, possibly, that of the grave, into which the disturbing influences of this war do not penetrate," Dickinson wrote one of
her most famous and piercing poems:

> The Soul selects her own Society—
> Then—shuts the Door—
> To her divine Majority—
> Present no more—
>
> Unmoved—she notes the Chariots—pausing—
> At her low Gate—
> Unmoved—an Emperor be kneeling
> Upon her Mat—
>
> I've known her—from an ample nation—
> Choose One—
> Then—close the Valves of her attention—
> Like Stone—

Whomever she chose to invite in—Susan, Kate, some amalgam
of loves in the face of her "Master"—Dickinson shut the door and
latched it for the remaining twenty-four years of her life. She alone
would achieve what all the Transcendentalists had attempted and
failed at—a purification of being by deliberate removal from the
bustling commonplaces of society. The Brook Farm utopia had collapsed in a cautionary public spectacle. Even Thoreau sustained his
famed Walden experiment in self-reliance for a mere year, during
which his mother and sister brought him fresh doughnuts every
Sunday morning.

But something momentous and profound did happen to her,
within her, in 1861—something she encoded in an arresting poem
from that period, her pronouns once again unsexed of a literal
reading:

> He fumbles at your Soul
> As Players at the Keys

Before they drop full Music on—
He stuns you by degrees—
Prepares your brittle Nature
For the Ethereal Blow
By fainter Hammers—further heard—
Then nearer—Then so slow
Your Breath has time to straighten—
Your Brain—to bubble Cool—
Deals—One—imperial—Thunderbolt—
That scalps your naked Soul—

When Winds take Forests in the Paws—
The Universe—is still—

In the autumn of 1861, Samuel Bowles—whose *Springfield Republican* had been the first literary journal to publish Dickinson's poetry and who had since become her close and affectionate correspondent—became afflicted with sciatica and sought a "water cure" in nearby Northampton. The month after the September "terror," he traveled to Amherst to visit the Dickinsons, but Emily refused to see him. In an apologetic letter, she beseeched him not to think that she didn't care: "I pray for your sweet health—to 'Alla'—every morning—but something troubled me."

Trouble, terror—Dickinson would not disclose the source of that "something," or her disclosure does not survive among the unburned letters. But Bowles was one of her three most intimate correspondents at the time, along with her cousins Loo and Fanny, friends of Maria Mitchell's. It is possible that she had confided in him the intensity of her heartbreak, if not its source. "We tell a Hurt to cool it," she would write in a poem. Among Bowles's own letters is one from that July to a recipient whose name has been scrubbed—an extraordinary letter of consolation to somebody anguishing with unrequited love, somebody who may well have been Emily Dickinson:

My dear—:
. . . . You must give if you expect to receive—give happiness, friendship, love, joy, and you will find them floating back to you.

Sometimes you will give more than you receive. We all do that in some of our relations, but it is as true a pleasure often to give without return as life can afford us. We must not make bargains with the heart, as we would with the butcher for his meat. Our business is to give what we have to give—what we can get to give. The return we have nothing to do with. . . . One will not give us what we give them—others will more than we can or do give them—and so the accounts will balance themselves. It is so with my loves and friendships—it is so with everybody's.

That Dickinson was the recipient is made all the more probable by a surviving letter of her own, written to one of her closest friends that same month—a letter embodying the very commitment of heart that Bowles encouraged:

Perhaps you laugh at me! Perhaps the whole United States are laughing at me too! *I* can't stop for that! *My* business is to love. I found a bird, this morning, down—down—on a little bush at the foot of the garden, and wherefore sing, I said, since nobody *hears*?

One sob in the throat, one flutter of bosom—"*My* business is to *sing*"—and away she rose! How do I know but cherubim, once, themselves, as patient, listened, and applauded her unnoticed hymn?

That year, in a letter to Higginson, she tendered a parallel sentiment—one of her most puzzling and profound: "My Business is Circumference." Here was a woman whose life's work was love, poetry, and "circumference." It may have been another coded reference to Susan, the resident mathematician of her heart; it may have been an allusion to Emerson, who had written two decades earlier in one of his most famous essays, "Circles":

The life of man is a self-evolving circle, which, from a ring imperceptibly small, rushes on all sides outwards to new and larger circles, and that without end. The extent to which this generation of circles, wheel without wheel, will go, depends on the force or truth of the individual soul.

20

BOUND BY NEITHER MIND NOR MATTER

In the years following her "terror," Dickinson penned hundreds of forceful poems—verses of unambiguous beauty that thrill and taunt with their ambiguous meaning. Writing at an almost manic pace, she seems to have found in poetry's generous allowance for symbolism and vagueness the one outlet for confiding, comprehending, and containing an experience of uncontainable emotional magnitude. Despite her elective isolation, word of her occupation traveled through Amherst and soon across New England—for the legend of her hermeticism is a rather selective retelling of the actuality of her life. While Dickinson herself seems to have enjoyed fomenting the myth with her almost performative evasion of visitors and her habit of conversing with guests from behind a wall, she also enjoyed mocking it. Around the time of her thirtieth birthday, when her cousin Loo mentioned the popular perception that the poet dressed only in white, Dickinson jibed: "Won't you tell 'the public' that at present I wear a brown dress with a cape if possible browner, and carry a parasol of the same!" As to the question of why there was a "public" to speak of in the first place, speculating about the life of a local thirty-year-old: Dickinson lived on Main Street, in one of the handsomest houses in town, often called the Mansion; everyone knew that the corner bedroom overlooking the busy stretch of the Boston mail route was occupied by the daughter of the Amherst College treasurer turned congressman, and that she was a poet.

Eventually, notable literati called on Dickinson, urging her to publish. She refused. After eight years of correspondence, Higginson himself came for a visit—one of only two in-person meetings the two would have throughout the long editorial relationship that would last until Dickinson's death. "If I read a book which makes my whole body so cold no fire ever can warm me," she told him, "I know *that* is poetry. If I feel physically as if the top of my head were taken off, I know *that* is poetry." He was thrown by the strangeness of her person, her pattering childlike step, her meteoric thought, the spasmodic artillery of her conversation. "My cracked poetess in Amherst," he would later call her. But coming from Higginson, this was an affectionate recognition of kinship rather than a slight. Long ago, his abolitionist ardor had driven him to plot the liberation of a former slave by placing a mattress beneath the courthouse window where the young man was held and encouraging him to leap onto it and into an escape carriage. When Higginson was criticized for the seeming insanity of his zeal, he proclaimed that "without a little crack somewhere, a man could hardly do his duty to the times."

A sickly child who circled the event horizon of death with alarming regularity—"half-dead," he remembered his young self—Higginson grew up determined to inoculate himself against frailty by becoming a man of action. Unlike Emerson and the other reformers whose swords were words, he believed that action had a necessary physical dimension. In an impassioned essay titled "Physical Courage"—one of his first contributions to *The Atlantic Monthly,* a journal originally conceived as an antislavery publication—Higginson lauded the seemingly superhuman corporal valor of the runaway slaves who braved the Underground Railroad:

> These men and women, who have tested their courage in the lonely swamp against the alligator and the bloodhound, who have starved on prairies, hidden in holds, clung to locomotives, ridden hundreds of miles cramped in boxes, head downward, equally near to death if discovered or deserted,—and who have then, after enduring all this, gone voluntarily back to risk it over again, for the sake of wife or child,—what are we pale faces, that we should claim a rival capacity with theirs for heroic deeds?

He went on to become a pioneer of physical fitness and an advance apostle of bodybuilding decades before the word was coined in a 1904 pamphlet. Having long ago competed in bodybuilding myself, I am not oblivious to how this particular sport can become a sandbox for working out confused sexuality, separating spirit and sinew to turn the body into a means of both subverting and submitting to the ideals of femininity and masculinity. It spoke to Higginson, who struggled with his own sexuality and was ideologically opposed to the gender norms that kept women oppressed. Perhaps he so admired Margaret Fuller because, despite her chronic ill health, she had flung herself body and spirit into Rome's raging revolution, trekked the mountains of Italy seven months pregnant, and died a death of such tragedy that it bordered on the heroic. Although Emily Dickinson's strength was not of sinew but of sentiment, he sensed that her verse was not just "alive" but muscular, chiseled with great discipline into beauty that seemed almost of a different species than the soft-bodied verse reposing on the pages of literary journals. More than that, it spoke to his other great passion—the embodied awareness of nature's splendor, as elemental to our creaturely nature as the physicality of our bodies. While Higginson's fervid political writings had garnered him esteem—and controversy—among the narrow echelon of reformers, his nature essays in the *Atlantic* were what seized the popular imagination and catapulted him into celebrity, drawing piles of fan letters. Samuel Bowles's *Springfield Republican* exulted that "no other like him explores the sylvan haunts with the foot of a child, the eye of an artist and the heart of a woman." Even Thoreau—Higginson's great hero—praised his nature essays. In a particularly lovely one, titled "The Procession of Flowers," Higginson insisted that the wonder of literature lay in the miraculous ability to make words radiate the sensorial reality of a fragrant azalea:

> One ought to be able, by the mere use of language, to supply to every reader the total of that white, honeyed, trailing sweetness, which summer insects haunt and the Spirit of the Universe loves. The defect is not in language, but in men. There is no conceivable beauty of blossom so beautiful as words.

In another essay, titled "My Out-Door Study" and published the year before Dickinson's first letter to him, Higginson had written:

> We talk of literature as if it were a mere matter of rule and measurement, a series of processes long since brought to mechanical perfection: but it would be less incorrect to say that it all lies in the future; tried by the outdoor standard, there is as yet no literature, but only glimpses and guideboards; no writer has yet succeeded in sustaining, through more than some single occasional sentence, that fresh and perfect charm. If by the training of a lifetime one could succeed in producing one continuous page of perfect cadence, it would be a life well spent, and such a literary artist would fall short of Nature's standard in quantity only, not in quality.

Within a year, he would enter into correspondence with an eccentric writer who had been perfecting her verse beyond meter, beyond mechanical mastery, limning nature with dewy originality. The year 1863—the year following their first contact—would become the most prolific of Dickinson's life. By the end of December, she had tucked into letters two hundred ninety-five surviving poems, possibly many more, despite having fallen ill with rheumatic iritis—a rare iris disorder, often concomitant with diabetes, that inflicts upon the eyes pain, extreme light sensitivity, and blurred vision. Dickinson had to leave Amherst to see a prominent eye specialist in Boston and would later recall the period as "a woe"—"the only one that ever made me tremble," she wrote. It cut her off from "the strongest friends of the soul—BOOKS." Still, she went on writing at a formidable rate, often exceeding two hundred poems per year. Some were meant for Susan's eyes alone, but many she shared with Higginson. Eventually, he showed Dickinson's poetry to Helen Hunt Jackson—one of the era's most respected creative writers and among its rare women successful by their own pen. Several years later, Jackson would pick up where Margaret Fuller had left off with *Summer on the Lakes* and write *A Century of Dishonor*—a daring book condemning the displacement and abuse of Native Americans. The esteemed Boston bookbinder turned publisher Roberts Brothers would reject the manuscript as too controversial.

Thirteen years earlier, they had initially rejected Louisa May Alcott's *Little Women* as too boring, until the publisher saw the novel shake his niece with laughter and tears and relented.

A century and a half later, I find a tattered paperback copy of *Little Women* in my grandmother's library in Bulgaria, among the books that belonged to her father, Georgi. I never met my great-grandfather—he died six days before I was born—but I got to know him through my grandmother's stories. An astronomer and mathematician born at the dawn of the twentieth century, into Bulgaria's nascent monarchy after five hundred years under the Ottoman yoke, he lived through two world wars only to see his homeland, ravaged by centuries of oppression and decades of war, succumb to Communism in the 1940s. When the Iron Curtain dropped, the dictatorial government took great pains to silence any cultural signal from the other side. In one of those small yet enormous acts of resistance, my great-grandfather hacked his transistor radio into the frequency of the BBC World Service and, well into his fifties, set about teaching himself English. He acquired an English dictionary and a few literary classics through some underground channel and began underlining words, filling the margins with translations, and code-cracking English grammar like a small-scale Alan Turing. By the 1960s, he had become fluent. When his nine grandchildren—including my father—were entrusted to his daytime care, he decided to pass this legacy of insurgency along by teaching them English. He would take them to the park and when the time came for their afternoon snack, he would withhold the sandwiches until the children asked for them in the Queen's English.

Of all my great-grandfather's smuggled books—Hemingway, Salinger, Fitzgerald—the one most replete with his tiny, neat marginalia is *Little Women*. Could Alcott have imagined what Jo would do for Georgi? Can any author ever imagine just how far literature reaches into unfathomed horizons of culture, what it transforms and whom it liberates?

Roberts Brothers fell light-years short of such imagination when they initially rejected Alcott, just as they did when they definitively rejected Helen Hunt Jackson. New York's Harper & Brothers would take the chance instead, publishing a book that would become an instant success and establish Jackson as the first serious literary advocate for Native American rights. She would soon be appointed Commissioner for Native Americans in California, becoming one of the first women to enter American politics in a leadership position.

But now she came to Dickinson as a fellow poet, one who felt it her duty—to literature, to beauty, to women's quest for recognition—to coax "the myth of Amherst" into the daylight of the printed page. In a letter to Dickinson from March 1876, Jackson tempered the gravity of her sentiment with a wink at the writer's responsibility to posterity:

> I have a little manuscript volume with a few of your verses in it—and I read them very often— . . . You are a great poet—and it is wrong to the day you live in, that you will not sing aloud. When you are what men call dead, you will be sorry you were so stingy.

That October, she attempted persuasion in person—one of the rare visitors the poet conceded to see face-to-face a decade and a half into the tunnel of her seclusion. Sitting across from Dickinson—who by that point had written well over a thousand poems—Jackson sensed a whole other species of genius, different not by degree but by kind. "Your hand felt like such a wisp in mine that you frightened me," she wrote to Dickinson after the visit, during which she had felt "like a great ox talking to a white moth, and begging it to come and eat grass with me to see if it could not turn itself into beef!" Apologizing for the impertinence of trying to persuade this strange moth to step into the sunlight—"How stupid"—Jackson seemed cornered into respecting Dickinson's resistance to publication. But she did not, could not understand it.

And how is it to be understood, anyway? Surely it wasn't mere humility. Dickinson was proud to be a poet, proud of her verse—so proud she bound her poems with a darning needle, shared them readily in letters to friends, tied them to loaves of bread she baked for ill neighbors, and was only half facetious when she envisioned that they "Will entertain the Centuries / When I, am long ago, / An Island in dishonored Grass— / Whom none but Daisies, know—"

Having read *Aurora Leigh* religiously, Dickinson may well have taken for a tenet Barrett Browning's assertion that "the worthiest poets have remained uncrowned till death has bleached their foreheads to the bone." It wasn't acclaim she skirted but the crown, the attendant visibility of fame—a mind-set diametrically opposed and almost alien to our current celebrity culture, which mistakes visibility for merit. This was another of Dickinson's rending paradoxes— she wanted to be recognized and appreciated, but she didn't want to be exposed—an aversion that may well have been encoded in her nature but was certainly indoctrinated through her nurture.

When Emily was twenty, Austin urged his sisters—twice—to come to Boston and hear Jenny Lind. "We don't care a fig for the museum, the stillness, or Jennie Lind," Emily scoffed in response. In the summer of 1851, as she was falling in love with Susan, she finally consented to let her father take the women of the family to hear the Swedish Nightingale. In a downpour, the foursome made their way to a Gothic cathedral—the only building large enough to contain the audiences Lind drew. Emily—who had never heard nor would ever again hear a musician in concert—was mesmerized by Lind's performance, but even more so by her person. "Herself, and not her music, was what we seemed to love," she wrote to Austin two days later, telling him of "the air of exile in her mild blue eyes," and of "how Jennie came out like a child and sang and sang again, how bouquets fell in showers, and the roof was rent with applause—how it thundered outside, and inside with the thunder of God and of men . . . how we all loved Jennie Lind."

Not all in the party loved what they saw—Emily's father, whom she described as reading only "lonely & rigorous books," was made uneasy by the sight of a woman onstage, apparently feeling that even talent on the level of genius was an insufficient reason for a woman to expose herself to public attention and charge for her work. Whatever other reasons Emily Dickinson may have had for secluding herself in her bedroom for the majority of her life and refusing publication, the formative climate of her father's conviction is not irrelevant.

Confounded by Dickinson's resistance, Helen Hunt Jackson now tried an acrobatic trick of empathic inversion: "You say you find great pleasure in reading my verses. Let somebody somewhere whom you do not know have the same pleasure in reading yours."

Perhaps Dickinson's reservations were rooted in a distrust of the public's capacity to understand, much less appreciate, her verse and her vision. She must have known she was unusual, unexampled. Her beloved Aurora Leigh had cleverly enumerated the classes of misunderstanding and misappreciation by which critics, publishers, and the reading public dispirit the soul of original art with commercialism and convention:

> My critic Hammond flatters prettily,
> And wants another volume like the last.
> My critic Belfair wants another book
> Entirely different, which will sell, (and live?)
> A striking book, yet not a startling book,
> The public blames originalities.
> (You must not pump spring-water unawares
> Upon a gracious public, full of nerves—)
> Good things, not subtle, new yet orthodox,
> As easy reading as the dog-eared page
> That's fingered by said public, fifty years,
> Since first taught spelling by its grandmother,
> And yet a revelation in some sort:
> That's hard, my critic, Belfair!

Aurora's greatest concern may well have been Dickinson's own— the tyranny of artificial cheerfulness that leaves no room for the darkness that Dickinson mined for her verse.

> My critic Jobson recommends more mirth,
> Because a cheerful genius suits the times,

And all true poets laugh unquenchably
Like Shakspeare and the gods. That's very hard,
The gods may laugh, and Shakspeare; Dante smiled
With such a needy heart on two pale lips,
We cry, "Weep rather, Dante." Poems are
Men, if true poems: and who dares exclaim
At any man's door, "Here, 'tis probable
The thunder fell last week, and killed a wife,
And scared a sickly husband—what of that?
Get up, be merry, shout, and clap your hands,
Because a cheerful genius suits the times—"?
None says so to the man,—and why indeed
Should any to the poem?

If there was genius in Dickinson's verse, and if she knew it, she knew equally that none of it was cheerful genius. To bend it to popular taste would be to blunt the edge of its authenticity, to make it something other than art—something Barrett Browning had questioned in *Aurora Leigh*:

If virtue done for popularity
Defiles like vice, can art for praise or hire
Still keep its splendour, and remain pure art?

Jackson persisted. She beseeched Dickinson to send her poem "Success" to Roberts Brothers for an anthology of anonymous poems by some of the most celebrated living authors in the English-speaking world. (The editors of the *Brooklyn Daily Eagle*, where the poem had first appeared fourteen years earlier—one of eleven to be printed in Dickinson's lifetime—had given it that title. Dickinson herself never titled her poems.) In October 1878, Dickinson finally consented. When the anthology was released at the end of the year to middling reviews, "Success" was singled out as the standout amid the otherwise disappointing collection. Reviewers speculated that it was by none other than Emerson.

Success—is counted sweetest
By those who ne'er succeed—

To Comprehend a Nectar—
Requires sorest need—

Over the next four years, Jackson sang Dickinson's praises to
the editor of Roberts Brothers—who was aware of the author's
identity—and encouraged him to publish more of her poetry. But
when Dickinson submitted other poems, the publisher politely dis-
tanced himself. After more than two decades of writing poetry in
private—poetry she wrote for and shared only with her select society of intimates—Dickinson, at forty-two, had offered herself up
to the public. The result was rejection. She would never attempt
publication again. A generation earlier, Margaret Fuller had captured this perennial gauntlet of the creative life: "An everlasting yes
breathes from the life, from the work of the artist. Nature echoes it,
and leaves to society the work of saying no, if it will."

Dickinson went on living out her yeses in the uncensuring sunlight of her private chamber. "Success," she would write in the final
year of her life, "is dust, but an aim forever touched with dew." Yet
it would be rash to assume that she stopped seeking publication
out of woundedness over the rejection. More likely, her brush with
the commercial enterprise of publishing affirmed her broader reservations about the cultural machinery of fame. "If fame belonged
to me," she had told Higginson at the outset of their correspondence, "I could not escape her." She was certainly ambivalent about
fame—"a fickle food / Upon a shifting plate," she called it in one
poem. In another, she wrote:

Fame is a bee.
It has a song—
It has a sting—
Ah, too, it has a wing.

Helen Hunt Jackson remained undeterred in her crusade to bring
Dickinson's poetry to the world. Having just weathered her own
rejection by Roberts Brothers only to find landmark success with
another publisher, she continued encouraging the poet to reconsider.
First she made a further appeal to Dickinson's moral responsibility

to her epoch: It would be "a cruel wrong" to withhold such genius from her generation, Jackson charged. Then she drew on Dickinson's preoccupation with death and playfully cast her verse as her ticket to immortality: "Surely, after you are what is called 'dead,' you will be willing that the poor ghosts you have left behind, should be cheered and pleased by your verses, will you not?—You ought to be." Jackson wasn't aware that Dickinson had already penned a retort in a poem painting fame not as the gateway to immortality but as its counterpoint, small of aim and suspended in time:

Some—Work for Immortality—
The Chiefer part, for Time—
He—Compensates—immediately—
The former—Checks—on Fame—

Higginson had been fascinated with Dickinson's poetry, but he deemed it unmarketable and discouraged her from publishing. Samuel Bowles had printed some of it, but anonymously and editorially mutilated. This was, after all, the era in which Walt Whitman, the nation's most esteemed living poet, elegized Longfellow, the nation's most esteemed just-dead poet, for the fact that "he strikes a splendid average, and does not sing exceptional passions, or humanity's jagged escapades"; that "he is not revolutionary, brings nothing offensive or new, does not deal hard blows"—in other words, that he is no Vesuvius. Helen Hunt Jackson would be one of only three readers—all women—to recognize Dickinson's volcanic genius during her lifetime. But when Jackson, having offered to be her literary executor, died suddenly several months before Dickinson, the task of recognition fell on the other two—women who bookended the poet's life in radically different ways: Susan, her first love, foremost muse, and lifelong reader, and Mabel Loomis Todd, whose improbable invasion of the Dickinson universe would rip the family apart but would seal Emily Dickinson's legacy as a literary artist without peer or precedent.

. . .

Twenty-six years younger than Austin and twenty-four younger than Emily, Mabel Loomis Todd waltzed into the Dickinsons' lives on the last day of August in 1881, after a two-week journey by boat, train, and carriage from Washington. "What have I done?" she shuddered in her journal. She had followed her husband, the astronomer David Peck Todd, who would rise to fame later that year for taking the first photographs of a transit of Venus—the rarest of all predictable cosmic events. Todd had taken a staggering pay cut in accepting an astronomy position at Amherst College, his alma mater, on the whispered promise that a wealthy patron was ready to invest $300,000—more than $7.5 million today—in a new observatory, which Todd would head. The promise would not materialize. Instead, a decade later, his wife would raise funds for the observatory by banking on her newfound fame as Emily Dickinson's self-appointed ventriloquist.

Mabel had grown up an only child in an era when families had scores of children. Her father—a poet, scientist, and lover of nature with a Transcendentalist bent—had taken wilderness walks with Walt Whitman and Henry David Thoreau, who once awkwardly cradled the baby Mabel in his arms. Her parents had strained their meager means to give their daughter three years of school in Georgetown, where she was inculcated with Southern manners and heavily immersed in science—astronomy, geometry, chemistry—before enrolling in the Boston Conservatory of Music. Her aunt had been one of the first women to graduate from a university. Her grandfather, a farmer and mathematician, had been one of Maria Mitchell's colleagues at the *Nautical Almanac*. Mabel's father would also work there for fifty years. While visiting him at the *Almanac,* Mabel would meet his young, suave colleague David Todd—a sybarite who often had his sight, and occasionally his hands, on several women at a time.

Twenty-one months later, Mabel and David were married.

At twenty-five, unbeautiful but striking, Mabel carried herself with astonishing self-possession. Large and lively reddish-brown eyes illuminated her Pekingese-proportioned face with the confidence of one who knows that personal beauty radiates not from physical fact but from a performance of being.

Born in the year of Susan and Austin's wedding, Mabel arrived into their lives shortly after their twenty-fifth anniversary. A painter, pianist, professionally trained singer, and published essayist, she brought ambition, charisma, and worldliness that stunned rural Amherst. Immediately, she gravitated to Susan Dickinson as "the most of a real society person" in town. "I am thoroughly captivated with her," Mabel enthused to her mother. "She is so easy and charming & sincere—and she understands me completely."

Within two years, she would wish Susan dead.

A year and eleven days after her arrival, Mabel would become Austin Dickinson's lover and would remain so until his death two decades later—a sort of alternative marriage that would become the single most decisive factor in how Emily Dickinson's poetry penetrated the world.

Long before the notion of an open marriage was accepted, or the term even existed, the Todds had one—happily. "We should have been born later, that is all," Mabel would write. "One or two hundred years from now the world would rejoice with us." David, who continued to have fleeting flings of his own, signed his letters to his wife "l/h"—*lover/husband*. Mabel recorded her dynamic sex life in her diary, using a set of symbols to mark lovemaking and her orgasms. (In his own diary, the virgin Hans Christian Andersen used a Christian cross to mark his self-pleasuring.) She kept track of the occasions on which she and David made love, beginning with the number 1 at the start of the new year and giving up count at 75 in August. Her lovemaking with Austin she would later record qualitatively: "A most exquisitely happy and satisfactory two hours." She reflected on the symmetry of the arrangement:

> I do not think David is what might be called a monogamous animal. While I know that he loves me to the full of his nature, he is not at all incapable of falling immensely in love with somebody else, & having a very piquant time of it.

Mabel and David had put into practice the philosophy Emerson had only dared, and barely, put into words half a century earlier. Emerson, who died the year Mabel and Austin fell in love, had once told Margaret Fuller that "the soul knows nothing of marriage, in the sense of a permanent union between two personal existences"—rather, "the soul is married to each new thought as it enters into it."

The thought of Austin Dickinson entered Mabel Loomis Todd's soul at first sight—she found him to be "fine (& very remarkable) looking—& very dignified & strong and a little odd." But it would be a year until her fixation on Susan shifted to Susan's husband, pivoted by Mabel's fascination with Austin's sister. In mid-September 1882, Mabel marveled in her diary:

> Emily is called in Amherst "the myth." She has not been out of her house for fifteen years. She writes the strangest poems, & very remarkable ones. She is in many respects a genius. She wears always white, & has her hair arranged as was the fashion fifteen years ago when she went into retirement.

The previous Sunday, Austin had escorted Mabel on her first visit to the Homestead—Emily had requested that the enticing newcomer, who had already enchanted Sue and Austin, come sing for her. And so she did—Mabel unleashed Beethoven from the piano and spilled the highest octaves of her steady voice into the hollow of the Homestead. "It was odd to think as my voice rang out through the big silent house," she later wrote in her journal, "that Miss Emily in her weird white dress was outside in the shadow hearing every word." When the song alighted to its final notes, Emily sent Mabel a glass of sherry and a poem she had written while Mabel sang. "I know I shall see her," Mabel resolved. "No one *has* seen her in all these years except her own family."

Mabel Todd would never see Emily Dickinson. In their closest encounter, a coffin lid would separate them. But she would become the mightiest animating force keeping "the myth" alive in the popular imagination for decades to come.

The following evening, September 11, Austin picked Mabel

up from the Todds' boardinghouse and walked her to his home, where she had been invited to a party. Under a heavy downpour, they paused as they passed the gate of the Evergreens. "I could not see even a step ahead," Mabel reflected on the first anniversary of the moment that would shape Emily Dickinson's meeting with the world. "But I did not want to see." The blinding brown of Mabel's eyes rose to meet the amber of Austin's, awned by his thick auburn eyebrows and the low rim of his black hat. Given Austin's constitutional reserve, it is highly probable that Mabel initiated the mutual profession: They were in love. A year later, she would echo Goethe's notion of "elective affinities" in reflecting on the possessing magnetism of their illicit liaison: "I entered it boldly and happily, led by something thoroughly outside of myself and my will."

Austin, too, would recall the inception as ineluctable and beyond the bounds of conscious reality:

> I took a hand I could not let go, and that did not let go mine. I walked along—was I in dreamland—or in the world of the real! I thought it must be dreamland—I feared to wake—and I could not believe, even when I *knew* I was awake. It was too much, too great.

He would later reflect on the paralyzing force of this euphoric excess: "My experience of life was too firm & encrusted to permit it. It contradicts everything, revolutionizes everything."

Mabel, unbounded by such Puritanical rigidity of moral sentiment, would exclaim of their private revolution: "Great Heavens, my darling, I am transported by it, almost overpowered. We love." She would go on to write of their relationship as one between "two persons who have loved so nobly, so utterly, so endlessly that the gods themselves must have delighted to watch." Theirs was a love unexampled in the history of the world and even in the imagination: "No love story approaches it."

In his own diary, Austin marked the evening of September 11 with one austere, momentous word: "Rubicon," likening the stormy crossing of the yard, of the bounds of marital fidelity, to the historic river crossing by which Julius Caesar broke the sacred law of the

Roman Republic and sparked a civil war—a point of no return that
gave rise to much of Western civilization, from classical sculpture
and the literature of the Romance languages to the modern calendar. Austin could not have fathomed the prescience of his choice
of metaphor, for the crossing he and Mabel made that night would
launch the famous "war between the houses"—the generations-long
victorless feud between the Homestead and the Evergreens, waged
with magmatic emotions on the battleground of Emily Dickinson's
writing, effecting a radical transfiguration of literature.

Mabel intuited the momentousness of what had happened, but
she couldn't have realized that in articulating its personal significance, she was also presaging its significance to literature for centuries to come:

> An opening so strange, so unexpected, and so ineffably beautiful
> could not.lead to anything commonplace or trivial. . . . A whole new
> future opened—possibilities quivered before me—although even
> then I scarcely comprehended its significance.

Shortly after the Rubicon, the Todds returned to Washington
for a brief visit with their eighteen-month-old daughter, for whom
Mabel's mother had been caring until they settled more firmly in
Amherst. It was from there that Mabel mailed her first letter to
Austin, who meanwhile had used his influence with the board of
trustees at the university to procure a significant salary increase for
David. After thanking him for the favor, Mabel wrests a metaphor
for the unpredictable cosmic force of their love from her curious
remarks on the Great Comet of 1882, which had loomed overhead
on the night of the Rubicon and was still blazing across the sky:

> I am so glad you take so hopeful a view of that comet—indeed I
> did myself after the day or two of rather sombre reflections which
> followed my first view of it. . . . My extreme buoyancy of spirits
> would, I think, carry me safely over the final day itself, and I could
> not help being happy if I knew absolutely that the end of all things
> approached. Nevertheless, I am very glad the comet is receding so
> rapidly from the Inn. I love to live.

Within a month, Mabel has transposed this cometic zest for life onto Austin, casting their love as part miracle and part inevitability, governed by the same forces that govern the universe:

I love you. I love you! Why should I! and why shouldn't I! Who made & who rules the human heart! Where is the wrong in preferring sunshine to shadow! Does not the unconscious plant lean toward light?

Austin responds in kind, echoing Melville's "divine magnet":

I am feeling this morning that you indeed are drawn to me by the same mysterious unbidden influence that draws me irresistibly to you.

And where is Susan in all of this? At first, not only unsuspecting of deceit but encouraging—after a neighbor teased Austin for the gallantry of walking Mabel home one night, Susan scoffed: "For pity's sake don't laugh at him. If there is any one person he actually likes, I am too rejoiced." Mabel herself joyously reported to her husband how the Dickinsons had opened to her "their home, their horses, & their hearts with a truly touching and magnificent generosity." She seemed to appease her moral dissonance with a peculiar kind of magical thinking, projecting herself into an alternate universe of possibility where she could both surrender to the impelling force drawing her to Austin and remain Susan's trusted, admired, and admiring friend. Or perhaps she was simply hoping that what was possible within her own marriage would also be possible within Austin's—even as she was falling in love with him, she was writing in her diary: "David & I are very happy together. We love each other freshly every day, and our life with each other is inexpressively joyous."

Even as Susan began suspecting that something beyond "liking" was taking place between her husband and the young astronomer's wife, even as she transmuted the inferno of her jealousy into an iciness so palpable and sharp it razed Mabel's fantasy of possibility— "utter coldness (combined with unimpeachable courtesy) [that] was well nigh unbearable"—Mabel insisted on her parallel universe, writing to Austin:

> Can you see how I can still love her very much? But I do—she stimulates me intellectually more than any other woman I ever knew. She is fascinating to me. I would do *any thing* to make her like me again. She has such pretty feminine hands and wrists, and she had some very pretty little quaint bracelets last night. I could have gone to her and kissed them at any moment.

Austin was equally shaken by the strange electricity between them, equally forced to reconcile what seemed like an existential incompatibility—the self he had been constructing these fifty-three years, a lawyer so stern and joyless and shackled by Puritanical moral dogma, and the stranger of a self being born through this new love, abloom with exultation and disrobed of inhibition. Like an autumn crocus, so splendidly insensible in its counterseasonal burst of vitality, Austin had come alive in the October of life. Astonished by the birthing of this unrecognizable new self, he wrote to Mabel in late 1882, struggling to understand what her love had awakened in him and why it had been dormant all his life in the first place:

> My experience of life was too firm & encrusted to permit it. It contradicts everything, revolutionizes everything, overturns everything in me—astonishes & overwhelms me as much as overjoys & intoxicates me. I love you, I admire you, I idolize you. I am exalted by your love for me. I am strong as not for a long time before—elastic, well. I walk the street airily & with high pride, for I am loved—loved as I love, loved where I love. You fill my heart & my mind & my life & my world.

After a three-month buildup of this intoxicating unconsummated fervor, he anguishes and exults:

> The loneliness & lonesomeness & longing for you last evening were beyond anything yet. . . . The cruelty of life never seemed half so cruel. Why are we endowed with all this wild love & longing & the

person to gratify then never laid hand upon! Such blankness & dreariness & darkness & chill!

And yet, my darling, my darling you have given me in these weeks more than all life before—incomparably more. I would have lived for these alone—lived exultingly. I would die for them.

There is a singular strangeness to those moments when we find ourselves unmoored from our own being, when something seems to pull us beyond ourselves and shock us into the recognition, however momentary, that the self is not the static monolith we take it to be but something dynamic and situationally sculpted into various possibilities of being. Some of our dormant multitudes come awake with a catlike stretch, slowly and lazily over years of personal development. Others leap into being with the jolt of an alarm sounded by a particular event or person who has entered our lives at a particular moment—rarely anticipated, almost never convenient, always transformational. On those rare, momentous mornings, one looks in the bathroom mirror and greets—sometimes grudgingly, sometimes gleefully—the gladsome stranger of oneself.

When Austin faced the self Mabel had awakened in him, it was nothing less than a rebirth:

Now I am another man—in another world, magnified, clarified, glorified. The earth & the past drop from me, into the innermost remoteness. With you I tread upon the stars.

Mabel trod with him:

[When] I recall all the unspeakable proof you have given me that you are mine as I am yours—that I am light and gladness to you, as you to me, and find I am possessed of a great joy which nothing can take from me.

Unable to understand the disorienting transcendence that stretched between them and pulled them toward each other, Austin eventually ceased trying to think his way through it and simply felt:

I fell to wondering *why* I loved you—why, after having gone so far stirred only in the most general way by fair & fine women on every side, I should suddenly have seen something in you different from any other, that waked me into new life, inspired me with new thoughts & feelings, filled my imagination with possibilities undreamed before, transformed the world—made everything exuberant, wild, thrilling, satisfying. I had always thought I liked [name erased, likely Susan] and yet you are the one. . . . The wonder will never cease, of course, for the secret is too deep for discovery—it eludes all search, is fixed in the original constitution of all things—like life, & light, it is, and it is—that must suffice.

As true as Austin and Mabel felt their love to be, it existed in secret—at least a secret from one key figure: Susan. To bypass her increasingly suspicious attention, their love letters traveled via an underground post operated by Austin's complicit sisters. Since Mr. Dickinson's death eight years earlier, Emily and Vinnie had been living together in the Homestead, caring for their mother, paralyzed by a stroke she had suffered on the first anniversary of her husband's death. "I never had a mother," the poet had written to Higginson two decades earlier. "I suppose a mother is one to whom you hurry when you are troubled." But now, with Mrs. Dickinson almost completely disabled, Emily took strange solace in the reversal of parent-child roles, which paradoxically opened up a channel of ungrudging love. "We were never intimate Mother and Children while she was our Mother," she wrote to a longtime friend, "but Mines in the same Ground meet by tunneling and when she became our Child, the Affection came."

When Mrs. Dickinson died in November 1882, seven months after Charles Darwin, a disconsolate Emily once again bristled at the false consolations of religion:

Mother's dying almost stunned my spirit. . . . She slipped from our fingers like a flake gathered by the wind, and is now part of the drift called "the infinite."
We don't know where she is, though so many tell us.

Emily didn't leave her bedroom to attend the funeral, but Mabel was there, further inserting herself into the family in her elegant mourning black.

With Mrs. Dickinson gone, Austin's sisters became an autonomous household unit shielded from all intrusion—a rather convenient shield. Vinnie came to serve as the go-between. She mailed Austin's love letters to Mabel under her own name and received Mabel's—addressed to her—at the sisters' post office box, to which only the three Dickinson siblings had a key.

As all secrecy tends to swell with time, engulfing more and more of life, the Homestead soon became not only the switchboard for the lovers' communication but the site of their communion. On Valentine's Day 1883, Austin and Mabel met at the Homestead. Before the burning fireplace in the dining room, near Emily's second writing desk by the shuttered northern window, on the other side of which a honeysuckle vine denuded of leaves stood vigil, they made love for the first time.

Mabel became a frequent visitor to the Homestead—sometimes for private encounters with Austin, sometimes to visit the Dickinson sisters who had become the gatekeepers to their love. Adding to the strange geometry of the arrangement was the fact that Emily never once appeared to meet Mabel in person—it was always Lavinia who greeted her. As Mabel played Bach and Beethoven on the square piano in the Homestead dining room, she imagined Emily perched atop the stairs, midway between her bedroom and the social hub of the house, savoring the music with hungry attention. After these performances, the absent-bodied poet would ask the day cook to bring Mabel a glass of wine with a rose or a slice of cake and an extemporaneous verse she had penned while listening. Mabel was mesmerized by this—as much by the mystery of it as by the peculiar verse, the unexampled genius of which she was coming to recognize with the elation of a scientific discovery. She returned this disembodied attention by sending Emily jelly, fresh flowers, and her own paintings—including one of Indian pipes, a native New England flower Dickinson had long loved, immortalized in the pages of her teenage herbarium. The poet responded with a cryptic note that only deepened the alluring mystery: "I know not how to thank you. We do not thank the Rainbow, although its Trophy is a snare."

Secluded in her bedroom, Dickinson might not have realized the real reason for Mabel's frequent visits. As much as she loved her brother and wished for his happiness, it is improbable that she would be willfully complicit in something that would wound Susan. Far more likely, she was simply too preoccupied to notice the affair—with an improbable new love of her own.

21

IN THE DARKNESS OF BEING

Emily Dickinson had met Judge Otis Lord, a friend of her father's and nearly the same age as Mr. Dickinson, about a decade earlier, when he had come to the Homestead from Salem to prepare her will. The two must have remained in touch, for when Judge Lord's wife died in 1877, he entered into lively correspondence with Dickinson that soon swelled with the promise of romance. Within a year, she wrote to Lord:

> My lovely Salem smiles at me . . . I confess that I love him—I rejoice that I love him—I thank the maker of Heaven and Earth—that gave him to me to love—the exultation floods me. I cannot find my channel—the Creek turns sea—at thought of thee.

Judge Lord was respected to the point of fear in the courtroom, but beneath his oratorical edge lay a kindly decency and a keen interest in the invisible interiority of the human experience. A decade before Maria Mitchell looked back on her life and reflected that she would rather have been known for authoring a great poem than for discovering a comet, Judge Lord wrote:

> The mysteries of the mind are more subtle than those of physics and much more readily elude pursuit and investigation, and he that becomes master of the human mind and human passions has achieved a greater triumph than he who has discovered a planet.

Like Dickinson, Judge Lord never joined the church; like her, he worshipped Shakespeare. Unlike most of her correspondents, upon whom the poet rained a fiery language and passionate sentiments no one could fully meet, Judge Lord returned her romantic undertones amplified. By the time Mabel and Austin crossed their Rubicon, Emily, in her fifties, had permitted the possibility of love with this man eighteen years her senior. "We both believe and disbelieve a hundred times an Hour," she wrote, "which keeps Believing nimble."

Dickinson's letters to Lord—like the Master Letters penned two decades earlier—survive only in drafts preserved among her own papers, which Austin discovered after her death and placed in a large brown envelope he gave to Mabel as part of his sister's literary legacy—the legacy with which Mabel would soon be entrusted. Whether what Dickinson drafted was what she ultimately mailed, or whether she mailed her letters to Judge Lord at all, is unclear. Another perplexity is why she seems not to have shared any of her poetry with Lord—that most intimate part of her, which filled her days and nights and being. In one of her letter drafts, she acknowledges a deliberate holding back, easy to read as sexual, but perhaps it was something far more intimate he had demanded and she had refused—her verse: "Don't you know you are happiest while I withhold and not confer—don't you know that 'No' is the wildest word we consign to Language?"

Dickinson was busy navigating her own labyrinth of refusal and surrender with Judge Lord while Austin and Mabel were domesticating the wildness of their no's. But in the autumn of 1883, three weeks after the first anniversary of their Rubicon, the precarious idyll of their alternative marriage was detonated by an unforeseen tragedy: Gib, Austin and Susan's youngest child, came down with typhoid fever. The long-haired sunshine of a boy, shy of nine and so adored by Emily, was Austin's most beloved child—the light of the household that made his long-loveless marriage to Susan bearable. Gib plummeted rapidly. For the first time in years—fifteen years, neighbors speculated—Emily crossed the grass between the Homestead and the Evergreens with lantern in hand. I have tried to imagine the quickening of mind and foot that carried her toward that which she had hedged against all her life—death, turbid and unholy.

When she entered the boy's sickroom at three in the morning on October 5, she collapsed at the sight of the inevitable. By dawn, Gib was dead. No other death would impact Dickinson this deeply—not even Judge Lord's, by a fatal stroke, five months later. She rose out of her own bereavement to comfort Susan, memorializing Gib in an arresting letter of consolation suspended between poetry and prose:

> No crescent was this Creature—He traveled from the Full—
> Such soar, but never set—
>   I see him in the Star, and meet his sweet velocity in everything that flies—His life was like the Bugle, which winds itself away, his Elegy and echo—his Requiem ecstasy—
>   Dawn and Meridian in one.

Dickinson's own health was failing—"nervous prostration," the doctor proclaimed of what would become her final illness. "I do not know the Names of Sickness," she told a friend with marked contempt for the impotence of medicine. "The Crisis of the sorrow of so many years is all that tires me." But she sidelined her own suffering to continue comforting Susan, writing just before Thanksgiving:

> The first section of Darkness is the densest, Dear—
> After that, Light trembles in—

The light had fled from Austin's days. He plummeted into a darkness that terrified Mabel. She tried to assuage his pain, but it felt beyond her reach. For weeks, she saw little of him. "It is terrible even to think of his grief," she wrote to her parents. By November, they had slowly resumed their romance. Susan, for whom Gib had been the last anchor of her marriage, seemed not to care. Austin now clung to Mabel with an almost desperate attachment—with Gib gone, she alone became the light of his life. Just after Thanksgiving, he wrote to her:

I *have* something to be thankful for, and grateful for, this sad day, with my boy gone, and except for you, alone. I have *you*. Would to God I had you closer—in my house, at my heart, in my arms! Would not this be too much? *Would* it!

Mabel took on the role of savior hungrily. Perhaps to alleviate the moral dissonance of the affair, she cast their love in the language of divinity—theirs was a union so numinous that no earthly scruples could maim their conscience. In her diary, she recorded:

[Austin] has expressly told me over and over again that I kept him alive through the dreadful period of Gilbert's sickness and death. He could not bear the atmosphere of his own house, & used to go to his sisters', & then he or Lavinia would send for me—& it was on those oases from the prevailing gloom in his life that he caught breath & gathered strength to go on. . . . He recovered from the blow enough to wish to live for *me*. . . . My life has a sort of consecration now, & all outward things seem changed. His love for me is something sacred; it dignifies me & elevates me. I thank God daily for it.

She reiterated the sentiment in her letters to Austin:

I rejoice more every day in the immensity of the love which you have given so magnificently. You have made me grander and nobler every day . . . I trust you as I trust God. The way in which you love me is a consecration—it is the holy of holies, and a thought, even commonplace, would desecrate it. I approach it even in my mind as a shrine, where the purest and noblest there is in me worships.

Austin readily took up the narrative thread:

My love and your love have expanded and exceeded one. All I am—and all I can be—I give to you. . . . My love for you today is a more solemn and sacred thing than ever before.

Twice her age, Austin had a dissonance of his own to palliate:

You are beyond your years—vastly, in knowledge and experience of the human heart, and in subtle distinction and realization of the deepest secrets of human life. If anything is true—and real, our love is. We are made to give joy to each other. I love you—I love you.

While grief leveled Susan's jealousy to apathy, David Todd leaned into his wife's alternative marriage. He was not merely aware of it—he condoned it, gave his consent to its sexual dimension, and came to consider Austin his best friend. Austin and Mabel, in turn, referred to David as their "mutual friend" in their love letters. Mabel wrote in her diary:

> And all the time my dear David & I are very happy & tender & devoted companions. My married life is certainly exceptionally sweet & peaceful & satisfying, & his nature is just the one to soothe & rest me. I love him better all the time, and appreciate him more.

Upon Austin's death a decade later, David would count the funeral as the saddest day of his entire life. "My best friend died tonight, & I seem stranded. . . . He touched and forwarded everything," he would sorrow in his diary, then fetch from the family vault Austin's love letters to read them to Mabel as she wept disconsolately.

But now the three rejoiced in their unusual bond. When Mabel's mother refused to accept this arrangement, Austin wrote in consolation: "Conventionalism is for those not strong enough to be laws for themselves, or to conform themselves to the great higher law where all the harmonies meet."

Caught up in the intoxication of it, Austin decided to deed a plot of Dickinson land to the Todds, who were still living in a boardinghouse—Mabel had persuaded him that meeting at his sisters' home was not sustainable in the long term for a love anchored to the eternal.

This seemingly banal real estate formality would become the cinder of the generations-long contention that would bedestine Emily Dickinson's literary legacy.

Because the three Dickinson siblings were equal heirs to the land, Austin needed to persuade his sisters to sign the deed. Emily refused—complicit as she had been in Austin's affair with Mabel, she was not oblivious to how it injured Susan, the only point in the quadrangle who had not consented to the geometry of polyamory. "Sue spends her time reading old letters, and assorting them," Austin wrote to Mabel with remove. I imagine her rereading Emily's early love letters as the marriage that had been a decades-long disappointment was now collapsing around her in public view. But she was yet to suffer her greatest loss.

In the early evening of May 13, 1886, after several months of illness that the prescribed cure of olive oil and chloroform had failed to relieve, Emily Dickinson gasped for breath and slipped out of consciousness. Her mind's eye would never open again. At 6 p.m. on Saturday the fifteenth, with Austin by her side, her lungs sawed one final, disbarked breath from the tree of life.

> Because I could not stop for Death—
> He kindly stopped for me—

It was Sue who dressed Emily for the funeral. She wrapped her in a white robe and rested alongside her in the small white casket a single pink lady's slipper—a rare orchid associated with Venus, beautiful and savage, a living Georgia O'Keeffe painting. Into the neck of the white shroud she tucked a small posy of violets—the flower Dickinson cherished above all others for its "unsuspected" splendor, to which she had dedicated the most dramatic page of her herbarium. "Still in her Eye / The Violets lie," she had written in one of her earliest and most intense poems dedicated to Sue, which ends with the declamation "Sue—forevermore!"

Higginson journeyed from Boston—his fourth visit to his "cracked poetess" in the quarter century of their friendship. With his long gait now wound by a restless urgency, he scissored through the fragrant lawn of the Homestead, abloom with violets, buttercups, and wild geraniums, and entered the darkened house. In the middle of the library lay the casket, almost cradlelike in its littleness. He was struck by the surreality of it all, but most of all by the "wondrous restoration of youth" in the face of the dead woman, who lay there without a single gray hair or wrinkle at fifty-five, her tresses still a vermilion eruption against the eternal white of the pillow. She looked thirty, Higginson wrote in his diary in half-belief. He found her, for the first time, beautiful.

At the service, he read one of Dickinson's favorite poems—"Last Lines" by Emily Brontë. "No coward soul is mine," the poem begins. "No trembler in the world's storm-troubled sphere."

Mabel was there, looking haggard at twenty-nine with a grief hardly befitting someone who had never once met the myth in the casket. Three days earlier, the Sunday after Dickinson's death, she had stood in the church choir dressed in black, barely able to sing. A cynical interpretation would take her mourning for a public spectacle, part of Mabel's ploy to insert herself into the Dickinson family. But perhaps she had genuinely bought into her own inflated fantasy of her relationship with the poet who never appeared but who sent her ghostly verses with cake and pressed flowers; perhaps she saw some of herself in Dickinson's bold defiance of convention; perhaps she thoroughly believed herself to be the only person who fully saw the poet's genius.

After the burial, Mabel recorded in her diary a sentiment of remarkable prescience and poetic splendor:

Rare Emily Dickinson died—went back into a little deeper mystery than that she has always lived in.

But alongside this impersonal appreciation of a genius was also a deeply personal anguish. Emily's death was a disquieting reminder that Austin, two years older than his sister, could be taken from Mabel at any moment—a loss the very thought of which insaned her. Their alternative marriage worked for her—until it didn't. Already, Mabel had been imagining herself in Susan's stead. She had neatly inscribed an envelope containing a photograph of her teenaged self with a three-word incantation, part wish and part time machine: "Mabel Loomis Dickinson." Not long after Emily's death, Mabel, seeing that Austin wouldn't divorce his wife even though he had in effect left her long ago, undertook a radical campaign to eclipse Susan: Mabel would weave herself into the Dickinson DNA by conceiving a child with Austin. When the plan, which they code-named "the experiment," went actively under way five years after their first February lovemaking, Mabel was thirty-one and Austin almost sixty.

A child was not in the stars. They persisted for weeks. Before the trials, Mabel took hot baths, which were believed to aid in concep-tion; they didn't. She grew depressed, unfathoming of how a love as divinely fated as theirs could meet such unholy hindrance. The language of failure entered their letters. Eventually, "the experi-ment" faded away the way most dreams die—not with a bang but a whimper.

But an even grander heirloom opportunity would soon present itself to Mabel.

Within days of Dickinson's death, Lavinia discovered in the small bureau by the sunlit southern windows of her sister's bedroom a shock of poems—hundreds and hundreds of coruscating compo-sitions, their explosiveness contained in tiny hand-sewn booklets, shrapnel scattered across envelope pieces and scraps of paper scrib-bled with fragments. Lavinia had always known, of course, that her sister wrote poems—but she had no sense of their multitude and magnitude. Suddenly, the entreaty Dickinson had whispered dur-ing her final illness blazed with urgency: "Oh Vinnie, my work, my work!"

Despite Higginson's longtime private encouragement, he had never seen Dickinson's poetry as fit for publication. Helen Hunt Jackson had been her sole public champion, tirelessly submitting verses to various journals and anthologies, succeeding only with "Success." With Jackson now nine months dead, Lavinia reasoned that the task of bringing her sister's work to the world should fall on her longest and most loyal reader: Susan.

It was Sue, after all, who had composed Emily's obituary, published in the *Springfield Republican* the day before the funeral. Full of love and gallant guardianship, it was both tender and terrific—an almost violent lashing out against the public eye that had glimpsed Dickinson's private world so partially and misunderstood her so completely. "Not disappointed with the world," Susan censured, "not an invalid until within the past two years, not from any lack of sympathy, not because she was insufficient for any mental work or social career—her endowments being so exceptional—, but the 'mesh of her soul,' as [Robert] Browning calls the body, was too rare, and the sacred quiet of her own home proved the fit atmosphere for her worth and work." For the fortunate few who had read her poems, she had "made palpable the tantalizing fancies forever eluding their bungling, fettered grasp." Her mind was "a Damascus blade gleaming and glancing at the sun." With it, "quick as the electric spark of her intuitions and analyses, she seized the kernel instantly, almost impatient of the fewest words by which she must make her revelation." This she made with "her swift poetic rapture . . . like the long glistening note of a bird one hears in the June woods at high noon, but can never see." The bird had alighted for Susan alone.

How Lavinia, her lifelong plumpness withered by worry in the final year of Emily's life, must have hurried across the lawn between the Homestead and the Evergreens with the forty booklets she brought to lend, adjoining these eight hundred poems to Sue's own chest of nearly three hundred received in letters and handed across the hedge over the years.

Susan began transcribing the poems, Dickinson's difficult hand a native language to her. On the last day of the last year of Emily's life, three weeks after what would have been her fifty-sixth birthday, Susan chose a poem about the rage of storm and submitted it to New York's most prominent editor for consideration. He rejected it. More rejections followed. Dickinson's eccentric verse was a defiant deviance of vision. It would be more than half a century before Bertrand Russell laid out his ten commandments of cultural progress, the seventh radiating the triumph and tragedy of Dickinson's poetry: "Do not fear to be eccentric in opinion, for every opinion now accepted was once eccentric."

But editors then, as editors now, feared eccentricity, feared that whatever is unclassifiable, whatever fits no existing template, whatever requires of the reader a modicum of exertion, is unmarketable. Susan halted, suspended between the rejections and her own unease about making public what she knew Emily had insisted on keeping private. The question of why she abandoned her efforts has never been adequately answered. Later, in her campaign to tarnish her rival's reputation, Mabel would attribute it to Susan's "unconquerable laziness." But my own sense is that Susan was torn between the impulse to safeguard the intimacy of Emily's poems—poems the publication of which she well knew Emily resisted all her life—and the clear sense of their immense literary value to posterity. She had slipped a sentence into the obituary pointing at the moral paradox of publication during Dickinson's lifetime: "Now and then some enthusiastic literary friend would turn love into larceny, and cause a few verses surreptitiously obtained to be printed." The ambivalence must have been too sundering when she was asked to become lead larcenist herself. She chose, instead, love.

Irritated by this choice, Lavinia soon turned against Susan—an antagonism the roots of which may have reached far deeper than the practical impediment of the stalled work. It is impossible not to wonder how Lavinia felt upon discovering her sister's eruption of poems, then upon realizing that Emily had written, dedicated, and given hundreds more to Susan over the decades, among them the poem that begins with "One Sister have I in our house—/ And one a hedge away" and ends in "Sue—forevermore!" How uneasy Lavinia must have been to recognize that while she was the legal heir to her sister's poetry, its true heirloom was Emily's love for Susan.

Mabel, privy to the predicament thanks to Austin's reports on Susan's stalled efforts, wasted no time capitalizing on the situation. On one of her regular visits to the Homestead in early 1887, just before she began wearing Austin's wedding ring on her right hand,

Mabel casually remarked to Lavinia that she had been teaching herself the miracle of turning script into print on a borrowed Hammond typewriter. This novelty, unlike all the other typewriters commercially available for nearly a decade, allowed the typist to actually see the text as she typed—something Hammond proudly advertised in mail-order catalogs with an image of the curved machine rolling out a sheet of paper with the words WORK IN SIGHT printed on it. Just as casually, Mabel asked Lavinia if she would like to see some of her sister's poems in print. Lavinia was enticed. She read a few poems aloud to Mabel. I imagine her hitting the keys of the Hammond's peculiar crescent of a keyboard with performative ceremony, the way she played Beethoven at the Dickinsons' piano, lower back arched and chest high, as though about to sing. Sufficiently enchanted, Lavinia entrusted Mabel with some poems to take home and type up, and soon withdrew the eight hundred she had given to Susan, turning them over to Mabel. How Susan must have sorrowed to be replaced by Mabel a second time, first in her marriage and now in the most significant relationship of her life.

Mabel would soon perform—this time literally perform—the poems for Higginson, in an effort to persuade him that the verse he felt was alive but feared was unmarketable was indeed posterity's rightful and revolutionary inheritance. He had already been discussing the possibility of publication with Lavinia, but crowning his numerous reservations was the formidable labor of copying the poems. In the autumn of 1889, Higginson visited for a cautious discussion of print, aware that Mabel had been busy transcribing— she had copied hundreds of poems by that point. He didn't hide his skepticism of the conceptual challenge beyond the practicality of transcription: "The public will not accept even fine ideas in such rough and mystical dress, so hard to elucidate." Mabel answered not with rhetoric but with the rapture of Dickinson's poetry itself. Erect in her corseted soprano, she held up a typewritten page and gave the dramatic appearance of reading aloud verses she was actually reciting, for she had been committing to memory the poems she most loved as she typed. Her confident melodic voice glided along the dashes, cascaded over the symbolic leaps, and dulceted the discordant punctuation, unbuttoning the "rough and mystical dress" to reveal the sensual richness of Dickinson's poetry.

Higginson was stunned. This verse must live.

If Mabel had failed to conceive a child with Austin, she could become the surrogate who brought his sister's creative labor to life—typing up and editing Emily Dickinson's poems would be Mabel Loomis Todd's claim to Dickinson legitimacy. This wouldn't be an unreasonable interpretation of her motives. It is, however, both unreasonable and ungenerous not to recognize that human motives come in multitudes, as reticulated and contradictory as our selves. Mabel's diaries and letters make clear that she viewed "rare Emily Dickinson" with a sincere admiration bordering on adulation.

After returning the borrowed Hammond, she purchased a World index typewriter for $15 and resumed painstaking work on the primitive machine, manually dialing the pointer to each letter before pressing it onto the inked rubber sheet to stamp a crude capital on the paper. Her desk became a Dickinson altar, a framed daguerreotype of Austin brooding over the typewriter as the hours spilled into days, months, years. Typing up hundreds of poems over which Mabel held no copyright—Lavinia did—was thankless work, sustainable over so long a stretch only by some element of unselfish love of art, however commingled it may have been with her self-interest.

By May 1890, Mabel Loomis Todd and Thomas Wentworth Higginson had selected two hundred typed-up poems for publication. Higginson deemed Houghton Mifflin, who had brought out Emerson's poetry debut, the ideal publisher for this unexampled little book. They rejected it. Todd then turned to Roberts Brothers, who had rejected seven poems Dickinson herself had timidly submitted after her "Success" had become the crowning achievement in their anthology of anonymous verse. The publisher spilled his reservations before the two editors: "It has always seemed to me that it would be unwise to perpetuate Miss Dickinson's poems. They are quite as remarkable for defects as for beauties & are generally devoid of the true poetical qualities."

But somehow he saw through the unorthodoxy to concede, with the help of an outside reader he hired to assess the work, that although this wasn't standard poetry, it radiated genius. Perhaps it was the combined pressure of Helen Hunt Jackson's persistent advocacy a decade earlier and Mabel Loomis Todd's confident approach now—did she perform the poems for him as she had for Higginson?—that swayed him to take a chance. Roberts Brothers agreed to publish the volume, but only if Lavinia Dickinson—the sole copyright owner—would pay for the printing and relinquish royalties on the first five hundred copies, and only if certain poems were omitted. This was extortion, both commercial and creative. Mabel, who had been laboring over the poems for three years and had absorbed them into the marrow of her own being, was aghast that "I died for beauty" was excluded. But the choice seemed to be between insensitive publication and no publication. The Dickinson camp—Mabel, Lavinia, and Higginson—chose to publish. The poems would be their own proof.

On November 12, 1890, a slim, handsome volume met the world with the simple legend *POEMS * Emily Dickinson* embossed in gold on the white leather cover above Mabel's painting of Indian pipes. The poems had suffered the very fate Dickinson had feared and fiercely resisted in her lifetime—her dashes had been shorn, her unconventional yet intentional capitalizations bulldozed, her deliberately untitled verses given toothless titles. The editors had even fiddled with some of the language to rein in the choreographed startlement of her off-rhymes.

And yet beneath the surface mutilations pulsed an irrepressible might that gripped literature by the cerebellum and shook out a new species of poetic consciousness.

Higginson exulted in the preface:

In many cases these verses will seem to the reader like poetry torn up by the roots, with rain and dew and earth still clinging to them, giving a freshness and a fragrance not otherwise to be conveyed. In other cases, as in the few poems of shipwreck or of mental conflict, we can only wonder at the gift of vivid imagination by which this recluse woman can delineate, by a few touches, the very crises of physical or mental conflict. . . . But the main quality of these poems is that of extraordinary grasp and insight, uttered with an uneven vigor sometimes exasperating, seemingly wayward, but really unsought and inevitable.

The volume was an astonishing success, much to Houghton Mifflin's chagrin. Five hundred copies vanished from the shelves on the first day of publication. Within the first year, the book had gone through eleven printings, and nearly eleven thousand copies had been absorbed into the body of culture.

That year, as the rapids of Dickinson's verse sprang into the world, William James's groundbreaking *Principles of Psychology* coined the notion of *stream of consciousness*. Soon, as English reviewers launched upon Dickinson attacks unequaled since those on Shelley and Keats a century earlier, Alice James, William James's brilliant bedridden sister, would write wryly in her diary, itself an unheralded triumph of literature:

It is reassuring to hear the English pronouncement that Emily Dickinson is fifth-rate, they have such a capacity for missing quality; the robust evades them equally with the subtle. . . . What tome of philosophy *resumes* the cheap farce or expresses the highest point of view of the aspiring soul more completely than the following—

How dreary to be somebody
How public, like a frog
To tell your name the livelong day
To an admiring bog.

American reviewers, perhaps taking special pride in the heroic force that had arisen from the national literature in the dead of night when no one was looking, met Dickinson on the enthusiastic soil of her readers, growing daily by the legion. Mabel carefully clipped and collected the praise that began populating the major papers. A month after publication, Higginson wrote to her in faithful disbelief:

> You are the only person who can feel as I do about this extraordinary thing we have done in revealing this rare genius. I feel as if we had climbed to a cloud, pulled it away, and revealed a new star behind it.

Exactly fifty years later, the mathematician G. H. Hardy would write:

> To have produced anything of the slightest permanent interest, whether it be a copy of verses or a geometrical theorem, is to have done something utterly beyond the powers of the vast majority of men.

22

SEARCHING FOR TOTALITY

One hundred thirty-one years after Emily Dickinson's death, I stand in her bedroom, chasing the ghost of her truth. I am struck by the contrast between the bellowing darkness of her poems and the fount of sunlight flooding in through the two fully windowed walls. I am struck, too, by the scale of it: Her mahogany sleigh bed is practically child-sized, her cherrywood writing desk almost a miniature at seventeen and a half inches square. I am reminded of recent findings in embodied cognition—the study of how external physical parameters influence our interior states—indicating that large open spaces and rooms with high ceilings enhance creativity, and I find myself wondering whether there might be an embodied-cognition analogue to Kierkegaard's assertion that "the more a person limits himself, the more resourceful he becomes." Deliberate constraints, after all, are a mighty catalyst of creative breakthrough: The rigid geometric grids onto which Agnes Martin unleashed her genius, Einstein's choice to limit the speed of light as the sole non-negotiable variable around which to build his relativity, the single room in which the whole of Hitchcock's *Rear Window* unfolds. Seventeen inches square. More than seventeen hundred poems.

Within the tiny perimeter of her physical environment, Emily Dickinson created infinities—of beauty, of meaning, of truth.

But what strikes me most of all is the orientation of her bedroom: southwest—not, as Dickinson herself repeatedly described it, west.

The two large windows on the southern wall, to the immediate left of her bed, overlook the bustle of Main Street. The two on the western wall frame the Evergreens, its buttery walls almost aglow through the maples, towering over the magnolia with jarring proximity. All day every day for thirty years, Emily Dickinson faced her fate through the parted white lace curtains—faced the home where her own brother was domiciled with the woman she loved all her life, so close yet so unpossessable. I stand there suddenly seized with the terror of it, the daily terror, encoded even in Dickinson's famous description of her bedroom as "a chamber facing West"—I see in it for the first time, feel in my bones, her deliberate turning away from the south of life and toward the west of Susan, her "Only Woman in the World," the pole star by which she oriented her life.

Downstairs in the library rests Disraeli's romance novel *Endymion,* titled after the famous Keats poem that begins with the line "A thing of beauty is a joy for ever." The book—a Christmas present from Sue thirty years into their relationship—is inscribed to "Emily, Whom not seeing, I still love."

In the final months of her life, as she lay seriously ill—mortally ill, Austin feared—Emily had written to Sue:

> Emerging from the Abyss, and reentering it—that is Life, is it not, Dear?
> The tie between us is very fine, but a Hair never dissolves.

It is often lamented that Dickinson was only fifty-five when she died, but as I stand there facing the Evergreens, facing the hollowing helplessness of this undissolvable yet unlivable love, it seems like nothing less than heroism to have survived so long with such unpalliable sorrow. With the whole of her being, Emily Dickinson was in love with her dearest friend—and nearest, devastatingly so—for thirty-six years.

Any close reader of Dickinson would be riven by this fact, of which Susan alone was in possession during Emily's lifetime and which was revealed even to her own kin only with the posthumous discovery of the mass of poems. Verse upon verse orbited Susan's devastating centrality to the cosmos of the poet's reality. It must have come as a shock to Lavinia and Austin, and as a great grief to Mabel, who wished her lover's wife dead rather than immortalized with such immense love.

And so somebody set out to erase Susan. Sometime between the publication of the first volume of poems in 1890 and the second in 1892, the darning thread of one booklet is carefully taken apart to remove one poem, the punctures of Dickinson's needle trimmed off to mask the fact that the page had once been sewn to others. The page thus removed, but preserved for the sake of the poem on the other side, contains the verse ending with "Sue—forevermore!" Black ink scratches out each line, most furiously concentrating upon the last. The poem survives only because Susan herself kept the copy Emily handed her over the hedge in the dawning days of their romance. Many of Emily's letters to Sue from that period, as well as letters to Austin brimming with effusions about the woman they both loved, have suffered similar disfigurements.

It has long been assumed that Mabel maimed the manuscripts. This is possible—having failed to replace Susan by becoming Mabel Loomis Dickinson, having failed to divert the Dickinson bloodline by mothering a child with Austin, she may have resorted to the one erasure in her power. But after an immersion in Mabel's diaries and letters, I find it improbable—not only because Mabel ultimately devoted a decade of her life to transcribing, preserving, and stewarding Dickinson's manuscripts—a Herculean effort for which she received a meager total of $200, being repaid primarily in the private satisfaction of giving voice to genius—but because she had already copied that particular booklet before the mutilation occurred. In a 1967 book on the editing of the manuscripts, the then director of Yale's Beinecke Rare Book and Manuscript Library, where the Todd papers reside, conceded that Mabel simply had too much reverence for the manuscripts to have mutilated them, and suggested instead that Austin had done it. But what would Austin have gained from this? Of all his sister's intimates, he had been the only one privy—as privy as she had permitted—to the extent of her love for Susan since the very beginning. By the time his lover of many years edited the

SEARCHING FOR TOTALITY 395

manuscripts, Austin had already removed himself from Susan so thoroughly that an excision from the collected poems would have achieved nothing further.

It is the most unsuspected actor I wonder about: Lavinia.

The poem severed from the booklet, after all, is the one beginning "One Sister have I in our house— / And one a hedge away," then proudly proclaiming Sue's supremacy in the poet's emotional universe: "I chose this single star / From out the wide night's numbers." How must Lavinia have felt to discover these words and their sundering sentiment in the wake of her sister's death—a sister who apparently classed her own kin as inferior in intimacy to the woman across the hedge? By the time of the mutilation, Susan had ceased speaking to Lavinia after the betrayal of entrusting her husband's lover with the invaluable heirloom Susan alone had witnessed ripen in Emily over the decades. While Mabel was typing up the poems Lavinia had withdrawn from Susan and turned over to her, Susan was reading her own copies aloud at her salons at the Evergreens, hoping to enchant the influential guests into aiding with publication. Lavinia was not invited to these gatherings. What better vengeance for exclusion than erasure?

Lavinia seems to have had no scruples about bending reality to her benefit. Several years later, when a lawsuit predicated on Austin's gift of Dickinson land to the Todds rose all the way to the state supreme court, Lavinia perjured herself, denying that she willingly signed the deed, while Mabel told the truth, however reluctantly, even at the cost of disgrace as her affair with Austin became a public spectacle. (Mabel's reputation was tarnished by the revelation, even though her spouse condoned the relationship. Austin's was not, even though his spouse was the only victim of betrayal in the arrangement.) But beneath the veneer of the real estate dispute lurked a larger and less neatly resolvable debate about the most valuable Dickinson property: Emily's poems and letters.

Mabel had begun transcribing the manuscripts as a labor of love, but a decade into the work she had become Emily Dickinson's chief scholar and steward, securing the publication of the groundbreaking volumes of poetry and fashioning herself into a spokeswoman for the myth she never met. She traveled across New England to give public lectures on Dickinson's work, wrote essays for magazines, and distributed pamphlets to women's colleges. Despite all this work, Lavinia refused to give Mabel a share in the copyright of the books that might not have existed without her—Higginson, Susan, Helen Hunt Jackson, and even Emily Dickinson herself had been met only with rejection. Mabel alone had secured publication. The plot of land, the Todds argued in court, had been granted them by Austin Dickinson—dead seven weeks before the motions toward the trial began—as a gift of gratitude for their years of work on his sister's poems. Although Lavinia had signed the deed, following instructions in her brother's unnotarized will, in court she claimed that she had been tricked into it and went to great lengths to devalue Mabel's instrumental role in Dickinson's ultimate claim to immortality.

Perhaps Lavinia wasn't afflicted with some singular selfishness but simply with the common ignorance of how impotent genius is without ambition. Mabel Loomis Todd had appended her ambition to Emily Dickinson's genius—this was not parasitism but symbiosis, vital to the survival of Dickinson's verse. Mabel's hero-villain role in the Dickinson drama is a microcosm of the human predicament. Our inner multitudes cleave us into contradictions never as perfectly parted as Emily Dickinson's hair in the daguerreotype that sealed her image. We are never one thing, our slumbering potentialities stirred into being by situations in which chance and choice conspire to make us the people we are said to have been.

There is, of course, no point to such speculations about motives in the records of collective memory. Memory and motive are the two edges of the blade by which we slice experience out of events and carve out history—personal, political, civilizational—from the trunk of life. Both are highly selective—memory retrospectively so and motive prospectively. And yet speculation has woven the whole of the Dickinson legend. Any narrative thread, followed long enough, grows frayed by conflicting claims several degrees removed from the loom of fact, tattered by the personal agendas of those who made the claims and those who repeated them half-verified, half-comprehended.

And what is fact, anyway, in the life of a woman of such tessellated truth? Even her handwriting—that most intimate script of personhood—underwent three dramatic transfigurations over the course of her lifetime: from the tiny, sharp, tight rightward slant of her teens and twenties to the rounder, larger, more upright curl of her thirties and forties to the stiff, wide-spaced almost-print of her final years. Looking at her manuscripts from these distinct periods side by side, I am staggered by the inconceivable fact that the same person penned them. And, in a sense, she didn't. Her life was lived—as every life is lived—not by Emily Dickinson, but by many Emily Dickinsons. Lavinia's sister was different from Austin's sister, different from Susan's almost-lover, different from Higginson's cracked correspondent, different from the woman who silently tended to the orchids in the glass chamber of her winter conservatory, different from the ghost who sent Mabel wine and verses from the bedroom above Beethoven. These are not costumes donned with artifice for different occasions—they are facets of a self, each illuminated when a particular beam hits at a particular angle. We are different people in different situations, each of our dormant multitudes awakened by a particular circumstance, particular chemistry, particular stroke of chance; each true, each real—a composite Master of our being.

Such speculations about the biographical mysteries of an artist's life must not be permitted to eclipse the work that has rendered their life attractive of speculation. Virginia Woolf would lament in her essay on the Brownings that "how far we are going to read a poet when we can read about a poet is a problem to lay before biographers."

By the time Mabel Loomis Todd edited and published the first volume of the poet's letters, she had devoted a fifth of her life to Dickinson's body of work—work she saw as blazing with "comets of thought." All along, David Todd had been helping her copy, transcribe, and error-check her painstaking typescripts—part of the couple's lifelong devotion to aiding each other's careers. Now it was Mabel's turn to help David. She set out to use her newfound literary fame as Emily Dickinson's voice in raising funds for the dream that had drawn David to Amherst thirteen years earlier—the observatory that had never materialized.

Like many astronomers' wives in the centuries before education and vocational opportunity became available to women, Mabel had served as her husband's de facto assistant in observations and reports, cultivating scientific acumen of her own in the process. Unlike most astronomers' wives, she had joined him on numerous eclipse expeditions around the world, absorbing the science of the spectacle along with its poetic grandeur. During an eclipse expedition to Japan, she had become the first woman permitted to climb beyond the sixth level of Mount Fuji.

In 1894—the year Dickinson's letters were published and swiftly christened "the book of the year" by the popular press—Roberts Brothers published a very different kind of unprecedented masterwork by Mabel Loomis Todd: the first-ever popular treatise on solar eclipses, describing the otherworldly experience of totality in poetic prose, alongside illuminating explanations of the science of the phenomenon and lively histories of notable eclipses since antiquity.

Todd opens her final chapter with a Dickinson verse—"Eclipses are predicted, / And science bows them in"—and adds: "Poets usually care little for the *modus operandi* of scientific phenomena; the lines above embrace the fact, the result, the gist of the whole matter, and that ought to be sufficient." She quotes the influential astronomer, physicist, and aviation pioneer Samuel Pierpont Langley: "The spectacle is one which, though the man of science may prosaically state the facts, perhaps only the poet could render the impression."

By 1894, Todd had spent seven years with Dickinson's poems. But she doesn't seem to have known, for she would have quoted it, that among the poems Dickinson tucked into her private letters was an exquisite description of nature's ecliptic eeriness—possibly the world's first poem about a solar eclipse, and certainly the world's most splendid.

On September 29, 1875, the path of totality had passed across

New England, sweeping the drama of a near-total solar eclipse through Amherst. This spectacle of nature might have been the rare miracle that would beckon Dickinson out of her solitary chamber. I imagine her cautiously pulling the ivory lace of her bedroom curtains to peer at the glooming firmament, then rushing out into the orchard and gasping at the sight of the cherry trees scattering a thousand crescents onto the lawn as the gaps between their leaves turned into tiny pinhole cameras—a stunning play of light and shadow during an eclipse, which had enthralled and puzzled even Aristotle.

However Dickinson saw the eclipse, she certainly saw it, and it impressed itself upon her imagination—impressions she captured in eight perfect lines limning its otherworldliness, absent from Todd's 1896 edition of her poems, present only in a letter Dickinson had sent to Higginson in August 1877:

> It sounded as if the streets were running—
> And then—the streets stood still—
> Eclipse was all we could see at the Window
> And Awe—was all we could feel.
>
> By and by—the boldest stole out of his Covert
> To see if Time was there—
> Nature was in her Opal Apron—
> Mixing fresher Air.

That month, astronomers at the U.S. Naval Observatory discovered the first moon of Mars, and soon the second, through the grand 26-inch telescope that had just dethroned Harvard's Great Refractor as the largest refracting telescope in the world. The moons were named after the dark twin brothers of Greek mythology—Phobos, the personification of fear, and Deimos, of terror. A hundred fifty years earlier, Jonathan Swift had drawn on Kepler and, quoting his third law, had envisioned two Martian moons in *Gulliver's Travels*. Reading the Washington papers that August, Walt Whitman enthusiastically recorded the discovery in his notebooks. "Mars walks the heavens lord-paramount now," he wrote ten days later, "all through this month I go out after supper and watch for him; sometimes getting up at midnight to take another look at his unparallel'd lustre."

In August 1977, exactly a century after Dickinson committed the grandest cosmic spectacle to words and astronomers discovered the moons of Mars, *Voyager 1* and *Voyager 2* launched into the cosmos. Within four decades, one spacecraft would overtake the other and become the first human-made object to break out of the sun's magnetic field and enter the enigma of interstellar space.

Aboard this triumph of science was a triumph of romance: the Golden Record—a time capsule of the human spirit encrypted in binary code on a disc, one on each *Voyager*, containing salutations in the fifty-four most populous human languages, one from humpback whales, and an ancient Greek saying that translates to "Greetings to you, whoever you are. We come in friendship to those who are friends." Compressed as data are photographs and drawings of life on Earth—a 117-picture poem distilling the meaning of humanity in a symbolic language of images that represent fragments but radiate a whole. Crowning the Golden Record is a selection of the planet's sounds, from an erupting volcano to a kiss to Beethoven's Fifth Symphony. There are echoes of Margaret Fuller's assertion that "all truth is comprised in music and mathematics" on this twelve-inch gold-plated copper disc carrying Beethoven along a shoreless cosmic sail steered by Kepler's laws.

Carl Sagan initiated the Golden Record project, envisioning a "cosmic greeting card" from humanity to some faraway alien civilization. Ann Druyan, its creative director, saw it as "a cultural Noah's Ark." Etched onto the protective cover shielding the record from dust and debris is a diagram mapping the location of our Solar System in relation to fourteen pulsars. Pulsars—city-sized, rapidly spinning stellar lighthouses of densely compressed nuclear matter magnetized with a strength exceeding Earth's magnetic field by a factor of a hundred million to a thousand trillion—were discovered exactly ten summers earlier by a young Northern Irish astronomer named Jocelyn Bell. The month of her twenty-fourth birthday, Bell noticed something strange—a "scruff" of sudden activity—in the ink-and-paper charts of data streaming in from the massive dipole telescope in her charge. It turned out to be a pulsar, furnishing the first evidence that neutron stars—the collapsed cores left behind by the final explosion of dying stars, first hypothesized a year after the discovery of the neutron in 1933—were real. Crucially, it meant that black holes—which even Einstein held as an enticing but purely mathematical and possibly unprovable theoretical construct—might also be real. This was an epoch-making leap in our understanding of the universe, fundamental to modern astrophysics. When the discovery was awarded the Nobel Prize in Physics, Bell's adviser took the credit—Bell was excluded from the award citation for the discovery she herself had made. In a stroke of insufficient yet poetic redemption, a decade later her discovery was being used as the sole basis for depicting Earth's coordinates in space on the *Voyager* plaque.

The stated mission of the Golden Record was to serve as a message from humanity to some other civilization that might surmount the towering improbability of finding it adrift amid the cosmic infinitude and having the necessary technology and consciousness to decode its contents. Eclipsing this sweetly naïve aspiration is the unstated aim of the project, an endeavor far more poetic than scientific—to mirror what is best and truest of humanity back to us, at a moment when we seemed to have forgotten that we share this small, improbable planet. Sagan considered the Golden Record proof of our being "a species endowed with hope and perseverance, at least a little intelligence, substantial generosity and a palpable zest to make contact with the cosmos"—proof that, at the zenith of the Cold War, humanity needed far more than did any hypothetical extraterrestrial civilization. "We are attempting to survive our time so we may live into yours," says President Jimmy Carter on the scratchy recording.

Against the backdrop of this grand civilizational ambition lay the most invisible, tenderest dimension of the project—the Golden Record was also the love story of two naked apes suspended in a sliver of time.

Carl Sagan saw the musical selection—Bach, Louis Armstrong, Mexican mariachi, Javanese gamelan, a Bulgarian shepherdess folk song, a sixteen-year-old Pygmy girl singing a rite-of-passage paean to puberty in the forests of Africa—as conferring upon our species "a kind of immortality which could not be achieved in any other way." But Ann Druyan, in her devotion to the project's creative completeness as a representation of humanity, was troubled by the inadequate representation of the Far East. Finally, after months of search, she found an ethnomusicologist who led her to the perfect missing piece—a twenty-five-hundred-year-old Chinese melody called "Flowing Streams." She telephoned Sagan in Tucson, where he had traveled for a lecture, to share the ecstatic news of the breakthrough. He wasn't in his room. She left a message.

An hour later, her phone rang. It was Carl. "I get back to my hotel room," he tells her, "and I find this message that says, 'Annie called.' And I say to myself: 'Why didn't you leave me this message ten years ago?'"

Druyan remembers the feeling, the physical feeling, of her heart skipping a beat.

"Some thoughts are fashioned like a bell," Elizabeth Barrett Browning had written in *Aurora Leigh*, "to ring once being touched."

It was the first day of June in 1977. Carl and Annie had known each other for years, always involved with other people—he was still in the final spin of a collapsing marriage—but a warm friendship had blossomed between them. While working together on the Golden Record, they had been alone often and spoken frequently, but always as friends and colleagues. Neither of them had dared acknowledge that in the course of their many soaring conversations about music and mathematics, they had been falling in love.

Annie spoke into the receiver with the unreasonable courage of one beneath whose feet a wondrous trapdoor of possibility had suddenly opened:

"For keeps?"

"You mean get married?"

"Yes."

They had never so much as kissed. They had never had any conversation of a personal nature before. Something about the Golden
Record's serenade to immortality had thrust them against the
urgency of a mortal existence, against the recognition of life, of love,
as a tiny, irretrievable, beautiful blip in the eternal score of the universe.

They hung up the phone.

A moment later, Carl called back.

"I just want to make sure: That really happened. We're getting
married, right?"

"Yes. We're getting married."

"Okay, just wanted to make sure."

Across the two thousand miles, they promised themselves to each
other for the slice of forever allotted them. Annie experienced it as a
Eureka! moment, how she imagined it must feel to make a scientific
discovery. Her sunny voice streams into my earphones:

> Carl and I knew we were the beneficiaries of chance, that pure chance
> could be so kind that we could find one another in the vastness of
> space and the immensity of time. We knew that every moment should
> be cherished as the precious and unlikely coincidence that it was.

On August 20, the first *Voyager* lifted off, carrying the Golden
Record containing among its sonic treasures the sound of Annie's
heartbeat and brain waves recorded at Bellevue Hospital—the
sound of a system pulsating with the electricity of cosmic love. She
had asked Carl if there was any use in compressing the impulses
of the brain and nervous system into sound to put on the record—
whether anyone in the far-distant future, human or alien, would
be able to decode the data, to convert it back to thought and feeling. He looked at her with his twinkling brown eyes. "A thousand
million years is a long time. Why don't you go do it? Because who
knows—who knows what's possible in a thousand million years?"

On August 22, Carl and Annie announced their engagement to the *Voyager* team. They were together—"madly in love," she recalls—for the remaining nineteen years of Carl's life. Among their many collaborations was the first definitive book on the science of comets. With their characteristic sense of the poetic, they described a comet as "a great clock, ticking out decades or geological ages once each perihelion passage, reminding us of the beauty and harmony of the Newtonian universe, and of the daunting insignificance of our place in space and time."

The day Carl Sagan died, the *Voyager* was sailing somewhere past Neptune, toward the boundary of interstellar space, beyond which lay the open cosmic sea of the unknown. Thirty-five Augusts after the launch, *Voyager 1* began crossing the wide, ruffled edge of the Solar System, still carrying what now lived up to Carl and Annie's vision of a truly interstellar record—a record they believed "intentionally expresses a kind of cosmic loneliness."

Carl Sagan made one other monumental contribution to our civilizational canon in the course of the *Voyager* mission, the primary purpose of which had been not as poetic vehicle for the Golden Record but as scientific probe to explore and document the outermost planets of the solar system. Among the 105 kilograms of scientific instruments aboard these twin poems of aluminum and electricity was a camera, bound for interstellar space less than a century and a half after Talbot's crude attempts to capture light and shadow. As the *Voyagers* sailed away from Earth at 35,000 miles an hour, they took spectacular technicolor images of the outer planets—the first-ever complete portrait of our cosmic neighborhood. They saw for the first time, in rapturous detail, the Jovian moons Galileo had glimpsed as faint spots and named after Roman deities nearly four centuries earlier. They saw Uranus, the color of Margaret Fuller's eyes, its aquamarine so arresting and thoroughly unexpected that it extracted audible gasps from the imaging team on the ground. They saw what no human imagination had fathomed before: Navigation engineer Linda Morabito, glancing back over the shoulder of the spacecraft to take one final photograph of Jupiter, was stunned by the sight of an enormous umbrella-shaped plume emerging from behind its moon Io. In an instant, she was seized by the certainty that she was seeing the first known evidence of active volcanism on a world other than Earth—a Vesuvius four hundred million miles from home.

Neptune was the final target of humanity's enormous prosthetic eye. Planetary scientist Heidi Hammel—a meticulous marginalian in her mission logs—captured the rapture of its striking blue orb, so kindred to Earth yet so otherworldly, in three letters and a symbol in her log notes: "WOW!"

With the imaging mission complete after Neptune, NASA commanded that the cameras be shut down to conserve energy. But Carl Sagan had the simple, revolutionary idea to turn the camera around and take one final photograph—of Earth itself.

Objections were raised—from so great a distance and at so low a resolution, there would be absolutely no scientific value to the image. But Sagan, convinced of the poetic worth, appealed all the way to the top and persuaded the administrator of NASA to grant permission. I can only imagine the words this poet laureate of the cosmos chose in making his case for the poetic over the purely scientific; I imagine him radiating the same confident charisma Mabel had radiated when she performed Dickinson's poems to persuade publication.

On Valentine's Day 1990, as the silent serpent of cancer was weaving its way through Sagan's body undetected, the *Voyager* pointed its cameras toward the inner Solar System from its distant vantage point four million miles away. Imaging scientist Candice Hansen-Koharcheck was the first person to look at the picture. The other planets, while faint, were easy to discern. But Earth seemed to have vanished in the light-streaked photograph. Hansen-Koharcheck, with her eye trained to the minutest grain of the solar system, found it—a blurry speck islanded in a stream of sunlight against the blackness of empty space. There amid the endless expanse of nowheres, amid the shoreless cosmic ocean of pure spacetime that floods the vast majority of the universe, was our tiny somewhere.

A century earlier, Emily Dickinson had projected herself to the faraway vantage point of the *Voyager*s:

I touched the Universe—
And back it slid—and I alone—
A speck opon a Ball—
Went out opon Circumference—
Beyond the Dip of Bell—

This landmark photograph would come to be known as "The Pale Blue Dot," after Carl Sagan's moving reflection that endures as a gift of perspective unmatched before or since:

From this distant vantage point, the Earth might not seem of any particular interest. But for us, it's different. Consider again that dot. That's here. That's home. That's us. On it everyone you love, everyone you know, everyone you ever heard of, every human being who ever was, lived out their lives. The aggregate of our joy and suffering, thousands of confident religions, ideologies, and economic doctrines, every hunter and forager, every hero and coward, every creator and destroyer of civilization, every king and peasant, every young couple in love, every mother and father, hopeful child, inventor and explorer, every teacher of morals, every corrupt politician, every "superstar," every "supreme leader," every saint and sinner in the history of our species lived there—on a mote of dust suspended in a sunbeam.

The Earth is a very small stage in a vast cosmic arena. Think of the rivers of blood spilled by all those generals and emperors so that in glory and triumph they could become the momentary masters of a fraction of a dot. Think of the endless cruelties visited by the inhabitants of one corner of this pixel on the scarcely distinguishable inhabitants of some other corner. How frequent their misunderstandings, how eager they are to kill one another, how fervent their hatreds. Our posturings, our imagined self-importance, the delusion that we have some privileged position in the universe, are challenged by this point of pale light. Our planet is a lonely speck in the great enveloping cosmic dark. In our obscurity—in all this vastness—there is no hint that help will come from elsewhere to save us from ourselves. The Earth is the only world known, so far, to harbor life. There is nowhere else, at least in the near future, to which our species could migrate. Visit, yes. Settle, not yet. Like it or not, for the moment, the Earth is where we make our stand. It has been said that astronomy is a humbling and character-building experience. There is perhaps no better demonstration of the folly of human conceits than this distant image of our tiny world. To me, it underscores our responsibility to deal more kindly with one another and to preserve and cherish the pale blue dot, the only home we've ever known.

Cycling sixty-two miles on my way to see the 2017 total solar eclipse in Oregon, I put on *Radiolab* to hear Annie Druyan reflect on the fortieth anniversary of the *Voyager* launch, which would fall on the day before the eclipse. A still-youthful voice crackling ever so subtly with the accumulation of life pours into my headphones. Listening to the time machine of Druyan's voice as I pedal to the point in the pixel I have chosen as my vantage point for totality, I keep thinking about Dickinson's eclipse poem.

It sounded as if the streets were running—
And then—the streets stood still—
Eclipse was all we could see at the Window
And Awe—was all we could feel.

By and by—the boldest stole out of his Covert
To see if Time was there—
Nature was in her Opal Apron—
Mixing fresher Air.

That the poet laureate of death should be the poet laureate of totality is only fitting. Dickinson sent this poem to Higginson as his wife lay dying. "We must be less than Death, to be lessened by it," she wrote to him, "for nothing is irrevocable but ourselves." And what lessens us more grandly than the cosmic spectacle of totality? Kerneled in the softness with which Dickinson holds existence and its counterpoint is a deep intuition about the hardest fact of science: In a few billion years, when our star burns itself out "by and by," it will bend time itself as this pale blue dot is revoked into an eternal stillness of nonbeing—the world will end in an endless total solar eclipse. No "God" will redeem the light that is forever lost—an awareness on which Dickinson shone a sidewise gleam in that first letter to Higginson as she wrote of her family: "They are religious, except me, and address an eclipse, every morning, whom they call their 'Father.'"

The only "eclipse" Emily Dickinson addressed with such supreme spiritual ardor is the one she called her Master—an unattainable beloved, a muse, a personal deity, a pulsar of inspiration that magnetized the poet's mind. There is something beautiful and sobering in the fact that we shall never know the identity of her Master with any degree of certainty, for at the center of the Master Letters cult is the false assumption that in a life of such immense emotional vitality, there was only one supreme object of love—the "Master"—and that this person is the key to the riddle of the interior life from which Dickinson's poetry sprang. If there is any indisputable evidence in the body of her letters—to Susan, to Kate Scott Anthon, to Otis Lord—it is that she loved frequently and ferociously, that if her loves were the flowers to which she consistently likened them, her garden grew wild with various species of various colors and forms.

One might wonder what the point is of all such speculations bleeding into historical tabloidism—art, after all, should speak for itself. But this is where the snake bites its own tail: There is no "itself" any more than there is a solid self that holds up to the scrutiny of disambiguation. Elizabeth Barrett Browning had decreed as much:

> The artist's part is both to be and do,
> Transfixing with a special, central power
> The flat experience of the common man,
> And turning outward, with a sudden wrench,
> Half agony, half ecstasy, the thing
> He feels the inmost: never felt the less
> Because he sings it.

The art arises from the entirety of the artist—from what Margaret Fuller called one's "fulness of being"—and no element therein can be scalpeled off as irrelevant to the whole. To understand the richness and complexity of the interiority that creates the externality of art is to have a richer appreciation of the art itself, its-indivisible-self.

Richard Feynman addressed this in a splendid refutation of a painter friend's insistence that any scientific knowledge about a flower detracts from the appreciation of its beauty. In a fragment of an interview now known as "Ode to a Flower," Feynman speaks passionately about how being able to imagine the cells and the magnificent processes taking place within them, to know how the colors of flowers evolved to attract insects, only amplifies the aesthetic appreciation. "The science knowledge"—he beams his boyish smile into the camera—"only adds to the excitement, the mystery, and the awe of a flower."

Virginia Woolf, too, beheld the cosmos of connections within a flower. In an autobiographical reflection, she recounts the moment of revelation in which she finally understood her task as artist: Walking in the garden one afternoon, her eyes fall on a flower and she is thunderbolted with the understanding that the flower is part of the mound of dirt from which it stems, and the dirt is part of the earth beneath, which belongs to the whole of the planet, and that what she is looking at is "part flower, part earth"—all one. Suddenly, the "cotton wool of ordinary life" lifts and she realizes that these fragments of truth cohere into a unified sense of meaning, and the task of the artist is to bring that meaning to light. In a passage that has reverberated through the hallways of my mind since the moment I first read it long ago, she writes:

> Behind the cotton wool is hidden a pattern . . . the whole world is a work of art . . . *Hamlet* or a Beethoven quartet is the truth about this vast mass that we call the world. But there is no Shakespeare, there is no Beethoven; certainly and emphatically there is no God; we are the words; we are the music; we are the thing itself.

In 1894, the year Emily Dickinson's letters entered the world, Elizabeth Peabody exited it. She was nearly ninety and had outlived all the other Transcendentalists. Transcendentalism—the ideology she herself had named, predicated on the patterned interconnectedness of being—would outlive her in turn, seeding some of the most formative ideals of the next century, among them the environmental conservation movement.

23

INTO THE UNFATHOMED

"The more clearly we can focus our attention on the wonders and realities of the universe about us the less taste we shall have for the destruction of our race," a slight woman with intent eyes the color of Mediterranean seawater declares with unassuming aplomb from behind a lectern a size too large. "Wonder and humility are wholesome emotions, and they do not exist side by side with a lust for destruction."

This is not the wishful thinking of a naïve idealist or the shrill cry of an alarmist, but a clarion call by the nation's most respected science writer, who has taken the podium to deliver her acceptance speech for the John Burroughs Medal and who would posthumously earn her country's highest civilian honor—the Presidential Medal of Freedom.

By the time Rachel Carson was awarded the prestigious medal for excellence in nature writing in the spring of 1952, the unknown marine biologist who had spent years working for the United States government's Fish and Wildlife Service had risen to worldwide celebrity with her trailblazing book *The Sea Around Us*, published several months earlier—a lyrical serenade to the unseen world beneath the surface of the ocean.

In addition to the John Burroughs Medal, *The Sea Around Us* earned Carson the National Book Award and established her as a singular bridge figure between serious science and serious literature, with Galileo's rigor and Thoreau's poetic gift. "In the regions we call Nature, towering beyond all measurement, with infinite spread, infinite depth and height," Whitman had lamented a century earlier, "how small a part . . . has literature really depicted." Carson had emerged a depicter of unprecedented virtuosity and clarity of vision. Within a decade, she would catalyze the conservation movement, introduce the word *ecology* into the lay lexicon, and awaken the modern environmental conscience with her epoch-making *Silent Spring*—one of those rare books, like Kepler's *Astronomia nova*, Margaret Fuller's *Woman in the Nineteenth Century*, and Darwin's *On the Origin of Species*, that change history by changing the human mind itself.

Although Carson made her name by writing about the oceans— she had authored three books about the sea by the time she emerged onto land with *Silent Spring*—she had beheld the ocean only in her mind's eye for the first two decades of her life. A solitary landlocked child, she spent her days roaming the woods of western Pennsylvania to revel in the fellowship of birds, insects, and flowers, all the while dreaming of the sea. One day, roaming the cliffs behind her family's farm, Rachel found a fossilized fish skeleton that sparked an electric longing to know how that mysterious marine creature had ended up a terrestrial ghost, where the ocean it inhabited long ago had gone, what such swaths of time meant beside the shallow tidal marker of a human life. Carson would later reflect:

I might have said, with Emily Dickinson:

I never saw a moor,
I never saw the sea;
Yet know I how the heather looks,
And what a wave must be.

One rainy August day during her senior year of college, Rachel Carson laid her blue-green eyes on the sea for the first time. She was journeying to the Marine Biology Laboratory at Woods Hole on Cape Cod—one of the first scientific institutions to regularly invite female researchers and scholars, founded several months before Maria Mitchell's death. (Gertrude Stein had been one of the six women, out of twenty-three students, in the institution's embryology class of 1897.) The ocean would remain Carson's lifelong love. Her encounter with the spruce-lined seashore through a curtain of fog at dawn, a pristine and primordial scene, gave her a sense of what the young Earth must have looked like:

> There was nothing, really, for human words to say in the presence of something so vast, mysterious, and immensely powerful. Perhaps only in music of deep inspiration and grandeur could the message of that morning be translated by the human spirit, as in the opening bars of Beethoven's Ninth Symphony—music that echoes across vast distances and down long corridors of time, bringing the sense of what was and of what is to come—music of swelling power that swirls and explodes even as the sea surged against the rocks below. . . .

Born in the year Einstein watched the construction worker plummet from the rooftop into relativity, Carson grew up in a family bereft of means, always knowing she wanted to be a writer. A voracious reader since early childhood, she was eleven when her story "A Battle in the Clouds"—a wartime tale inspired by a letter from her brother Robert, who had enlisted in the World War I Army Air Service—was accepted for publication in the wildly popular *St. Nicholas Magazine*. The young people's magazine was a platform for the early writings of such literary titans as Edna St. Vincent Millay, F. Scott Fitzgerald, E. E. Cummings, and William Faulkner. Rachel was paid $3.30 for her story—a penny a word. At eleven, she was officially a professional writer.

That month, President Wilson stood before the Senate and called for the approval of the suffrage amendment granting women the right to vote. "We have made partners of the women in this war," he exhorted. "Shall we admit them only to a partnership of suffering and sacrifice and toil and not to a partnership of privilege and right?" Rachel Carson was thirteen when the amendment was ratified.

She kept submitting stories to *St. Nicholas*, which published several more by the time she graduated from high school. Her senior thesis, titled "Intellectual Dissipation," admonished against the squandering of our most precious human faculty—the "thinking, reasoning mind." At the heart of her thesis was a conviction that would govern the remainder of her days—a deep faith in the power of great books to transform and ennoble, casting real literature as "something that would raise you a little higher than you were yesterday, something that would make you willing and able for your part in the work of the world."

Decades later, Carson would mature into the recognition that "it is not half so important to *know* as to *feel*," for "if facts are the seeds that later produce knowledge and wisdom, then the emotions and the impressions of the senses are the fertile soil in which the seeds must grow." At the zenith of her career, she would observe:

> The most memorable writings—though they be addressed to the intellect—are rooted in man's emotional reaction to that life stream of which he is a part.

In the autumn of 1925, Carson enrolled in Pennsylvania College for Women in Pittsburgh with the intention of studying literature, aided by a $100 scholarship she had won in a state competition that would cover half the tuition for her freshman year. But room and board cost another $575—a Sisyphean financial push for the Carson family. Mr. Carson, like the Peabody sisters' father a century earlier, had tried his hand at a series of trades over the years but had failed to provide for his family. It was Mrs. Carson, like Mrs. Peabody, who made ends meet by giving piano lessons. Beethoven reverberated through the Carson home daily to put food on the table. Eleven months after Emily Dickinson's death, Maria Carson had graduated from the Washington Female Seminary with honors in Latin. Determined to give her daughter the education that would free Rachel from ever having to depend on a husband, Mrs. Carson took on more piano students, then sold all her china. When one of Rachel's classmates came to dine with the family, she was taken aback by being served on the kind of plastic dishes given away as promotional gimmicks by cereal brands. A neighbor would later recall stopping by for a spontaneous visit at dinnertime and finding the family gathered around a single bowl of apples. When the annual college tuition rose to $300, the Carsons had nothing left to give. Rachel took out loans that mounted to an impossible $1,400 by the middle of her senior year—a year in which fewer than 4 percent of American women graduated from a four-year university. She offered the college two of her family's vacant lots—remnants of her father's failed attempt at real estate—as collateral against the debt, signing the agreement exactly nine months before the 1929 financial crash.

Suspended by so tenuous a thread of opportunity, Rachel brought to scholarship an obsessive work ethic, aided by her mother, who came for regular visits and invested hours in typing up her daughter's papers. Introverted and besotted with books, Rachel spent her scant free time not socializing with her young peers—except for the occasional game of field hockey, in which she was a formidable goalie in her blue bloomers and black stockings—but in the company of guiding spirits long gone. At eighteen, she preferred the literature of earlier eras. Like Maria Mitchell, she loved Milton; like Margaret Fuller, Shakespeare. She cherished Melville and especially admired Twain for his "hatred of hypocrisy." A colleague would later recall that "there was something about her of the nineteenth century." Throughout her life, Carson would keep by her bedside a copy of Thoreau's journals, which she would read as a "pleasant ritual" at night.

As intentional as Carson was about the direction of her college education, the most significant event of her intellectual and emotional development arrived the way most transformative things enter our lives—through the back door of the mansion of our plans.

Consumed with the demands of her English major during her freshman year, Rachel had put off the curriculum's science requirement. At the start of her sophomore year, she enrolled in an introductory biology course taught by Professor Mary Scott Skinker—a formidable mind encased in a body of arresting, almost alien beauty. Born in the year Emily Dickinson's poems entered the world and still in her early thirties, the tall, glamorous, brilliant Professor Skinker was an uncompromising educator. During her tenure at the college, Skinker would more than triple the offerings of the biology department she chaired—from three basic courses to ten, including advanced classes in disciplines from the frontiers of science: genetics, microbiology, and embryology. Her tough grading struck terror—especially after she gave a C to the most popular girl in the class, whose wealthy family pressured the college president into pleading with Skinker to change the grade; she did not. Still, her students worshipped her—she seemed like an apparition from another era, another world. On Saturdays, she came to dinner in elegant formal wear, with a flower pinned to her waist or her chest—a new species every week—which the girls assumed came from some mysterious suitor. On weekdays, she delivered enthralling lectures on natural history and evolution that awakened in her students an awareness of the glorious interleaving of all life and seeded a novel understanding of the continuity of existence—the present day was not a sealed jar adrift on the river of time but a cabinet containing fossils of every single day that preceded it. Decades later, Skinker's formative influence would seep into Carson's definition of biology as the understanding that "the stream of life, flowing out of the dim past into the uncertain future, is in reality a unified force, though composed of an infinite number and variety of separate lives."

At nineteen, Rachel was as taken with this revelatory view of life as she was with the beguiling biologist. Under this dual bewitchment, Rachel changed her major from English to biology. As she continued writing for the university's student magazine, winning prizes for her stories, and publishing the occasional poem, she began spending blissful hours dissecting specimens in the tiny laboratory atop the ivy-festooned three-story brick building that housed classrooms, dormitory rooms, and the university's art studio. At the intersection of science and literature, Carson found a focal point for the beam of her searching and sensitive intellect. "I have always wanted to write," Rachel told her lab partner late one night in her formaldehyde paradise. "Biology has given me something to write about." This was the inception of Carson's lifelong conviction that literature and science live in vital symbiosis in illuminating the nature of reality, which she would articulate a quarter century later in her National Book Award acceptance speech:

> The materials of science are the materials of life itself. Science is part of the reality of living; it is the what, the how, and the why of everything in our experience. It is impossible to understand man without understanding his environment and the forces that have molded him physically and mentally.
>
> The aim of science is to discover and illuminate truth. And that, I take it, is the aim of literature, whether biography or history or fiction; it seems to me, then, that there can be no separate literature of science.

This may seem like an obvious truth today, but in 1926 it was a countercultural notion. C. P. Snow's now-legendary lecture "The Two Cultures"—a watershed case for the necessity of desegregating science and the literary arts, of bridging investigation with imaginative experience—was still more than three decades away. In a footnote to it, Snow—who was a university senior himself when Rachel Carson changed her major to biology—would remark that a third of Russian engineering graduates were women and would lament of the West:

> It is one of our major follies that, whatever we say, we don't in reality regard women as suitable for scientific careers. We thus neatly divide our pool of potential talent by two.

Two months before Rachel's twenty-first birthday, her roommate procured for her a date for the university's annual prom—a young man named Bob from a nearby men's college. Despite the silver slippers a size too small—a common practice for young women at the time, a vestige of the punishing gender norms that led Chinese women to bind their feet for millennia—Rachel had a "glorious time," transfixed by the vision of Mary Scott Skinker in a miniskirt and a chiffon velvet blouse the color of a ripe peach, a kaleidoscope of light radiating from the rhinestone pinned at her waist.

"Miss Skinker was a perfect knockout," Ray—as Rachel signed her letters—reported after the prom. There was no mention of Bob, whom she saw just a couple more times that spring. She would never date again.

But the elation of Rachel's newfound passion plunged to despair when, a few months after she switched her major, Miss Skinker summoned her to deliver rending news: She was to take a leave of absence from the college to study at Woods Hole before pursuing a Ph.D. at Johns Hopkins University. In her senior year Rachel would be bereft of her mentor and muse.

Rachel was devastated. She refused to accept the separation and immediately decided to follow Skinker, applying to the graduate program in zoology at Johns Hopkins. She was admitted. But reality eclipsed this pleasant fantasy of reunion. Carson realized she simply couldn't afford to abandon her degree at PCW and amass even more debt at another university. Reluctantly, despondently, she stayed as Miss Skinker left. With a friend, Rachel founded a science club named for the departed muse's initials in Greek—Mu Sigma Sigma—and had a local jeweler make small, pretty membership pins engraved with the letters. She kept in close touch with Skinker, who would help her navigate the currents of a scientific career for years to come. After Carson graduated, Skinker encouraged her to apply for a fellowship at Woods Hole, where she herself had earned a research seat. She fortified the encouragement with a formal recommendation that opened the gate to the prestigious Marine Biology Laboratory for her protégée, who was granted an eight-week fellowship. Freckles constellated Carson's fair skin as she spent hours under the August sun, bent over the tide pools swarming with astonishing life-forms—an experience that planted the seed that would blossom into *The Sea Around Us* more than two decades later.

Carson hadn't given up her Johns Hopkins dream. Earlier that summer, she had reapplied and, again with a recommendation from

Skinker, was admitted with a full scholarship—one of only seven such scholarships the university offered to promising scholars with a proven penchant for independent research. It was an event significant enough for the local newspaper to note that "the honor of this award is seldom conferred upon women."

Before departing for Woods Hole, Carson journeyed to the Baltimore campus for an orientation, then joined Skinker for a vacation in the Blue Ridge Mountains, where the two women—Rachel now twenty-one and Mary thirty-seven—spent their days at the tennis court and on horseback, and their nights by the fireplace of the cabin they shared.

But while it was Skinker who had steered Carson toward the Woods Hole adventure that gave her that first glimpse of the ocean, it was a verse by a long-dead poet that had first incited Carson's aquatic imagination during her college years. Working on an English assignment late one night as a thunderstorm raged outside her dorm room, Rachel devoured Tennyson's 1835 poem "Locksley Hall"—one of the first works Emerson had been able to read after the shock of little Waldo's death had deadened him to literature, which had given him "a momentary sense of freedom & power" in the midst of his bereavement. An epiphany came over her like a seizure as she reached the closing lines depicting the ocean engulfed by a savage storm:

Comes a vapour from the margin, blackening over heath and holt,
Cramming all the blast before it, in its breast a thunderbolt.

Let it fall on Locksley Hall, with rain or hail, or fire or snow;
For the mighty wind arises, roaring seaward, and I go.

How could she have lived without ever laying eyes on this supreme evocation of nature's might and splendor? Carson would later recount the intense emotional stir of reading that final line, pointing to the moment as a revelation that unlatched the unsuspected chamber of her being from which her life's work would spring:

That line spoke to something within me, seeming to tell me that my own path led to the sea—which then I had never seen—and that my own destiny was somehow linked with the sea.

But as she turned toward marine biology, she never turned away from writing, nor from her greatest literary love: poetry. In fact, her first serious attempts at publication as an adult were with verse. Among her papers is a vast collection of rejection slips—*The Atlantic Monthly, Poetry, The Saturday Evening Post, Century Magazine, Good Housekeeping*—dated from her senior year of college onward. Somewhere along the way, Carson must have arrived at the same conclusion as Aurora Leigh—that "no one lives by verse that lives," and that if she were to survive as a writer, she must write prose. But unlike Barrett Browning's Aurora, Carson realized that poetry lives in innumerable guises beyond standard verse and made the radical decision to graft the poetic onto the scientific.

Over the next few years, Carson immersed herself in the science of the seas. For her thesis on the fish kidney, the function of which was then poorly understood and subject to controversial theories, she made painstaking *camera lucida* drawings under the microscope as she peered at specimens she had dissected and stained. To pay her way through the master's program, she took jobs as lab assistant and biology instructor—the only female one in the department—before graduating with a degree in zoology in 1932 and entering a Ph.D. program, also at Johns Hopkins.

But midway through Carson's doctoral studies, tragedy piled atop tribulation. First, the financial strain of keeping up with the tuition became too severe, and she had to leave the program. Then, one summer morning in her twenty-eighth year, her father died suddenly in the backyard of the family home. With her mother disabled by severe arthritis, Rachel was rendered head of household. Her brother and sister, neither of whom had finished high school, had left the nest long ago. After two divorces, her sister had eventually returned to live under Mrs. Carson's roof with two young daughters. Not yet thirty, Rachel had four dependents and a mass of student loans.

She applied for a low-level position at the United States Bureau of Fisheries and was hired as a field aide for $6.50 a day. When her supervisor noticed her literary gift, he tasked her with writing short scripts for the government agency's program *Romance Under the Waters* airing on CBS Radio. Meanwhile, she began submitting longer pieces about marine life to the Baltimore *Sun,* which, arrested by so uncommon a fusion of science and lyrical prose, made her a regular contributor to their *Sunday Magazine.* On the first day of March 1936, one hundred years after Maria Mitchell received her first paid job at the Nantucket Atheneum, Rachel Carson received the first check of her adult life for a piece of writing: $20.

Thanks to a series of civil service exams in parasitology, wildlife biology, and aquatic biology that Skinker, then employed by the government herself, had encouraged her to take, Carson qualified for a full-time position as a junior aquatic biologist. She scored above all other applicants and was hired at $2,000 per year, assigned to a dark ground-level Washington, D.C., office that felt "like working in the bottom of a well." There, Carson first became aware of and alarmed about the rapid decline in fish populations after the surge of industry in the first decades of the twentieth century.

Impressed with her work on the radio scripts, Carson's boss tasked her with writing "something of a general sort about the sea" to introduce the bureau's work to the popular reader, expecting that she would summarize the agency's scientific research and annual reports. Instead, she transmuted the facts of science into a kind of poetry, something so lyrical that her chief told her—"with a twinkle in his eye," she would later recount—that it didn't work as a government report. But he encouraged her to submit it to *The Atlantic Monthly* as an essay.

Before she had a chance to do that, tragedy struck again—her sister died of pneumonia at forty, leaving her two young daughters in Carson's care.

I have often wondered how a writer whose published prose radiates such exuberant emotional richness could remain so intently stoic in her personal writings, her letters never dwelling on the inordinate share of misfortune life had dealt her and would continue to deal. Writing couldn't have been a mere "passion"—it must have been for her, as it is for many of us who write, redemption, self-salvation, a lifeline. In science she must have found the consolation of the wider lens that humbles the temporal turmoils of any single life against the eternal cosmic backdrop of all life—the "grandeur" of view that had solaced Darwin in the wake of loss.

Shortly after her sister's death, Carson submitted her essay to the *Atlantic*, where it was accepted and published in the September 1937 issue as "Undersea"—a lyrical journey to what Walt Whitman had called, in one of his least known poems, "the world below the brine," a world more mysterious in 1937 than the Moon. The byline read R. L. Carson—a century after S. M. Fuller, Carson, too, worried that her gender would undermine the authority of her prose. Of the twenty-one contributors to the issue, Carson is the only one whose name would be widely recognized in the following century.

In this unprecedented masterpiece, she invited the reader to explore the most enigmatic recesses of Earth from the perspective of nonhuman creatures—Whitman's "beings who walk other spheres." Carson wrote:

Who has known the ocean? Neither you nor I, with our earth-bound senses, know the foam and surge of the tide that beats over the crab hiding under the seaweed of his tide-pool home; or the lilt of the long, slow swells of mid-ocean, where shoals of wandering fish prey and are preyed upon, and the dolphin breaks the waves to breathe the upper atmosphere. Nor can we know the vicissitudes of life on the ocean floor, where sunlight, filtering through a hundred feet of water, makes but a fleeting, bluish twilight, in which dwell sponge and mollusk and starfish and coral, where swarms of diminutive fish twinkle through the dusk like a silver rain of meteors, and eels lie in wait among the rocks. Even less is it given to man to descend those six incomprehensible miles into the recesses of the abyss, where reign utter silence and unvarying cold and eternal night.

To sense this world of waters known to the creatures of the sea we must shed our human perceptions of length and breadth and time and place, and enter vicariously into a universe of all-pervading water.

. . .

Writing in his journal a century earlier, in the year Maria Mitchell discovered her comet and taught him to use a telescope, Emerson lamented that there had yet to be invented a way of transmuting the facts of the natural world into beautiful literature:

> Literature should be the counterpart of nature & equally rich. I find her not in our books. I know nature, & figure her to myself as exuberant, tranquil, magnificent in her fertility,—coherent, so that every thing is an omen of every other. She is not proud of the sea or of the stars, of space or time; for all her kinds share the attributes of the selectest extremes.

Carson eulogized this notion of an ecology of being, beckoning the reader to appreciate the intricate interconnectedness of all life to which Mary Scott Skinker had awakened her a decade earlier:

> Every marine animal, from the smallest to the sharks and whales, is ultimately dependent for its food upon these microscopic entities of the vegetable life of the ocean. Within their fragile walls, the sea performs a vital alchemy that utilizes the sterile chemical elements dissolved in the water and welds them with the torch of sunlight into the stuff of life.

It was a revelation that science could be a literary subject, that it could speak—nay, sing—to the common reader with melodic might, so gracefully and graciously rejecting the false trade-off between the authority of science and the splendor of literary art. Rachel Carson would model for generations of writers the dignified refusal to give up either in the service of the other.

24

WHERE SPLENDOR DWELLS

Within a week, an envelope from the editor in chief of Simon and Schuster arrived at Carson's desk, inviting her to expand the essay into a book. *Under the Sea-Wind* was published four years later—a series of lyrical narratives about the life of the shore, the open sea, and the deep oceanic abyss. Determined to avoid the human bias of popular books about the ocean, which had always been written from the perspective of a human observer—a fisherman, a deep sea diver, a shore wanderer—Carson explored each of the three areas of marine life through the perspective of a particular, personified creature, christened by the scientific name of its genus. Three decades before the primatologist Jane Goodall was ridiculed for giving chimps names during her pioneering studies of primates in Gombe—work that later humbled our anthropoarrogance by revolutionizing our understanding of nonhuman consciousness—Carson writes of Silverbar, the sanderling soaring in migration from the Arctic Circle to Patagonia; Scomber, the Atlantic mackerel journeying from New England to the Continental Shelf; and Anguilla, the eel on a voyage to spawn with millions of his kin in the abysses of the Sargasso Sea south of Bermuda. Out of this rich personified narrative emerges the book's central hero: the ocean itself.

Carson wrote in a memo to her publisher:

Each of these stories seems to me not only to challenge the imagination, but also to give us a little better perspective on human problems. They are stories of things that have been going on for countless thousands of years. They are as ageless as sun and rain, or as the sea itself. The relentless struggle for survival in the sea epitomizes the struggle of all earthly life, human and nonhuman.

But chance interceded once again. Just as effusive reviews began flooding in for *Under the Sea-Wind*—"a beautiful and unusual book," *The New York Times* enthused—Japan's attack on Pearl Harbor claimed the nation's mind. Just before the bombing, one reviewer had written:

Our own battles for existence seem less a matter for dismay and more a simple reason for fortitude when compared in the mind with the ceaseless ebb and flow of life and death that are under all the sea winds.

The paradox of terror is that it contracts our scope into a smallness of attention that frantically filters in only confirmation of our grounds for fear and filters out our grounds for hope. The beauty of the natural world, the ancient kinship with our fellow beings, and the reassurance of cosmic timescales that dwarf any momentary crisis may have been exactly what a terrified nation needed, but *Under the Sea-Wind* was filtered out of the nation's attention. Carson saw her three years' labor as a casualty of the war. Her only solace was the book's ardent reception by the scientific community. Prominent biologists and naturalists wrote to commend her on the uncommon feat of popularizing without diluting science.

And yet the broader indifference stung. After seven years of discontent at the publisher's growing carelessness with the book's life in the world, Carson broke free of her contract. But she was too destitute to afford to buy back the publishing rights for $150. The disappointment, she wrote to Simon and Schuster, had almost broken her spirit and discouraged her from ever writing another book. But some deeper fidelity to the beauty and significance of her subject buoyed her as she began thinking about a far more ambitious book.

Meanwhile, Carson—one of only two women scientists employed by the government agency—had been steadily ascending the ranks, rising from her original appointment as junior aquatic biologist to senior biologist at the bureau, now reconfigured as the United States Fish and Wildlife Services. She trawled the technical journals and saved newspaper clippings about breakthroughs in the science of ocean currents and waves, about advances in sonar, radar, and other wartime technology that could be enlisted in the richer understanding of nature.

In the autumn of 1944, Carson submitted to *Collier*'s a fifteen-hundred-word piece bridging evolution and modern technology by drawing a sixty-million-year connection between the bat's sonic navigation system for nocturnal flight and the novelty of radar. The essay was a triumph. Several other magazines republished it. The Navy used it in their internal materials as "one of the clearest expositions of radar yet made available for public consumption." It unbolted the gates to the magazine world for Carson.

Carson pitched to *Reader's Digest*—who had reprinted the bat piece—another story, this time exploring the darker side of the relationship between nature and modern technology. She had been following new research on the negative effects of DDT—the pesticide so widely and indiscriminately used that cities sprayed entire neighborhoods, the government hosed down acres of forests, and agricultural airplanes rained it down upon children lunching in the schoolyard amid cornfields. At the Patuxent Research Refuge in Prince George's County, DDT doused the forest canopy and drifted toward the Patuxent River. Following the spraying, researchers monitored the wildlife in the area and watched birds, butterflies, fish, frogs, and foxes suffer and perish. After reading their cautionary report on the "two-edged sword" of industrial chemicals that were intended to eradicate so-called harmful species but ended up harming all of life, Carson offered *Reader's Digest* a lucid look at the dangers of DDT: "what it will do to insects that are beneficial or even essential; how it may affect waterfowl, or birds that depend on insect food; whether it may upset the whole delicate balance of nature if unwisely used."

Reader's Digest was uninterested. Carson would incubate her growing concern for another decade and a half. For now, she reasoned that one attracts more flies with honey than with vinegar and proposed to her boss at the Fish and Wildlife Service a twelve-part series of brochures spotlighting and celebrating the national wildlife refuge system. Under the plain, purposeful title *Conservation in Action,* Carson strewed these government brochures with her surprising bursts of lyrical prose about the splendors of nature and the hard-earned glories of evolution. The series, unprecedented in government publication, earned Carson promotion to editor in chief for the agency.

Carson continued submitting essays to popular magazines. In what began as a government press release about the migration patterns of chimney swifts and ended up as a feature article in *Collier's,* she envisioned what we now call biomimicry—the replication of nature's processes and systems in technological solutions to human problems: "If aviation engineers would apply the wisdom of the chimney swift, several troublesome problems of aeronautics could be solved." She was paid $55 for the piece—a sum so negligible as to be almost humiliating, but having just returned from the hospital after an appendectomy, Carson gratefully put the small amount toward her medical bills.

She kept thinking about her next book, until its subject coalesced from the particulate cloud of her lifelong inspirations and fascinations: the ocean as the seedbed of life and our profound dependence on it. A decade into her writing career, Carson began looking for a literary agent. In early 1948, after careful deliberation, she signed with Marie Rodell—a Vassar-educated novelist and editor who had just launched her own literary agency in New York and who would go on to procure the publication of Martin Luther King, Jr.'s, first book. "I, as an agent, do not handle this thing by Rachel Carson, and that thing by Rachel Carson," Rodell would soon write. "I

handle Rachel Carson." She would become not only Carson's fiercest champion but one of her dearest friends. By summer's end, "Sincerely, Rachel Carson" had melted into "Love, Ray."

That year, Carson was elected to the board of the Audubon
Society—an honor particularly gladdening, for birds had been her
first love and would always remain the chief animating force of her
love of all life. Among Carson's colleagues on the board was Mabel
Loomis Todd's daughter, Millicent Todd Bingham, who after a four-
year immersion in the science-heavy curriculum Maria Mitchell had
established at Vassar had gone on to become the first woman to
earn a doctorate in geography from Harvard.

But the year ended on a somber note. Just as Carson was gathering momentum on her new book, she received news that Mary Scott
Skinker lay dying of cancer. Carson flew to Chicago to spend two
sorrowful weeks at the bedside of the woman who had awakened
her to herself. Skinker died a week before Christmas at the age of
fifty-seven. Grief-stricken, Carson turned to the only medicine she
had ever known—writing about the grandeur of life.

By early 1949, she had completed three sample chapters of the
new book, which Rodell pitched to Oxford University Press. The
editor in chief was taken with prose that embodied what Carson
herself would later describe as "the magic combination of factual
knowledge and deeply felt emotional response" in a letter of advice
to a young woman who had asked her what it takes to become a
writer.

On June 3, 1949, Carson signed a contract with Oxford for an
advance of $1,000, to be paid in two installments. The follow-
ing month, she set out from Woods Hole for "ten days of unusual
adventure"—as part of her job at the Fish and Wildlife Service, she
was to join a government research vessel for a fish census and then
report on it. But the assignment was befogged when officials realized
the marine biologist sent to observe the census was a woman—no
woman had ever been allowed aboard the ship before. Eventually,
some bureaucrat decided that while one woman aboard a vessel
with fifty men was impermissible, two would be all right. Carson

invited Marie Rodell along, who half-joked that she would write about her experience in a piece titled "I Was a Chaperone on a Fishing Boat." (A decade and a half later, in the year of Carson's death, the pioneering oceanographer Sylvia Earl—one of the first marine scientists to use scuba diving equipment and to this day the only human being to have walked the deepest ocean floor—joined a six-week expedition to the Indian Ocean, on which she was the sole woman. A newspaper headline proclaimed: "Sylvia Sails Away with 70 Men, But She Expects No Problem.")

As the *Albatross III* sailed past Maria Mitchell's home island, Carson found herself apprehending for the first time "the unutterable loneliness of the sea at night as seen from a small vessel"—a creaturely awareness at which one could arrive only as a naked ape draped in mist and foaming saltwater far from shore:

> When I stood on the afterdeck on those dark nights, on a tiny man-made island of wood and steel, dimly seeing the great shapes of waves that rolled about us, I think I was conscious as never before that ours is a water world, dominated by the immensity of the sea.

In the spring of 1950, exactly a hundred years after Margaret Fuller boarded the *Elizabeth,* Carson arrived at the title for the book she had been incubating her entire life and composing over three years' worth of the nights and weekends punctuating her demanding government job: *The Sea Around Us.* By the time she completed the book, Carson had scoured hundreds of technical papers, corresponded with scores of specialists, worked with dozens of librarians to find obscure documents and rare books on oceanography, and consulted more than a thousand different printed sources. All of this she distilled into what may best be described as a book-length prose poem about the science of the seas.

That winter, Carson received news that she had been awarded the prestigious Westinghouse Prize for science writing, which came with a $1,000 check, for a chapter from the book-to-be titled "The Birth of an Island." Elated, she wrote to Rodell insisting that she

take the typical agent's commission on the prize money. Touched
by this warm generosity—agents are owed commission only on
publications—Rodell refused. Carson pressed lovingly:

> I don't know anything about your old Agent's Association rules, but
> my reasoning tells me that you are entitled to your share of anything
> that comes in on a book you've handled. If I can't give you a check
> without getting you disbarred, you must at least tell me something
> handsome you want, that I can get you as a little share of the loot.

For Rodell's thirty-ninth birthday later that month, Carson gave
her a subscription to *Natural History Magazine* and a beautiful edition of a biblical text, along with a handwritten note: "May they
remind you of my love and the very real gratitude for all the things
you have done for me in many ways."

Rodell began submitting sample chapters to various publications. Interest was lukewarm. A midtier science magazine considered printing an abridged version of one chapter, offering $50 for
it. As Carson was wrestling with the fear that the new book would
suffer the indifference of her last, a providential offer came from a
most improbable denizen of the literary universe: Edith Oliver—
a young actor turned *New Yorker* editor, who would later rise to
a three-decade tenure as the magazine's eminent drama critic. Carson's chapter on waves had crossed Oliver's desk and left her besotted. She requested more chapters to read, then made before William
Shawn, the magazine's editor, a fervent case for Carson's writing as
not only emblematic of *The New Yorker*'s literary tradition but as
a rare chance to extend that tradition into the editorially unmined
world of science.

Shawn was as taken with Carson's prose as Oliver. Like Mary
Somerville more than a century earlier, Carson explored how the various sciences—biology, geology, physics, chemistry—came together
in a holistic understanding of nature. Like Emerson and Dickinson, she wrote about the natural world with a poet's precision and
splendor of sentiment. The combination was unlike any Shawn had
encountered before. By midsummer, *The New Yorker* had accepted

not one but nine chapters of the book, offering Carson a total of $7,200—more than her annual government salary. (Meanwhile, *Reader's Digest*, five years after rejecting Carson's DDT article, rejected the chapter on climate as lacking popular appeal.) Released across three consecutive issues of *The New Yorker* in June 1951 as a "Profile of the Sea," the series precipitated more praiseful letters to the editor than any other profile in the magazine's quarter-century history. Enclosed with their check was a note to Rodell from Shawn himself about "Miss Carson's superb article":

> We are delighted about publishing this. Thank you for sending us that original chapter, on Waves, and starting us off on the whole happy venture.

Just as the jubilant news from *The New Yorker* was coming in, the elated author was reminded that nature deals fortune and misfortune with an even, disinterested hand. A routine physical exam revealed a small tumor in Carson's left breast. Without any fuss, she approached it as a pragmatic problem to be solved: She found a surgeon she trusted; she had the operation; she asked her doctor whether the tissue biopsy showed evidence of malignancy—he said it did not and recommended no further treatment. "The thing they took out of me was okay," Carson assuaged Rodell's cascading concern, "though about walnut-size and very deep. I'm sore as heck, but otherwise very spry."

And yet this reminder of her creaturely finitude kindled in Carson a new sense of urgency. Although her correspondence habitually downplayed her struggles and minimized her anxieties, she did reveal a glimpse of this psychic recalibration in a letter to her friend and fellow nature writer Edwin Teale:

> This time I'm not going to sit back for seven years before starting another [book]! I seem now to have, as writers should, a sense of urgency and passing time—and so much to say! Of course Thoreau had the whole idea in a sentence—"If thou art a writer, write as if thy time were short, for it is indeed short, at the longest."

On Monday, July 2, *The Sea Around Us* was published into a world already abuzz with excitement after its electric debut in *The New Yorker*. The day before, a commendatory review had crowned the cover of the Sunday *New York Times*. Praise poured in from the pages of nearly every esteemed publication, along with fan letters from every corner of the country—letters Carson would load into the trunk of her car and take home, determined to answer as many as she could, always prioritizing those from students and young women who asked her advice on making their way as writers.

Carson had accomplished the improbable feat of enchanting lay readers and scientists alike. A leading Harvard oceanographer wrote with admiring amazement to commend her on having found "a good many facts" that were completely new to him, even though he had been studying the ocean for fifty years. In a short letter addressing Carson as "Dr.," the pioneering Caltech seismologist Hugo Benioff wrote: "The Sea Around Us is the most beautifully written and lucid book on a scientific subject that I have ever read. I hope you will write many more like it."

A geology professor, after drawing analogies between Carson's writing and Goethe's, told her: "One of the finest compliments your book may experience, perhaps, is the eagerness with which our eight year old boy listens to the chapters as we read them to him."

One summer morning, the phone rang at Carson's home. She wasn't there. Her mother picked up to receive the singsong gusto of Alice Roosevelt Longworth—President Theodore Roosevelt's daughter and a gravitational force in Washington society. She told Mrs. Carson, who reported the conversation to her daughter as soon as they hung up, that *The Sea Around Us* was "the most marvelous thing she had ever read"—a marvel that had kept her up all night as she reread the book twice by sunrise.

There were also letters of tragicomical testament to Carson's feat against her cultural odds. One man, too busy making assumptions to note the name on the spine, wrote bluntly: "I assume from the author's knowledge that he must be a man." Another took these assumptions to a point of unwitting parody, addressing his letter to "Miss Rachel Carson" but opening it with "Dear Sir" before explaining that although he had enjoyed the book, he wasn't going to reverse his lifelong conviction that men have superior intellectual powers and was therefore choosing to address Carson in the masculine. Upon meeting Carson for the first time, one of the male editors working for her own publisher exclaimed: "You are such a surprise to me. I thought you would be a very large and forbidding woman."

The vast majority of the letters, however, were from admirers of her work—hundreds, then thousands of them, letters the common sentiment of which Carson summarized as "an immense and unsatisfied thirst for understanding of the world about us, and every drop of information, every bit of fact that serves to free the reader's mind to roam the great spaces of the universe, is seized upon with almost pathetic eagerness."

A malignancy of that selfsame "pathetic eagerness" accounted for the scant criticism Carson received, which echoed the very criticism that had been hurled at Copernicus, Kepler, and Galileo centuries earlier: She had dared to challenge the notion of "God" as creator and to unsettle the sense of certainty to which humanity so desperately clings. These criticisms would continue as Carson became increasingly vocal about the propagandist forces in society, occasionally rising to an almost comical crescendo. In a letter penned in the final year of Carson's life, after a page and a half of fulsome praise, the editor of *The Sunday School Times*—a publication in its 105th year, he took care to point out—would proffer:

> May I take the liberty of saying that I wish you might see all these natural wonders, of which you have written so well and fully, as coming from the hand of an almighty God, according to the first few chapters of Genesis, rather than as the product of evolution. I had to study this subject at the University, and the professor was fair enough to give me a mark in the top bracket, though I told him frankly that I did not believe in the theory. Of course I did the required work. For forty-five years I have found the greatest comfort and satisfaction in daily Bible study. . . . If you have not already done so, may I ask you, in all kindness, to give some serious thought to these things?

Carson would later address this class of criticism in a letter to a friend:

> As a biologist, I shall indeed try to stick to what we can observe and test—always realizing, of course, that what we do know now is only a tiny fragment of what Really Is! . . . I spent my years of graduate work at Johns Hopkins. Whatever else I may have learned there, this was the unforgettable lesson: we do not really know anything. What we think we know today is replaced by something else tomorrow.

25

TO LIVE AND TO VANISH

Twenty days after its publication, *The Sea Around Us* entered the *New York Times* best-seller list at number five, then steadily ascended to number one, where it was to remain for more weeks than any other nonfiction book ever had. The *Times* chose it as the outstanding book of the year. By the end of December, a quarter million copies had been sold. Numerous international translations and a Braille edition followed. The publisher, who had failed to anticipate the book's success, struggled to keep up, going through six strained printings as book buyers complained about the shortage and readers added their names to months-long waitlists. The Oxford University Press did, however, purchase rights to republish Carson's *Under the Sea-Wind*, which a decade earlier had sold fewer than seventeen hundred copies before slipping out of print. It now joined *The Sea Around Us* on the *New York Times* best-seller list, with forty thousand copies ordered before the new edition was even out. With fifteen years of magazine writing under her belt and a decade after the publication of her first book, Rachel Carson was declared an overnight success.

When she was awarded the $3,000 Guggenheim Fellowship she had applied for the previous autumn for her next project, she returned it, feeling it would better serve another artist in direr need now that the income from her own work could sustain her.

An editor at Knopf asked Carson's recommendation for a writer

to compose the cosmic counterpart to her marine masterpiece—
"a thoroughly grounded astronomer ... able at the same time to
write more than ordinarily well." Acknowledging that Carson's was
no common feat, he wrote: "Books like yours are not written to
order; they grow on the writer." *The Sea Around Us* had been growing on Carson like a coral reef, imperceptibly yet steadily, in the
twenty-one years since that formative trip to Woods Hole.

On January 29, 1952, a disbelieving Carson received the National
Book Award for, the award citation read, enchanting the common
reader with "a hitherto unconsidered field of scientific inquiry of
great importance to the spiritual and material economy of mankind.
It is a work of scientific accuracy presented with poetic imagination
and such clarity of style and originality of approach as to win and
hold every reader's attention." At the ceremony, the drama critic
John Mason Brown welcomed Carson to the stage with his introductory remarks:

> Miss Carson [has] made those odd creatures of the sea, those bipeds
> known as men and women, interested the world over in the mystery
> of our beginnings and the profundity and beauty of something far
> greater than mortals, with their petty egotisms and vanities, can hope
> to know. . . . She has atomized our egos and brought to each reader
> not only a new humility but a new sense of the inscrutable vastness
> and interrelation of forces beyond our knowledge or control. She has
> placed us as specks in time and yet inheritors of a history older, and
> certainly deeper, than many of us realized. . . . Where prose ends
> and poetry begins is sometimes hard to say. But I do know that Miss
> Carson writes poetic prose or prose poetry of uncommon beauty.

A century earlier, Frederick Douglass had insisted that "the dead
fact is nothing without the living expression"—that it is "truth but
truth disrobed of its sublimity and glory: a kind of frozen truth,
destitute of motion itself and incapable of exciting emotion in others." Douglass believed that the writer "who speaks to the feelings,
who enters the soul's deepest meditations, holding the mirror up to
nature ... will be sure of an audience."

Carson rose from the table she shared with the poet Marianne

Moore and walked with measured steps to the stage, where she delivered her stunning acceptance speech. A century after Maria Mitchell had observed, while leading a pioneering all-female eclipse expedition, how difficult it always is "to teach the man of the people that natural phenomena belong as much to him as to scientific people," Carson said:

> We live in a scientific age; yet we assume that knowledge of science is the prerogative of only a small number of human beings, isolated and priestlike in their laboratories. This is not true. It cannot be true. The materials of science are the materials of life itself. Science is part of the reality of living; it is the what, the how, and the why of everything in our experience. It is impossible to understand man without understanding his environment and the forces that have molded him physically and mentally.
>
> [. . .]
>
> The winds, the sea, and the moving tides are what they are. If there is wonder and beauty and majesty in them, science will discover these qualities. If they are not there, science cannot create them. If there is poetry in my book about the sea, it is not because I deliberately put it there, but because no one could write truthfully about the sea and leave out the poetry.

A century earlier, Emerson had articulated the same sentiment in his landmark essay "The Poet," penned over the course of the two years he walked the woods of Concord with Margaret Fuller:

> The sea, the mountain-ridge, Niagara, and every flower-bed, pre-exist, or super-exist, in pre-cantations, which sail like odors in the air, and when any man goes by with an ear sufficiently fine, he overhears them and endeavors to write down the notes without diluting or depraving them.

Now the fine ear transmuting the beauty of nature into poetry belonged to a woman. *The New York Times* compared "the slender, gentle lady who is editor of the United States Fish and Wildlife Service" to Homer and extolled her as "a publishing phenomenon as rare as a total solar eclipse." Rights were signed for a major cin-

ematic adaptation of *The Sea Around Us.* Although the film would
win an Academy Award, Carson was appalled by her Hollywood
experience—she had to submit numerous pages of scientific corrections to the script, many of which weren't honored in the final
movie—and she never repeated it. In an outraged letter to Marie
Rodell, she shared a resonant passage from a recent *New York
Times* article about the television adaption of William Faulkner's
story "The Brooch":

> The advance fanfare over "The Brooch" obviously was an attempt
> to capitalize on Mr. Faulkner's justly-earned fame; yet what the audi-
> ence saw was substitute merchandise not of the quality advertised.
> This intellectually subversive approach to literature is an old TV trick
> and it is time it was stopped. . . . Don't say you are going to do "The
> Brooch" and then not do it. If the principle of brand labeling has a
> validity in selling canned vegetables, it has an equal validity in offer-
> ing literary works.

And then Carson added with smoldering fury:

> Although Faulkner apparently, in momentary weakness, cooperated
> in perverting his own work, I have never given any suggestion of
> approval to what [the Hollywood people] have done.

Of the innumerable offers that barraged her, Carson accepted a
select few. She traveled to Nantucket to do a book signing at the
Maria Mitchell Association, housed in the astronomer's childhood
home. She wrote the liner notes for a prominent symphony orchestra recording of Debussy's *La Mer.* In her speech at the National
Symphony luncheon to celebrate its release, she reflected on the
relationship between great music and "the beauties and mysterious
rhythms of the natural world," and told the gathered musicians:

> I believe quite sincerely that in these difficult times we need more
> than ever to keep alive those arts from which men derive inspira-
> tion and courage and consolation—in a word, strength of spirit. . . .
> The symphony orchestras that present and interpret the music of the

ages are not luxuries in this mechanized, this atomic age. They are,
more than ever, necessities.

Standing in the receiving line for an honorary doctorate from her
alma mater, Carson turned to a former classmate who now directed
the college's alumni office and confided in a whisper that while she
appreciated the recognition, she would always feel far more herself wading barefoot through a tide pool than pecking a hardwood
stage with stilettos.

In New York, autograph hunters besieged her. In Myrtle Beach,
where she had traveled with her mother to accept the John Burroughs Medal, one barged into their motel room early in the morning, shoved past Maria Carson, and handed Rachel two books
to autograph as she lay in bed, freshly awakened by the tumult.
When *Harper's Bazaar* sent a photographer for a profile of her and
a journalist came "threatening"—Carson's word—to follow her to
Woods Hole, she felt herself "getting very tired of this nonsense."

None of the praise meant more to Carson than a beautiful, generous, and redemptive review of her once-neglected *Under the Sea-
Wind* by Henry Beston—one of her great literary heroes, whose
work she had discovered in a dusty corner of Baltimore's Pratt
Library as a student and had reread many times in the two decades
since.

There is a singular succor in receiving a kind and encouraging word
from one's heroes and creative elders. A century before Carson
became the Whitman of science, such soul-boosting beneficence had
befallen Whitman himself. In July 1855—shortly after Ida Russell's
sudden death—he self-published the monumental poetry collection
Leaves of Grass, inspired by Emerson's essay "The Poet." Despite
Whitman's elated hopes for the book, it landed with the thud of
paltry sales and negative reviews from the handful of critics who
paid any attention to it at all. When his father died later that month,
Whitman's heartbreak festered into a deep depression. "Every thing
I have done seems to me blank and suspicious," he wrote in his

journal. "I doubt whether my greatest thoughts, as I supposed them, are not shallow—and people will most likely laugh at me. . . . I am filled with restlessness.—I am incomplete." Whitman might have found solace in knowing that no creative person is immune to these interior tumults invisible to the outside world—not even his greatest hero. At the peak of his entanglement with Margaret Fuller, Emerson had written in his own journal:

> I am awkward, sour, saturnine, lumpish, pedantic, & thoroughly dis-agreeable & oppressive to the people around me. Yet if I am born to write a few good sentences or verses, these shall endure & my disgraces utterly perish out of memory.

Seventeen days after *Leaves of Grass* entered a world inhospitable and indifferent to it, a letter arrived that changed everything—a letter from Emerson himself. The sage of Concord, who had emerged as America's reigning literary tastemaker after Margaret Fuller's death, wrote to the obscure poet in Brooklyn:

> Dear Sir,
> I am not blind to the worth of the wonderful gift of Leaves of Grass. I find it the most extraordinary piece of wit and wisdom that America has yet contributed. I am very happy in reading it, as great power makes us happy. It meets the demand I am always making of what seemed the sterile & stingy Nature, as if too much handiwork, or too much lymph in the temperament, were making our Western wits fat and mean. I give you joy of your free and brave thought. I have great joy in it. I find incomparable things said incompara-bly well, as they must be. I find the courage of treatment which so delights us, & which large perception only can inspire.
> I greet you at the beginning of a great career, which yet must have had a long foreground somewhere, for such a start. I rubbed my eyes a little, to see if this sunbeam were no illusion; but the solid sense of the book is a sober certainty. It has the best merits, namely, of fortify-ing & encouraging.

Whitman was so moved by the letter that he carried it at his breast, neatly folded into his shirt pocket. He read it to his live-in lover, a young Irish stagecoach driver. When he published a second edition of *Leaves of Grass* a year later, he invested his meager means in a lavish ornament: Stamped in gold on the spine was "I Greet You at the Beginning of a Great Career R. W. Emerson." In the opening pages, he reprinted Emerson's letter in full. Without Emerson's generous encouragement, the private consequences of which were for the despairing poet perhaps even greater than its public endorsement, we might have had no Whitman.

Beston was in many ways Carson's Emerson—a role model whose lyrical, Transcendentalism-infused prose had become a lifelong inspiration for hers. How his words must have honeyed her soul:

> The poetic sense is the justification of man's humanity; it is also the justification of his inexplicable world. No matter what astronomers make of the sun, it is always more than a gigantic mass of ions, it is a splendor and a mystery, a force and a divinity, it is life and the symbol of life. It is Miss Carson's particular gift to be able to blend scientific knowledge with the spirit of poetic awareness, thus restoring to us a true sense of the world.

Not all reviewers, however, focused on Carson's unexampled body of work as a scientist and a poet of nature. Many dragged her physical person into the scope of evaluation. A reviewer in the *Boston Post*, as though surprised by his own assertion that she was both bold and feminine, could only fathom such a combination in a mythic creature, not a real woman:

> Apparently there are few photographs of Miss Carson anywhere on view, but we have worked this out. Rachel is probably no lady scientist at all, but an enchantress who lives in a cave under the sea, and there the light is awfully bad for pictures of authors.

Even the *New York Times* reviewer couldn't resist adding to his laudatory piece:

> It's a pity that the book's publishers did not print on its jacket a photograph of Miss Carson. It would be pleasant to know what a woman

looks like who can write about an exacting science with such beauty and precision.

Beneath the obtuse genderedness of these remarks was the simple fact that in falling in love with Carson's books, a whole nation was falling in love with their author. (Melville's infatuation with Hawthorne a century earlier had begun with the observation that "no man can read a fine author, and relish him to his very bones, while he reads, without subsequently fancying to himself some ideal image of the man and his mind.")

Carson's literary success had rendered her financially solvent after a lifetime of struggle. After fifteen years of service, she quit her government job. On the formal papers, under reason for resignation, she stated plainly: "To devote my time to writing." She then set out to fulfill her childhood dream of living by the ocean. After searching along the New England coast, she fell in love with West Southport—a picturesque island in Maine, nestled among evergreens and oaks in the estuary of the Sheepscot River, where seals frequented the beach and whales billowed by as though torn from the pages of her beloved Melville. With her royalties, she bought a plot of land on which to build a summer home. It would also become the laboratory for her next book, on which she had already begun working—an ambitious guide to the seashore, the strange and wondrous boundary Whitman had once extolled as "that suggesting, dividing line, contact, junction . . . blending the real and ideal, and each made portion of the other." In what would eventually become *The Edge of the Sea*, Carson would take an ecological lens to "the story of how that marvelous, tough, vital, and adaptable something we know as LIFE has come to occupy one part of the sea world and how it has adjusted itself and survived despite the immense, blind forces acting upon it from every side." Her dream home would become her locus of exploration:

I can't think of any more exciting place to be than down in the low-tide world, when the ebb tide falls very early in the morning, and the world is full of salt smell, and the sound of water, and the softness of fog.

Seeping into her excited report to Marie Rodell is Carson's reverence for nature as an unpossessable miracle not beholden to humans:
"I am about to become the owner (strange and inappropriate word)
of a perfectly magnificent piece of Maine shoreline." Carson would
spend many a blissful and fertile hour there. Like Maria Mitchell observing the stars in the biting cold of the Nantucket night,
Carson would wade the icy, barnacle-encrusted tide pools of West
Southport for hours on end, collecting specimens and examining
them with a magnifying glass, sometimes until the freezing waters
so numbed her body that Bob Hines—the artist illustrating her seashore guide, a longtime friend from her government job—had to
carry her ashore.

So great was Carson's celebrity that her land purchase made the
local news.

Leafing through the Southport Island paper one morning, Dorothy Freeman was astonished to read that the author of the book
with which she had fallen in love a year earlier was about to be
her neighbor. Just before Christmas 1952, Freeman mailed a warm
note of welcome to Carson's publisher, hoping it would reach her.
By that point, Carson was receiving hundreds of letters each week.
That she read Freeman's at all is no small matter of chance. That
she responded is a chance-sculpted choice—How many other letters were on her desk that day? What other pressures demanded
her time? Had something put her in a particularly magnanimous
mood?—that would shape the central fact of her emotional life.

A vivacious, educated woman born in the final year of the nineteenth century, the fifty-five-year-old Freeman had held a government job in Emily Dickinson's hometown and taught at the youth
organization 4-H—"head, heart, hands, and health"—before meeting Stanley Freeman. She had risen to regional director—the first
woman to do so—but when she wedded Stanley, she had to resign,
as married women were not permitted to teach at 4-H. A housewife for the twenty-nine years of her loving and devoted marriage,
Dorothy had become a self-educated naturalist with a keen interest

in birds and marine life. *The Sea Around Us* had serenaded the most alive part of her.

Dorothy was stunned to receive a response from Rachel Carson— a warm thank-you note inviting her to visit Carson and her mother once the cottage was finished in early June.

Just after dinnertime on Sunday, July 12, 1953, with the early evening sun spilling through the evergreens and the invisible moon denuding the shore in low tide a few feet below, Dorothy and Stan Freeman nervously descended the rocky path to the gray-blue cottage stretching long and low at the edge of a rocky bluff. They must have looked at each other before knocking—Which one of them tendered a knuckle to the wooden door?—then waited.

Rachel Carson rose from her book-lined desk by the vast window overlooking the bay, walked past the microscope-crowned worktable strewn with specimens gathered that morning, and welcomed her guests into the main room that still smelled of freshly carpentered pine. Hours melted by the redbrick fireplace as the small party bonded over their shared love of nature, the singular splendor of the New England coast, and the fact that Dorothy was also caring for an elderly mother at home. Carson was delighted to hear that the tall, handsome Stan was a self-taught photographer, with a particular passion for marine wildlife. But she was especially taken with Dorothy—not exactly beautiful, but magnetic in her animated yet unaffected demeanor and empathic warmth. Something wonderful entered Carson's life that evening—as wonderful yet imperceptible as the hairline crescent of the new moon rising over the dark horizon by the time Dorothy and Stan left late into the night. "I knew when first I saw you," Rachel would later tell Dorothy, "that I wanted to see much more of you—I loved you before you left Southport."

What Dorothy saw behind the persona of the famous author was a humble person with kind, pensive eyes, disoriented by her new celebrity, radiating a subtle but palpable air of melancholy uncapturable by any photograph. Perhaps she saw Carson the way Whitman saw Lincoln when the two men locked eyes in the streets of Washington one midsummer day ninety years earlier:

I see very plainly Abraham Lincoln's dark brown face, with the deep-cut lines, the eyes, always to me with a deep latent sadness in the expression. . . . None of the artists or pictures has caught the deep, though subtle and indirect expression of this man's face. There is something else there. One of the great portrait painters of two or three centuries ago is needed.

For Whitman, Lincoln belonged to the class of people whose human essence portraiture could never capture—people who, beyond categories of beauty, are animated by "superior points so subtle, yet so palpable, making the real life of their faces almost as impossible to depict as a wild perfume or fruit-taste, or a passionate tone of the living voice." Photography was still young then, but Whitman intuited its inescapable limitation—a limitation radiating from every photograph of Rachel Carson.

Dorothy and Stan, touched if bewildered by the warmly offered friendship of a national celebrity, made another visit before the season's end—an expedition to the tide pool below Carson's cottage, which Mrs. Carson and Marie Rodell joined. After the adventure in the cool September waters, they sat by the fireplace with a pot of tea and visited Carson's study. Through the microscope, Dorothy peered at the alien Braille of a starfish and into "a new world"—a world "wonderful, beautiful, and unbelievable." The night before the Freemans were about to leave Southport Island for the winter, Carson couldn't resist the impulse to see Dorothy one last time, and she walked through the woods to their house to seal the farewell with a kiss.

After they parted, Rachel and Dorothy entered into a correspondence that would soon become the emotional epicenter of each of their worlds, lasting for the remainder of Carson's life and engendering some of her most radiant writing. "Somehow," she would tell Dorothy, "the sharing of beautiful and lovely things is so much more satisfying with *you* than it has ever been for me with anyone else."

The rapid and uncommon intensity of affection that erupted

between the two women was fanned by the longing to spend more time in each other's physical presence—they estimated they had been together for a mere six and a half hours on the island, a fact that only amplified Dorothy's insecurity about the sudden blooming of such an intense attachment to a person so adored by millions. In a letter from early December, Carson addressed Dorothy's fears with a bold embrace of assurance, firm and forthright in her unquestioning ardor:

> As you must know in your heart, there is such a simple answer for all the "whys" that are sprinkled through your letters: As why do I keep your letters? Why did I come to the head that last night? Why? Because I love you! Now I could go on and tell you some of the reasons why I do, but that would take quite a while, and I think the simple fact covers everything.

The day before New Year's Eve 1953, Carson was invited to give a lecture on the impact of climate change on the oceans to the American Association for the Advancement of Science in Boston. The Freemans had returned to their winter home an hour south of the city, so Rachel and Dorothy deemed it a perfect opportunity to spend more time together. "Although I'd like nothing better than to step off the train into your arms (much, much better than a publisher's red carpet)," Carson wrote, "it would be foolish to plan it." She'd be too caught in the whirlwind of the daylong symposium and too nervous before her own talk. Instead, she suggested that Dorothy meet her at the hotel after the lecture, then they would drive together to the Freemans' home.

As Carson walked off the stage to a resounding ovation, she was stopped midstride by the sight of Dorothy standing quietly in the back of the lecture hall. With their eyes locked, Rachel approached her without a word, greeted her with an impulsive kiss, and whispered: "We didn't plan it this way, did we?"

They went back to Carson's hotel for an hour—two bodies in physical space, behind a closed door, behind the curtain of partial records we mistake for history. All that survives of their relation-ship are the letters they exchanged while they were apart. But what transpired while they were together? The words that flowed between them, the torrents of touch, the glances each containing a galaxy of feeling, a universe of sentiment—unrecorded, unrecordable.

On the drive to the Freemans' home, Rachel and Dorothy stopped at the edge of a pond to delight in the swimming ducks and to steal a few more moments alone as they tried to process the "elective affinity" that magnetized them to each other. Carson would later recount, half amused and half embarrassed, how she tried to "skirt around the edge of the subject" so tentatively that she supposed Dorothy didn't know what she meant. But Dorothy did know—with that feeling-knowledge that Carson herself would articulate in her posthumously published book on wonder, in which she asserted that "it is not half so important to *know* as to *feel*." That timid pondside taste of mutual discovery became the seed for what Doro-thy would soon call "the Revelation" as the two women finally put into words what they had not dared, or perhaps had not known how to, name. Several weeks later, Carson would write:

Yes, we were a little shy, weren't we, especially at first—but it was rather sweet that way and perhaps as it should have been for the first time you and I were together!

In the embering late afternoon light, they made their way from the pond to the Freemans' home. Rachel stayed the night. On the first day of 1954, after returning home to Silver Spring in Maryland, she addressed Dorothy as "my darling" for the first time and wrote:

Reality can so easily fall short of hopes and expectations especially where they have been high. I do hope that for you, as they truly are for me, the memories of Wednesday are completely unclouded by any sense of disappointment, or of hopes unrealized. And as for you, my dear one, there is not a single thing about you that I would change if I could!

Aglow with the "complete and overflowing happiness in the whole thing," Carson wrote out a Keats sonnet she felt captured "the feeling that exists" between them:

> A thing of beauty is a joy forever:
> Its loveliness increases; it will never
> Pass into nothingness; but still will keep
> A bower quiet for us, and a sleep
> Full of sweet dreams.

She added:

> I am certain, my dearest, that it will be forever a joy, of increasing loveliness with the years, and that in the intervals when being separated, we cannot have all the happiness of Wednesday, there will be, in each of our hearts, a little oasis of peace and "sweet dream" where the other is.
>   I can see your eyes this minute—bless your dear heart!

Carson would later refer to this milestone in their relationship as "the thirteen hours." This scientist who thought on the vast time scales of the universe and wrote of evolutionary eons measured out her private life in hours, acutely aware of just how rare and how precious love is, just how improbable for any two lives to intersect in a meaningful way in the blink of human existence.

Still Dorothy continued to struggle with the puzzling miracle of why Carson, a public figure idolized and beloved by millions, had chosen her alone as the object of such intimate trust. Carson facetiously encouraged Dorothy to think of her public persona as "the other woman," then offered serious and sensitive assurance:

> There is a "why" in a recent letter that you say not to answer; and I won't, except to say that everything is explained by the fact that you are you, and I can imagine no substitute for you in my life.

The dawn of every love seems haloed by the sense—the beautiful illusion—of fatedness, as the lovers discover in elated disbelief the staggering number of things they have had in common since long before they met: the favorite poem, the esoteric obsession, the freckle on the same spot of the same thigh. They seem to have lived two strands of the same life, long ago unwreathed by some cruel chance and only just now entwined into wholeness. They seem to be thinking the same thoughts. This sense pervaded Rachel and Dorothy's intensely deepening attachment. "Darling," Rachel wrote, "I wonder if I'll ever get used to the fact that you think my thoughts before I've expressed them?" They came to refer to the serendipities and astonishing coincidences twining their parallel lives as "stardust"—synchronicity, we would call it today, though both the term and the idea behind it were then practically unknown.

The concept of synchronicity is the product of a most improbable friendship—that between the psychiatrist Carl Jung and the physicist Wolfgang Pauli.

Long before he won the Nobel Prize in Physics for his exclusion principle—the tenet of quantum physics stating that multiple identical particles within a single quantum system cannot occupy the same quantum state at the same time—and around the time he theorized the neutrino, Pauli was thrust into existential tumult. His mother, to whom he was very close, died by suicide. His tempestuous marriage ended in divorce within a year—a year during which he drowned his unhappiness in alcohol. Caught in the web of drinking and despair, Pauli reached out to Jung for help.

Jung, already deeply influenced by Einstein's ideas about space and time, was intrigued by his brilliant and troubled correspondent. What began as an intense series of dream analyses unfolded, over the course of the remaining twenty-two years of Pauli's life, into an exploration of fundamental questions regarding the nature of reality through the dual lens of physics and psychology. Each used the tools of his expertise to shift the shoreline between the known and the unknown, and together they found common ground in the analogy between the atom, with its nucleus and orbiting electrons, and the self, with its central conscious ego and its ambient unconscious.

While there is a long and lamentable history of science—physics in particular—being hijacked for mystical and New Age ideologies, two things make Jung and Pauli's collaboration notable. First, the analogies between physics and alchemical symbolism were drawn not only by a serious scientist, but by one who would soon receive the Nobel Prize in Physics. Second, the warping of science into pseudoscience and mysticism tends to happen when scientific principles are transposed onto nonscientific domains with a false direct equivalence. Pauli, by contrast, was deliberate in staying at the level of analogy—that is, of conceptual parallels furnishing metaphors for abstract thought that can advance ideas in each of the two disciplines, but with very different concrete application. From this sandbox of physics and psychology emerged the birth of synchronicity—an ordering system for similarities and acausally connected events that the observer experiences as having a meaningful connection on the basis of his or her subjective situation, a meeting point of internal and external reality. The word first appeared in a 1948 letter from Pauli to Jung, referencing a conversation they'd had in person the day before. "Quite a while ago," Jung would later write to Pauli, "you encouraged me to write down my thoughts on synchronicity. . . . Nowadays, physicists are the only people who are paying serious attention to such ideas."

Pauli, who foresaw "a close fusion of psychology with the scientific experience of the processes in the material physical world," shared in Jung's enthusiasm for the cross-pollination of perspectives:

> In truth, nature is so fashioned that—analogous to Bohr's "complementarity" in physics—any contradiction between causality and synchronicity can never be ascertained. . . . How do the facts that make up modern quantum physics relate to those other phenomena explained by you with the aid of the new principle of synchronicity? First of all, what is certain is that both types of phenomenon go beyond the framework of "classical" determinism.

Jung had borrowed the word "archetype" from Kepler, drawing on the astronomer's alchemical symbolism. More than three centuries after Kepler's alchemy, Pauli's exclusion principle became the basic organizing principle for the periodic table. The alchemists had been right all along, in a way—they had just been working on the wrong scale: Only at the atomic level can one element become another, in radioactivity and nuclear fission. Even the atom itself had to transcend the problem of scale: The Greek philosopher Democritus theorized atoms in 400 BC, but he couldn't prove or disprove their existence empirically—a hundred thousand times smaller than anything the naked eye could see, the atom remained invisible. It wasn't for another twenty-three centuries that we were able to override the problem of scale by the prosthetic extension of our vision, the microscope.

What had originally attracted Pauli to the famous psychiatrist was Jung's work on symbols and archetypes—a Keplerian obsession that in turn obsessed Pauli, who devoted various essays and lectures to how Kepler's alchemy and archetypal ideas influenced the visionary astronomer's science. In physics, he saw numerous analogies to alchemy: In symmetry, he found the archetypal structure of matter and in elementary particles, the substratum of reality that the alchemists had sought; in the spectrograph, which allowed scientists for the first time to study the chemical composition of stars, an analogue of the alchemist's oven; in probability, which he defined as "the actual correspondence between the expected result . . . and the empirically measured frequencies," the mathematical analogue of archetypal numerology.

But Pauli recognized that the dawn of quantum physics, in which he himself was a leading sun, introduced a new necessity to reconcile different facets of reality. In one of his Kepler lectures, he reflected:

> It would be most satisfactory of all if physics and psyche could be seen as complementary aspects of the same reality. To us [modern scientists], unlike Kepler and Fludd, the only acceptable point of view appears to be one that recognizes *both* sides of reality—the quantitative and the qualitative, the physical and the psychical—as compatible with each other, and can embrace them simultaneously.
> [. . .]
> In my own view it is only a *narrow* passage of truth (no matter

whether scientific or other truth) that passes between the Scylla of a blue fog of mysticism and the Charybdis of a sterile rationalism. This will always be full of pitfalls and one can fall down on both sides.

Four decades before the revered physicist John Archibald Wheeler, who popularized the term *black hole*, made his influential assertion that "this is a participatory universe [and] observer-participancy gives rise to information," Pauli wrote to Jung:

Modern microphysics turns the observer once again into a little lord of creation in his microcosm, with the ability (at least partially) of freedom of choice and fundamentally uncontrollable effects on that which is being observed. But if these phenomena are dependent on how (with what experimental system) they are observed, then is it not possible that they are also phenomena (extra corpus) that depend on who observes them (i.e., on the nature of the psyche of the observer)? And if natural science, in pursuit of the ideal of determinism since Newton, has finally arrived at the stage of the fundamental "perhaps" of the statistical character of natural laws . . . then should there not be enough room for all those oddities that ultimately rob the distinction between "physics" and "psyche" of all its meaning?

And yet Pauli was careful to recognize that "although microphysics allows for an acausal form of observation, it actually has no use for the concept of 'meaning'"—that is, meaning is not a fundamental function of reality but an interpretation superimposed by the human observer. Synchronicity, which Pauli preferred to call "meaning-correspondence," is a heightened manifestation of that human interpretation.

Jung delivered the first public lecture on synchronicity in the year *The Sea Around Us* was published—the book that drew Dorothy Freeman into Rachel Carson's life. But even as the two women marveled at all the "stardust" stippling the ether in which the orbits of their lives had so improbably and so meaningfully intersected, Dorothy, bestirred by this "overpowering emotional experience," continued to suffer over the half-spoken *why* and to worry that the attention Carson showered upon her was detracting from the famous author's literary work.

One winter night after the "thirteen hours," Carson gave a long, beautiful answer by way of a parable: A destitute man who had only two pennies spent one on bread and the other on "a white hyacinth for his soul"—the flower to which Kepler had likened his precious boy taken by smallpox. Carson's writing career was her bread, after a lifelong struggle to put food on the table, but Dorothy was her white hyacinth. Their love provided a sustenance of the spirit at least as vital as the sustenance of the body. Rachel assured Dorothy that she loved her not for any particular quality or particular service she was performing in her life, but for the very essence of her soul.

Rachel and Dorothy would go on to celebrate the date of the letter, February 6, as a special anniversary. But besides the deep personal revelation, the "hyacinth letter," as they came to call it, also contains the most direct statement Carson would ever make about the loneliness of the creative life:

I don't suppose anyone really knows how a creative writer works (he or she least of all, perhaps!) or what sort of nourishment his spirit must have. All I am certain of is this; that it is quite necessary for me to know that there is someone who is deeply devoted to me as a person, and who also has the capacity and the depth of understanding to share, vicariously, the sometimes crushing burden of creative effort, recognizing the heartache, the great weariness of mind and body, the occasional black despair it may involve—someone who cherishes me and what I am trying to create. . . . The few who understood the creative problem were not people to whom I felt emotionally close; those who loved the non-writer part of me did not, by some strange paradox, understand the writer at all! And then, my dear one, you came into my life! . . . I knew when I first saw you that I wanted to see much more of you—I loved you before you left Southport—and very early in our correspondence last fall I began to sense that capacity to enter so fully into the intellectual and creative parts of my life as well as to be a dearly loved friend. And day by day all that I sensed in you has been fulfilled, but even more wonderfully than I could have dreamed. . . .

I feel such a joyous surge of wonder every time I stop to think how in such a dark time and when I least expected it, something so lovely and richly satisfying came into my life.

She then inverts the equation and, in a touching testament to the insecurity that throbs in the underbelly of all love, wonders what she could possibly be giving Dorothy, unlonely in her happily companionable marriage:

Of course—there is another side to all this. I know so well what this experience means to me—but I can't see that *I* can possibly be giving *you* anything comparable in return! But darling—before you begin to protest—let me say that I, unlike you, simply accept the fact that evidently—in a way I don't understand—I have filled some need in your life. What it is doesn't matter—unless or until you want to tell me. Perhaps you don't even know. That part isn't important—I'm just deeply grateful that I can mean so much to you.

A week later, on the eve of Valentine's Day, Carson revisits the subject and contemplates the self-expanding nature of love, so counter to the asphyxiating belief that it is a finite resource, that loving one person is invariably at the expense of loving another—a belief upon which the contractual monogamy of marriage is founded. She writes:

My darling. . . . One of the things about you that impressed me from the beginning was the lovely quality of your family life. . . . No one could be with you and Stan even a short time without realizing how devoted and congenial you are. And I wonder whether the very fact that you have experienced, and have yourself poured out, so much love, has not made you all the more receptive to the devotion offered by this newcomer in your life. You wrote so beautifully, weeks ago, of how one's capacity to give love grows with the exercise of it, so perhaps the more love we have received, the more we are able to absorb and in that sense no one ever has enough. And I do know that the facts that we are, to an incredible degree "kindred spirits," and that for many reasons we need all that we mean to each other, probably lie at the heart of our love. But the more I think about all we both have said, the more I feel that there is also something that perhaps will always remain elusive and intangible—that the whole is something more than the sum of the various "reasons."

Carson quotes from Henry Beston's review of *Under the Sea-Wind*, which had so touched her—"the sun is always more than a gigantic mass of ions, it is a splendor and a mystery"—then adds:

> Our analysis [of our love] has been beautiful and comforting and satisfying, but probably it will never be quite complete—never encompass the whole "splendor and mystery."

That May, Rachel and Dorothy spent five nights together at Carson's cottage, reading E. B. White to each other—his *Charlotte's Web* had been published the same year as *The Sea Around Us*—and talking by the fireplace into the morning hours, suspended in the peculiar state of timelessness that creative work and love share. There was something pleasantly insaning about the inarticulable nature of their bond—something that made them feel further bonded by being, as Carson put it, "both 'crazy' in the same way, and at the same time." "After all," she told Dorothy, "our brand of 'craziness' would be a little hard for anyone but us to understand." Theirs was the kind of "craziness" that comes from veering from the convention-paved path into that liminal Uranian space where love exists beyond category, beyond the cultural and biological imperative, beyond what even the most precise and poetic language can hold.

Letters continued to stream between their two homes—usually handwritten on elegant stationery, very rarely typed, occasionally bursting with the surprise of a carefully pressed flower. Aware of the astonishing volume of letters and of the swelling intensity of sentiment they contained, Rachel and Dorothy deemed it best to separate each round of correspondence into two parts—one letter intended to be read by anyone in the household, comprising personal news and general discussions of literature, nature, and their other shared interests; then, folded inside it, a private letter in which their uncontainable effusions could have free rein—letters "about Us." They came to call these letters "apples"—a term laced

with equal parts natural sweetness and biblical sinfulness, reflective of the ambivalence they felt about a love they knew not how
to explain or classify. (A century earlier, the Puritanically prudish
Emerson had considered apples his one guilty pleasure and great
moral weakness.) Dorothy and Rachel's "apples" were kept in the
"strongbox"—the stash of correspondence closely guarded from all
household members and intended eventually to be burned, though
Carson would never do so, perhaps regarding them, as Mabel had
regarded the love letters from Austin she couldn't bring herself to
destroy, as "holy."

Despite the escalating intimacy of the private letters, Dorothy
wished to keep nothing from Stan and took the risk of reading him
excerpts from one of the "apples." He met the revelation only with
gladness, which a relieved and half-apologetic Dorothy reported to
Rachel. Carson, for her part, responded with assurance—not only
did she not mind that Dorothy had shared the letter, but was happy
that she had done so and heartened by Stan's response. "Perhaps
this is the little final touch of the perfection in the whole episode,"
she wrote, then further reassured Dorothy:

> It means so very much to me to know that you have such an under-
> standing husband. And darling . . . I was so glad you read him the
> letter—or parts of it. I *want* him to know what you mean to me.

Stan seemed to have understood that he wasn't being thrust into
a losing equivalence—that Dorothy's love for Rachel was not competitive with her love for him but belonged in a class of its own, the
discovery of which had expanded her very being. A new vista of the
heart had opened up for the woman he loved and he could only be
glad of it.

In a most extraordinary letter penned two years into the relationship, Dorothy would articulate with immense depth of emotion the
significance of her marriage, and Stan and Rachel's complementary
roles in her world. Writing in an April downpour at dusk, as an
invisible bird is singing in the tree outside her window "plaintive
and poignant like a canary full of sadness," Dorothy tells Rachel:

This is an experiment. I have just lived through an hour of suspension in time that I would like to express. Perhaps you will understand—perhaps you won't—why I am writing it to you. I feel the need to put it on paper—somehow if I say it to you, I may come more nearly to saying what I want to say than if I make a simple record for myself. I am shut away in the back bedroom in the corner that belongs in my heart only to you—you know where and why.

Dorothy had gone upstairs to take a nap, but had found herself gnawed by guilt—for having left her widowed elderly mother alone on her fifty-ninth wedding anniversary the previous night, and most of all for having been cross with Stan that morning, his feelings visibly hurt. She had "asked his forgiveness in his arms" and he had granted it, but she hadn't forgiven herself. And now she was burrowed in the bedroom with a philosophy-laced adventure novel exploring "human destiny" and presenting "a mysterious study of personality." An enchanting, unfamiliar symphony came pouring in from the radio. (Carson must have been listening to the radio at the same time—there were only so few stations then, and of them only one was playing the Philharmonic at that particular hour—for in the margin of Dorothy's letter, in Rachel's hand, the piece is identified as Mahler's Symphony no. 3 in D Minor.) Dorothy writes:

Suddenly, at one of the most dramatic moments in the book before its climax—the music overpowered me so that I had to stop reading. Floods of tears just streamed from my eyes. The music had been subdued and at times a rich human voice had become part of it. At the time it reached me it was carrying an exquisite melody in the high strings with dark shadings in the lower strings. It seemed to complement the book completely. Then I began to think of Stan asleep in the other room and suddenly underneath the lovely melody was a pattern of discord in the brasses, incongruous and intruding—almost a warning to me it seemed. And then I knew that I've got to tell Stan how wonderful has been my life with him, how good he has been to me, how rich our life together has been. He's made me so happy—given me so much. I feel I have in no way repaid him for his years of devotion. Of course, I know I am thinking deep inside me, "What if I should lose him?" And so to-night I'm going to try to put into words all this that I feel. It will be good to do for there is never enough expression, in words[,] of one's gratitude, is there?

But the very thing that had unlatched in Dorothy this consecrating recognition of her love for Stan sprang from the dimension of her being to which Rachel alone had access:

I know most of what has affected me this afternoon is the book—I have marked so many passages for Us for there is no one else who could share this with me but you.
   Perhaps back to reality—or is it illusion?—I shall not be so moved and when I read it to you I may wonder why all this.
   But as I said at the beginning I have been suspended in Time.

Dorothy shared with Rachel a radiant reality that was theirs alone:

Darling, you and I on our Island are looking at a light so bright— invisible to others—a glorious, miraculous light that has brought to me and I hope and believe to you, untold happiness.

In the spring following the "hyacinth letter," Carson commenced a tradition of wearing a flower corsage from Dorothy whenever she gave a public talk. She often illustrated her lectures with Stan's photographs—the Freemans had been accompanying Carson on many of her specimen-collecting expeditions as she worked on her new seashore book. (Encouraged by Stan's offer to teach her underwater photography, Carson treated herself to a 35mm Exakta camera—a fossil of human ingenuity, which in the geologic blink of a hundred years had leapt from the ephemeral lattice of light and shadow captured in Talbot's rickety "mousetrap" to a small portable device capable of bringing the ocean onto land.)
   Increasingly selective in the invitations she accepted, Carson chose not by pay or prestige but by values—from the annual Audubon Society gathering, an epicenter of the naturalist world, to a small local fund-raiser for transforming an old jail into a children's museum. On the eve of the date that sixteen years later would become Earth Day—the annual celebration of environmental

responsibility inspired by Carson's legacy—she gave a talk before a meeting of women journalists, which encapsulated her guiding ethos so succinctly that it was posthumously published under the heading "A Statement of Belief." Carson told the thousand women gathered in the Ohio auditorium:

> I am not afraid of being thought a sentimentalist when I say that I believe natural beauty has a necessary place in the spiritual development of any individual or any society. I believe that whenever we destroy beauty, or whenever we substitute something man-made and artificial for a natural feature of the earth, we have retarded some part of man's spiritual growth.

One bright May morning shortly after the talk, Carson made her first visit to the home of Henry Beston. She had been so nervous in approaching her literary idol that she had waited two years before writing to tell him just how much his generous review of her first book had meant to her. Beston responded immediately with an invitation to his farmhouse in Maine. Meeting her hero would be a life event so monumental for Carson that she wanted to share it—as she wanted to share everything—with Dorothy. They drove to Maine together, accompanied by the birdsong orchestra of spring cusping on summer. After they left, Beston's wife surprised Carson with the revelation that Henry had been "deeply pleased and touched" by her letter. What tonic of gladness, what validating sweetness must have invaded Carson's being as she read Mrs. Beston's words: "I think there is no one in the world whose praise he values more."

I wonder if Carson pinned the letter above her desk, beneath the bookshelf where Beston's *Outermost House* was enshrined, to steady herself as she spiraled further and further into self-doubt. The new seashore book on which she had been working for more than two years, already far behind her original contract with Houghton Mifflin, had become a maddening struggle. Carson had always considered herself a slow writer and a meticulous reviser, but now she was slogging along so painfully that she joked she might make better progress if she began each page of the book with "Dear Dorothy." She confided in her beloved that she feared whatever she wrote next might not rise to the impossible bar set by the success of *The Sea Around Us*. From that lonely and vulnerable place that only artists know, she told Dorothy:

> The heart of it is something very complex, that has to do with ideas of destiny, and with an almost inexpressible feeling that I am merely the instrument through which something has happened—that I've had little to do with it myself. . . . As for the loneliness—you can never fully know how much your love and companionship has eased that.

Carson had always loved the opening lines of William Blake's poem "Auguries of Innocence":

> To see a World in a Grain of Sand
> And a Heaven in a Wild Flower
> Hold Infinity in the palm of your hand
> And Eternity in an hour.

This, perhaps, is why the first chapter she completed was on sand, in which she saw a miraculous reminder of "the unhurried deliberation of earth processes that move with infinite leisure, with all eternity at their disposal."

When Marie Rodell submitted the chapter to *The New Yorker*, William Shawn telephoned with an immediate offer not only for the chapter but for serial rights to the entire book. "She's done it again," the editor exclaimed to Rodell. Elated by the news, Carson mailed Dorothy a special gift to thank her for the love that had buoyed her through the storm of self-doubt—inscribed first editions of *Under the Sea-Wind* and *The Sea Around Us*, each accompanied by a brief "apple." After telling Dorothy the story of the Tennyson line that had sent her to the sea, Carson wrote:

> And so, as you know it has been. When finally I became its biographer, the sea brought me recognition and what the world calls success. It brought me to Southport. It gave me You.
> So now the sea means something to me that it never meant before. And even the title of the book has a new and personal

significance—the sea around Us. Keep this for me, dear, and understand all it means.

My deep love—Rachel

In March 1955, Carson finally sent the near-complete manuscript
of the new book to Paul Brooks, her patient editor at Houghton
Mifflin, who told her that this was some of her finest writing, with
many passages "superior to anything in *The Sea Around Us*."

When *The Edge of the Sea* was published in October, the dedication printed on the page following the table of contents read:

To Dorothy and Stanley Freeman
who have gone down with me into the low-tide world
and have felt its beauty and its mystery.

How many books have been composed—are being composed—as
love letters to someone's Dorothy?

Carson had a symphonic way of writing about the interdependence of every note of nature—a way greatly informed by her deep
relationship with music, which she believed only Dorothy fully
understood. Beethoven, Bach, Mendelssohn, Mahler, and Tchaikovsky percuss their letters, and many of the precious hours they
spent together in physical space were scored by the concertos, sona-
tas, and symphonies they both cherished. They came to consider
Tchaikovsky's Symphony no. 6—which he had titled "The Passionate Symphony"—their own. The spring after *The Edge of the Sea*
was published, Carson bought tickets for them to hear Leonard
Bernstein conduct Tchaikovsky with the New York Philharmonic.
"The combination of Bernstein and Our Symphony seems too wonderful to miss," she wrote to Dorothy. This shared passion was
central to Carson's sense of being so singularly seen and understood by her beloved, as a creator and a complete human being of
which music was an indelible part. She shared Margaret Fuller's
conviction that "the thought of the law that supersedes all thoughts,
which pierces us the moment we have gone far in any department
of knowledge or creative genius, seizes and lifts us from the ground
in music."

In one letter, penned during a frustrating period of work on an anthology of nature writing Carson had agreed to edit, she sent Dorothy an "apple" containing a sublime account of creative break-through under Beethoven's benediction. More than a century after Fuller celebrated music for "the stimulus and the upbearing elastic-ity it offers for the inspirations of thought," Carson recounted:

> Listening to Beethoven, the mood became, I suppose, more cre-ative, and rather suddenly I understood what the anthology should be—the story it should tell—the deep significance it might have. I suppose I can never explain it in words, but I think you understand without words. It was a mood of tremendous exaltation, I wept. I paced the floor. And I wanted to have you beside me so badly it tore me to pieces! There now, darling—this is for us alone, for I am still shy about revealing such moods to the World. But only when I have felt myself so deeply moved, so possessed by something outside myself, can I feel that inner confidence that what I am doing is right.

Again and again she would turn to Beethoven when stymied by writer's block. In another letter to Dorothy, Carson relays the moment of creative breakthrough in a passage that she would later rework into one of her most beautiful essays:

> All the bits and pieces were there waiting for the central, unifying idea. If I'm satisfied with this now, it's at least partly due to an evening of Beethoven last night, when, in the study, I played his 6th, 7th and 9th symphonies and the violin concerto. Some little bit of his marvel-ous creativeness seems to seep through into my brain cells when I lis-ten to him—or perhaps I should say into my emotions. Will you listen to the very first few bars of the 9th and see if the chills run up your spine as they do mine? To me it is the perfect expression, in music, of my first morning at Ocean Point, where there was nothing but fog and rocks and sea, and the time might well have been Paleozoic.

She told Dorothy that she was hoping to imbue her own writing with this feeling.

Several weeks after *The Edge of the Sea* was released to an expectant choir of acclaim, *Woman's Home Companion* published

Rachel Carson's most personal piece of public writing. Under the title "Help Your Child to Wonder," she invited parents to preserve the curiosity about nature, the sweet veneration of it, that inheres in every human being, blunted as we grow up under the forces of so-called civilization. Carson drew on her own experience with her beloved grandnephew Roger, who had been visiting her since he was a toddler and had accompanied her and the Freemans on many a joyful excursion into the barnacled tide pools of the seashore she studied and revered. Recounting a clear moonless night she had shared with Dorothy one summer on the Seaport Island headland—a place where "the horizons are remote and distant rims on the edge of space"—she wrote:

> We lay and looked up at the sky and the millions of stars that blazed in the darkness. The night was so still that we could hear the buoy on the ledges out beyond the mouth of the bay. Once or twice a word spoken by someone on the far shore was carried across on the clear air. A few lights burned in cottages. Otherwise there was no reminder of other human life; my companion and I were alone with the stars. I have never seen them more beautiful: the misty river of the Milky Way flowing across the sky, the patterns of the constellations standing out bright and clear, a blazing planet low on the horizon. Once or twice a meteor burned its way into the earth's atmosphere.
>
> It occurred to me that if this were a sight that could only be seen once in a century or even once in a human generation, this little headland would be thronged with spectators.

Shortly after the publication of the piece, Roger's single mother—Carson's orphaned niece Marjorie, who had grown up under her roof—died from complications of the chronic diabetes and severe arthritis that ran in the family. Amid the shock of another loss, Carson, about to turn fifty, adopted Roger. She was to mother a young child while mothering her own mother. Maria Carson was fading in her late eighties, yet refusing help from anyone but her daughter—stubbornness that had precluded Carson from hiring full-time household help, so that she now contained the multitudes of scientist, author, lover, mother, caretaker, and housekeeper.

. . .

All the public saw was the famous author who had once again triumphed at the intersection of poetry and science. As *The Edge of the Sea* alighted in the world, critical praise and honors came cascading, trailed by invitations for lectures and acceptance speeches. Carson became even more selective, prioritizing women's associations and nonprofit cultural institutions over glamorous commercial stages. When she did speak, her words became almost a consecration, as in a speech she delivered before a convocation of librarians:

> When we go down to the lowest of the low tide lines and look down into the shallow waters, there's all the excitement of discovering a new world. Once you have entered such a world, its fascination grows and somehow you find your mind has gained a new dimension, a new perspective—and always thereafter you find yourself remember[ing] the beauty and strangeness and wonder of that world—a world that is as real, as much a part of the universe, as our own.

Addressing the National Council of Women, which had given *The Edge of the Sea* its annual book award, Carson prefigured the new dimension her own mind was about to gain—a dimension that would establish her legacy and reorient the whole of culture:

> Any literature that is worthy of the name is the result and expression of a free and fearless pursuit of truth. The writer makes himself a sensitive instrument of impressions of the world within himself and about him. In proportion to the greatness of his art, we are informed and enriched, and the world as a whole advances toward light, out of darkness. For only as truth is substituted for the shadows of doubt and fear and distrust that now impel man to turn against himself— only as truth is discovered and expressed—can we be truly free.

Carson was growing more and more bestirred by the darker truths of humanity's relationship with nature—truths increasingly silenced by the political and economic forces she watched govern a tractable society into willful deafness. Since her formative years, she had only wished to be a writer and a scientist, but now a new sense of political responsibility was waking in her. Like Maria Mitchell, who a century earlier had gradually outgrown her reservations about being a "platform woman" and had stood up for the causes she saw as essential to the world she wanted to live in, Carson realized that it is impossible to care deeply about any slice of the universe, as every scientist must in order to study it rigorously, without standing for the whole by defending any part under assault. Upon resigning from the Fish and Wildlife Service four years earlier, she had cited the need for devoting her time to writing. This was undoubtedly a major reason—but it was not her only reason. As a government employee, Carson had to contain her public stance on political matters within narrow limits—limits that soon ceased to contain her growing alarm over the government's increasingly reckless policies regarding nature.

Carson resigned as the conclusion of the heated 1952 election season loomed with alarming inevitability. Its result ended the Democrats' two-decade reign of the White House. When Eisenhower took office, the Republican administration swiftly began instituting policies that effected the destruction of nature, casting it as a commodity of industry. The Fish and Wildlife Service—the sole government agency responsible for the protection and preservation the natural world—was atop their target list. After appointing a businessman as secretary of the interior, the Republican government removed the longtime director of the Fish and Wildlife Service, Albert M. Day—a trained field scientist and a passionate, visionary conservationist whom Carson considered a kindred spirit and mentor—and replaced him with a nonscientist political pawn who would sign off on removing hard-won environmental protections in order to turn nature into "natural resources"—a euphemism for profitable commodities.

Carson believed that such exploitation of nature for ruthless commercial and political gain "should be deeply disturbing to every thoughtful citizen." In August 1953—the summer she met Dorothy—she poured her sobering rhetoric into a letter to the editor of *The Washington Post*. Since Carson was already the most esteemed science writer in the country, it was picked up by the wire of the Associated Press, syndicated widely, and reprinted in *Reader's Digest*—the era's equivalent of going viral. Carson's voice was a clarion call to resistance:

> The real wealth of the Nation lies in the resources of the earth—soil, water, forests, minerals, and wildlife. To utilize them for present needs while insuring their preservation for future generations requires a delicately balanced and continuing program, based on the most extensive research. Their administration is not properly, and cannot be, a matter of politics.

The agencies responsible for those resources, she argued, should be governed by people with the proper expertise and experience to understand and heed the findings of the scientists in their charge. Her words of admonition reverberate with ominous prescience across the decades between her time and ours:

> For many years public-spirited citizens throughout the country have been working for the conservation of the natural resources, realizing their vital importance to the Nation. Apparently their hard-won progress is to be wiped out, as a politically minded Administration returns us to the dark ages of unrestrained exploitation and destruction.

A century after Walt Whitman remarked that "America, if eligible at all to downfall and ruin, is eligible within herself, not without," Carson ended her letter with a kindred sentiment:

> It is one of the ironies of our time that, while concentrating on the defense of our country against enemies from without, we should be so heedless of those who would destroy it from within.

Several months after the publication of *The Edge of the Sea*, a book in which Carson had noted the systematically documented and "well recognized" fact of global climate change, this seething cauldron of environmental concern came to a boiling point and became the subject of her next and final book—the masterwork that would ignite the modern environmental movement.

Ever since *Reader's Digest* had rejected her DDT story idea more than a decade earlier, Carson had remained alert to the dangers of chemical poisons and the increasing recklessness of pesticide spraying for so-called pest control. She keenly followed scientific studies on the effects of pesticides on wildlife and clipped all newspaper articles she could find on the subject, which came in growing numbers as more and more communities around the country reported the mass deaths of birds, fish, frogs, small mammals, cattle, horses, and household pets following pesticide spraying. Scientists found that even earthworms—the creatures Dickinson had eulogized as "our little kinsmen" and Darwin had celebrated in his final book as having plowed and created the earth as we know it, without whose work agriculture "would be very difficult, if not wholly impossible"—were dying by the legion from pesticide poisoning. The mere 20 percent that survived carried the chemical in their bodies and transmitted it to the birds who ate them, poisoning them in turn. The human animal, too, was far from safe. Reports of horrifying cases were piling up: the thirty-eight-year-old illiterate farmer who, not realizing the chemical with which he sprayed his tobacco crop was toxic, let himself get soaked with it and was dead within fifteen hours; the young entomologist studying pesticides at a university who neglected to put on his protective mask one morning, grew nauseous at the lab by the afternoon, and died at home by evening; the ten-year-old who found a bottle in the woods and drank from it, not knowing it was filled with tetraethyl pyrophosphate—an insecticide developed in the late 1940s and hailed by newspapers as "the answer to the 17-year locust plague" afflicting the Midwest; the child foamed at the mouth and was dead within fifteen minutes. Such cases were far from isolated horror stories—in California alone, state records reported more than a thousand human poisonings by pesticide per year.

The chemical most widely used for pest control was DDT—dichloro-diphenyl-trichloroethane, for the insect control application of which the Swiss chemist Paul Müller had received the

Nobel Prize a decade earlier. The use of DDT had accelerated during World War II, when showers of it further dehumanized Jewish refugees thought to be carrying lice. In 1943, the U.S. Army doused more than a million civilians with DDT in an effort to contain a typhus epidemic in Naples. Although other factors may well have led to the successful curtailment of the outbreak, DDT took on the sheen of a silver bullet against insect-borne diseases and was soon applied as liberally as mercury had been prescribed a century earlier, its side effects just as untested and its long-term consequences as unconsidered.

In 1957, aware of Carson's longtime disquiet about pesticides, Marie Rodell alerted her to a case in Long Island, where fourteen citizens were taking the federal government to court in an effort to save their land from being sprayed against gypsy moths, citing growing concern over the environmental hazards of DDT and lack of evidence that gypsy moths were problematic in the area in the first place.

The trial was organized by a local poet and farmer named Marjorie Spock. At eighteen, Marjorie—the younger sister of the pediatrician Benjamin Spock—had rebelled against her family's pressure toward a traditional life by moving to Switzerland to study biodynamic agriculture—the term "organic" as related to produce wouldn't come into popular use for another decade—with the Austrian philosopher and social reformer Rudolf Steiner. There she met and fell in love with another student of Steiner's—Mary Richards, who went by the nickname Polly. Disabled by a lifelong digestive disorder, most likely to have been celiac disease, Polly could consume only the purest food. When the couple moved back to America in their twenties, they settled not far from Whitman's hometown in Long Island and sustained themselves with modest organic farming— a lovely vegetable garden and a couple of dairy cows.

In the summer of 1957, government airplanes began raining DDT mixed with fuel oil on Marjorie and Polly's little farm as frequently as every two hours, supplanting "the delicate and wild odor of the woods" Whitman had once celebrated in the Long Island air with the miasma of chemicals and jet fuel. Appalled at this toxic violation of their civil liberty and afraid for their very lives, the couple saw no choice but to sue for an injunction. Spock hired a skilled legal team and recruited other residents of the pesticide-barraged area, including J. P. Morgan's daughter, Theodore Roosevelt's son, and Robert Cushman Murphy, the prominent naturalist and former curator of birds for the American Museum of Natural History.

After twenty-two weeks in court, an Eisenhower-appointed judge refused to allow seventy-five uncontested findings of scientific fact in evidence and denied the citizens' appeal. The defeat ultimately cost Spock and Richards $100,000, but their case established a model for citizen resistance against the government's assault on nature.

Carson, having followed the proceedings, was galled by the verdict, her alarm further amplified when she learned that *Reader's Digest*, which had rejected her DDT exposé thirteen years earlier, was planning an article in favor of pesticide spraying. She asked Rodell to put her in contact with Spock, who was thrilled by Carson's interest in the case. She then began calling government offices tasked with studying the effects of aerial spraying on wildlife, reaching as high as the U.S. Congress in the hope of finding an official willing to talk to her.

A Deep Throat of sorts finally emerged from the Food and Drug Administration and whispered to her the rumor, which the agency was still investigating, that a major baby food manufacturer had ceased using a particular vegetable owing to pesticide contamination. As she gathered evidence, Carson wrote to the editor of *Reader's Digest* to admonish him against "the enormous danger—both to wildlife and, more frighteningly, to public health—in these rapidly growing projects for insect control by poisons, especially as widely and randomly distributed by airplanes." Once again, her admonition fell on deaf ears.

In January 1958, the *Boston Herald* published a spirited letter by a friend of Spock's from New Hampshire, herself an organic gardener and naturalist, reporting the decimation of wildlife by pesticide spraying, cautioning against the potential deadly consequences to humans, and inciting citizens to take a stand against this "mass poisoning." The paper published several responses, including one from a man involved in the spraying program who declared pesticides "entirely harmless" and dismissed the woman's letter as "hysterical."

Olga Owens Huckins, former literary editor of the *Boston Post*, sent the editor of the *Boston Herald* a searing account of the gruesome deaths that birds in the sanctuary behind her home had died the previous summer after a mosquito control airplane had rained poison over their small shoreside town:

> The "harmless" shower bath killed seven of our lovely songbirds outright. We picked up three dead bodies the next morning right by the door. They were birds that had lived close to us, trusted us, and built their nests in our trees year after year. The next day three were scattered around the bird bath. (I had emptied it and scrubbed it after the spraying but YOU CAN NEVER KILL DDT.) On the following day one robin dropped suddenly from a branch in our woods. We were too heartsick to hunt for other corpses. All of these birds died horribly, and in the same way. Their bills were gaping open, and their splayed claws were drawn up to their breasts in agony.

Addressing the argument that DDT is the lesser evil in the war on mosquitoes, Huckins noted that the spraying had actually produced pesticide-resistant mosquitoes far more vicious than those of previous seasons and insisted that the solution to the problem was not to double the strength of the poisons but to stop spraying altogether until there was sufficient evidence, "biological and scientific, immediate and long run, of the effects upon wild life and human beings."

Huckins sent a copy of her letter to Carson—they had been epistolary friends ever since Carson had written to thank her for a beautiful review of *The Sea Around Us* seven years earlier. She begged Carson to help her find someone in Washington who might be able to help. In the course of sourcing that someone for her friend, Carson would later recall, she began seriously considering a book on the subject.

Shortly after receiving Huckins's letter, Carson reached out to E. B. White, whose lyrical nature essays she and Dorothy had read aloud to each other in their private hours but who also wielded the light-saber of his radiant mind with merciless might at what he saw as morally troublesome. In his *New Yorker* editorials, the beloved author of *Charlotte's Web* and *Stuart Little* had been among the first to caution against the dangers of humanity's arrogant misuses of science against nature. Two years earlier, he had admonished:

> I think man's gradual, creeping contamination of the planet, his sending up of dust into the air, his strontium additive in our bones, his discharge of industrial poisons into rivers that once flowed clear, his mixing of chemicals with fog on the east wind add up to a fantasy of such grotesque proportions as to make everything said on the subject seem pale and anemic by contrast. . . . I belong to a small, unconventional school that believes . . . that *no* chemical waste is the correct amount to discharge into the fresh rivers of the world.

Carson alerted White to the Long Island case, telling Dorothy it was just "the sort of thing he could be devastating about if he chose"— a corrective devastation she hoped to see on the pages of the country's most influential magazine.

White responded right away. Pesticides, he told Carson, were but one part of the vast problem of pollution, which ought to be "of the utmost interest and concern" to every wakeful citizen. "It starts in the kitchen and extends to Jupiter and Mars," he observed with prescience apprehended only in hindsight. But White, who professed not to know "a chlorinated hydrocarbon from a squash bug," thought Carson far more scientifically qualified for the task and intimated that she should cover it for *The New Yorker* herself.

But Carson had reached out to White because, despite her unwavering moral conviction about the cause, she was simply too threadbare to take on the task. She was consumed with the care of her eighty-five-year-old mother. She was learning to mother her new six-year-old son. She was gnawed by guilt over a contract she had signed four years earlier with Harper & Brothers for a book on the origins of life for a new series titled *World Perspectives*—envisioned by the philosopher Ruth Nanda Anshen, it was to feature books by the world's great "spiritual and intellectual leaders who possess full consciousness of the pressing problems of our time with all their implications," with a board of editors including Niels Bohr and Robert Oppenheimer. Carson would never complete this book on evolution, as she was increasingly unsettled by the hazards of DDT, the arrogant destruction of nature, and the hijacking of science as an instrument of political and military power.

Carson confided in Dorothy that this problem had rendered her "mentally blocked for a long time" as she struggled to figure out how to celebrate life in an authentic way against the dark backdrop of its destruction—a disconnect that troubled her more and more as she witnessed the advent and subsequent misuse of atomic science. She wrote:

> Some of the thoughts that came were so unattractive to me that I rejected them completely, for the old ideas die hard, especially when they are emotionally as well as intellectually dear to one. It was pleasant to believe, for example, that much of Nature was forever beyond the tampering reach of man.

Carson had witnessed the terrible aftermath of the atomic bomb, which had decimated not only innumerable human lives but entire ecosystems. The detonation in Japan immediately killed every living thing within a seven-kilometer radius and melted the serene stone countenance of every Buddha at the local temples. Radioactive fallout tainted the oceans and the skies, permeating the soil in which plants grew, invading the cells of the animals that subsisted on them, and lodging itself in the very body of nature.

It had all begun one November day twenty years earlier, not with the impulse for destruction but with the purest impulse of science— that hungry fusion of wonder and curiosity with which we seek to understand the universe. It had begun, of course, long before that, for every beginning is an arbitrary point stabbed into the continuum that binds all events and all ages.

26

BETWEEN THE SCALE OF ATOMS
AND THE SCALE OF WORLDS

On a bright July morning in 1901, at a plaza named for Beethoven in Vienna's old city, a pale young woman presents herself at a distinguished boys' school, elated exhaustion encircling her large dark eyes. At twenty-three, she is about to take the Matura—an examination boys must pass before being admitted to a university; boys, because until this summer, Austrian universities have been closed to women. But Lise Meitner is ready. It has been nine years since the end of the only formal education available to her. She has labored tirelessly, compressing eight years' worth of mathematics, logic, literature, Greek, Latin, zoology, botany, and physics into twenty months in preparation for the Matura now that she is finally permitted to take it.

Meitner aced the exam and went on to study at the University of Vienna with the physicist and philosopher Ludwig Boltzmann, whose visionary statistical mathematics furnished the first predictive model of how the properties of atoms shape the properties of matter. Months after Boltzmann's death, Meitner received her Ph.D., becoming one of the first women in the world with a doctorate in physics.

Despite her credentials, the only job offer she received was from a gas lamp factory. She declined and left Vienna for Berlin, hoping to study with the quantum theory pioneer Max Planck. But she seemed to have entered a time machine—German universities still had their doors bolted to women. The achingly shy Meitner had to beseech for special permission to attend Planck's lectures.

Months after Rachel Carson's birth, twenty-nine-year-old Lise Meitner met Otto Hahn—a progressive German chemist her own age, unopposed to working with women, and cut of the same cloth: Both scientists were restless about the multitude of unanswered questions at the smallest scale of reality, defiant of the notion that they might be unanswerable, and determined to answer them—together. But women were prohibited from entering, much less working at, Berlin's Chemical Institute. In order to collaborate, Meitner and Hahn had to work in a former carpentry shop converted into a laboratory in the basement of the building. Hahn was allowed to ascend to the upper floors, but Meitner was not—a metaphor not worth belaboring.

Over the course of their thirty-year collaboration, the two scientists would fill each other's gaps with their respective aptitudes— Meitner, trained in physics, was a brilliant mathematician who thought conceptually and could design highly original experiments to test her ideas; Hahn, trained in chemistry, excelled at punctilious lab work. Eventually, Meitner branched out on her own, publishing an astounding fifty-six papers between 1921 and 1934. Her reputation as a pioneer of nuclear physics and one of the preeminent experimentalists of her time prompted Einstein to herald her as the Marie Curie of the German-speaking world.

By the time Marie Curie herself died, her two Nobel Prizes having failed to save her from the destiny of all organic matter—"her body bombarded for years," Adrienne Rich would write, "by the element she had purified"—her pioneering research on radioactivity had birthed a whole new way of understanding the elemental building blocks of everything that ever was and ever will be. The discovery of the neutron in the early 1930s only intensified the sense that the physical nature of reality was encrypted in this enigmatic substratum of matter. In a rare feat of calibrating personal ego to the myriad external conditions that factor into achievement, James

Chadwick, discoverer of the neutron, would later relay his conviction that Meitner would have discovered it first had she had certain advantages available to him but not to her—little had changed in the three centuries since Kepler contemplated his mother's fate.

Meitner would furnish the next leap—one humanity would take, twist, and plummet into a moral abyss. As Meitner's career was taking off, the Nazis began usurping Europe. Meitner and Hahn's third collaborator—a junior scientist named Fritz Strassmann—had already become a target of political persecution for refusing to join Nazi organizations. In 1938, just as the three scientists were performing their most visionary experiments to shed light on the structure and behavior of matter, Nazi troops marched into Austria. Meitner refused to hide her Jewish heritage, nor could she simply leave, for the Nazis had already instituted anti-Semitic laws prohibiting university professors from exiting the country.

When she was threatened with being arrested and thrown into a concentration camp, she fled under cover of night with little more than ten marks in her purse and Otto Hahn's mother's diamond ring—he had given it to his friend to use to bribe a border guard should her life come to depend on it. On July 13, Meitner made a narrow escape across the Dutch border. From Holland, she sought refuge in Denmark and stayed with her colleague Niels Bohr, who had established a program to support refugee scholars. Meitner finally found a permanent home at the Nobel Institute for Physics in Sweden. How little seemed to have changed in the suppression of ideas under the tyranny of religious dogma in three centuries—after witnessing the trial of Galileo, Descartes had also fled to Sweden to avoid a similar fate.

That November, Hahn traveled to Copenhagen to deliver a lecture at the Niels Bohr Institute. There, four of the world's supreme scientific minds—Hahn, Bohr, Meitner, and her nephew and collaborator, Otto Frisch, also a refugee—convened a secret meeting to discuss some perplexing experimental results Hahn and Strassmann had obtained: After bombarding the nucleus of a uranium atom (atomic number 92) with a single neutron, they had ended up with the nucleus of radium (atomic number 88), which acted chemically like barium (56), an element with close to half the atomic weight of radium—a transmutation that didn't make physical sense. That a tiny neutron moving at low speed would destabilize and downright shatter something as robust as an atom, knocking down its atomic number and altering its chemical behavior, seemed as mythical as David taking out Goliath with a slingshot.

Half a century earlier, Emily Dickinson had written:

> It troubled me as once I was,
> For I was once a child,
> Deciding how an atom fell
> And yet the heavens held.

Meitner, one of the world's best physicists, told Hahn, one of the world's best radiochemists, that his chemical reaction made no sense on physical grounds and urged him to repeat the experiment. But she continued pondering the perplexity.

On Christmas Day, during a walk with her nephew, the epiphany arrived. In recounting the occasion in his memoir, Otto Frisch inadvertently provided the perfect metaphor for how women have historically made progress in science relative to their male peers:

> We walked up and down in the snow, I on skis and she on foot (she said and proved that she could get along just as fast that way).

To make sense of the apparently nonsensical results, Meitner and Frisch came up with the concept they would call *nuclear fission*—a term used for the very first time in the seventh paragraph of the paper they published the following month. The notion that a nucleus of one element can split and be transformed into another element was radical—no one had fathomed it before, except the alchemists in their crude way. Meitner had provided the first understanding of how and why this happened.

The year she was forced to flee for her life, Enrico Fermi was able to escape Italy's anti-Semitic laws by emigrating to America after receiving the Nobel Prize for having allegedly created new radioactive elements by bombarding thorium and uranium atoms with slow neutrons—results that Meitner was about to disprove, for these turned out to be not new elements but fission products. The consensus in the scientific community today is that Fermi was erroneously awarded the prize. Meitner was awarded nothing.

Nuclear fission would prove to be one of the most powerful— and most dangerous—discoveries ever made. This triumph of the human intellect over the mysteries of nature became a failure of human morality as it led to the invention of the atomic bomb. In fact, Meitner was later cruelly referred to as "the Jewish mother of the atomic bomb," even though her discovery was purely scientific and predated its malevolent application by many years, and as soon as she saw the plans to put it to destructive ends, she adamantly refused to work on the bomb. Meitner saw the atomic bomb as a grave turning point for humanity and would spend the remainder of her life protecting the purity of science from the impure impulses of its abusers. When she returned to Vienna at the age of seventy-five to deliver a lecture, she reflected on the heart of the scientific world-view: "Science makes people reach selflessly for truth and objectivity; it teaches people to accept reality, with wonder and admiration, not to mention the deep joy and awe that the natural order of things brings to the true scientist."

In her final years, Meitner issued a bittersweet lamentation for the era that had ended with the atomic bomb and its hideous hijacking of science:

> One could love one's work and not always be tormented by the fear of the ghastly and malevolent things that people might do with beautiful scientific findings.

This ghastly malevolence also troubled Rachel Carson as she dived deeper and deeper into the pesticide research. The very term seemed no longer appropriate to her, for designating any organism as a "pest" to be decimated for the benefit of another organism— the human animal—was an affront to the elemental interconnectedness of nature. She thought *biocide* better captured the impossibility of violating Earth with such poisons "without making it unfit for all life."

Nobody was talking about this moral dimension of science. Nobody was placing a hand on humanity's shoulder and turning us away from this destructive hubris, shaking us into awareness, into humility, into wakefulness to the fragility of a miraculous world that flourished long before we trampled it with our arrogant footsteps and should continue to flourish long after we have gone.

On the first day of April 1958, exactly 111 years after Margaret Fuller chanced across Giovanni Ossoli at St. Peter's Cathedral, Rachel Carson had three long telephone conversations—with a science editor at *Newsweek* who also had an interest in the subject; with *The New Yorker*; and with Paul Brooks, her editor at Houghton Mifflin. When she hung up, she wrote to Dorothy to tell her that she was writing a book about the pesticide problem, tentatively titled *The Control of Nature*. She didn't yet know that what she was about to write would be something far vaster—a symphonic invitation to change course while this pale blue dot still had a chance at redemption.

Dorothy, protective of Rachel's genius, worried that what she called "the poison book" would tether Carson to an ugly subject, bemiring her talent and her reputation. But Carson saw in this unbeautiful subject a new frontier for a different kind of beauty— the beauty of moral courage. "I never predicted the book would be a smashing success," she would later tell Dorothy. "It was simply something I believed in so deeply that there was no other course." She shared with Dorothy a quote she felt captured it all perfectly— words that Carson, like many people, misattributed to Abraham Lincoln, but that were in fact the opening lines of a 1914 poem by Ella Wheeler Wilcox: "To sin by silence, when we should protest, makes cowards out of men."

Before her lay a formidable project electric with promise— intellectually challenging in ways that helped her grow as a scientist, invigorating for a literary artist tasked with anchoring the facts of an ugly subject to the beauty of nature's larger underlying truth, and morally ennobling in its aim of humbling humanity into remembering that we are but a speck in a vast and magnificent universe.

Carson began assembling a team of scientists whose research she could cite in shoring up her case against the attacks from corporate and political interests she could foresee from the start. She was soon in correspondence with nearly every prominent scientist whose work touched the vast territory of pesticides and its many adjacent frontiers.

Field biologists and zoologists sent her detailed reports of bird mortality following DDT spraying. One hundred years after Darwin published *On the Origin of Species,* Rachel Carson issued a disquieting reminder of the interleaving of all life in another letter to *The Washington Post*:

> To many of us, this sudden silencing of the song of birds, this obliteration of the color and beauty and interest of bird life, is sufficient cause for sharp regret. To those who have never known such rewarding enjoyment of nature, there should yet remain a nagging and insistent question: If this "rain of death" has produced so disastrous an effect on birds, what of other lives, including our own?

Carson's moral outrage and sympathetic creaturely heartache over the silencing of songbirds would eventually give the book-in-progress its final title: *Silent Spring.*

Unafraid of hard work and creative challenge, Carson illustrated her predicament with a Wonderland allusion: "My own work goes on at a furious pace but I feel like the Red Queen who had to run as fast as she could just to stay where she was." By October, she was hard at work collecting specific data on declines in bird populations due to DDT—"factual comparisons that will hold up under fire." Staying up late to write after doing housework and rising before dawn "to get in an hour of thinking and organizing before the household stirs," Carson wrote to her editor: "I guess all that sustains me is a serene inner conviction that when, at last, the book is done, it is going to be built on an unshakable foundation."

But just as Carson was gaining an optimistic confidence in the difficult direction she was taking, her mother, now approaching ninety and crippled by arthritis, suffered a stroke, followed by acute pneumonia. Within a week, an oxygen tank breathed life into Maria Carson's body as she lay unconscious in her bedroom at the Silver Spring home that mother and daughter had shared for twenty years.

An hour before dawn on the first day of December 1958, Rachel rose from her mother's bedside, where she had been sitting for a long time, and walked into the unlit living room to peer our through the picture window. The Milky Way constellated the clear winter sky with its almost shocking splendor—that primordial river of stars Walt Whitman had celebrated as "some superhuman symphony, some ode of universal vagueness, disdaining syllable and sound—a flashing glance of Deity, address'd to the soul." On a planet orbiting one of the two hundred billion stars in it, a thinking, feeling creature was facing the fate of all matter—the atoms that had given it life were about to retreat into stardust.

Moments after Rachel returned to the bedroom, Maria Carson died holding her daughter's hand.

In the wake of her bereavement, Carson elegized her mother in a letter to Marjorie Spock that reads like a self-portrait:

> Her love of life and of all living things was her outstanding quality. . . . And while gentle and compassionate, she could fight fiercely against anything she believed wrong, as in our present Crusade! Knowing how she felt about that will help me to return to it soon, and to carry it through to completion.

The more she buried herself in the research, the more the problem appeared to be one not of science but of economic and political systems, giving "a strange, Alice-in-Wonderland quality" to the destruction of the natural world by commercial forces that render a conned public complicit. A decade earlier, Carson had foreshadowed this ominous strangeness at the close of her National Book Award acceptance speech:

[I] wonder if we have not too long been looking through the wrong end of the telescope. We have looked first at man with his vanities and greed and his problems of a day or a year; and then only, and from this biased point of view, we have looked outward at the earth he has inhabited so briefly and at the universe in which our earth is so minute a part. Yet these are the great realities, and against them we see our human problems in a different perspective. Perhaps if we reversed the telescope and looked at man down these long vistas, we should find less time and inclination to plan for our own destruction.

Now she inverted the telescope. In a sentiment of remarkable prescience in the context of climate change denial half a century later, Carson articulated the formidable task before her:

It is a great problem to know how to penetrate the barrier of public indifference and unwillingness to look at unpleasant facts that might have to be dealt with if one recognized their existence.

In early 1960, her progress on the book decelerated as she delved into a most unpleasant aspect of her subject—the implication of a causal relationship between DDT and cancer risk. In her research files following the Long Island trial two years earlier, at which a medical witness for the defense had adamantly denied any link between DDT and blood mutations, Carson had saved the following letter from an outdoorsman suggesting at least a correlation:

On a hunting trip in Northern British Columbia the latter part of August 1957, we sprayed a tent for twenty-one nights with DDT. We did not sufficiently aerate the tent. When I got back home in September, my marrow and white and red corpuscles were terribly impaired. I nearly lost my life. I have had forty-one infusions in my arm, each lasting from four to six to eight hours, in Philadelphia, and I am slowly coming back.

A note in Carson's looped hand stretches across the bottom margin of the man's letter: "Died of leukemia, May 1959." What she didn't know is that cancer's clandestine mutations were already coursing through the very fingers that held the pen.

In the spring of 1960, after a series of debilitating illnesses—a severe sinus infection, an ulcer, pneumonia that had dragged on for weeks and kept her from working—Carson discovered two masses in her left breast. As she neared completion of the two chapters dealing with the link between pesticides and cancer, she headed in for surgery to remove them, expecting the kind of minor operation she had undergone a decade earlier. Dorothy, having just been discomposed by Stan's most recent hospitalization—one of several in his four-year spell of ill health, which left his recovery uncertain and held Dorothy in the grip of anticipatory loss—sent Rachel a Sara Teasdale poem to read before her surgery. "Peace flows into me," it began, "as the tide to the pool by the shore." But beneath the assuring surface of her poem choice, Dorothy was plunged into worry. "Hurry to get well," she wrote before signing her letter with an anxious entreaty: "I need you—and love you."

Carson wrote to Marjorie Spock that she was going into the hospital "for a few days." When she emerged two weeks later, she told Spock with characteristic understatement that the "hospital adventure" had morphed into "a setback of some magnitude." She spared Spock the measure of the magnitude: A radical mastectomy had been performed after one of the tumors appeared "suspicious enough" to warrant it. She called Dorothy immediately after the surgery. We shall never know what words curled their awkward fingers around the ungraspable sorrow and tenderness in the hearts on both ends of that line, but Dorothy's letter to Rachel the following day gives some sense:

> I can think of nothing else to-day but you. . . . Darling, if ever you thought you know what you mean to me, multiply that to infinity and you may have some idea!
>   I love you so,
>   Dorothy

After the operation, Carson explicitly asked the surgeon whether the mass removed had metastasized. He told her it had not. He saw before him not a scientist and a human being with agency asking him a question of life and death—he saw a woman and a patient, and he answered with a lie. Nothing had changed in the twenty years since Arline Feynman's doctors had lied to her about her terminal illness. Carson's cancer had metastasized to her lymph nodes. She was dying.

Ten years earlier, after the surgery that removed the tumors she believed were benign—which may well have been a lie, too—Carson had taken respite on the Atlantic shore and recorded in her field notebook while watching a one-legged sanderling on the beach one morning:

> I could see that his left leg is a short stump less than an inch long. I wondered if some animal maybe a fox, had caught it in the Arctic, or whether it had gotten into a trap. . . . He would hop, hop, hop, toward the surf; probing and jabbing busily with opened bill, turn and hop away from the advancing foam. Only twice did I see him have to take to his wings to escape a wetting. It made my heart ache to think how tired his little leg must be, but his whole manner suggested a cheerfulness of spirit and a gameness which must mean that the God of fallen sparrows has not forgotten him.

As soon as Carson realized the lie, she sought medical advice from Dr. George "Barney" Crile, Jr.—a physician at the Cleveland Clinic, whose book on cancer she had stumbled upon in the course of her pesticide research. She had come to admire Dr. Crile as "more than a medical man"—he was a fellow biologist with wide knowledge and appreciation for the delicate interconnectedness of "the little understood but all important ecology of body cells." He devised a treatment plan for Carson and connected her with a pioneer of radiation therapy—a treatment still novel at the time, a little more than a decade in mainstream medical use, having harnessed the selfsame science upon which the atomic bomb was built to save human lives. Carson remained lucid about the costs and benefits that inhere in any interference with nature. She would later tell Dorothy from the midst of another brutal round of radiation: "I know that 2-million-volt monster is my only ally in the major battle—but an awesome and terrible ally, for even while it is killing the cancer I know what it is doing to me."

Carson endured the pain and fatigue inflicted by the monster with uncomplaining courage. "In the intervals I hope to work hard and productively," she assured her editor. "Perhaps even more than ever, I am eager to get this book done." Her determination collided with the creaturely limits of a body unequal to the restless urgency of her mind. By the holiday season, Carson was leveled by a severe case of the flu, followed by a staphylococcus infection that mauled both of her knees and one ankle. This marked the onset of the rheumatoid arthritis that bedeviled her genealogy and would bedevil the remainder of her days. When she was rushed to the hospital in February 1961, she faced her own suffering with characteristic stoicism, but she was heartbroken to watch ten-year-old Roger weep next to her in the ambulance. I, too, have sorrowed for this boy, fatherless since birth and orphaned of his biological mother, who was herself an orphan, now facing the death of his new mother—how much loss can a single heart hold? (Paul Brooks, Carson's editor for *The Edge of the Sea* and *Silent Spring*, would raise the thrice-orphaned boy after Carson's death.)

Carson was bedridden for five weeks, unable to stand, then slowly moved on to a wheelchair, then a walker, then a cane, and finally, as she reported to a friend, to "the blessed state of being able to walk almost normally." She outlined the bodily disability with matter-of-fact equanimity but, anxious to get on with the book, bemoaned the loss of time as "maddening."

Just as she began turning a corner of temporary recovery, an acute eye inflammation rendered her unable to work for more than a circadian sliver each day. The manuscript was nearly complete, but Carson was a meticulous reviser. She went over every page again and again with her burning eyes, perfecting each sentiment and the sentence that carried it, honing the poetic precision of each word. The painstaking progress felt "rather like those dreams where one tries to run and can't." Beneath the placid surface of her composure in the face of nonexistence roiled a volcanic restlessness to bring into being something without which the world itself could not go on existing—an island of difficult, lifesaving truth amid the ocean of civilizational delusion.

More than a decade earlier, Carson had written in *The Sea Around Us*: "The birth of a volcanic island is an event marked by prolonged and violent travail: the forces of the earth striving to create, and all the forces of the sea opposing." Her own person was now a violent landscape where these opposing forces played out as she fought with every fiber the corporeal destruction of cancer in that final creative act that would transfigure the whole of culture.

In January 1962, after two decades of incubation and four years of methodical work transcending every bodily limit, Rachel Carson turned in her manuscript to *The New Yorker*. The daylight had fled from the windy winter day when her telephone rang and the voice of William Shawn, the editor in chief, streamed into the evening to tell her that she had transfigured the unlovely subject of pesticides into beautiful literature—"a brilliant achievement."

When Carson hung up, she tucked Roger into bed, kissed him good night, took her beloved black cat Jeffie into the study, shut the door behind her, and put on her favorite Beethoven violin concerto. "Suddenly," Carson recounted the evening to Dorothy the next day, "the tension of four years was broken and I let the tears come." She reflected on her ineluctable impetus:

Last summer . . . I said I could never again listen happily to a thrush song if I had not done all I could. And last night the thoughts of all the birds and other creatures and all the loveliness that is in nature came to me with such a surge of deep happiness, that now I had done what I could—I had been able to complete it—now it had its own life.

Carson continued her quiet battle against what Dorothy called "the shadows in the background." The radiation had failed to curtail the spread of cancer—there was another swollen lymph node in her armpit and new pain in her neck and spine. Although the X-rays revealed nothing, Carson conveyed to Dorothy the maddening curse that the disease casts on the mind as the body turns on itself: "The trouble with this business is that every perfectly ordinary little ailment looks like a hobgoblin, and one lives in a little private hell until the thing is examined and found to be nothing much."

Carson braved the inferno by holding on to two lifelines. One was Dorothy's love: "Do you know how much I love you for what you have meant to me at this time—and always? This note is tiny but it carries an immense load of love."

The other was the moral imperative that had motivated her to compose *Silent Spring*.

There is no overstating the triumph of having remained motivated by beauty in taking down the ugliest malignancies of human nature's grasp for power. Carson never faltered in the splendor of her prose, but she channeled through it a courageous and meticulously substantiated charge against the assault on nature by government and industry. She had long defied the notion that this must be the cost of progress—a terrible trade-off that had become implicit to the cultural narrative. A decade earlier, she had told the thousand-person gathering of women journalists: "Beauty—and all the values that derive from beauty—are not measured and evaluated in terms of the dollar." She had had a jarring firsthand brush with the hijacking of nature for commercial gain: Among the myriad offers that had barraged her after the success of her sea books was a particularly lucrative one from the Dow Chemical Company, who wanted her to write twenty-five words for a plaque to go on an aquarium inside their new chemical plant on the Texas Gulf Coast. When Marie Rodell responded with the prediction that her client was "extremely unlikely" to be interested, Dow told her unambiguously that they were willing to pay any price—Carson need only name it. Carson refused to name a price—but she walked away with a terrifying taste of the lengths to which chemical companies would go to buy themselves a favorable public image.

Carson saw no moral choice but to defend what she held dearest by catalyzing a new kind of conscience. Her aim with *Silent Spring* was threefold—to transmute hard facts into literature that stands the test of time, to awaken a public hypnotized into docility to the perils of substances so mercilessly marketed as panaceas by chemical companies, and to challenge the government to rise to its neglected responsibility in regulating these perils. She admonished against the fragmentation, commodification, and downright erasure of truth in an era when narrow silos blind specialists to the interconnected whole and market forces sacrifice truth on the altar of revenue. When citizens protest and try to challenge those forces with incontestable evidence, they are "fed little tranquilizing pills of half truth." In a sentiment of striking resonance half a century later, Carson exhorted: "We urgently need an end to these false assurances, to the sugar coating of unpalatable facts." Above all, she countered the pathological short-termism of commercial interests with a sobering look at "consequences remote in time and place" as poisons permeate a delicate ecosystem in which no organism is separate from any other and no moment islanded in the river of time.

In June 1962, five days before the first installment of *Silent Spring* made its debut in *The New Yorker,* Carson summoned the remnants of her strength to take her very first cross-country jetliner flight and deliver a long-awaited commencement address at Scripps College in California, which she titled "Of Man and the Stream of Time." It was a crystallization of her moral philosophy, a farewell to the world she so cherished, and her baton-passing of that cherishment to the next generation. She told graduates:

> Today our whole earth has become only another shore from which we look out across the dark ocean of space, uncertain what we shall find when we sail out among the stars.
>
> [. . .]
>
> The stream of time moves forward and mankind moves with it. Your generation must come to terms with the environment. You must face realities instead of taking refuge in ignorance and evasion of truth. Yours is a grave and sobering responsibility, but it is also a

shining opportunity. You go out into a world where mankind is challenged, as it has never been challenged before, to prove its maturity
and its mastery—not of nature, but of itself.

Therein lies our hope and our destiny.

Kepler had believed that the earth digested and breathed like a living being, and that it had a soul—beliefs for which he was ridiculed
for centuries, until Rachel Carson came along and located that soul
in the breath of life distributed across a vast and varied ecosystem
of beings, its marine heart beating to the pulse of tides. Darwin had
demonstrated our evolutionary kinship with other organisms across
the long arc of time, but it was Carson who bent the human imagination toward the poetic truth inside the scientific fact, bringing
to the cold intellectual awareness a warm feeling-tone that awakened the modern environmental conscience. Fuller had written to
Emerson: "Only through emotion do we know thee, Nature! We
lean upon thy breast, and feel its pulses vibrate to our own. That
is knowledge, for that is love. Thought will never reach it." It was
Carson again who officiated the marriage of ecology and ethics that
had begun with the intellectual flirtations of the Transcendentalists.

27

BETWEEN THE TIME OF MONARCHS
AND THE TIME OF STARS

Carson spent her time in California going over the proofs *The New Yorker* had sent her. The day after the Scripps College commencement—Dorothy's sixty-third birthday—she learned that the Book-of-the-Month Club, which reached an enormous mass of subscribers, had selected *Silent Spring* for October, following its scheduled publication in September. Aware that the subject of pesticides affected farmers and families in the agricultural expanses of Middle America far more directly than it did New York's intellectual elite, Carson rejoiced that the selection would "carry [*Silent Spring*] to farms and hamlets all over the country that don't know what a bookstore looks like—much less the *New Yorker*." From three thousand miles away, she told Dorothy:

> It is very, very good and tonight I am deeply and quietly happy. . . .
> Do you know how much I love you—and how much it means to have
> you to share all this?—Goodnight—Happy Birthday—and my love,
> always.

Silent Spring was powerful and polarizing the way only a substantive challenge to the status quo can be. Carson had pulled back the curtain on the $800 million pesticide industry, a major interest in the agricultural subsidies of a complicit government, and its ruthless publicity campaign dispensing those "little tranquilizing pills of half truth." Letters from readers bombarded *The New Yorker* at an astonishing rate matched only by the barrage of letters to the USDA from legions of furious citizens who suddenly felt betrayed and endangered by their own government. Like Darwin's masterwork, which threatened the manipulative authority of the ruling force of his time—the Church—Carson's masterwork challenged the ruling force of hers: industry and the unscrupulous commercial interests that govern capitalism.

Silent Spring's wake-up call reverberated through the major opinion instruments of the country. *The New York Times,* siding with Carson, addressed what would become the most common warping of her thesis by those who sought to discredit it or who simply hadn't read it and were reacting on the basis of rash secondhand impressions—a cultural malady we forget is not singular to the age of social media, though that has undoubtedly aggravated it manyfold. Correctly predicting that Carson would be accused of being an alarmist by those who preferred to hold the problem in convenient denial, the *Times* wrote:

> Miss Carson does not argue that chemical pesticides must never be used, but she warns of the dangers of misuse and overuse by a public that has become mesmerized by the notion that chemists are the possessors of divine wisdom and that nothing but benefit can emerge from their test tubes.

Carson, in fact, did acknowledge that there were potential applications of pesticides under very limited circumstances—such as the successful control of the typhoid outbreak in Italy—but she admonished that over the long run, chemical poisons become not only dangerous but ineffective as insects develop resistance and mutate into superspecies that require harsher and harsher poisons to control. Her primary targets were not the substances themselves but the heedless policies that allowed for their indiscriminate use devoid of proper testing and consideration of long-term effects at the level not only of local symptoms but of ecology at large. Chemical insecticides lacked any precision of targeting—in trying to eradicate one "harmful" insect species, they were decimating what Carson had once called "the instruments that make up the elemental earth orchestra." She conceived of more sophisticated alternatives to this brutality—science, she believed, should be wielded with conscientious sophistication, not with the loutish sweep of untested industrial chemicals. "As crude a weapon as the cave man's club," Carson wrote, "the chemical barrage has been hurled against the fabric of life—a fabric on the one hand delicate and destructible, on the other miraculously tough and resilient, and capable of striking back in unexpected ways." The triumph of *Silent Spring* was not merely one of facts, but of facts that had never before been considered in relation to one another.

Several months earlier, and a century after the indiscriminate prescription of mercury had maimed thousands in Sophia Peabody's generation, another epidemic of pseudoscientific overconfidence untamed by proper testing had swept across Great Britain, West Germany, and Canada: Thousands of babies were born with missing limbs and other gruesome birth defects traced to thalidomide—a sedative liberally prescribed to pregnant women as a "cure" for morning sickness and sleeplessness. The drug hadn't infested the American market, thanks to the rigorous skepticism of one scientist: Frances Oldham Kelsey, a pharmacologist and physician with the FDA, who had refused to accept the evasive answers the manufacturer had given to her detailed questions about drug safety. Kelsey likely saved thousands of lives with her rigorous persistence—a service to humanity for which John F. Kennedy awarded her the nation's highest honor of Distinguished Federal Civilian Service for "her exceptional judgment [that] has prevented a major tragedy of birth deformities." As he hung the medal around Kelsey's neck, the president addressed the nation and the scientist before him:

> I know that we are all most indebted to Dr. Kelsey. The relationship and the hopes that all of us have for our children, I think, indicate to Dr. Kelsey, I am sure, how important her work is and those who labor

with her to protect our families. So, Doctor, I know you know how much the country appreciates what you have done.

Kelsey, who lived to the age of 101, was only the second woman to receive the presidential medal. Kennedy later signed into effect a landmark regulatory law for pharmaceuticals based on Kelsey's work.

In July 1962, two weeks after *The New Yorker* published its third and final installment of Carson's *Silent Spring*, *The Washington Post* ran a lengthy piece on Kelsey's triumph titled " 'Heroine' of FDA Keeps Bad Drug Off Market." It began:

This is the story of how the skepticism and stubbornness of a Government physician prevented what could have been an appalling American tragedy, the birth of hundreds or indeed thousands of armless and legless children.

When a reporter reached out to Carson for comment, she responded with a formulation of the central argument in *Silent Spring*: "It is all of a piece, thalidomide and pesticides—they represent our willingness to rush ahead and use something new without knowing what the results are going to be."

On the pages of Long Island's *Newsday*, a driven twenty-six-year-old investigative reporter by the name of Robert Caro—who a decade later would take down Robert Moses with his formidable biography *The Power Broker*—crystallized the controversy ignited by "famed biologist and author Rachel Carson":

The lid is about to blow off a behind-the-scenes controversy over swelling scientific evidence that chemical pesticides, enthusiastically promoted by the United States Agriculture Department despite 16 years of warnings, have decimated species of wildlife and now threaten man with cancer, leukemia and abnormal gene development.

In his five-part amplifier of Carson's clarion call, the young journalist managed to get an interview with Secretary of Agriculture Orville Freeman, who gave the rote response that the benefits of pesticides outweighed the costs. He claimed that Carson had ignited unnecessary "panic and hysteria," hurling at her the bomb of uterine etymology that has been hurled at nearly every woman in the history of the world who has raised her voice against any form of injustice or abuse.

Such denial was one of the two main strategies employed by the culprits in Carson's indictment. Those whom the book riled were but a fraction of those who welcomed her courageous telling of truth, but it was a rich and powerful fraction who spared no means in claiming attention. They met the indictment with the human animal's two most predictable reactions to threat: fight and flight. Government officials and industry spokesmen fled from the inconvenient truths *Silent Spring* had unveiled and made every effort to hijack the public along for the flight. Behind the polite veneer of sound bites, they were preparing for a bloody personal fight.

Carson's longtime friend and former Fish and Wildlife Service colleague Shirley Briggs warned her that while Orville Freeman was buying time with the party line that pesticides were beneficial and well regulated, his Department of Agriculture was readying an attack on her credibility and sifting through the *New Yorker* pieces for cause for libel. Pesticide makers were not far behind—the DuPont Corporation requested advance copies of *Silent Spring,* most likely in preparation for a lawsuit. Velsicol, another major pesticide manufacturer, threatened Houghton Mifflin directly, promising litigation if they didn't stop the publication of *Silent Spring* or publish it only without any negative mention of their products. They went as far as to claim that criticism of pesticides was part of a Communist conspiracy. A man from California echoed these accusations in a letter to *The New Yorker,* then added in complete seriousness: "We can live without birds and animals, but, as the current market slump shows, we cannot live without business." Eight years later, with the legacy of *Silent Spring* rooted in popular culture, Joni Mitchell would offer a splendid counterpoint in the lyrics to her song "Big Yellow Taxi":

Put away the DDT
I don't care about spots on my apples

Leave me the birds and the bees
Please!

The man concluded his letter to *The New Yorker* with this befuddling statement:

As for insects, isn't it just like a woman to be scared to death of a few little bugs! As long as we have the H-bomb everything will be O.K.
    PS. She's probably a peace-nut too.

But absurd as the charges of Communist ties were, Carson's industrial-strength critics pushed them so insistently that the FBI commenced an investigation of her, the result of which ran to two unimpressive pages that were classified Confidential and eventually destroyed with remnants of other futile investigations.

Carson assured her publisher of her confidence in the solidity of her science—*Silent Spring* was buttressed with hundreds of meticulously sourced references stretching across fifty-five pages of citations. The USDA failed to find any fault in her science and Velsicol eventually dropped the litigious bullying, only to end up on the other side of a lawsuit—several months later, twenty people in Memphis grew ill after inhaling fumes emanating from a stream near a Velsicol chemical plant and two dozen workers were hospitalized after inhaling gas from the plant. In the final month of Carson's life, a USDA investigation would reveal that a major fish kill along the Mississippi, where Harriet Hosmer and Mark Twain had once admired the pristine beauty of the river, was the result of a leak of endrin—a pesticide thirty times deadlier than DDT—from the same Velsicol plant. It had coated the sewers of Memphis with three feet of poison and reached all the way to the New Orleans public water supply.

By August, a month before the book was published, *Silent Spring* was on the president's agenda. When asked about the threat of pesticides during a televised White House press conference, John F. Kennedy—whose presidential campaign had included the Carson-influenced promise of conserving seashores as wildlife refuges—responded that he had tasked several government agencies with investigating the matter as a direct consequence of Carson's book. Two months earlier, a representative of the Department of the Interior had met with Carson, hoping to enlist her help in communicating scientific ideas to the general public. What Kennedy didn't tell the press was that the federal government had already set up a special interagency panel to work with the president's Science Advisory Committee on an intensive investigation of pesticides.

Although the president's science adviser had been paying attention to the *New Yorker* installments, it is likely that *Silent Spring* claimed Kennedy's attention through a channel closer to home. Five years earlier, when the judge in Long Island had denied residents their request for an injunction against DDT spraying, Marjorie Spock and her partner had appealed the case, taking it all the way to the Supreme Court, which declined to hear it. But there was one strong dissenting voice: Supreme Court Justice William O. Douglas—a man with a strong environmental conscience, who had quoted from Carson's *Washington Post* op-ed in his dissent from the Court's decision not to take the case.

Douglas had been Bobby Kennedy's wilderness hiking companion for years. By the time *Silent Spring* disquieted the nation, Douglas had become the president's most influential unofficial adviser on environmental matters. Having never forgotten the unjust outcome of the Long Island case, he devoured an advance copy of *Silent Spring* and readily endorsed it for Houghton Mifflin as "the most revolutionary book since *Uncle Tom's Cabin*." When he saw Carson at a White House conference on conservation in May, which she attended between radiation treatments as a distinguished guest, Douglas professed his enthusiasm for the book as a long overdue vindication of the crusade against the reckless use of DDT and offered to write the catalog copy for the Book-of-the-Month Club edition of 150,000 copies. In it, he lauded the book as an immensely persuasive call "for effective control of all merchants of poison," endorsing it with a commanding proclamation: "This book is the most important chronicle of this century for the human race."

Silent Spring was published on September 27, 1962. It was reviewed by every major publication and widely excerpted. *The*

New York Times echoed Justice Douglas and likened it to "a 20th-century *Uncle Tom's Cabin*," a literary masterwork that "tingles with anger, outrage and protest." The *Times* preempted what would become a frequent refrain of Carson's critics—that the book is "unfair" and "one-sided" in its assessment of pesticides—with the keen observation that "*Uncle Tom's Cabin* would never have stirred a nation had it been measured and 'fair.' "

While most serious publications sided heavily with Carson, some parroted the position of chemical companies—who were, as it happens, some of their most lucrative advertisers. *The Economist* predicted that no one would take the book seriously and its sole consequence would be damage to Carson's "professional reputation as a reliable scientific journalist." *Time,* citing a years-old study on the safety of DDT amply challenged since, deemed the pesticide "harmless," called the book "unfair, one-sided, and hysterically overemphatic," and proclaimed Carson's meticulously researched case "patently unsound"—an "emotional and inaccurate outburst." *Reader's Digest,* which had rejected Carson's DDT exposé pitch nearly twenty years earlier, canceled the contract for condensation they had signed with Houghton Mifflin two months before the book's publication and instead ran an abridged version of the *Time* review. (In 1969, years after Carson's death, *Time* would print a photograph of her in its Environment section, accompanied by a belated redemption: "Since Rachel Carson exposed the pesticides' threat seven years ago, in *Silent Spring,* evidence of the chemicals' pernicious effects on birds, plants, fish, animals and occasionally man has continued to grow." *Time* would later vote Carson one of the one hundred most influential people of the twentieth century.)

The most ruthless attacks came from the chemical and agricultural industries. *Monsanto Magazine*—with a circulation close to the Book-of-the-Month Club's—printed a parody of the opening chapter, which they titled "The Desolate Year." Where Carson had painted a bleak apocalyptic landscape "deserted by all living things" after poisons had savaged trees and animals and families, Monsanto tried to mimic Carson's lyrical prose in painting the reverse—a Dark Age when insects and other "pests" have inherited the Earth.

The cofounder and chairman of the National Nutrition Council—a pro-industry organization funded in large part by annual dues paid by Monsanto and the nation's other leading pesticide manufacturers—declared *Silent Spring* "baloney." The Nutrition Foundation, a similar outfit with close ties to industrial agriculture and executives from major junk food manufacturers on its board, launched a concerted attack on Carson's credibility with propagandistic untruth bleeding into the absurd:

> Publicists and the author's adherents among the food faddists, health quacks, and special interest groups are promoting her book as if it were scientifically irreproachable and written by a scientist. Neither is true. The book presents almost solely selected information that is negative and uses such bits from a period of many years, building a vastly distorted picture. The author is a professional journalist—not a scientist in the field of her discussion—and misses the very essence of science in not being objective either in citing the evidence or in its interpretation.

The Nutrition Foundation joined forces with the National Agricultural Chemicals Association, which had allotted a quarter of a million dollars to improving "the image of the industry" in the wake of *Silent Spring*. After assembling and distributing all the negative reviews of the book they could find, having come up empty-handed in the search for sufficient dissent from legitimate scientists, they supplied their own refutation in a pamphlet titled *Fact and Fancy*—a collection of alternative "facts" designed to undermine the research Carson had highlighted. In a similar vein, an agriculture magazine published a piece titled "How to Answer Rachel Carson," equipping its readers with canned talking points should they have to defend Big Agriculture against the evidence presented in *Silent Spring*. It employed the most common tactic of Carson's critics: refuting arguments the opponent hasn't actually made. Disregarding the passage in which Carson explicitly stated that the book was not meant as a wholesale renunciation of every pesticide in every circumstance—she had pointed to the lifesaving uses of chemical controls in typhoid and malaria outbreaks—some went as far as accusing her of being antiscience. The grave irony is that she opposed not science but the most unscientific stance there is—the arrogance of false certitude unsupported by evidence and the dangerous delusion of pretending to have answers we don't actually have.

Astonishingly, when I shared an essay on the writing of *Silent Spring* more than half a century after its publication, someone on Twitter responded—in far less time than it would have taken to read the twenty-five-hundred-word essay—by parroting these pseudorefutations and blaming Carson for millions of malaria deaths. Such is the staggering half-life of untruth once lodged in the tissue of culture.

Carson's most visible public critic was an antihero by the name of Robert H. White-Stevens—a commercial chemist decidedly theatrical in his pathos-mongering, his pomade-sleeked hair, thin mustache, and thick black eyebrows bushing above black horned glasses that rendered him a film noir villain character. White-Stevens's primary argument against *Silent Spring* was a muddling of causation and correlation—he asserted that disease and famine dominate in areas of the world where pesticides are not used. White-Stevens was either oblivious to or intentionally obfuscating the glaring confound of economic development and its more recently uncovered correlate of girls' education—poorer countries simply couldn't afford pesticides, and it is poverty that predicts negative population health and crop yield.

No amount of propaganda was going to unwake the public on so vast a scale as *Silent Spring* reached within days of its publication. "Democracy Still Works," proclaimed a Washington paper. "Rachel's Song Is Loud and Clear." The first printing of a hundred thousand copies swiftly sold out and the book ascended the *New York Times* best-seller list. By Thanksgiving, it was at number one. Letters of gratitude, which Marie Rodell hauled to Carson in enormous bags, flooded Houghton Mifflin. Readers commended her on the "continued devotion to the preservation of the finer things of life for humanity." Ruth Adams, editor of *Prevention* magazine, lauded *Silent Spring* as an invaluable weapon of citizen empowerment:

And by Rachel Carson! Not a crank, not a faddist, not a communist. But a best-selling author, a real live scientist on the top level whose conservative, beautifully-written works are in all our school libraries. . . . Just the kind of person who should write such a book! I'm so glad you did.

In exposing abuse worthy of outrage, Carson had managed to mobilize not through anger but through compassion, to speak lucidly of terror while effecting, somehow, tenderness. A woman writing from the middle of Pennsylvania captured this singular achievement:

Dear Miss Carson:

I am a social worker—my working days are filled with plans for the needs of people in trouble. In this field one's efforts are often frustrated by blocks caused by the expediencies of comfortable people, those with deeply rooted prerogatives, with politics and politicians, with the prestige and label seekers.

Yesterday on a train after a particularly harrowing day, I read the short description of your philosophy by Cleveland Amory in *McCall's* magazine—of your care to protect small dependent creatures of the sea and of your Mother's concern for all forms of life.

Without realizing how or why, the weariness dropped away and I felt new again as one does early in the morning.

Dozens of international editions followed. In England, where a London newspaper had reported that "a 55-year old spinster has written a book that is causing more heart-searching in America than any book since Upton Sinclair's *The Jungle* forced Chicago to clean up its abattoirs," the conservationist Lord Shackleton—son of the pioneering polar explorer Ernest Shackleton, who had once so bluntly rejected women from his expeditions—offered to write the introduction for the British edition. He lauded Carson for shedding light on the "ethical and aesthetic values" so essential to the salvation of nature and for bringing "her training as a biologist and her skill as a writer to bear with great force on a significant and even sinister aspect of man's technological progress."

A woman wrote to Carson from Amsterdam:

After two world wars I know only too well how wickedly stupid and ruthless most people in power are and that they are only out for their own immediate gain and never for the common good in the long run. On the other hand, once public opinion has been roused, something might be done. . . . I think you have done work of the greatest possible value for mankind and without your horribly convincing picture it would have remained impossible to take any action at all.

Another woman echoed the sentiment, writing from Seattle: "To speak against a powerful wrong puts one in a lonely and misunderstood position. But—how thankful we are—that there are such people as Miss Carson who are willing to do what is right."

Such people have always been rare even among the great minds of the ages. While Kepler was printing the first six pages of *The Dream* in the final year of his life, hoping his subtle parable would at last invite humanity to consider the controversial Copernican perspective, René Descartes set out to expound the Copernican model in a book titled *The World,* intended to synthesize the essence of his entire philosophy. He worked on it for four years, but upon witnessing Galileo's fate in the summer of 1633, the mind-body divide vanished into ether as Descartes weighed the threat that his ideas would incite corporeal torture. He abandoned the project—publish and perish, he inferred.

In a letter from late November 1633, Descartes tells his friend Marin Mersenne that he had intended to send him a copy of Galileo's *Dialogue on the Two Chief World Systems* as a New Year's gift but discovered that the book had been burned and Galileo convicted and tried. "I was so surprised by this," Descartes writes, "that I nearly decided to burn all my papers, or at least let no one see them." He remarks in shock that the notion of Earth's motion, the inconvenient fact of which wrought Galileo's misfortune, is at the center of his own life's work. "If this view is false, then so are the entire foundations of my philosophy," he mourns to Mersenne, "for it can be demonstrated from them quite clearly. And it is such an integral part of my treatise that I couldn't remove it without making the whole work defective." But he decided that rather than making himself vulnerable to censorship—or worse—by publicly advocating for what he knew to be true, he wouldn't publish a book "which had a single word that the Church disapproved of." He preferred, he said, "to suppress it rather than to publish it in mutilated form." Publishing the truth unmutilated was clearly not one of the options Descartes considered—a decision all the more baffling, given there was no Inquisition in his native France and sympathy with Galileo's views was quickly trickling down from pro-Copernican Holland. More likely, he simply disliked the idea that the book wouldn't sell, or that his reputation would be engulfed in controversy. (His motto, as he writes to Mersenne the following April, was "he lives well who is well hidden.")

> To sin by silence, when we should protest, makes cowards out of men.

Descartes, like all of us, contained the dormant potentialities for intellectual courage and intellectual cowardice, and he spent most of his life wakeful to the former. And yet he shirked from supporting a truth he knew well to be true. Perhaps, after all, we aren't divided so much into mind and body as into mind and mind. And few forces can propel humanity forward more reliably than the cleaving together of kindred minds in solidarity to a shared truth.

Carson had dedicated *Silent Spring* to the French-German philosopher and physician Albert Schweitzer. A year after *The Sea Around Us* had established her as nature's supreme steward, Schweitzer had received the Nobel Peace Prize for his philosophy of "Reverence for Life." Of the numerous accolades she received for *Silent Spring*, the one that meant the most to her was the Schweitzer Medal of the Animal Welfare Institute. In accepting the award, Carson reflected on the central conviction she shared with Schweitzer:

> We are not being truly civilized if we concern ourselves only with the relation of man to man. What is important is the relation of man to

all life. This has never been so tragically overlooked as in our present age, when through our technology we are waging war against the natural world. . . . By acquiescing in needless destruction and suffering, our stature as human beings is diminished.

A century earlier, Emily Dickinson had written in one of her poem-letters to Susan:

It is not Nature—
dear, but those
that stand for
Nature.
The Bird would be
a soundless thing
without Expositor.

Ninety-five pages into *Silent Spring*, Rachel Carson distilled her central thesis, which would become the founding ethos of the modern environmental movement:

The question is whether any civilization can wage relentless war on life without destroying itself, and without losing the right to be called civilized.

Three weeks after the book's publication, Carson received an invitation from the White House to attend a Kennedy Seminar at the home of the secretary of the interior. Expecting an attack from agricultural interests frontman Orville Freeman, she arrived armed with a meticulously reasoned speech. Reading from eleven neatly typed double-sided notecards, she proceeded to offer "imaginative, creative, and scientifically sound" alternatives to the blunt weapon of chemical pesticides. Among the most imaginative of them was a prescient vision for biological controls that would curtail the reproduction of a particular species without harming other organisms. Exactly fifty-five years later, the Environmental Protection Agency—the founding of which was a direct consequence of Carson's work—would announce the approval of a pioneering technique for controlling the population of disease-carrying mosquitoes by releasing lab-raised males infected with a bacterium that renders the females sterile. Carson concluded her presentation with a vital challenge to the government: "These approaches . . . require support—the support of increased funds, the support of public understanding. In this direction, I am convinced, lies the best hope for our future."

The New York Times declared that if Carson succeeded in her mission of taking the government out of industry's back pocket and holding it accountable for the protection of nature and its citizens, she would be "as deserving of the Nobel Prize as was the inventor of DDT." Indeed, had Carson lived even a few more years, she might even have surmounted the Nobel committee's historic gender bias— where are Lise Meitner's, Vera Rubin's, and Jocelyn Bell Burnell's Nobel Prizes?—and received the Nobel Peace Prize.

Even *Peanuts* celebrated Carson. In one comic strip, Lucy excitedly shows off her new baseball bat to Charlie Brown, who asks whose name is on it: "Mickey Mantle? Willie Mays?" "It must be a girl's bat," says Lucy. "It says 'Rachel Carson.'" In another, Lucy quotes geological facts from Carson's books to an exasperated Schroeder: "Rachel Carson! Rachel Carson! You're always talking about Rachel Carson!" Lucy fires back: "We girls need our heroines!" Having received more congratulatory calls from friends after the *Peanuts* nod than after her National Book Award, Carson joked: "I've found that true immortality seems to rest in being included in a comic strip."

Behind the public facade of good spirits, Carson sorrowed that, increasingly stripped of bodily agency, she now had to have other people accept the awards on her behalf. "I keep thinking," she confided in a friend, "if only I could have reached this point ten years ago! Now, when there is an opportunity to do so much, my body falters and I know there is little time left."

Barraged by press inquiries and interview requests, Carson habitually turned them down. Instead, she wrote back to readers whose letters had moved her and continued prioritizing students. During the frenzied final months of completing *Silent Spring,* she had

even taken the time to contribute an essay to the student literary
annual of a Chicago high school, who had asked her to contribute
her advice on writing. The piece, which was never published elsewhere and survives as a draft in Carson's papers at Yale's Beinecke
Library, remains the most concrete articulation of her philosophy
as a writer:

> In writing about the sea I have learned the important truth that a
> writer's subject is always far bigger and more important than the
> writer himself. This would be true of something as seemingly trivial
> as a butterfly's wing no less than of a majestic subject like the sea.
> For the writer—if he is to be worth reading—is merely the instrument
> through which a truth is expressed. He does not create the truth,
> but he gives it expression and illuminates it for us with something
> of himself.
>
> If these most important aims are to be accomplished, the writer
> must never attempt to impose himself upon his subject. He must
> not try to mold it according to what he believes his readers or edi-
> tors want to read. His initial task is to come to know his subject inti-
> mately, to understand its every aspect, to let it fill his mind. Then at
> some turning point the subject takes command and the true act of
> creation begins. What results is a mysterious blend of writer and sub-
> ject. Given the same subject and two writers the results will of course
> be different, just as the theme of a symphony falls upon our ears dif-
> ferently when stated by the strings or by the woodwinds. But as the
> theme is more important than the instruments, so in writing what is
> said is more important than the writer who says it. The discipline of
> the writer is to learn to be still and listen to what his subject has to
> tell him. Those who have experienced such unity with great universal
> truths know that a writer's role in expressing them is privileged and
> rich in satisfactions.

It was as such an instrument of truth that Carson composed *Silent
Spring*, but she now saw the cacophony of misunderstanding and
deliberate misinterpretation the chemical industry was capable of
orchestrating. Reluctantly, she agreed to two major media appear-
ances. One was a profile in *Life* magazine, which she initially resisted,
until Marie Rodell cleverly pointed out that the chemical lobbyists

would never turn down such a platform if invited—antihero Robert H. White-Stevens, after all, was grasping after every opportunity to promote pesticides and malign Carson. The journalist assigned to the *Life* story—a woman—would go on to describe Carson as "unmarried but not a feminist," taking an identity-politics liberty of interpretation with a statement of Carson's quoted parenthetically in the selfsame sentence: "I'm not interested in things done by women or by men but in things done by people." Under the heading "A Calm Appraisal of 'Silent Spring,'" *Life* fanfared: "Like all good crusaders, Rachel Carson presents a one-sided case." The magazine summarized the tumult wrought by "Hurricane Rachel" and the counterattacks by the chemical industry. Although there was an acknowledgment that Carson's book was "amply buttressed by research," which rendered her a "formidable adversary," *Life* ultimately failed to take a stand and instead made an attempt at a noncommittal midpoint:

> Somewhere between the desert depicted by Rachel Carson and the jungle predicted by the chemical warfarers there is a middle ground where chemistry, biology, wildlife and mankind can achieve a peaceful coexistence and the bees may continue to hum. The problems are complex: they cannot be solved either by bird watchers or by chemists. They must be attacked by ecologists and biologists, who will assess all environments and give the public the full answers it needs.

Between ads for aspirin and cigarette lighters, photographs of Carson showed her in her study with her beloved cat Jeffie and in nature with a set of binoculars, apparently classing her with bird watchers and not with biologists.

The second media request Carson accepted, just as reluctantly, was an appearance on the popular television program *CBS Reports*, the producer of which was interested in putting the issue of pesticides before the nation's eyes. Houghton Mifflin's publicity team armed Carson with instructions for her on-camera presence: try not to look "too stern," don't wear red lipstick, and smile, smile, smile while discussing this grim subject.

In November, the CBS crew arrived at Carson's home in Silver

Spring for a multiday interview. Visibly ill under a shiny black wig, she swallowed the agony of sitting under the bright camera lights for hours that stretched tenfold their length. With poised exactitude, Carson delivered her sobering message. She spoke with a serious serenity, her naturally warm face unmarred by even a single artificial grin. Taken as the CBS host was by Carson's eloquence, infallible logic, and authoritative presence, he was jarred by her physical state into a new sense of urgency in getting the program on the air. As the crew was leaving, one of the cameramen turned to the producer: "Jay, you've got a dead leading lady."

Urgency thundered upon Carson herself when, out on a shopping trip to get Roger a record player for Christmas, she blacked out and collapsed atop a display of records, her limp body pressed against the floored Beethoven. An examination revealed that she had developed angina in addition to the cancer. A hospital bed was installed in her Silver Spring home. She was ordered to stay indoors, walk as little and possible, climb no stairs, and cease all housework. Cancer invaded her vertebrae, inflicting back pain so intense she could barely stand. She began a new round of radiation, enduring a new spell of severe nausea.

In her annual Christmas letter to Dorothy, Rachel acknowledged what a "mixed year" it has been for both of them, with the joy of *Silent Spring*'s almost incomprehensible triumph and the cascading terror inflicted by her cancer and Stan's ongoing hospitalizations. "For me," she told Dorothy, thanking her for being in effect her life-partner, "either would have been a solitary experience without you." She ended her letter with words of love and the hope that the new year would bring them "more joys than sorrows and renewed joys in being together—in belonging to each other."

As Carson adamantly kept her private trials private, the public attacks on her continued. The man who had served as Eisenhower's secretary of agriculture and who would later become Prophet of the Mormon Church asked "why a spinster with no children was so concerned about genetics." He didn't hesitate to offer his own theory: because she was a Communist. The lazy hand grenade of "spinster" had been thrown and would be thrown at Carson many times, having been clenched in the unevolved fist of culture for more than a century since the landmark Woman's Rights Convention was derided as comprising "old maids, whose personal charms were never very attractive." When a reporter from the Baltimore *Sun*—Carson's editorial alma mater—asked her why she had never married, she replied simply, "No time." She then echoed Mary Somerville's lamentation that she could have benefited from the luxurious privilege of male writers, who can focus solely on their work while their wives take on domestic and secretarial duties. Indeed, as much as Dorothy was Rachel's closest approximation of a spouse, their relationship was decidedly free of this domestic dimension, which may have deprived Carson of the relief of shared household duties but may have also allowed their love to remain in that numinous space of adoration unburdened by laundry. "Do you wonder I worship you?" Dorothy had written at the end of a long love letter. Worship is hard—not impossible, but hard—at the altar of the kitchen sink with its towering presbytery of unwashed dishes.

Carson was thrust into the harsh creaturely reality of her illness—the pain that had dogged her left shoulder for two months, which she had attributed to arthritis, turned out to be new cancer growth, which had now invaded her collarbone and her neck. With that supreme survival instinct of optimistic denial, she entreated Dorothy—entreated herself—not to get "bogged down in unhappiness about all this," resolving instead to inhabit their remaining time together with unassailable presence:

> We are going to be happy, and go on enjoying all the lovely things that give life meaning—sunrise and sunset, moonlight on the bay, music and good books, the song of thrushes and the wild cries of geese passing over.

In mid-January, Carson delivered before the New England Wildflower Preservation Society a speech she titled "A Sense of Value in Today's World." Addressing an organization tasked with saving the species young Emily Dickinson had once pressed into her herbarium, Carson extracted from "the fragile, transient loveliness of wildflowers" something larger and essential to culture—a call for moral courage in protecting the future from the unlovely greed of the present:

> We must be able to separate the trivia of today from the enduring realities of the long tomorrows. Having recognized and defined our values, we must defend them without fear and without apology.

As the holiday season rose and set, with an air date for the *CBS Reports* segment still unannounced, Carson began to worry that the producers were changing the angle and choosing to side with her choir of critics, increasingly vociferous in their agitation. But she was not without her champions. She received a handwritten note from Albert Schweitzer, thanking her for having dedicated *Silent Spring* to him.

Among the prominent scientists and writers who sided with her was one improbable admirer—the theologian and Trappist monk Thomas Merton. In January 1963, he sent Carson a letter that conveyed how interconnected the deepest truths of existence are, how they transcend all boundaries of discipline and credo to bring us into naked contact with reality itself—and with our responsibility to the web of life. Reaching out with "every expression of personal esteem" and commending Carson on the "fine, exact, and persuasive book," Merton wrote:

> [*Silent Spring*] is perhaps much more timely even than you or I realize. Though you are treating of just one aspect, and a rather detailed aspect, of our technological civilization, you are, perhaps without altogether realizing, contributing a most valuable and essential piece of evidence for the diagnosis of the ills of our civilization. . . . Your book makes it clear to me that there is a *consistent pattern* running through everything that we do, through every aspect of our culture, our thought, our economy, our whole way of life.

A century after Whitman observed that Emerson's greatest gift was not that of "poet or artist or teacher" but of "diagnoser" of society, Merton wrote that in order for society to begin correcting its pernicious symptoms, its elemental ills must be exposed—a civilizational self-awareness Carson had effected with unparalleled diagnostic virtuosity. He wrote:

I would almost dare to say that the sickness is perhaps a very real and very dreadful hatred of life as such, of course subconscious, buried under our pitiful and superficial optimism about ourselves and our affluent society. But I think that the very thought processes of materialistic affluence (and here the same things are found in all the different economic systems that seek affluence for its own sake) are ultimately self-defeating. They contain so many built-in frustrations that they inevitably lead us to despair in the midst of "plenty" and "happiness" and the awful fruit of this despair is indiscriminate, irresponsible destructiveness, hatred of life, carried on in the name of life itself. In order to "survive" we instinctively destroy that on which our survival depends. . . . Technics and wisdom are not by any means opposed. On the contrary, the duty of our age, the "vocation" of modern man is to unite them in a supreme humility which will result in a totally self-forgetful creativity and service.

In the last week of March, with half a million copies of *Silent Spring* sold, CBS finally mailed Carson the press release listing the other persons interviewed—the seemingly inescapable Robert H. White-Stevens to represent the chemical industry, a handful of scientists to weigh in on the research, and a number of high-ranking government officials, including the surgeon general, the commissioner of the FDA, and the secretary of agriculture to address the issue of regulatory policy. Carson penciled a symbol next to each name: "+ means at least reasonably on my side, 0 means neutral and if anything disposed to be negative, – means . . . strongly negative," she explained to Dorothy, and she told her that, looking over the balance, there was every reason to expect the program to be skewed heavily against her. Meanwhile, CBS was bombarded with thousands of letters, believed to be the product of a letter-writing campaign orchestrated by the chemical industry, demanding that the program be "fair" to pesticides. Three of the five major advertisers—two food manufacturers and the makers of Lysol chemical disinfectant—withdrew two days before the broadcast. Undaunted, CBS decided to expand the program.

CBS Reports: The Silent Spring of Rachel Carson aired on April 3, 1963—five years and two days after Carson began the Everestine climb that became *Silent Spring*. Edited into a point-counterpoint format, the program reads like a debate, with Carson and White-Stevens on either side and a cabal of government representatives between them. Leaning back in her chair, Carson delivers her points with measured composure, her words meticulously chosen and saturated with meaning yet streaming out effortlessly. White-Stevens inclines eagerly toward the camera, emphasizing each proclamation with a fiendish full-body nod and a lift of his bushy eyebrows. A white lab coat asserts his performative authority as he calls the writings of "Miss" Rachel Carson "gross distortions of the actual facts."

Carson reads passages from *Silent Spring* as the camera interpolates between resplendent scenes of nature—glistening schools of fish, birds feeding their young in a nest, waves breaking on foggy spruce-lined shorelines evocative of the primeval Earth—and footage of pipes draining chemicals into the ocean, store shelves stretching into an endless selection of the 55,500 legal pesticides, airplanes raining DDT upon rivers and forests and homes, birds and fish convulsing in dying agony. Carson's steady voice asks: "Can anyone believe it is possible to lay down such a barrage of poisons on the surface of the Earth without making it unfit for all life?"

White-Stevens addresses this devastation of ecosystems by industrial chemicals with the claim that wildlife numbers generally recover quickly—a claim that, if turned around on the human animal, appalls to the bone: Human "numbers" also recover quickly in evolutionary time, and yet we call the deliberate decimation of our own species murder, terrorism, genocide.

In between Carson and White-Stevens, Orville Freeman fumbles to articulate the government's confused stance, and the head of the FDA adamantly denies that pesticides found in produce are problematic.

CBS had orchestrated a deliberate contrast, the overall effect of which was the very opposite of what Carson had feared. In this debate waged on the national stage, she emerged the clear victor, making the chemical lobbyists appear like hysterical propagandists out to delude for profit and the government officials like incompetent, spineless bureaucrats unworthy of the public's confidence. The program host concluded by pointing out the fundamental difference between Carson and her critics—their respective views, one rooted in humility and the other in arrogance, about humanity's place in and relationship to nature. When White-Stevens proclaims into the camera that the disruption of the balance of nature is not a problem but a prerogative of humanity, that "the modern chemist, the modern biologist, the modern scientist" should aim unabashedly at "controlling" nature, the camera cuts to Carson, Minerva-like in her delivery of nuanced wisdom:

> To these people, apparently the balance of nature was something that was repealed as soon as man came on the scene—you might just as well assume that you could repeal the law of gravity. The balance of nature is built on a series of relationships between living things, and between living things and their environments—you can't just step in with some brute force and change one thing without changing many others. This doesn't mean, of course, that we must never interfere, that we must not attempt to tilt that balance of nature in our favor. But when we do make this attempt we must know what we're doing—we must know the consequences.

The program ended with a variation on the sentiment with which Carson had concluded her Scripps College commencement address. Her poignant, penetrating words, now addressing not just a single graduating class but the entire nation, perhaps the entire planet facing a shared future, transcending the particulars of her time and her subject. More than half a century later, they apply with unblunted precision to ethically complex applications of science as wide-ranging as gene editing and artificial intelligence:

> We still talk in terms of conquest. We still haven't become mature enough to think of ourselves as only a very tiny part of a vast and

incredible universe. . . . We're challenged, as mankind has never been challenged before, to prove our maturity and our mastery—not of nature, but of ourselves.

Immediately after the program, praise poured in to the CBS headquarters—calls and letters from hundreds of viewers grateful for what was essentially a tremendous gift of public service and citizen empowerment. The FDA, USDA, and Public Health Service were flooded with the opposite—outcries against the government's complicity in this chemical assault, demanding change. Shortly after the broadcast, the secretary of the interior—one of Carson's most vocal public champions—ended his speech at the ribbon-cutting of the government's first laboratory for the study of pesticides and wildlife with these words: "A great woman has awakened the Nation by her forceful account of the dangers around us. We owe much to Rachel Carson."

Among the estimated ten to fifteen million viewers who witnessed Carson's triumph on national television was John F. Kennedy. Within days, the White House hastened to complete the long-promised report on pesticides by the President's Science Advisory Committee. When it was finally released without warning a fortnight before what would be Carson's final birthday, it read like a forty-three-page vindication of *Silent Spring*. Stating that until the publication of Carson's book, "people were generally unaware of the toxicity of pesticides," the report held both government and industry accountable and stressed the urgent need for regulatory laws. That evening, CBS broadcast a follow-up program titled *The Verdict on the Silent Spring of Rachel Carson*, highlighting the major findings of the report between footage of Carson reading and White-Stevens responding from the previous broadcast. The host ended with the unambiguous verdict:

Miss Rachel Carson had two immediate aims. One was to alert the public; the second, to build a fire under the government. She accomplished the first aim months ago. Tonight's report by the presidential panel is prima facie evidence that she has accomplished the second.

Silent Spring sang hymnal proof of Whitman's conviction that true democracy is accomplished at least as much—if not "doubly as much"—by "fitting and democratic sociologies, literatures and arts" as it is by political laws. Carson had course-corrected government by employing the art of literature in the service of socially wakeful science.

After the CBS broadcast, Dorothy proudly said she was certain that Rachel Carson's name would be remembered longer than Gordon Cooper's—the astronaut who became the second American to orbit Earth when he piloted the final manned space mission of the *Mercury* program, and of whom I had never heard. *Faith 7*, the spacecraft that carried Cooper, had launched on the day of the CBS broadcast, which was interrupted seven times for updates on the flight. But it was Carson who held the nation's attention. "I don't suppose there is a household in this country where your name is unknown," Dorothy cheered. Still, tied up with caring for the convalescent Stan at home, she sorrowed at not being there to witness her beloved's triumph:

> I am denied the big things, the biggest of which would be to be with you in this triumphal hour. To see you last night (I am now writing at 6 A.M.) on the screen gave me a sense of frustration that I could not touch you! And how I should have enjoyed seeing you descend the curving stairs in the spotlight and hearing the applause.

That applause had reverberated through the ranks of government. Connecticut senator Abraham Ribicoff was tasked with chairing a committee to conduct a large-scale review of environmental hazards. Two weeks after the CBS broadcast, he invited Carson as key witness at the hearing slated for June. She accepted, well aware that testifying in Washington would require that she relinquish her precious hours with Dorothy at the edge of the sea she so loved. Despite their hope against hope, both must have known that this would be their final summer together. Carson had been counting down the moments until their reunion. "What deep happiness to look into your eyes!" she had written to Dorothy in anticipation of their season. But now Carson began doubting that she was in any condition to make the journey to Southport Island, which would put six hundred miles between her and her doctors. Perhaps Dorothy might visit her in Maryland instead. "So much I feel welling up that I want to say," she wrote. "If you can come it will all pour out."

By the end of the month, Carson was "weary in every bone." Acute chest pain had been piercing her heart for days. On the last night of April, as her heart raced with angina and a strange new blurring of vision made it difficult to see, she feared she might not live until morning. She sorrowed not for herself but for her beloved. "One by one, those you love are being taken from you," she wrote to Dorothy, whose cat Willow had just died. Anguished by the notion of leaving Dorothy without a farewell, without all that lay unexpressed expressed, she climbed out of bed to compose the "apple" of all "apples"—a letter articulating with uncensored candor what her beloved had meant to her all these years. She wrote:

> I have had a rich life, full of rewards and satisfactions that come to few and if it must end now, I can feel that I have achieved most of what I wished to do. That wouldn't have been true two years ago, when I first realized my time was short, and I am so grateful to have had this extra time.
>
> My regrets, darling, are for your sadness, for leaving Roger, when I so wanted to see him through manhood, for dear Jeffie whose life is linked to mine.
>
> But enough of that. What I want to write of is the joy and fun and gladness we have shared—for these are the things I want you to remember—I want to live on in your memories of happiness. I shall write more of those things. But tonight I'm weary and must put out the light. Meanwhile, there is this word—and my love will always live.

But when daybreak came and Rachel felt her symptoms subside, she folded the letter and tucked it into the "strongbox." Instead, she wrote to Dorothy from her home hospital bed:

> Darling . . .
> I want to write you, yet I am hesitant about everything I would say, for to speak of all that surrounds me will only make us long all the

more for what we hoped was to be. And I can't think what else to say! I know you feel the same way.

There are other things I need to say to you, but they should be said with my arms around you—so how can I write you of them? I feel I must see you, somehow, somewhere.

Then, returning to her native borderland of reason and romanticism, she added:

It is such a paradox that to write of the lovely things that mean so much to us both is only to worsen the ache in our hearts—but, at least, darling, we must be glad that in all this loveliness—the song of a woodthrush in a fairy world of dogwood, whippoorwills on a moonlight night, beautiful music—each of us lives for the other.

But as naturally as Dorothy had twined her two loves over the last decade, she suddenly faced a fraying physical fact: In early May, Stan was hospitalized again, hurling her once more into the ongoing terror of his uncertain recovery. She couldn't leave him alone, and she couldn't bear being apart from Rachel:

It is a terribly hard situation, darling. Here I am, trapped, because I dare not leave one of the two, while the longing and need to be with the other is almost beyond endurance.

Gracious and loving as ever, Rachel assured her that she must remain with Stan as he convalesced. At the end of May, Rachel and Roger flew to the island—driving was unthinkable—to spend five days with the Freemans. One hundred twenty hours. She made up her mind that she would spend the summer at Southport after all. With the scalpel-like awareness that it might be her last, she couldn't imagine spending it without Dorothy.

But first she had to return to Washington to appear before the congressional committee on pesticides.

On June 4, 1963, Carson climbed into the passenger seat of her Oldsmobile and had her assistant take her from Silver Spring to Capitol Hill—the pain in her back, spine, shoulder, and neck was by now too unbearable for Carson to drive even this short distance herself.

Under the bright television lights, all traces of physical agony fled from the authoritative presence that took the witness stand in the windowless, wood-paneled Room 102 of the Senate building. A crowd packed onto the stained once-carmine carpet, weaving between the cameramen and spilling out the door of the tiny chamber. One hundred and one years after Abraham Lincoln greeted *Uncle Tom's Cabin* author Harriet Beecher Stowe with the words "This is the little woman who wrote the book that started this great war," Senator Ribicoff greeted Carson: "Miss Carson . . . we welcome you here. You are the lady who started all this. Will you please proceed."

Speaking calmly into the press posy of six microphones before her, Carson proceeded to deliver a stunning forty-minute testimony predicated on revealing the delicate interconnectedness of nature and tracing the far-reaching devastation inflicted by poisonous chemicals once they enter an ecosystem. She called for a "strong and unremitting effort" to reduce and eventually eliminate pesticides. While her testimony was strewn with facts, it was palpably poetic in its elegy for ecology. It embodied that perfect line John F. Kennedy would deliver four months later in his eulogy for Robert Frost: "When power corrupts, poetry cleanses." Having built her life on the refusal to see poetry and science as separate, Carson effected an unprecedented cleansing of power with her twin talents.

At the end of her testimony, she took a question from an Alaskan senator in the audience, who wanted to know her views on the prospect of a government agency tasked with safeguarding nature. Carson gave her strong recommendation that such an agency be established—a landmark development that would take the government another seven years to institute. Carson would never live to see the creation of the Environmental Protection Agency, nor its ban of DDT, both the direct result of her work.

Her congressional testimony, after which she was flooded by letters from citizens thanking her for having spoken inconvenient truth to power, was a crowning moment for the sense of duty that had propelled Carson through the arduous years leading up to *Silent Spring*. Having executed her responsibility as a citizen, scientist, and steward of life for the last five years, she was free and restless to return to Southport, to the sea, to Dorothy.

No record survives of the weeks containing Rachel and Dorothy's last summer hours together—the absence of letters suggesting that they spent every precious moment in each other's presence. Tide pool excursions were now a thing of the past—compression fractures in Carson's spine made it difficult to walk, painful even to stand. Dorothy thought she looked like alabaster. They spent afternoons together in a little clearing in the woods near Carson's cottage, watching the clouds float across the sky, listening to the avian orchestra in the trees, and reading to each other from their favorite books—Henry Beston, E. B. White, Rachel's beloved 1908 children's novel *The Wind in the Willows*.

One shimmering day in early September, Dorothy took Rachel to their favorite spot on the tip of the island, where they had once watched meteors blaze ephemeral bridges of light across the riverine haze of the Milky Way. With their arms around each other, they slowly made the short, aching walk to the wooden benches perched atop the shore and sat under the blue late morning skies. Above the crashing waves, under the wind-strummed spruces, Dorothy and Rachel sat in intimate silence and watched a majestic procession of monarch butterflies flit toward the southern horizon on their annual migration—living meteors of black and gold. Half a century later, monarchs would take flight aboard the International Space Station, and the Fish and Wildlife Service, where Carson had found her dual devotion, would call for their inclusion in the protections of the Endangered Species Act—one of several dozen environmental protection laws passed in the 1970s as direct and indirect consequences of *Silent Spring*.

That afternoon, Rachel sent Dorothy a lyrical "postscript" to their morning—she had always felt that, for a writer, the inarticulable lends itself better to writing than to speaking. Detailing the splendors that had etched themselves onto her memory—the particular hue of the sky, the particular score of the surf—she wrote:

Most of all I shall remember the monarchs, that unhurried westward drift of one small winged form after another, each drawn by some invisible force. We talked a little about their migration, their life history. Did they return? We thought not; for most, at least, this was the closing journey of their lives.

But it occurred to me this afternoon, remembering, that it had been a happy spectacle, that we had felt no sadness when we spoke of the fact that there would be no return. And rightly—for when any living thing has come to the end of its life cycle we accept that end as natural.

For the Monarch, that cycle is measured in a known span of months. For ourselves, the measure is something else, the span of which we cannot know. But the thought is the same: when that intangible cycle has run its course it is a natural and not unhappy thing that a life comes to an end.

That is what those brightly fluttering bits of life taught me this morning. I found a deep happiness in it—so I hope, may you. Thank you for this morning.

"I prefer the time of insects to the time of stars," the Nobel Prize–winning Polish poet Wisława Szymborska would write many seasons later. Carson understood that the time of insects and the time of stars exist along a shared continuum, with the human animal, so grand in its ambitions and yet so perishable in its finite allotment of time, perched midway between them, beholden to both. A world without insects would be as dark as a world without stars, shorn of the shared stardust that makes a world a world.

28

TRACING THE THREAD OF BEING

When summer set on Southport Island, Carson began packing the cottage for the reluctant seasonal migration back to Silver Spring. She must have known, with the cellular awareness of a body frailing behind the denial-bolted portal of the conscious mind, that she would never return. We are congenitally blind to the lasts of life— a survival mechanism of the human psyche driven by the same stubborn dissent from impermanence that drives our dreams of immortality.

She moved with great difficulty—a new pelvic fracture rendered every step an agony. When the day of departure arrived, her long-time friend and Fish and Wildlife Service colleague Bob Hines, who had worked closely with her as the artist for *The Edge of the Sea*, all but carried her to the car. They drove twelve torturous hours to Silver Spring, deciding that the overnight trip, grueling as it was, would be easier to endure than stopping to check in to and out of a motel.

Back in Maryland, Carson ignored the barrage of requests from journalists, but she continued answering letters from students and wrote back to a new mother who asked about a baby food company that uses only pesticide-free produce—the term "organic" in relation to food wouldn't come into popular use for another four years. Bedridden, she fulfilled an information request from a student working on an article for a Pennsylvania high school science club magazine called *The Alchemist*. With sweet naïveté, the young man invited Carson to contribute another article soon. "We will be happy to put it in the next year's issue," he wrote.

There would be no next year for Carson.

In October, she began a new course of testosterone treatments she hoped would alleviate her pain just enough to make transcontinental travel endurable—she had promised to deliver a lecture in San Francisco and was determined to keep her word. Marie Rodell offered to escort her. Flying over the Grand Canyon for the first time, Carson was filled with awe at this spectacular monument to the relationship between land and sea, carved deep into Earth's geological record.

When Carson arrived, she gave her hosts the usual explanation of her wheelchair—acute arthritis. Ever since her cancer diagnosis, she had chosen not to let on that she was seriously ill—a fact only a handful of her intimates knew, and never to the full extent, for she habitually minimized her suffering. She even instructed Dorothy to tell inquiring neighbors that she was healthier than ever. Now, with not only her writing but her person the object of attacks, she took even greater care to conceal her illness, well aware that this, too, could be exploited in the merciless campaign to discredit her. Indeed, even arthritis was hurled against her. After Carson delivered an elegant speech on pesticides and ecology to a full house at the regal Fairmont Hotel in downtown San Francisco, a local newspaper breezed past the science and the significance of her points to describe her as "a middle-aged, arthritis-crippled spinster" who "hobbled off the platform" with her cane. Another paper, turning a deliberately deaf ear to the fervent ovation into which Carson had hobbled off, characterized her as "diminutive and extremely mild," unable to "command attention in a bunch of Brownie Girl Scouts."

After the lecture, Carson decided to realize her lifelong longing to see the California redwoods and set out to visit Muir Woods. "Between every two pine trees," John Muir had written in the margin of his copy of Emerson's essays, "there is a door leading to a new way of life." That way was the way of grasping and actively inhabiting the inherent interdependence of nature, to which Carson had devoted her life. "When we try to pick out anything by itself, we find it hitched to everything else in the universe," Muir had written.

David Brower, executive director of the Sierra Club and a long-time fan of Carson's, offered to take her on a tour of the Muir Woods. He would later encapsulate her genius with perfect suc-cinctness: "She did her homework, she minded her English, and she cared."

As Brower pushed her wheelchair between the majestic thousand-year-old trunks, Carson savored what Whitman, on his own first journey west a century earlier, had described as "the bracing and buoyant equilibrium of concrete outdoor Nature, the only perma-nent reliance for sanity of book or human life." Hiking through Muir Woods half a century after Carson's visit, with a volume of Whitman in my backpack, I run my fingers over the coarse, fragrant bark of these venerable trees that have outlived her and will out-live me.

Shortly after Carson returned from California, President Kenne-dy's assassination shook the nation. Carson was devastated, unable to think of anything else, unable to see it the way Whitman had strained to see Lincoln's assassination a century earlier:

> The soldier drops, sinks like a wave—but the ranks of the ocean eternally press on. Death does its work, obliterates a hundred, a thousand—President, general, captain, private—but the Nation is immortal.

Ever since her first writings about the sea, Carson had found the closest thing to immortality in the tidal cycles of change that continually destroy one element, one organism, and reabsorb its atoms into another. This had always been the way of the universe, nature's way. But there could be no promise of immortality in Ken-nedy's unnatural death, wrought by a cancer in the human spirit. She found herself "numb and dazed," unable to write a single word for days. Sensing the source of her silence, Dorothy articulated what Rachel could not: "In these past days I think we have felt apart from the world—in time and in space, living within our homes and yet so close to world-shaking events."

Seventy-some latitude degrees south, Jorge Luis Borges received the news at the National Library of Argentina. Stupefied, he walked out to wander the neighborhood in gutted disbelief, stopping in the street to share embraces with people he did not know who did not know him—a creaturely response to collective tragedy comparable only to collective joy, as on the day of the Kennedy-envisioned Moon landing. Borges found in both events "a sort of communion among men." He would later recall the common fabric of the two experiences—the lunar, the lunatic:

> There was the emotion over what had occurred, and there was also the emotion of knowing that thousands of people, millions of people, maybe all the people in the world, were feeling great emotion over what was occurring.

Kennedy had been invited to Gettysburg to give a speech commemorating the hundredth anniversary of the Gettysburg Address, but he declined in order to travel to Dallas and mediate rising tensions within the Democratic Party. Dwight Eisenhower, a resident of Gettysburg, spoke in his stead and called for upholding Lincoln's legacy of "a nation free, with liberty, dignity, and justice for all." Five months earlier, Martin Luther King, Jr., had been violently arrested in Alabama on the charge of parading without a permit while leading a nonviolent protest. In his famous letter penned in the Birmingham city jail, Dr. King called for recognizing the ecology of justice:

> Injustice anywhere is a threat to justice everywhere. We are caught in an inescapable network of mutuality, tied in a single garment of destiny. Whatever affects one directly, affects all indirectly.

Sixteen hundred hours before King's assassination, 864,353 after Lincoln's, and 72 after the Gettysburg speech he didn't deliver, Kennedy was shot in Texas. What if he had gone to Maryland instead? Chance and choice.

Meanwhile, the great Catalan cellist and conductor Pablo Casals was on his way to the White House to receive the Presidential Medal of Freedom—a rare honor for a foreigner. Two years earlier, just after Kennedy took office, Casals had visited the White House to perform a stunning cello rendition of "The Song of the Birds"—an old Spanish folk melody that he told the President symbolized his hopes for freedom and peace in the world. In an act of resistance to Francisco Franco's dictatorship in his native Spain, Casals had been refusing for years to perform in countries that recognized the Spanish despot's ultranationalist government. But he made an exception for Kennedy, seeing in him a beacon of democracy, art, and the human spirit. The day of the assassination plunged Casals, who had lived through two world wars and gruesome dictatorial violence, into an abyss of darkness he had never experienced, for he saw in the particular loss an ugliness reflecting on the whole of humanity. The "monstrous madness" of it would stay with him for the remainder of his life. It was alive as ever when he recounted at the age of ninety-three: "I have seen much of suffering and death in my lifetime, but I have never lived through a more terrible moment. For hours I could not speak. It was as if a beautiful and irreplaceable part of the world had suddenly been torn away."

Three days after the assassination, as a devastated nation was processing its shock and grief, the United Jewish Appeal of Greater New York transformed its twenty-fifth annual fund-raising gala, "Night of Stars," into a memorial. Vice President Lyndon B. Johnson had been scheduled to speak but canceled. Instead, Leonard Bernstein delivered the address to eighteen thousand of the country's most distinguished artists, writers, and other public figures— a passionate tribute to JFK's support of the arts and a piercing meditation on violence. At the New York Philharmonic the night before, Bernstein had conducted Mahler's Second Symphony—the *Resurrection*—in tribute to the memory of JFK. He now addressed the broader significance of the choice:

There were those who asked: Why the *Resurrection Symphony*, with its visionary concept of hope and triumph over worldly pain, instead of a Requiem, or the customary Funeral March from the Eroica? Why indeed? We played the Mahler symphony not only in terms of resurrection for the soul of one we love, but also for the resurrection of hope in all of us who mourn him. In spite of our shock, our shame, and our despair at the diminution of man that follows from this death, we must somehow gather strength for the increase of man, strength to go on striving for those goals he cherished. In mourning him, we must be worthy of him. . . . We loved him for the honor in which he held art, in which he held every creative impulse of the human mind, whether it was expressed in words, or notes, or paints, or mathematical symbols.

Bernstein quoted from a speech Kennedy would have delivered a few hours after the assassination: "America's leadership must be guided by learning and reason." The loss, he said, was only deepened by the awareness that it had been the product of the exact antipodes of learning and reason—"ignorance and hatred." I can picture the undulating furrow of his eyebrows, which always provided their own animate score to the symphonies he conducted:

Learning and Reason: those two words of John Kennedy's were not uttered in time to save his own life; but every man can pick them up where they fell, and make them part of himself, the seed of that rational intelligence without which our world can no longer survive. This must be the mission of every man of goodwill: to *insist, unflaggingly*, at risk of becoming a repetitive bore, but to *insist* on the achievement of a world in which the mind will have triumphed over violence.

Almost exactly a year before the assassination, at a benefit concert titled "An American Pageant of the Arts," Bernstein served as master of ceremonies and presented before President Kennedy a seven-year-old Chinese-born, French-raised cellist by the name of Yo-Yo Ma, who performed a 150-year-old concertino by Jean-Baptiste Bréval alongside his eleven-year-old sister, Yeou-Cheng, on the piano. The boy had been brought to Bernstein's attention by

Casals, who had heard him play and instantly recognized genius. Bernstein's voice boomed with warm pride as he introduced one of the greatest musicians of the century to come: "Now here's a cultural image for you to ponder as you listen: a seven-year-old Chinese cellist playing old French music for his new American compatriots."

It was during that selfsame benefit, broadcast nationwide, that Kennedy rose above his moment, above all moments, to make his most enduring offering to culture:

> I am certain that after the dust of centuries has passed over our cities, we, too, will be remembered not for victories or defeats in battle or in politics, but for our contribution to the human spirit.

When Carson finally composed herself from the shock of the tragedy, she told Dorothy that she was seized with a sorrowful sense of loss cutting so near the bone of the spirit that she felt as though a member of her own family had been murdered. But even with death so near, the will for life pressed on. Ten days earlier, Carson had glimpsed a strange spot of white in her garden. She had leaned down, a detonation of pain in each of her vertebrae, and gently pushed the withered late autumn grass apart to discover a pot of hyacinths, forgotten there since the previous spring. In late November, several improbable buds of this glory of spring had pushed up from the bulbs. Carson took the pot into her bedroom, where—against reason, against season—it was now abloom with white hyacinths. "White hyacinths for my soul," she told Dorothy.

As she hungered for consolation in the wake of the assassination, Carson did something unusual. Lying distraught in bed one night, unable to sleep, she tried to find something to read that would soothe her into somnolence. She walked over to the bookshelf and, in one of those rare bolts of inspired desperation, pulled out a yellowed copy of *Under the Sea-Wind*, her own first book. Reading from it, she found herself slowly relaxing and in that loosening finally understood, not with the mind but with the marrow, what her readers found in her books—that dwarfing of human dramas against the perspective-dilating backdrop of geological and cosmological time. "O the cares of man, how much of everything is futile," Kepler had inscribed as his motto three centuries earlier. She was reminded of a passage she had penned as an epilogue in an early draft of *The Edge of the Sea*, which eventually became a short, existentially hued chapter titled "The Enduring Sea"—Dorothy's favorite of any of Carson's writings. Perched at the window of her study long before cancer and Kennedy, with the sounds of the rising tide serenading eternity below, she had contemplated how space and time converge in the sea:

> The differences I sense in this particular instant of time that is mine are but the differences of a moment, determined by our place in the stream of time and in the long rhythms of the sea. Once this rocky coast beneath me was a plain of sand; then the sea rose and found a new shore line. And again in some shadowy future the surf will have ground these rocks to sand and will have returned the coast to its earlier state. And so in my mind's eye these coastal forms merge and blend in a shifting, kaleidoscopic pattern in which there is no finality, no ultimate and fixed reality—earth becoming fluid as the sea itself.

This contact with the timeless rose and fell in Carson as the shoreline of her mortality edged this side of the horizon. Some days she was buoyed by the potent elixir of tenacity and denial, soaring into the possibilities of what she still hoped to accomplish. Other days she plummeted into deep depression. Whitman had recognized this above-average ebb and flow of emotion as the blessed curse of the artist—all who reach "sunny expanses and sky-reaching heights" are apt "to dwell on the bare spots and darknesses." "I have a theory that no artist or work of the very first class may be or can be without them," he declaimed.

Sensing how troubled Rachel was about what would happen to Roger and Jeffie after her death, Stan volunteered that he and Dorothy would take care of both boy and cat. Stan had been a father figure for Roger—the only one he'd ever had—since the boy first began visiting Southport Island as a toddler. But touched as

Rachel was by Stan's large-hearted offer, she was not ready to face the question at all, gripped by that creaturely survival instinct of denial when confronted with the imminence of nonsurvival.

She asked Dorothy and Stan to meet her in New York, where she was to receive a constellation of honors. The first was the highest medal of the National Audubon Society for her incalculable public service to conservation. It had never been awarded to a woman before. Two days later, at the reception for the American Geographical Society medal, Stan photographed Dorothy and Rachel beaming in their elegant silk gowns—a joyous occasion Carson would recall the next day as "the 19 hours," feeling more acutely than ever the flight of her time, their time. But the honor that most moved her that month was her admission to the American Academy of Arts and Letters, whose membership was limited to fifty artists. Among them were only three living women, including Pearl S. Buck—the first American woman to receive the Nobel Prize in Literature—and the poet Marianne Moore, with whom Carson had shared a National Book Award table a decade earlier. Carson was honored by all the recognition she received for the scientific and civic dimensions of her work, but this she cherished in a different way. Typically bestowed upon novelists and poets, this honor was a recognition of her contribution as a literary artist—the childhood dream she had refused to surrender even as she turned to science.

But the jubilation of the month was blackened just before Christmas when Jeffie died. Carson was devastated. "I have found that deep awareness of life and its meaning in the eyes of a beloved cat," she had written years earlier. But she also felt the dark relief of not having to worry about what would become of Jeffie—as she had to worry with Roger—once she returned her own atoms to the sea.

Christmas had always been Rachel and Dorothy's special time. They must have known this would be their last. In the annual Christmas letter that had been their private tradition for a decade, Dorothy reflected on their years of love. She dated it "Christmas 1963 AC"—for "After Carson," a testament to how profoundly Rachel's love had changed her life. Her words streamed with the parallel currents of adoration and anticipatory loss:

Ten years, dar, since that first Christmas message. What can I say now, ten years later, that I didn't say in 1953? The words may be different but the theme—I need you, I love you—is the same. As I needed you then for understanding, and for the kind of companion-ship that no one else has been able to give, I need you now as much, and even more. As I loved you then, for yourself, and for all you rep-resent, I love you now—with warmth and earnestness and longing.

And so I give my Christmas thanks for this ten years—years that have enriched, yes, and even changed my life. Such years—of joy and sorrow for us both. As we shared the joys, no less have we shared the sorrows. Sometimes I wonder how I could have endured the depths without your sustaining love. Without you, in those shadowy days I know life would not have been worth living.

The sentiment harked back to the poem Dorothy had sent Rachel as she headed into her mastectomy operation three and a half years earlier, which ended with these lines:

My hopes were heaven-high,
They are fulfilled in you.
I am the pool of gold
When sunset burns and dies—
You are my deepening skies;
Give me your stars to hold.

Not knowing exactly when Rachel would discover the Christmas letter, Dorothy ended it with these words:

Whatever time it is when you read this, please know my arms are fig-uratively about you. So close your eyes and know that you are loved.

She enclosed in the letter a clipping from the December 21 issue of the *Saturday Review*, in which the author had written:

How many of the thousands of books published . . . actually move or change the course of civilization? . . . Offhand, I can think of *Silent Spring* as another example of the effect of a book on more than just bookseller and reader.

Just after Christmas, Dorothy drove to Silver Spring for a four-day holiday visit. They listened to Beethoven together, read to each other, and tried to savor the bittersweet nectar of their diminishing store of hours. After Dorothy left, Rachel reached across time to their first stardusted "thirteen hours," after which she had promised her love to Dorothy with the Keats verse that begins "A thing of beauty is a joy forever." Looking back on that promise, she wrote:

> That has proved to be supremely true, darling, through all the ten years since I quoted it. As long as either of us lives, I know our love will "never pass into nothingness" but will keep a quiet bower stored with peace and with precious memories of all that we have shared.
> I need not say it again but I shall—I love you, now and always.

A fortnight later, while Stan was sitting at the kitchen table and delighting in the sight of birds in the feeder he had just filled with seeds, his heart stopped. His surgery the previous year had left Dorothy optimistic after so many years of ill health. His death—so sudden, so folded into the mundane—seemed surreal. Rachel, at this point in the final weeks of her own life and ravaged by pain, flew to West Bridgeport for Stan's funeral. Anxious to do whatever she could for Dorothy, she wrote to her from the airplane as soon as she was in the air heading back to Silver Spring—on her most cherished notepaper, made by developmentally disabled children in Ohio; their teacher, a friend of Marie Rodell's, had sent a pad to Carson, who was so moved by the project that she wrote back and asked if she could buy it in quantity.

Dorothy and Rachel talked on the phone nightly in the wake of Stan's death. By every reasonable standard, he should have outlived Rachel. But there had never been anything standard or reasonable about their three lives—about the way their lives had entwined, about the way they were now unraveling. "No one's fated or doomed to love anyone," Adrienne Rich would write. "The accidents happen."

One evening, hanging up after another long conversation, Rachel and Dorothy had both felt the need to say one last "good night"—

a need that had crossed in a double busy signal. That night, reflecting on the sweetness and symmetry of this mutuality, Rachel exhorted in a letter:

> Darling, let's resolve that we are going to make use of every possible bit of time to be together. For all of us, not just for me, time is a precious gift, and it is one that can't be hoarded, but must be used well and joyously as it slips through our fingers.

Within a month, the cancer had spread to Carson's liver. She called on her friend the Reverend Dr. Duncan Howlett—a fellow writer, civil rights leader, and Unitarian minister. A great admirer of her work, Howlett had preached sermons based on her books. In the midst of the attacks on *Silent Spring,* he had told Carson that he considered her a prophet of her era on a par with Jeremiah. Now he was to receive her dying wish. With a steady eye to her vanishing hours, Carson said she was to be cremated, her ashes scattered at Southport Island. She asked him to read at the modest funeral service the existential passage from *The Edge of the Sea* that Dorothy so loved.

In the low late afternoon light of April 14, 1964, Rachel Carson suffered a heart attack. The sun was just about to set over the hilltops alive with spring when she drew her last breath, molecules that had once pulsated in the lungs of Kepler, of Dickinson, of Fuller, of every other human who had ever breathed the atmosphere of this pale blue dot.

Rachel's body was still warm when her brother Robert, selfabnegated absentee from the family for decades, stormed into the house, pushed past the weeping Roger and Carson's housekeeper, and began making decisions that countered every wish and will of his sister's. Within hours of her death, he tore through her papers and destroyed everything he thought controversial. He barged into Roger's bedroom and confiscated what he felt should not belong to the grief-stricken twelve-year-old boy, even though Carson had left her son all her personal effects. Then, negating Rachel's wish to be cremated, he sent her body to a funeral home for preparation and began making arrangements for a national spectacle of a burial at the Washington National Cathedral. Marie Rodell couldn't stop him. Dorothy didn't even try. In a different time, she would have had the spousal say, that supreme right bestowed only by love but yet unratified by legislature. Now, leveled by loss and powerless by law, she had no claim. She could only collect herself enough to go to the funeral home and view the body that had housed a hyacinthine soul.

Meanwhile, news of Carson's death traveled across radio waves and newspaper headlines, throwing readers into a state of Borgesian collective grief. No one had known she had been seriously ill. In a multipage obituary, *The New York Times* chronicled her achievements as a champion of science and an agent of cultural change, and mourned with uncharacteristic affection this "small, solemn-looking woman with the steady forthright gaze of a type that is sometimes common to thoughtful children who prefer to listen rather than to talk." Another obituary proclaimed: "Because of this gentle, valiant lady, mankind may to some degree leave its stupid, callous, ruthless trail to seek a better."

That summer, President Lyndon Johnson would sign the Wilderness Act, establishing a National Wilderness Preservation System for America—a landmark achievement unprecedented anywhere in the world, designating large swaths of federal land to be left untouched by human ruthlessness.

Condolence letters from strangers began streaming into Houghton Mifflin and Marie Rodell's office. A woman who had attended Carson's speech at the International Council of Women a year earlier recounted the standing ovation by "women of 58 countries speaking multiple tongues yet complete in their understanding of her message to the world." On letterhead identifying him as a "business card specialist," a man professed "a feeling of personal loss" in receiving the news of Carson's death and wrote that *The Sea Around Us* would remain "a timeless epitaph to a wonderful woman." Another man reported learning of Carson's death "with a terrible sense of shock" and told Rodell: "Please accept our deep feeling of sympathy in your great loss and in the nation's." A woman wrote: "Besides being a gay, gentle, gallant person, I think she had more eternity in her than most. To such rare ones, it seems, somehow, that one must say hello and not goodbye."

The reluctant public goodbye took place on the morning of Friday, April 17. Carson's brother never called Reverend Howlett. Instead, the fourth bishop of Washington—a man who had opposed the ordination of women to the priesthood and maintained his membership in organizations that excluded nonwhites—led a funeral procession of a hundred fifty mourners. He refused to read the passages Carson had requested—passages in which her reverence for nature bore strong evolutionary overtones. Instead, he read prayers her brother had selected as six men, including Senator Ribicoff and Carson's old friend Bob Hines, carried the bronze casket beneath the grand dome.

Carson's own brother had perpetrated what she had most dreaded throughout her ascent to unexpected fame—the crushing of her private person under the weight of a public persona. The person in the bronze casket was not Rachel but the person she and Dorothy called "the other woman." The service was so stark a caricature of so much she deplored that it jolted those who loved Carson—Dorothy, Marie Rodell, Bob Hines, her housekeeper, her research assistant—to band together and push back against her brother's demand that she be buried next to their mother rather than cremated. Perhaps fearing a public scandal that would unmask his hijacking of his famous sister's image, he finally half-relented, agreeing to the cremation but demanding that half of Carson's ashes go into the cemetery.

Rodell was so appalled by this cascade of disrespects that, overtaken by a kind of mother-bear instinct, she sidestepped Robert and called Reverend Howlett after the public funeral. That Sunday, Carson's intimates gathered at All Souls Unitarian Church for a very different memorial. Howlett opened with his conviction that Carson was one of the true prophets of the time, then prefaced the passages she had requested with a reading of the monarch butterflies letter, which Dorothy had given him for the occasion.

For all the damage Carson's brother had done, he hadn't managed to violate the "strongbox." It must have felt like a gray miracle to Dorothy when she found in it the unsent letter Rachel had written that frightening night a spring earlier, when she feared she might not live until morning. What unfathomable currents of love and sorrow must have coursed through her as she read:

> Darling—if the heart does take me off suddenly, just know how much easier it would be for me that way. But I do grieve to leave my dear ones. As for me, however, it is quite all right. Not long ago I sat late in my study and played Beethoven, and achieved a feeling of real peace and even happiness.
>
> Never forget, dear one, how deeply I have loved you all these years.
>
> Rachel

On a clear blue morning in early May, Dorothy drove to the tip of Southport Island with the other half of Rachel's ashes beside her. She walked to the spot where they had watched the monarchs and took a breath before scattering into the high tide the stardust that had once constellated into a beloved soul. As the ashes drifted into the ocean, she threw behind them a white hyacinth.

Fourteen years earlier, after her first surgery to remove the tumors she thought were benign, Carson had gone to the shore to recuperate for a week, walking on the beach every morning and filling her field notebook with observations. I touch the edge of the small lined page onto which her loose, undulating hand spills:

> Walked south on the beach—a cloudy, grey morning with showers of rain. . . . Saw tracks of a shore bird probably a sanderling, and followed them a little, then they turned toward the water and were soon obliterated by the sea. How much it washes away, and makes as though it had never been. Time itself is like the sea, containing all

that came before us, sooner or later sweeping us away on its flood and washing over and obliterating the traces of our presence, as the sea this morning erased the foot-prints of the bird.

Rachel Carson was days shy of her fifty-seventh birthday when she was swept away by the sea. Exactly fifty-seven years before her birth, Margaret Fuller decided that it was time to leave Italy, traverse the oceanic abyss, and return to America.

29

FROM SHORELESS SEEDS TO STARDUST

On July 18, 1850, after two months at sea, the *Elizabeth* perches triumphant between Cape May and Barnegat off the New Jersey coast. Margaret Fuller, still elated by Nino's miraculous recovery and infected with the collective cheer in anticipation of tomorrow's arrival in New York, packs her notebooks and her more minor possessions into her trunks, kisses Nino goodnight, then carefully lays out the outfit she has chosen for him to wear when his grandmother receives him into her arms.

As the last light of the setting sun draws a thin orange line between the steely waters and the thickening blanket of clouds, low thunder bellows this side of the horizon, announcing what Rachel Carson would call "the sea's power and its capacity for doing the unexpected . . . [a] reminder of how little we know, and of the mystery that is eternally the sea's."

By nine o'clock, an accelerating wind is beating the sails. The favorable gust in which all had so rejoiced swirls into a storm. By midnight, the storm has swelled into a hurricane. Waves of sudden ferocity send shudders through the ship as the current sweeps it north of the intended route. At 2:30 a.m., the novice captain measures twenty-one fathoms. Deeming it still safe for the ship's passage, he retires to his bunk. An hour later, the *Elizabeth* strikes sharp bottom—the lighthouse the captain had mistaken for the New Jersey coast turns out to belong to the rocky shore of Fire

Island, past which the young Rachel Carson would sail on her first encounter with the ocean.

The mainmast and the mizzenmast are immediately felled. Wave after wave sweeps over the deck with the undulating rage of a Beethoven symphony, washing away all the lifeboats as the ship hurtles toward the rocks. The heavy marble in its belly breaks through the hull and the hole begins gulping water at inconceivable speed.

Chaos envelops the *Elizabeth* as the passengers sense themselves hurled toward death. They rush to the main cabin and try to steady themselves against the windward side. Some are praying, some cursing, some enduring silently. In the distance, the lighthouse blinks like the enormous eye of some unfeeling cyclops.

Margaret Fuller is no longer a disembodied intellect but a body filled with a tempest of feeling, under siege by the elements that made it. Her hair has cascaded loose over her shoulders—a soaked Zenobia, white nightgown licked to her skin by the swirling cataclysm of rain and saltwater. She is singing to the drenched and terrified Nino—what song, and in what language?—as passengers and crew huddle around the surviving foremast.

For several hours, as the ship creaks apart and fills with water, they await help from the shore. They can see men gathering on the beach, but there is no lifeboat in sight. Some of the sailors leap into the ocean to save themselves.

Davis, the intrepid first mate to the novice captain, suggests a mechanism for rescuing the passengers one by one—each is to lie on a plank holding on to rope handles while Davis swims behind it, guiding the makeshift raft to the shore three hundred feet away. Captain Hasty's widow goes first. After two near-drownings, she washes up ashore, barely alive. Davis returns and urges Fuller to go next, but she refuses unless her whole family can be saved together, hoping a lifeboat would arrive from the shore.

Hours pass. The withdrawing tide placates the waves for a momentary window of opportunity for easier escape, but Fuller and Ossoli remain adamant that they will not be separated. A lifeboat appears on the beach, but no one launches it. Twelve hours into the storm, Davis resigns to their obstinacy and orders the remaining crew to save themselves. Four sailors defy and remain aboard to help. What makes a person go this way or that, the way of valor or self-salvation? One of them persuades Fuller to hand him Nino in a canvas bag, which he ties to his neck with the promise to save the boy or die with him, so that she may try the plank. The tide now having turned, the storm is raging with full ferocity again.

That spring, Fuller had noted in her journal the news of a ship-wreck in which a Parisian friend had perished, and had written with an eye to her own homeward voyage:

> Safety is not to be secured, then, by the wisest foresight. I shall embark more composedly in our merchant-ship, praying fervently, indeed, that it may not be my lot to lose my boy at sea, either by unsolaced illness, or amid the howling waves; or, if so, that Ossoli, Angelo, and I may go together, and that the anguish may be brief.

I can picture her habitually squinted eyes now open with full aquamarine intensity in the early morning hours as she looks over her shoulder at her son, body reluctantly facing the glistening edge of the deck.

But before she can mount the plank, a massive wave hits the ship, breaking the surviving foremast and sweeping the deck and everyone on it into the raging sea. For a moment, Margaret's night-gown balloons into a puff of white before blending with the froth-ing waters.

Above the storm clouds, a comet visible with the naked eye blazes across the July sky at a hundred thousand miles per hour. Below, stardust to seafoam to stardust.

Twenty minutes later, Nino and his sailor-guardian wash up ashore—dead, still warm—along with one of Fuller's trunks. The surviving sailors lay the child they so adored in a seaman's chest and, weeping, bury him in the sand. Margaret's and Ossoli's bod-ies are never found. Of her papers, only their love letters survive, spared in the one trunk unswallowed by the sea. Fuller's proudest work, which would have been the sole journalistic chronicle of the Italian revolution, is washed into the sea.

. . .

Ten days before the shipwreck, Herman Melville has purchased *Natural History of the Sperm Whale*—a book published in the year of photography's invention, which would become his primary scientific source material for *Moby-Dick*. As Fuller's body is being carried to the ocean floor, Melville writes in the seventh chapter of the epic novel he would dedicate to Nathaniel Hawthorne:

> A muffled silence reigned, only broken at times by the shrieks of the storm. Each silent worshipper seemed purposely sitting apart from the other, as if each silent grief were insular and incommunicable.

Sixteen chapters later, he writes:

> All deep, earnest thinking is but the intrepid effort of the soul to keep the open independence of her sea. . . . As in landlessness alone resides the highest truth, shoreless, indefinite as God—so better is it to perish in that howling infinite, than be ingloriously dashed upon the lee.

Eighty-seven years later, Rachel Carson would write of "the inexorable laws of the sea" in the *Atlantic* debut that launches her literary career, published when she is the age that Fuller was when she was shipwrecked:

> Individual elements are lost to view, only to reappear again and again in different incarnations in a kind of material immortality. Kindred forces to those which, in some period inconceivably remote, gave birth to that primeval bit of protoplasm tossing on the ancient seas continue their mighty and incomprehensible work. Against this cosmic background the life span of a particular plant or animal appears, not as a drama complete in itself, but only as a brief interlude in a panorama of endless change.

Fuller herself had intuited this inescapable cycle of destruction and creation, writing to her brother from war-torn Rome:

Foolish the fancy that because one lovely garden perished in the
storm, rich nature could not create another.

Another foolish fancy: the losing game of what-ifs that bedevils
all hindsight. For instance: When the *Elizabeth* plummets to the
howling infinite, the *United States Nautical Almanac* is still five
years into the future. Would the ship have fared differently if it had
been navigated by Maria Mitchell's celestial computations rather
than a frazzled sailor's intuition? Would Fuller have sailed at all if
Emerson's impassioned entreaty to stay had reached her? And if the
ship had arrived unscathed, would the idyll of that improbable love
have lasted ever after—or would Margaret, reunited with Waldo
and reimmersed in the cultured world she had once reigned, have
grown disenchanted with Ossoli's docile sweetness devoid of intellectual vitality?

Caroline Healey Dall, who identified deeply with Fuller since
the day she walked into her "Conversations" at the age of nineteen, contemplated this question in her diary after the shipwreck.
Dall envisioned the disillusionment that likely awaited Fuller—
a woman whose life had been marked by unremitting intellectual
restlessness—had her romance with Ossoli not been cut short by
death after only three years:

> I feel that Margaret was happy to die, before the mist dissolved. The
> true union must be not only a union of heart and flesh—but of mind.
> We must think together.

Several years earlier, in the thick of his entanglement with Margaret, Waldo had written in his journal under the heading LIFE:

> A ship is a romantic object but as soon as one embarks, the romance
> instantly quits that vessel & hangs on all other ships, on every sail in
> the horizon; but the old curse makes your deck a few dull planks,—no
> more.

Behind each door of what-if lies an unanswerable question that
unhinges an infinite Rube Goldberg machine of probabilities. The

life we have is the only one we will ever know, and even that with tenuous certainty.

Three nights before the *Elizabeth* sinks—as the deadly mycobacterium is weaving its way through Annie Darwin's body in England, as France is mourning the sudden loss of Louis Daguerre to a heart attack, as Emily Dickinson is beginning to fall in love with Susan Gilbert in Amherst, as Harriet Hosmer is dreaming up her sculpture of *Hesper, the Evening Star* in Boston—John Adams Whipple uses Harvard's Great Refractor telescope to make the first daguerreotype of a star: Vega, the second-brightest star in the northern celestial hemisphere, object of one of Galileo's most ingenious experiments supporting his proof of heliocentricity. "Nothing should surprise us any more, who see the miracle of stars," Elizabeth Barrett Browning wrote in *Aurora Leigh*.

An emissary of spacetime, Vega's light reaches the telescope's lens from twenty-five light-years away to deliver an image of the star as it had been a quarter century earlier—the year the teenage Margaret declared herself to be "determined on distinction."

Henry James—the seven-year-old brother of Emerson's godson William James—is traveling on a ferry from Manhattan to Long Island with his father when Washington Irving, a family friend, delivers the news of the shipwreck. Fuller would become the "Margaret-ghost" haunting Henry James's *The Bostonians*. James would commend her for "having achieved, so unaided and so ungraced, a sharp identity," as a "singular woman" who had been "a sparkling fountain to other thirsting young." It is not improbable that Walt Whitman, who had just begun composing *Leaves of Grass,* is also aboard the ferry—he so cherished ferries as "inimitable, streaming, never-failing, living poems" that he often rode them without going anywhere in particular, merely savoring "the great tides of humanity" traversing the New York waters.

Emerson, blackened by the news, writes in his journal the day after the shipwreck:

Margaret dies on rocks of Fire Island Beach within sight of and within sixty rods of the shore. To the last her country proves inhospitable to her; brave, eloquent, subtle, accomplished, devoted, constant soul! . . . There should be a gathering of her friends and some Beethoven should play the dirge.

Fathoms deeper than this loss for the world is his private loss—Margaret had been the prime point of his unrealized Platonic pentagon of "ideal relations" and the person with whom he most closely approximated, though never fully reached, the grace of feeling understood:

She bound in the belt of her sympathy and friendship all whom I know and love. . . . Her heart, which few knew, was as great as her mind, which all knew. . . . I have lost in her my audience.

But the conflicted push and pull that had frayed the elasticity of affection between Waldo and Margaret plays out one final time. As life had done them part, so death: Unable to bring his body to the site of the tragedy and try salvaging whatever might remain of the only person whose soul spoke the secret language of his, Emerson brings his intellect instead, choosing to remain in Concord in order to begin composing what would become a part eulogy, part biography of Fuller. He hands seventy dollars to the thirty-three-year-old Thoreau and sends him off to Fire Island in his own stead, commanding him to "go, on all our parts, & obtain on the wrecking ground all the intelligence &, if possible, any fragments of manuscript or other property."

When Thoreau arrives at Fire Island, he begins interviewing survivors and itemizing Fuller's belongings. One more of her trunks has now been found, empty—"whether emptied by the sea," Thoreau writes, "or by thieves, is not known." He nearly dies on an oyster boat manned by three drunken fishermen whom he has hired to take him to where he believes the looters live. Finding nothing of Margaret's, he watches the surreal spectacle of children playing in hats scavenged from the wreckage.

As Thoreau paces the shoreline for more than a week, the horizon now level with lifeless silence after the storm has swallowed distinction into primordial nothingness, is he thinking of Goethe's poem "Meeresstille"—"Calm at Sea"—which Beethoven had once set to music and which Margaret must have read, and quite possibly even tried translating, during her German period?

> Silence deep rules o'er the waters,
> Calmly slumbering lies the main,
> While the sailor views with trouble
> Nought but one vast level plain.
>
> Not a zephyr is in motion!
> Silence fearful as the grave!
> In the mighty waste of ocean
> Sunk to rest is every wave.

Having lost its home star, the *Tribune* dispatches its most promising young reporter to the scene—the poet and travel writer turned journalist Bayard Taylor. That autumn, Taylor would garner literary acclaim by winning a poetry competition with his poem "The Swedish Nightingale," an ode to Jenny Lind on the occasion of her American tour; that winter, he would come unhinged by loss as his young wife dies of tuberculosis months after their wedding.

At Fire Island, the twenty-five-year-old Taylor surveys the wreckage and tries to fathom the cause of this two-part tragedy in which the ferocious power of nature and the foibles of human nature have conspired—first the wreck itself, which he attributes to the ineptitude of the captain; then the merciless passivity of the bystanders. He interviews the surviving sailors, who testify that the first human activity they saw ashore after daybreak was that of plunderers carrying away cargo that had washed up, indulging their "ignorant and unscrupulous greed" instead of launching a rescue effort. The only lifeboat, at the lighthouse, was a mere three miles away, but no effort was made to fetch it until noon, and it was never launched. There is no room for journalistic impartiality—with grievous blame,

Taylor charges that had the islanders rowed the lifeboat toward the ship first thing after daybreak, before the tide rose, every life could have been saved. He reports that locals, upon witnessing the buzzing search for Fuller, exclaimed that had they known the woman on the sinking ship was of such celebrity, they would have gone to her rescue. A sentiment this hollowing makes me wonder whether Fuller, who so fiercely believed that every human life was worthy and capable of greatness—that genius was "common as light" when given a chance—would have wished herself saved by such criminally discriminant mercy.

Word of Fuller's death travels from Emerson to Carlyle to the Brownings. Elizabeth Barrett Browning, shocked by the "dreadful event," hastens to immortalize her admiration:

> High and pure aspiration she had—yes, and a tender woman's heart—and we honored the truth and courage in her, rare in woman or man.

But then, after venturing that Fuller's forever-lost record of the revolution would have been her only written work on a par with her unequaled conversation, Browning adds: "Was she happy in anything, I wonder? She told me that she never was."

Even Longfellow, who never warmed to Fuller as a person, sorrows at the loss for literature, for the nation, for the world:

> What a calamity! A singular woman for New England to produce; original and somewhat self-willed; but full of talent and full of work. A tragic end to a somewhat troubled and romantic life.

After devouring the memorial book Emerson had edited, Carlyle gasps:

> Such a predetermination to eat this big universe as her oyster or her egg, and to be absolute empress of all height and glory in it that her art could conceive, I have not before seen in any human soul.

Although Fuller's body is never recovered, her Emersonian circle of friends erect a monument to her at Mount Auburn—the majestic cemetery in her native Cambridge, the first grave of which was dug the year Emily Dickinson was born. I go searching for Fuller's tombstone one wet autumn morning a million and a half hours after her death, listening to the sonata of raindrops on the pond as I weave through the maze of paths. Hundred-year-old oaks and maples tower above me, their golden-orange leaves a flock of monarch butterflies on the rain-blackened branches.

I find the monument, as tall as me, unboastful, on a sloping stretch of grass beneath a white oak that could not have been more than a seed when Fuller died. I run my fingertips over the weathered marble, over the unflattering profile drawn from the sole daguerreotype of her, over the letters on the memorial plaque:

IN MEMORY OF
MARGARET FULLER OSSOLI
BORN IN CAMBRIDGE, MASS., MAY 23, 1810

BY BIRTH A CHILD OF NEW ENGLAND
BY ADOPTION A CITIZEN OF ROME
BY GENIUS BELONGING TO THE WORLD

IN YOUTH
AN INSATIATE STUDENT, SEEKING THE HIGHEST CULTURE
IN RIPER YEARS
TEACHER, WRITER, CRITIC OF LITERATURE AND ART
IN MATURE AGE
COMPANION AND HELPER OF MANY
EARNEST REFORMER IN AMERICA AND EUROPE

My fingers glide over the sixth line again, then again—a haptic refrain: BY GENIUS BELONGING TO THE WORLD. It strikes me, this existential ecology, as the simplest, most perfect measure of an actualized life—far fuller than fame and success, more generous than personal love and its greedy affinities, more precise than happiness and its confused aims.

.   .   .

Meanwhile, someplace in the world, somebody is making love and another a poem. Elsewhere in the universe, a star manyfold the mass of our third-rate sun is living out its final moments in a wild spin before collapsing into a black hole, its exhale bending spacetime itself into a well of nothingness that can swallow every atom that ever touched us and every datum we ever produced, every poem and statue and symphony we've ever known—an entropic spectacle insentient to questions of blame and mercy, devoid of *why*.

In four billion years, our own star will follow its fate, collapsing into a white dwarf. We exist only by chance, after all. The *Voyager* will still be sailing into the interstellar shorelessness on the wings of the "heavenly breezes" Kepler had once imagined, carrying Beethoven on a golden disc crafted by a symphonic civilization that long ago made love and war and mathematics on a distant blue dot.

But until that day comes, nothing once created ever fully leaves us. Seeds are planted and come abloom generations, centuries, civilizations later, migrating across coteries and countries and continents. Meanwhile, people live and people die—in peace as war rages on, in poverty and disrepute as latent fame awaits, with much that never meets its more, in shipwrecked love.

I will die.

You will die.

The atoms that huddled for a cosmic blink around the shadow of a self will return to the seas that made us.

What will survive of us are shoreless seeds and stardust.

ACKNOWLEDGMENTS

My magmatic gratitude to Emily Levine, for igniting my love of poetry; to James Gleick, for being the first to correct my pronunciation of "Maria Mitchell" and for insistently calling this project a "book" since the very beginning, despite my protestations to the hilt; to Dan Frank, for his boundless generosity, thoughtfulness, and kindness; to Amanda Stern and Sunny Bates, for invaluable feedback and fellowship in critical moments; to Amanda Palmer and Neil Gaiman, for the home away from home, where many of these pages were written; to Debbie Millman, Natascha McElhone, Emily Spivack, Jennifer Benka, and Alan Lightman for the constancy of encouragement; to Britta van Dun, Ruth Burtman, and Lisa Grant, for stewarding my sanity; to Dustin Yellin, Jackie Yellin, and Karen Maldonado for opening their hearts and their home to an itinerant writer.

To Janna Levin, for everything.

BIBLIOGRAPHY

Every voracious reader knows that there is no Dewey system for the Babel of the mind. You walk amid the labyrinthine stacks and ideas leap at you like dust bunnies drawn from the motes that cover a great many different books read long ago. In a sense, I have brought every book I have ever read and every thought I have ever thought—that is, all of myself—to this project. This makes it impossible to itemize a lifetime of consciously and unconsciously absorbed material in an exhaustive bibliography. But of what I did consciously seek out, I have relied predominantly on primary source materials—the letters, diaries, and personal writings of my figures, most of which are in the public domain—with biographies and other secondary scholarship as a complementary aid; to the authors of the latter I remain grateful.

What follows is a bibliography of the sources I deliberately referenced, arranged by figure and in descending order of source reliance.

PRIMARY FIGURES

Johannes Kepler
The Harmony of the World by Johannes Kepler, translated by E. J. Aiton, A. M. Duncan, and J. V. Field
Kepler's Dream by John Lear
Kepler by Max Caspar
BBC *In Our Time*: "Johannes Kepler"
The Astronomer and the Witch: Johannes Kepler's Fight for His Mother by Ulinka Rublack

Maria Mitchell
Life, Letters, and Journals by Maria Mitchell
Maria Mitchell: A Life in Journals and Letters by Henry Albers
Our Famous Women: Maria Mitchell by Julia Ward Howe
Among the Stars by Margaret Moore Booker
Maria Mitchell and the Sexing of Science: An Astronomer Among the American Romantics by Renee Bergland
The Maria Mitchell Association archives, with special thanks to Jascin Finger

Margaret Fuller
The Letters of Margaret Fuller, volumes I–VI, edited by Robert N. Hudspeth
Woman in the Nineteenth Century by Margaret Fuller
Summer on the Lakes by Margaret Fuller
Papers on Literature and Art by Margaret Fuller
Memoirs of Margaret Fuller Ossoli, edited by Ralph Waldo Emerson, William Channing, and James Freeman Clarke
These Sad but Glorious Days: Dispatches from Europe, 1846–1850 by Margaret Fuller
Margaret Fuller: Whetstone of Genius by Mason Wade
Eminent Women of the Age: Margaret Fuller Ossoli by Thomas Wentworth Higginson
Love Letters of Margaret Fuller, edited by Julia Ward Howe and James Nathan
Margaret Fuller: A New American Life by Megan Marshall
The Lives of Margaret Fuller by John Matteson
Essays and Lectures by Ralph Waldo Emerson
Ralph Waldo Emerson: Selected Journals 1820–1842, edited by Lawrence Rosenwald
The Dial, volume 1, edited by Margaret Fuller

Harriet Hosmer
Harriet Hosmer: Letters and Memoirs, edited by Cornelia Carr
Harriet Hosmer: A Cultural Biography by Kate Culkin
Our Famous Women: Maria Mitchell by Julia Ward Howe
Harriet Hosmer (1830–1908): Fame, Photography, and the American "Sculptress," Ph.D. thesis by Margo Lois Beggs
Lives of Girls Who Became Famous: Harriet Hosmer by Sarah Knowles Bolton

Emily Dickinson
The Letters of Emily Dickinson, edited by Thomas H. Johnson
The Complete Poems of Emily Dickinson
Lives Like Loaded Guns by Lyndall Gordon
Austin and Mabel by Polly Longsworth
The Life of Emily Dickinson by Richard Sewall

Open Me Carefully: Emily Dickinson's Intimate Letters to Susan Huntington Dickinson, edited by Martha Nell Smith and Ellen Louise Hart

White Heat: The Friendship of Emily Dickinson and Thomas Wentworth Higginson by Brenda Wineapple

The Gardens of Emily Dickinson by Judith Farr

The Editing of Emily Dickinson by R. W. Franklin

Rachel Carson

Always, Rachel: The Letters of Rachel Carson and Dorothy Freeman, edited by Martha Freeman

Beinecke Rare Book and Manuscript Library: The Rachel Carson Papers

The House of Life: Rachel Carson at Work by Paul Brooks

On a Farther Shore: The Life and Legacy of Rachel Carson by William Souder

Lost Woods: The Discovered Writing of Rachel Carson, edited by Linda Lear

The Sea Around Us by Rachel Carson

The Edge of the Sea by Rachel Carson

Silent Spring by Rachel Carson

The Sense of Wonder by Rachel Carson

Rachel Carson: Witness of Nature by Linda Lear

PERIPHERAL FIGURINGS ·

Specimen Days by Walt Whitman

Black Hole Blues and Other Songs from Outer Space by Janna Levin

How the Universe Got Its Spots by Janna Levin

Memoirs and Correspondence of Caroline Herschel, edited by Margaret Herschel and Mary Cornwallis Herschel

Genius: The Life and Science of Richard Feynman by James Gleick

Atom and Archetype: The Pauli/Jung Letters, edited by C. A. Meier

Migraine by Oliver Sacks

The Discoveries by Alan Lightman

Origins: The Lives and Worlds of Modern Cosmologists by Alan Lightman and Roberta Brawer

The Glass Universe by Dava Sobel

Personal Recollections, from Early Life to Old Age by Mary Somerville

The Civil Wars of Julia Ward Howe: A Biography by Elaine Showalter

The Portable Frederick Douglass, edited by John Stauffer and Henry Louis Gates, Jr.

BBC *In Our Time*: "The Invention of Photography"

Radiolab: "Where the Sun Don't Shine"

PBS: *The Farthest: Voyager in Space*

Capturing the Light: The Birth of Photography by Roger Watson and Helen Rappaport

The Peabody Sisters by Megan Marshall

Passages from the American Notebooks by Nathaniel Hawthorne

Passages from the English Notebooks by Nathaniel Hawthorne

Passages from the French and Italian Notebooks by Nathaniel Hawthorne

Letters, Diaries, Reminiscences & Extensive Biographies by Nathaniel Hawthorne

The Divine Magnet: Herman Melville's Letters to Nathaniel Hawthorne, edited by Mark Niemeyer

The Letters of Robert Browning and Elizabeth Barrett Browning

INDEX

Darwin, Charles *(continued)*
241–42, 243–44, 245; *On the Origin of Species*, 244, 245, 412, 479, 490
Darwin, Emma, 236, 243, 245
Darwin, Erasmus: *The Botanic Garden*, 247, 318; *Zoonomia*, 247
Davy, Humphry, 114, 248
Day, Albert M., 465
DDT and other pesticides, 477–517, 520; *biocide* suggested by Carson as better term for, 477–78; biological controls as alternative to, 502–3; Carson's attempt to interest E. B. White in writing book on, 470–71; Carson's congressional testimony on, 513, 515–17; causal relationship between cancer risk and, 481–82; Communist ties ascribed to critics of, 493, 494, 506–7; deaths ascribed to use of, 467, 469–70, 479, 510; Douglas's concerns about, 495, 496; government ban on DDT, 516; government complicity in use of, 489–90, 492–93; indiscriminate use of, as focus of Carson's criticism, 490–91; Kennedy administration and, 494–95, 502–3; lawsuit in Long Island and, 468–69, 471, 481, 495; Nobel Prize awarded to inventor of, 467–68, 503; pesticide makers' litigious bullying and, 493, 494; as problem not of science, but of economic and political systems, 480–81; *Reader's Digest* article favoring use of, 469; *Reader's Digest*'s rejection of Carson's exposé on, 426–27, 467; scientific studies on, followed by Carson, 426–27, 467–70, 477–79; sexist attacks on critics of, 470, 493,

494; thalidomide compared to, 491–92; valid limited uses of, 490, 497
death, 244–45; living with awareness of, 334–35; loss experienced after, 244–45; as natural end of life cycle, 518; natural selection and, 245. *See also* immortality, longing for
Debussy, Claude, *La Mer*, 438–39
democracy, American, 164, 166, 513
Democritus, 451
De Quincey, Thomas, 347
Descartes, René, 60, 108, 309, 475, 500–501; *The World*, 500
Dial, The, 137–40, 141, 148, 155–56, 157–58, 159, 161, 164, 184, 197
Dickens, Catherine, 244
Dickens, Charles, 244–45
Dickens, Dora, 244
Dickinson, Austin (brother of Emily), 245, 308, 323–24, 331, 332, 341, 344, 361, 393, 394, 396, 407–8, 456; Emily's literary legacy and, 378, 394–95; plot of Dickinson land deeded to Todds by, 381–82, 395, 396; son's death and, 378–80; Susan courted by, 320–26; Susan's marriage to, 326, 351, 378, 379, 381, 382, 383–84, 395; Todd's relationship with, 367, 368–76, 378, 379–82, 383–84, 395, 456; Todd unable to conceive child with, 384, 388, 394
Dickinson, Edward (father of Emily), 325, 329, 331, 340, 361–62, 377
Dickinson, Emily, 21, 65, 97, 98, 118, 184, 212, 225, 302, 306–65, 374–99, 412, 430, 443, 467, 476, 507, 544; Anthon's relationship with, 344–49, 350–51; bedroom

Russell, Ida, 52–57, 63–64, 148,
149, 308; at Brook Farm, 54–55;
death of, 57, 439; Mitchell's
relationship with, 51–53, 55–57,
70, 71, 174, 344

Sacks, Oliver, 240–41
Sackville-West, Vita, 66–67
Sagan, Carl, 12, 24, 400–407;
Druyan's relationship with,
402–4; Golden Record and,
400–403, 404; *Voyager*'s
photograph of Earth and,
405–7
St. Louis University School of
Medicine, 264, 268
St. Nicholas Magazine, 413–14
Salem witch trials, 64–65
Sand, George, 162, 186–88
Saturday Review, 528
Saturn, 34, 40, 297
Schopenhauer, Arthur, 148
Schweitzer, Albert, 501, 508
Schweitzer Medal of the Animal
Welfare Institute, 501–2
science: connection of fragmented
fields of, 80; moral dimension
of, 477–78; as part of reality
of living, 437; warped into
pseudoscience and mysticism,
450. *See also specific fields,
topics, and scientists*
science fiction: Kepler's *The Dream*,
12, 13–14
Scientific Revolution, 75–76
"scientist," coining of word, 81
Scott, Charlotte, 299
Scripps College, 487, 511
sculpture: daguerreotypes of, 251,
252–53, 276; daguerreotypes
of human sitters in style of,
253; Hiram Powers and, [page
number]; *See also* Hosmer,
Harriet (Hatty)

Sedgwick, Elizabeth, 266, 294
Sedgwick School, Lenox, Mass.,
266–67, 273, 278
Sellwood, Emma, 272–73
Shackleton, Ernest, 21, 499
Shackleton, Lord (son of Ernest),
499
shadowgrams, 248
Shakespeare, William, 65, 98, 173,
197, 301, 309, 333, 378, 415
Shawn, William, 430–31, 460,
485
Shelley, Percy Bysshe, 78, 288,
390
"Ship of Theseus" thought
experiment, 7
Silent Spring (Carson), 412,
477–517, 528; accolades for, 496,
498–99, 501–2; as Book-of-the-
Month Club selection, 489, 495;
Carson's congressional testimony
and, 513, 515–17; Carson's
decision to write, 470–72, 478;
Carson's moral imperative and,
477–78, 486–88; *CBS Reports*
segment on, 505–6, 508, 509–13;
central thesis of, 502; chemical
and agricultural industries'
attempts to refute findings
in, 493, 494, 496–98, 504–5,
509–12; dedicated to Schweitzer,
501, 508; international editions
of, 499–500; Kennedy's response
to, 494–95, 512; *Life* profile and,
504–5; Merton's praise for,
408–9; as powerful and
polarizing challenge to status
quo, 489–90, 492–93; release
of, 495–96; scientific research
as basis for, 426–27, 467–72,
477–79; ugly subject anchored to
beauty of nature in, 478–79, 486;
writing of, 478–85, 503–4. *See
also* DDT and other pesticides